Commodity Market Services and Publications

The publishers of "FORECASTING COMMODITY PRICES" specialize in preparing and publishing books and services for use by those who are concerned with price trends and background data for the commodities traded on all futures markets and numerous cash markets.

■ COMMODITY YEAR BOOKS (published annually)

Each annual volume contains new basic data on more than 110 different commodities, including price charts plus price records in tabular form; statistical tables of production, distribution and consumption; and original studies of factors that influence price movements and changes in supply and demand.

■ ECONOMICS OF FUTURES TRADING

This new book by an outstanding commodity market authority, is a "how to do it" book for commercial interests, a guide for speculators, and a college level textbook for a course in commodity futures markets and trading.

■ MODERN COMMODITY FUTURES TRADING

A practical book, devoted primarily to the techniques and methods for successful trading in the commodity markets. It explains trading methods, what makes prices go up and down, seasonal price patterns, chart trading, and much more.

■ COMMODITY YEAR BOOK STATISTICAL ABSTRACT SERVICE

This four-times yearly publication provides the latest available statistics for updating the statistical tables appearing in Commodity Year Book. It is published in January, April, September and November.

■ FUTURES MARKET SERVICE

A weekly analysis and forecast of price trends in the individual futures markets and the general commodity price level. Included are up-to-date charts and statistical data portraying price movements.

■ COMMODITY CHART SERVICE

A comprehensive commodity chart service published weekly which consists of well over 190 different daily charts plus additional chart studies provided at periodic intervals. The charts show the daily price movements of active futures deliveries traded on the United States and Canadian futures markets, plus "volume" and "open interest" data in chart form. A weekly "technical comment" section discusses significant chart formations and probable forthcoming price trends.

■ DAILY COMMODITY COMPUTER TREND ANALYZER

For those who closely follow the commodity futures markets, this unusual service identifies important price trends and where they are likely to change. It is also a complete price record of high, low and closing prices as well as volume and open interest for each of over 160 futures contracts in 40 different commodity markets. The report is mailed shortly after the markets close every trading day.

■ SPECIAL CHART COLLECTIONS

From its extensive library of charts and statistics, the Bureau publishes numerous collections of price records in chart form for commodities traded on the futures markets.

For More Details Write to the Publishers for Commodity Research Catalog

Commodity Research Bureau, Inc.

ONE LIBERTY PLAZA, NEW YORK, N.Y. 10006

FORECASTING COMMODITY PRICES

How the Experts analyze the Markets

Harry Jiler, Editor

Prepared and Published by
Commodity Research Bureau, Inc.
ONE LIBERTY PLAZA · NEW YORK, N.Y. 10006

INTRODUCTION

This is the second anthology of original studies of commodities that have appeared in the various editions of Commodity Year Book.

The first collection, entitled "Guide To Commodity Price Forecasting," was published in 1965 and it contained selected articles from Commodity Year Book volumes prior to that year. The studies, that are presented in this book, are derived from Commodity Year Book editions ranging from 1965 through 1974.

In view of the dramatic changes that have taken place in the commodity world during recent years, considerable work has been necessary to make the book of greater value as an aid to commodity price forecasting under conditions that prevail today. The original authors were contacted and asked to revise their studies; a job that needed almost a complete rewrite in a number of instances. Their cooperation has been most gratifying and we wish to express our appreciation here.

Among the most valuable contents of the book are the charts showing the daily price movements of each commodity for a number of years. This facilitates a study of seasonal price movements and other recurrent characteristics of each commodity. It also enables technicians to analyze and verify various chart patterns. These charts represent many hundreds of hours of work and we know of *no other publication in the world* where such a collection can be found.

We are indebted to Seymour Gaylinn and the chart staff of Commodity Research Bureau, Inc. for their painstaking efforts in bringing numerous charts up-to-date, which illustrate some of the articles in the following pages. The editors also take this occasion to express thanks for the excellent job of production coordination by Irving Schnider, also of the Commodity Research Bureau staff. The technical guidance of these experts constituted a major contribution in the preparation of this book.

The order in which the articles appear in the following pages has no special significance, and it is not at all necessary that they be read in sequence. Each study stands by itself and, accordingly, can be consulted by the reader at any appropriate time.

COMMODITY RESEARCH BUREAU, INC.

ISBN 0-910418-05-5
Library of Congress Catalog Card Number 75–18103

THE AUTHORS

Brief background information, about each of the experts who contributed to this book, is shown below. (The detailed table of contents is on the following page.)

FRED BAILEY: Fred Bailey is president of Bailey & Associates, McLean, Va., and a well-known writer and consultant specializing in agricultural economics and commodities.

MALCOLM CLOUGH: Mr. Clough worked for more than 30 years as an economist in the U.S. Department of Agriculture in the area of feed price analysis and as editor of the Economic Research Service publication, "Feed Situation." He is currently a consultant, devoting most of his time to analyses of the corn and soybean meal markets.

VINCENT J. CONWAY: Mr. Conway has been with the Commodity Division of Merrill Lynch, Pierce, Fenner & Smith, Inc. for eight years. Currently their Senior Metals Analyst, he has made extensive studies on numerous metals including gold.

WALTER L. EMERY: Walter L. Emery started his commodity career with the then active commodity firm of Orvis Brothers & Co. For almost twenty years he was with Shearson, Hammill & Co., where he was Director of Commodity Research. He has been a staff member of Commodity Research Bureau, Inc. since 1970.

ROBERT FEDUNIAK: Mr. Feduniak received BS & MS degrees from Stanford University, and University of California. After serving as branch manager and market analyst for B. J. Lind & Co. 1971–72, he joined Bache & Co. in 1972 and is currently Vice President in charge of Commodity Research and the Guided Commodity Trading Program. He is also Contributing Editor for *Commodities* and *Financial World* magazines.

DAVID INKELES: Dr. David M. Inkeles, a former commodity analyst for E. F. Hutton & Co. Inc., has been a prolific contributor to various issues of The Commodity Year Book. His early training was in economics at Yale but since the late 1960's he has pursued an interest in medicine. After earning an MD degree from Albert Einstein College of Medicine, he has been completing advanced training in diseases and surgery of the eye. Dr. Inkeles has continued to maintain his professional status in the Commodity world by consulting and economic writing.

ROBERT T. KECK: Mr. Keck is a Vice President and National Commodity Sales Manager for Bache & Co. Formerly Director of Commodity Research at Bache, he has had nine years of experience in many facets of commodity markets.

FRANK LESSITER: Mr. Lessiter grew up on a Michigan livestock farm that has been owned by his family since 1853. A veteran follower of the livestock industry, he has served five years as Editor of *National Livestock Producer* magazine.

MICHAEL L. MADUFF: Mr. Maduff is Managing Partner of Maduff & Sons in Chicago; a member of the American Meat Institute, the Chicago Mercantile Exchange and most other commodity exchanges. His firm and its predecessors were among the first to ever make or take delivery of Pork Bellies on the Chicago Mercantile Exchange. Mr. Maduff is an active broker, trader, hedger and merchandiser of Bellies and other pork products. He also manages farming and livestock operations in Iowa, Kansas and South Dakota. He has been a guest lecturer on commodities at numerous universities and an expert consultant to various governmental bodies.

JAMES P. OLMEDO, JR.: Mr. Olmedo, formerly a technical and marketing consultant in the forest products field, compiled the lumber and plywood study when he was a commodity analyst with Merrill Lynch, Pierce, Fenner & Smith, Inc. He is at present manager of commodity hedging at International Paper Company.

HAROLD L. OPPENHEIMER: General Oppenheimer is Chairman of the Board of Oppenheimer Industries, Inc., a Kansas City based firm which is America's largest ranch and cattle management concern. In the U.S. Marine Corps he served in three wars and has received several citations, including the Bronze Star. He also holds the Presidential Unit Citation, Vietnamese Cross of Gallantry and the Legion of Merit.

A native of Kansas City, Gen. Oppenheimer was graduated cum laude from Harvard University at the age of 19. A spokesman for the cattle and ranch real estate industries, Gen. Oppenheimer has written several books on agribusiness.

CLARENCE H. ROSENBAUM: Mr. Rosenbaum, a commodity and food analyst, is on the staff of the *Journal of Commerce*. He was formerly chief operating executive of a Midwestern wholesale food distributing firm, where his responsibilities included buying of such commodities as sugar, processed fruits and vegetables, coffee, cocoa products, fats and oils, flour, and other related food products.

WILLIAM STERN: Mr. Stern, a partner of General Cocoa Company, one of the world's leading international cocoa merchants, has been with this firm all his business life since leaving the Army in 1947. He served for three years as President of the Cocoa Merchants Association of America, Inc. He also writes the General Cocoa Company weekly newsletter.

WILLIAM C. STRUNING: Dr. Struning is Director of Research at the Pan American Coffee Bureau and Professor of Business Quantitative Analysis at Seton Hall University.

ROD SWOBODA: Mr. Swoboda is a staff member of Farm Business, Inc., a Washington, D.C., firm of agricultural market analysts, editors and consultants headed by Ray Reiman. They have authored more than 4,600 articles dealing with farm commodities.

TABLE OF CONTENTS

UNDERSTANDING THE ICED BROILER
FUTURES MARKET

BY FRED BAILEY AND ROD SWOBODA

The marriage of farm and factory that has given birth to the modern broiler industry was no shotgun affair. From the outset, it was a logical and perhaps inevitable union: The unequaled labor and management skills of the American farmer, coupled with the capital and assembly line wizardry of American business. The union has flourished. "Boomed" might be a better word.

"Boomed" it has! At the close of World War II, the average American ate a scant five pounds of broiler meat a year. In 1974 it's estimated he consumed nearly 38 pounds. Although surging feed costs slowed broiler production somewhat in 1973 and 1974, the long-term trend is still expected to rise.

Requiring only a shade more than two pounds of feed to produce a pound of meat, broilers are—past, present and future—one of the "growingest" growth industries in all of agriculture.

Yet in many ways, the broiler industry is a hybrid. Despite a mechanical mother, the incubator, and its push-button living conditions, the succulent young broiler remains an agricultural commodity. And, as such, its market remains subject to the same gyrations of supply and demand that perennially plague producers and processors of other commodities.

As if to accentuate that its ties continue to be farm as well as factory; broiler output has recently varied from one year to the next by as much as 16%. And price fluctuations within a single year are frequently as great as 30 to 40%. Such variations are closely tied with those for most other farm "crops."

Not surprisingly, production and price uncertainties create special problems in what has become a high-volume and low-margin, assembly line operation. The constant companion of price change is price risk. And the larger the volume and the smaller the margin, the greater the risk.

To provide a mechanism for insurance against the risk inherent in price change, the Chicago Board of Trade, in August of 1968, initiated futures trading in iced broilers. Creation of this new market stemmed, in large measure, from the urging of the broiler industry.

To understand the futures market for broilers, it is necessary to understand broilers: The how, when, where, and how much of their production, marketing and pricing.

A Not-So-Humble History

The modern broiler's history is hardly humble. So fond was Napoleon of young chicken that his battlefield chef reportedly turned out a bird at twenty-minute intervals because there was no way to tell when the commander of the army would return to dine. A special chicken dish, served after a victory during the Italian campaign in 1801, won Napoleon's fancy to such an extent that it was named after the battle—Chicken Marengo.

Even long before Napoleon's time, however, chicken was considered such a delicacy that a Roman Emperor issued an order that hens and cocks be consumed in moderation. Resourceful Romans thus desexed the cock (incidentially producing the first capon), thereby keeping within the law while continuing to eat chicken to their heart's content.

Chicken fanciers dot the pages of history. Sir Francis Bacon, so the story goes, died of pneumonia contracted from a chilly experiment of trying to preserve a chicken by filling it with snow. Henry IV of France desired his peasants to have a chicken in every pot every Sunday. And Herbert Hoover, echoing the thought, promised the people of America "A chicken in every pot and a car in every garage."

But while chicken has long been a delicacy, it has until recent years been a *rare* delicacy. At the time of Hoover's oft-quoted campaign promise, broiler production totaled fewer than 30 million birds a year. Even by 1947, production was only 310 million birds. Currently, it's nearer to 3 billion.

Birth of an Industry

Until 25 years ago, virtually the entire U.S. output of chicken meat came from farm chickens, including old hens which had outlived their usefulness as egg producers. Not until 1952, in fact, did production of commercial broilers exceed that of farm chickens.

Almost suddenly, chicken meat became a product rather than a byproduct. And thus began a marshalling of efforts to produce a better product at less cost.

Today's poultry meat industry does precisely that. The facts and figures on the following pages tell *how*. And in telling how, they provide an insight into the economic machinery of the broiler market.

Vertical Integration

These two words describe the structure of the broiler industry. Well over 90% of present broiler output is accounted for by integrated operations—operations in which several, or all, phases of production, processing, and marketing are under centralized management and/or ownership.

Integration, for the broiler industry, was a "natural." Formerly, farmers grew their own birds, found their own markets, and figured their own profit objectives. But with the increasing demand for broilers, plus improvements in feeds, management and disease control, commercialization began to develop. The farmer who wished to grow broilers on a large scale suddenly found that he needed capital, technological aid and management advice.

The feed dealer became the source of credit. With continued growth of the industry, feed dealers in turn became dependent on feed manufacturers as a credit source. To spread their risk, both feed dealers and manufacturers integrated vertically by acquiring hatcheries and processing plants. This was the start of many forms of integration.

Today, several types of integration exist. The illustration below shows the functions of a typically integrated broiler firm.

Although some firms encompass all functions shown in the illustration, the most common arrangement is for the integrating company—usually a feed company or food chain—to contract with independent producers to supply hatching eggs and to grow out the live broilers.

Under such an arrangement, the independent contractor owns his own buildings and equipment. In the case of a hatching egg farm, he is supplied with breeder stock from the integrator's hatchery, feed from the integrator's feed mill, plus a variety of technical and management services. Essentially the same arrangement is made with other farmers who contract to grow out live broilers provided by the integrator's hatchery.

The grow-out contractor is assured of a market for his output at a guaranteed minimum profit. Many contracts provide bonuses for efficient production.

In some cases, the integrating firm is also engaged in retailing of the birds, though this is not generally so.

The Few and the Large

Concentration is the name of the game in today's broiler industry. Primarily through mergers and acquisitions, the number of poultry slaughtering plants has continued to shrink. Latest available statistics—for the year 1972—show only about 227 such plants still in operation. Only ten firms accounted for 30% of total U.S. production. And half of the broilers produced came from only 27 firms.

The table shows the degree of concentration.

Size category	Number of firms	Percent of Output by group	cumulative
I	10	30	30
II	17	20	50
III	30	20	70
IV	21	10	80
V	26	10	90
VI	19	5	95
VII	104	5	100

While precise figures are lacking, integrated broiler operations are continuing to become fewer and larger.

Economics of Geography

Center of broiler production in the U.S. is in the South, where three states—Georgia, Arkansas, and Alabama—account for upwards of two-fifths of total output. Ten states currently supply nearly 90% of all broiler meat.

State	Number of broilers, 1973
Arkansas	501,845,000
Georgia	412,986,000
Alabama	399,324,000
North Carolina	290,448,000
Mississippi	239,130,000
Maryland	190,673,000
Texas	173,330,000
Delaware	140,967,000
California	83,193,000
Maine	75,642,000
Total top ten	2,507,538,000
TOTAL U.S.	2,923,498,000

The South's magnetic appeal to the broiler industry was its low costs. As King Cotton began to desert the area for higher-yielding opportunities elsewhere, poultry moved in. Labor—both for the building of broiler houses and for the growing out of broiler flocks was both plentiful and inexpensive.

Production—The Nine-Week Wonder

From the incubator to skillet-ready requires only a brief nine weeks. But what today's broiler lacks in

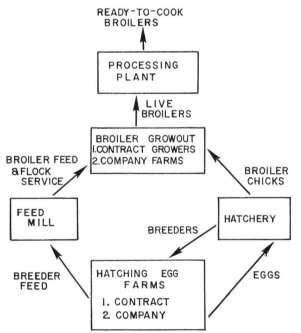

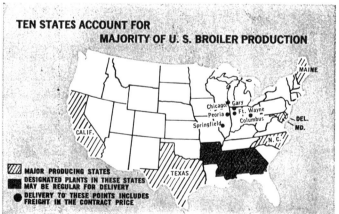

longevity, it makes up for in pampering. Modern broiler houses, particularly on those farms dealing in pure line breeds, provide practically every luxury except for wall-to-wall carpeting.

A visit to many up-to-date production facilities reveals rows of aluminum-roofed buildings, with sunlight glinting off thermopane windows. These windows, which act as insulation devices, have retractable sunshades to utilize efficiently the heat of the sun.

The same luxury dwellings are soundproof, and there are litter-cleaning devices and ones for overhead feeding that insure an uncluttered floor.

Best of all is the cuisine, prepared with scientific precision to produce the most meat at the least cost. In 1941, 4½ pounds of feed were required to produce one pound of edible poultry meat. Today, as a tribute to the teamwork of poultry nutritionists and breeders, only one half that amount—about 2.1 pounds of feed is needed to produce a pound of meat.

More efficient feeding saves time and money. Formerly, it took 12 to 16 weeks to raise a chicken to market weight. Today's nine-week-old birds are of large size and better quality. The reduction in growing time means that 25% more broilers can be produced in the same amount of space. That's a hefty cost saving, too.

Not only does automation dominate the broiler's nine-week life, it even *precedes* it. By three weeks. At that time, eggs from hatchery egg farms are shipped to hatcheries and placed in incubators resembling refrigerators with glass windows. The large modern hatchery may produce more than a million eggs every three weeks. It has rooms with row upon row of incubators, each of which holds tens of thousands of eggs. Temperature in incubators is rigidly controlled at 98°F., and the humidity at 97%.

Every hour, the incubator plays "rockabye" with the eggs in a three-stage cycle. Automatically, eggs are tilted back, set straight, then tilted forward. This process prevents the embyro from sticking to the eggshell.

After 18 days, eggs go to a hatching unit for another three days, permitting them more room than the trays with tightly packed eggs. When chicks are a day old, they part forever from their metallic mothers. They are vaccinated and debeaked to prevent pecking, then go either to feed suppliers or individual growers for nine weeks of feeding out.

Marketing

The processing plant is the link between farm and supermarket. Until 1942, most chickens were sold "New York dressed." That is, the feathers had been removed but no further processing had been done. In some cases, the butcher cleaned the chicken, in others cleaning the bird became a do-it-yourself project for the homemaker. In either case, the homemaker would have to remove the pinfeathers, singe the bird and remove the viscera. Today's processing plant now handles these jobs, and every broiler-fryer that reaches the market has been cleaned and eviscerated. Housewives may even select the favored pieces and buy only these.

In a sense, the processing actually begins on the farm, for the whole cycle is so well organized that today's chicks are virtually born to order. To insure a constant and uniform supply of birds, processors and those responsible for growing consult to determine how many chicks should be started each week. In this way, suppliers keep economic pace with consumer demand. The birds are moved from farm to plant in trucks, and the timing is as carefully arranged as an army maneuver. The trucks arrive at intervals during the day to synchronize deliveries with processing and avoid a waiting period.

On arrival at the processing plant, the birds are killed and then scalded at 130°F. for just 1½ minutes before plucking. They travel on a continuous chain conveyor, which takes them through all the stages of cleaning. The chickens are repeatedly washed by copious amounts of water; some plants use up to 800 gallons per minute. These processes are for the most part done automatically, from the first scalding to the singeing that removes the most minute pinfeathers. After cleaning and plucking, the chickens are eviscerated—one of the few processes still done by hand.

The skin is removed from the gizzard, leaving a clean piece of ready-to-cook meat. The heart, liver, gizzard and usually the neck are packed together, chilled in slushed ice for half an hour, and packed within the bird.

As soon as the birds are dressed, they are submerged in slushed ice, where they remain for half an hour to two hours, depending upon plant procedure. Once removed from their icy bath, they again go on into ice—this time in the box for shipping. Each box holds about sixty-five pounds of chicken. Some modern plants can turn out from 3,000 to 9,000 birds per hour. Once packed, the boxes are loaded onto trucks and sped to market.

Broilers from Maine are sent to Boston and local New England markets. The rest of the Northeast (Baltimore, Philadelphia, Washington, D.C., New York) is supplied principally by Delmarva. The midwestern market used to be supplied from Delmarva. Some of the broilers from the Southeast go to the Northeast, but principally they are trucked to Florida, Atlanta, New Orleans, Dallas, Chicago, Detroit, Cleveland and Columbus markets. The South Central states, especially Alabama, Arkansas, and Mississippi ship to Jacksonville, Miami, New Orleans, Dallas, Chicago, St. Louis, Omaha, Salt Lake City, Los Angeles, San Francisco, and Seattle. Most broiler production in Texas and California is consumed locally.

The Boom in Consumption

Build a better mousetrap, the adage says, and the world will beat a path to your door. The same goes for building a better bird. And, indeed, through the efforts of breeders and nutrition experts, today's broiler has literally been "built" to consumer specifications. What's more, it has been built at a lower cost, with savings passed along to the housewife.

Just as the adage predicted, the world has beaten a path to the broilerman's door. The production, price, and per capita consumption figures on the next page offer dramatic proof.

The Demand for Broilers

Demand can be simply defined as the pounds of broiler meat which will be purchased at various levels of price. An increase in demand boosts the amount which will be purchased at a given price. A demand decrease reduces the amount.

Year	Production (pounds)	Farm Price Live Weight (in cents)	Per Capita Consumption (in pounds)
1950	1,944,524,000	27.4	8.7
1951	2,414,767,000	28.5	10.4
1952	2,623,934,000	28.8	11.7
1953	2,904,174,000	27.1	12.3
1954	3,236,248,000	23.1	13.7
1955	3,349,555,000	25.2	13.9
1956	4,269,502,000	19.6	17.5
1957	4,682,738,000	18.9	19.1
1958	5,430,674,000	18.5	22.1
1959	5,472,795,000	16.1	22.7
1960	6,017,000,000	16.9	23.7
1961	6,841,000,000	13.8	25.9
1962	6,917,000,000	15.2	25.2
1963	7,284,000,000	14.6	27.0
1964	7,524,000,000	14.2	27.5
1965	8,106,000,000	15.0	29.4
1966	8,750,000,000	15.3	32.2
1967	9,181,199,000	13.3	32.7
1968	9,326,341,000	14.2	33.1
1969	10,047,769,000	15.2	35.2
1970	10,819,032,000	13.6	37.4
1971	10,817,748,000	13.7	37.1
1972	11,480,101,000	14.3	38.8
1973	11,216,989,000	24.1	37.7
1974*	11,260,000,000	21.6	37.7

* Estimated.

The foregoing, of course, is true for any commodity. Similarly, the developments which traditionally increase—or decrease—demand for broilers are those which, for the most part, affect the demand curve of many other agricultural commodities.

Here are six that belong on every price analyst's checklist:

1. Population. Increased population—currently climbing at the rate of about 1% a year—exerts an upward influence on broiler demand. In forecasting, changes in population are generally taken into account by computing demand on a Per Capita basis.

2. Disposable income. As with most consumer products, the price of broilers is usually directly related to the amount of money consumers have for spending. Increased income bolsters broiler demand. Distribution of incomes is particularly pertinent in the case of broilers, since families low on the income ladder tend to be the largest per capita consumers of broiler meat.

3. Consumer preferences. During recent years, the demand for beef has increased at a rapid clip. Demand for pork, after a period of steady decline, appears to have leveled off. Per capita demand for broilers has not changed sharply. The increased consumption, as shown in the above table, has occurred almost entirely at the expense of price.

4. Supply and price of competing products. Other types of meat—pork, lamb, and turkey—compete directly with broilers for the consumer's food dollars. To some extent, other protein food products—such as cheese and eggs—are substitutable for broilers, and to this extent are competitive. The supply and price levels of other meats and meat substitutes are important factors influencing both the short-run and long-run demand for broilers.

5. Seasonal factors. Peak demand for broilers is during the summer months. This stems, at least in part, from the traditional popularity of chicken for barbequeing and picnics. Demand is normally at its weakest during the Thanksgiving and Christmas period, when turkeys take over.

6. Other demand influences. Government purchases of broiler meat for school lunches, food distribution programs, and military procurement can—and sometimes do—have an impact on demand. To a limited extent, export developments are also a demand influence, although only about 1% of U.S. broiler production is exported. Purchases for cold storage are still another "sometimes" factor in figuring demand. Frozen broilers, however, have not been well accepted by consumers.

The chart on page 10 shows the demand "curve" for broilers during the period 1953–74. It offers impressive evidence that changes in consumption have been due primarily to changes in price rather than to an increase in demand. Demand changes—such as those due to changes in price and supply of competing meats—have been reflected mainly in short-run broiler price variations.

How to Anticipate the Supply of Broilers

Published—and readily available—statistics provide a convenient and accurate barometer of short-run levels of broiler supply. That is, the supply for up to approximately one year ahead. Here are the figures to watch:

1. Chicks placed. This indicates the number of chicks placed in "grow out" facilities each week and is a valuable indicator of what the marketable supply of broilers is likely to be 9 to 10 weeks later.

2. Eggs set. Estimates of the probable market supply can be extended by an additional three weeks —to about three months ahead—by studying reports of the number of eggs set in incubators. Three weeks, you'll recall, is the time required to produce a chick from an egg.

3. Breeding flock. The number of birds in the nation's laying age (7 to 15 months) breeding flock provides a clue to longer-run supply prospects. Regularly-published statistics indicate the number of birds in the present flock, the number of pullets added to breeder replacement flocks, the number of breeders tested, and the number slaughtered.

These figures can be significant. Pullets added to replacement flocks are those chicks which, about seven months later, will be ready to join breeder laying flocks. Normally breeder hens are *tested* about one to two months before joining the laying flock. That is, at about five to six months of age.

The "laying age" breeder flock is generally considered to be those hens from seven to 15 months of age.

Anyone attempting to analyze prospective broiler supplies should keep in mind that the number of birds in the replacement and hatchery egg flocks provide a measure only of the number of broilers which *can* be produced three months or more into the future— not necessarily the number which *will* be produced. In other words, such numbers are an indication only of maximum industry *capacity* during a given time period. If profit prospects are unfavorable, actual production may be cut back.

Admittedly, such measures are not absolute. The number of eggs produced for incubator can be expanded, for instance, if a large number of pullets are brought into the laying flock earlier than usual, or if the present breeding hens are kept longer than usual.

The question might well be asked, "What *causes* broiler production to be expanded or contracted? The answer, primarily is *profits*. As the profitability of producing broilers improves, production is increased. When it worsens production is decreased. This, at least, has been the short-run reaction.

Over the longer run of the past decade or so, the broiler supply curve has shifted upward. That is, the number of broilers which the industry has been willing to produce at given profit margins has increased. Indeed, over the long-run, production has increased despite *smaller* profit margins. This has been done largely through increases in per-firm volume, the ability to produce a pound of meat with much less feed, and the willingness of the industry

to accept smaller per-unit profits. Most observers doubt that this trend will continue. It is expected that more and more broiler production will be concentrated in fewer and fewer firms.

How Prices Are Determined

The point hardly requires elaboration that broiler prices reflect the interaction of current broiler supply and current broiler demand. This price-making process occurs weekly in the nation's major wholesale broiler markets. These major markets, for which the U.S. Department of Agriculture regularly reports prices are: Baltimore, Washington, D.C., Boston, Chicago, Cincinnati, Cleveland, Columbus, Denver, Detroit, Los Angeles, New York, Philadelphia, Pittsburg, St. Louis, and San Francisco.

The actual process of price determination is highly informal. On Thursday and Friday of each week,

BROILERS   CHICAGO (Weekly High, Low & Close of Nearest Futures)   CENTS PER POUND

sellers (processing plants) and buyers (food chains, institutions, wholesalers, etc.) negotiate by phone the price and quantities for the following week's deliveries.

Both buyers and sellers are well informed of current supply and demand conditions. Buyers, for example, know the number of birds in flocks scheduled for immediate slaughter. Likewise, sellers know the approximate number of birds which buyers will need in order to meet demand.

Each Friday, through its market information network, the USDA compiles and publishes preliminary statistics showing the range of prices and the quantities negotiated. On Monday, final figures on quantity and weighted average prices are compiled.

A perhaps more pertinent point is *how* broiler prices respond to fluctuations in supply and demand over periods of time. Take another look at the chart showing the relationship between per capita consumption (supply) and broiler prices.

Most notable is the fact that at high levels of consumption, such as those experienced in recent years, price changes are small in proportion to changes in per capita consumption. Roughly speaking, price declines by about ½-cent for each three pounds that per capita supply increases. At the lower levels of consumption typical of the mid-to-late 1950's, only a small increase in supply is needed to push prices lower. Prices decreased by about one cent for each pound increase in per capita supply. But when production per person slipped in 1973 and 1974, prices rose spectacularly.

Ups and Downs of Prices

While annual price averages respond obediently to variations in per capita supply, week to week and month to month price fluctuations are another story. Increases or decreases of 25% or more in a span of only several weeks are not uncommon. For the broiler industry, such price instability impedes orderly planning of production and marketing, and exposes sellers to the constant risk of sudden losses. Conversely, for the speculator, wide and rapid price movements create an abundance of opportunities for profit-taking.

Consider the past several years—the ups and downs of broiler prices and the reasons behind them.

The causes behind the greatest price swings in broiler market history—from 41¢ per pound in May, 1973, to well above 70¢ in August, 1973—may have altered the traditional supply-demand and broiler price relationships, say some analysts. Although price variations have toned down from the wide-swinging patterns of mid-1973, they still reflect sensitivity to consumer meat buying resistance and producer livestock holding actions.

On the demand side, theories are circulating that spinoffs from 1974's economic problems—such as the widening and higher price spreads between different kinds of meats and poultry—now throw the old price-making relationships off kilter.

But consumption patterns and the varying meat-mix of eaters at different prices aren't the only trends that show tendency to take a different track. Production patterns—due to perhaps more meat and poultry

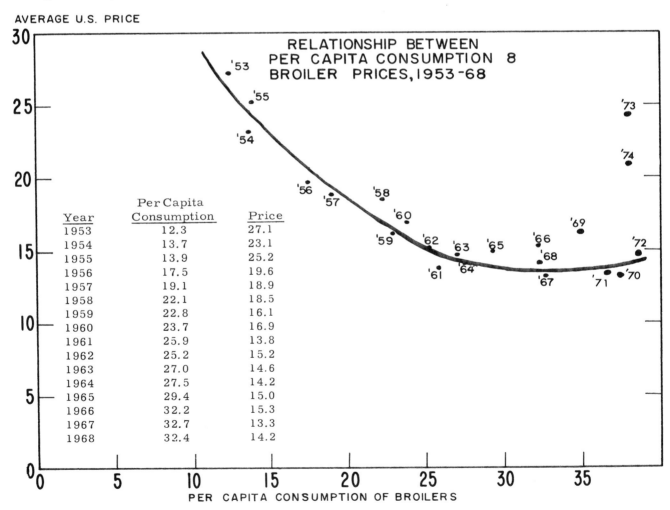

AVERAGE U.S. PRICE

RELATIONSHIP BETWEEN
PER CAPITA CONSUMPTION 8
BROILER PRICES, 1953-68

Year	Per Capita Consumption	Price
1953	12.3	27.1
1954	13.7	23.1
1955	13.9	25.2
1956	17.5	19.6
1957	19.1	18.9
1958	22.1	18.5
1959	22.8	16.1
1960	23.7	16.9
1961	25.9	13.8
1962	25.2	15.2
1963	27.0	14.6
1964	27.5	14.2
1965	29.4	15.0
1966	32.2	15.3
1967	32.7	13.3
1968	32.4	14.2

PER CAPITA CONSUMPTION OF BROILERS

profit uncertainty than ever before—also show signs of changing.

Broiler prices declined sharply in the fall of 1973 after reaching those record highs in the summer. The 9-city wholesale price in 1973 averaged 42¢ a pound, up 14¢ from 1972.

The all-time high of nearly 74¢ a pound reached in early August was more than 2½ times a year earlier. But by mid-November, more red meat as well as poultry weighed on the market, and broiler prices slumped to 33¢ per pound.

Early 1974 broiler prices increased but fluctuated widely. The 9-city wholesale average hit 43½¢ per pound in early January, then dropped to 35¢ by mid-month before recovering to 42¢ a pound for the last week of the month.

During the first 9 months of 1974, broiler production climbed 5% over the previous January–September period. Prices jumped up and down, although they stayed mostly under the previous late winter, spring and summer's rates. But then weather-beaten crops and the resulting soaring feed costs spun the broiler situation into an abrupt about-face.

Fall's production dive wiped out gains of winter, spring and summer—and stifled expectations that supplies for all of 1974 would have little trouble topping 1973's output.

The sharp plunge in marketings kept fall prices from taking their usual slip. In fact, at times in the fall of 1974, prices exhibited uncharacteristic amounts of strength. Though average prices for the period did show some decline from summer, they still averaged almost a dime a pound above year-earlier marks at times.

Despite such price support, however, 1974 broiler profits still stayed "in a bind." Costly feed was the culprit. As a result, broiler meat output for the entire year, according to still-changeable estimates, was a mere third of a percentage point above 1973.

Indicated 1974 broiler production was slightly below the record bulge grown in 1972, but nowhere near the amount indicated when January–April output jumped off to a 7.5% start over 1973.

Price-wise, 1974 went out in the same see-saw style with which it came in. Broilers leaped from a fall low of 35¢ per pound on December 15 to 45¢ on December 30. This nearly matched the previously-set top price for the year. Prices then started 1975 by sliding below the 40¢ mark.

The above prices are, as mentioned, *cash* prices. However, it follows that—since futures prices reflect cash price expectations—the extent of price variation in futures markets may frequently exceed that occurring in cash markets. (See charts on page 12.)

Keeping Informed

Abundant information is available for keeping abreast of current and prospective economic conditions in the broiler industry. More than a dozen daily, weekly, and monthly magazines and news services report and interpret industry developments.

Eleven separate USDA publications and reports provide statistical and interpretive information. These include: *Poultry and Egg Situation*, which provides outlook and statistical material five times a year; monthly reports on *Poultry Slaughter and Processing, Hatchery Production, Pullet Chicks for Broiler Hatchery Supply Flocks, Turkeys and Chickens Tested, Cold Storage*, and *Livestock Slaughter and Meat Production*. The *Livestock and Meat Situation* is published six times a year and the *Feed Situation* five times. *A Summary of Poultry Market Statistics* is published annually.

Individuals interested in USDA publications should write to the Office of Management Services, U.S.D.A, Washington, D.C. 20250.

The Iced Broiler Futures Market

Because volume in the broiler industry is large and profit margins are small, even nominal price variations can spell economic catastrophe. To enable the industry to establish prices in advance of marketing —or even in advance of actual production—the Chicago Board of Trade provides a futures market in iced broilers.

Price and production variability is the situation the broiler industry has faced in the past and will continue to face in the future. It should be very attractive to speculators, and it provides adequate reason for the industry to use the futures market to limit the impact of price changes.

Since broilers are a highly-perishable commodity, futures trading utilizes shipping certificates—roughly comparable to a warehouse receipt. The shipping certificate is a secure promise on the part of an authorized shipper that he will ship the contract grade and weight of broilers from production under carefully delinated conditions. The certificates come into being in the expiring month for the purpose of settling outstanding contracts.

As a practical matter, the shipping certificate is of little direct concern to the speculators (or to most hedgers) since very few intend to settle their contracts by making delivery. Most will settle by making an offsetting futures market transaction.

As an aid to prospective traders in the iced broiler futures contract (ticker symbol Ib), here's a rundown on the important facts and figures:

Trading unit: Whole, eviscerated, broiler-fryer chickens, ice-packed, ready-to-cook, and graded USDA Grade A. Individual birds must be in the 2½–3.5 pound range, 28,000 pounds constituting a contract.

Price multiples: prices quoted in dollars and cents per cwt. Price changes registered in multiples of 2½ cents per cwt., equivalent to $7.00 per contract.

Trading months: January, March, May, July, September, and November.

Delivery points: From designated processing plants in Alabama, Arkansas, Georgia or Mississippi with freight paid to towns shown on map. Milwaukee, Wisconsin, delivery costs 1/10¢ per lb. premium. Youngstown, Akron, Cleveland and Toledo, Ohio; Detroit, Lansing, Grand Rapids and Flint, Michigan; Madison, Wisconsin, call for ¼¢ per lb. premium. Other points may be arranged by mutual agreement.

Instrument of Delivery: Shipping certificate. Certificate holders may order shipment at any time and are guaranteed delivery to designated locations within 9 to 20 business days after giving loading orders. From February through July premium charge of $3.00 per contract per day is assessed from the day after date of certificate delivery until the business day after receipt of loading orders. No premium is charged from August through October; a $6.00 premium per contract per day is charged Nov. through Jan.

March Broilers (Iced) Futures Delivery
1970 to 1975

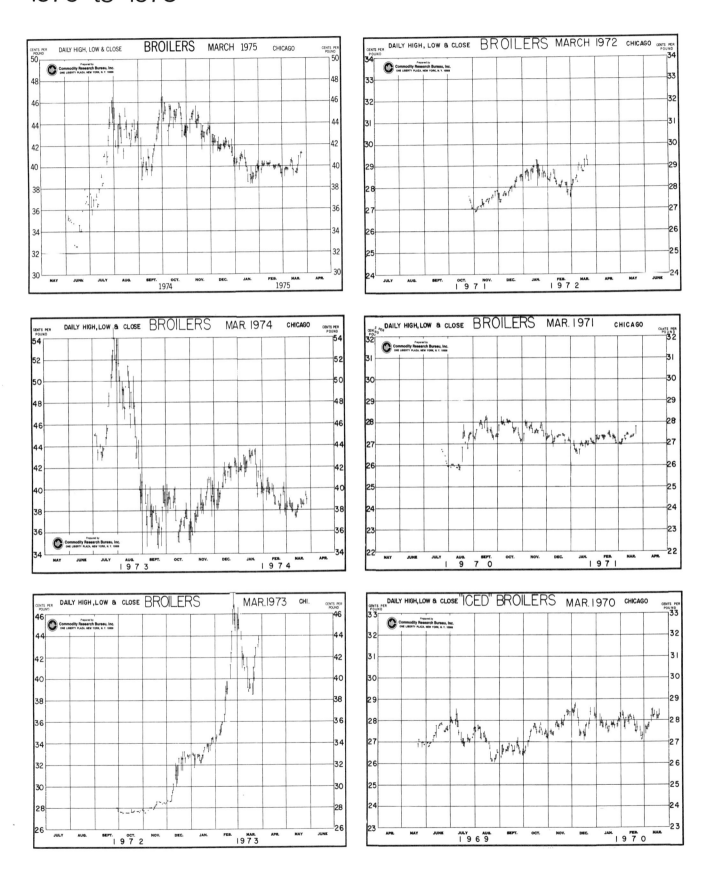

ANALYZING PRICE MOVEMENTS OF LIVE
BEEF (CATTLE) FUTURES

BY BRIG. GEN. H. L. OPPENHEIMER

When the gong rang November 30, 1964, to open trading in beef futures on the floor of the Chicago Mercantile Exchange, there was consternation in the American livestock industry. The highly organized packing houses had previously stated that they would boycott the exchange and they did. The various trade associations of ranchers, feeders, and marketing groups were silent and uneasy. Rarely had an event in American commodity trading caused such a stir.

Volume got off to a good start and has continued to be satisfactory, but the really big numbers that would be caused by the consumers (packers and chain stores) hedging with long contracts and the producers (farmers and feedlots) hedging with short sales were missing. When asked, these groups said, "we want to wait and see." What they meant was that they were afraid—afraid of the unknown.

Why did this commodity opening cause editorials all over the country; since then why has it been a principal subject of debate; why did the mere fact that it was coming rouse such an emotional and hostile response in certain areas?

First, the numbers are big. You are not playing penny-ante poker. Cattle raised for beef are the largest single segment of American agriculture. Even in 1953, 1963, and 1973/74, when cattlemen had poor years, sales of cattle and calves grossed almost as much income to producers as combined sales of wheat, corn and cotton.

Second, beef prices have been unregulated and unsupported by the government, with the exception of the beef price freeze in 1973. This is a wild and woolly free market, with the devil taking the hindmost.

Third, the production end of the industry is highly volatile. It often has disastrous years while other sectors of the economy prosper. May, 1964, saw an 18-year low in fed steer prices with bankruptcies and mortgage foreclosures being the order of the day. In mid-August of 1973 top prices were in the range from $58–$62. These high prices were a prelude to another major falloff in prices, which continued through the end of 1974 and lingered into 1975, as prices stabilized.

Fourth, there is no industry so hide bound by custom, tradition and the past. There are many who think it is immoral for a newcomer to buy a ranch or open a feedlot if his grandfather wasn't in the business.

Fifth, there is no agricultural commodity, or for that matter, there are few other major commodities, in which a dozen major packers and about the same number of super grocery chains completely dominate the purchasing end of the industry, and 5,000,000 disorganized and independent farmers and feeders represent the production end. This is the complete reversal of the automobile industry, in which you have four major domestic producers and "X"-million purchasers.

Sixth, there is not too much correlation between the price of a feeder steer at 30¢ per pound going to a feedlot and a choice steak at the butcher counter at $1.80 per pound. This will be discussed in some detail later, but it is due to two principal factors:

1. The time lag of four to seven months between the time an animal goes to feed and the time it goes to the packer.

2. The disproportionately high ratio of processing and retailing costs to the raw product cost.

This article is divided into the following sections:

A. The life cycle of the steer from the gleam in his father's eye to steak on the table, with the time elements and production costs along the way.

B. Market play and the economic factors involved.

C. The background of futures trading in cattle and some objections of the industry to seeing it done in volume on a central exchange.

D. Actual mechanics. The reasons futures contract trading can be made to work and the actual mechanics of how it can be utilized by the small packer and feeder to eliminate his risks and obtain better financing.

A. Life Cycle of a Steer

Once an old bull and a young bull were walking down a valley and they saw a group of heifers on a hill high above them. The young bull said, "let us run up the hill and service a heifer." The old bull said, "let us walk up the hill and service them all."

From this event in New Mexico to a cut of prime steak at the Golden Ox in Washington, D.C., a time lapse of two and a half years is required. This is one-fourth of the traditional 10-year cycle in cattle prices. The gestation period of a cow is nine months. At birth the calf weighs 60–90 lbs. At seven months of age he weighs 350–450 lbs. and is ready for weaning. From a calendar year standpoint in the Great Plains area of the United States, the mother was six months pregnant on January 1, gave birth on April 1, got rebred on July 1, and weaned her calf on October 1. If you give yourself a plus or minus factor of 45 days, you will hit 70% of the United States cattle industry for seasonal timing. The calf may be "rough wintered" in New Mexico for 180 days, during which he gained 100 lbs., and "summered" in the Kansas blue stem for another 180 days, during which he gains 225 lbs. He is now 19 months old and weighs 725 lbs.

From Kansas he is shipped to a Panhandle feedlot and gradually worked into a full corn ration. There he averages two and a half pounds per day of gain for 180 days, or 450 lbs. At the end of this period he is marketed as a 1,175 lb. medium choice steer, 20 months of age. Thirty months have elapsed since his mother was bred. His original production cost to a weaned 400 lb. calf is tied up with the maintenance of his mother.

Dividing the $120–$140 by the 400 pounds he weighs, your weaned calf has cost you 30¢–35¢ per pound. Some years it is cheaper to buy a calf; some years it is cheaper to raise him.

To run the calf from 400 lbs. to 725 lbs., or from six months to eighteen months, will cost you 27¢ to 30¢ per pound, or about $90. No consideration is given to return on your capital during this period. You now have a value of $225 and a 725 lb. steer yearling (18 months old). This comes to approximately 30¢ a pound.

You are about to leave breeding and go into feeding. These two bear little relationship to each other, have different tax treatments, require different skills, and their operations are often not even located in the same sections of the country.

In the feedlot you run into a high risk, high expense, speculative business. Once you have put a few months feed into the steer, and are committed to about a six month feeding program, you are stuck with the situation regardless of what the market looks like. If you stopped, you could lose all the money you have put in.

On gain, some people brag about getting three and a half pounds per day. In bad weather and a poor operation, many people get less than one and a half pounds per day. For calculating purposes, use two and a half pounds per day and be pleasantly surprised if you do better. On full feed, with corn at $2.75 per bushel, this will cost 49¢ per pound of gain, or $1.23 per day in an average commercial lot (includes labor, equipment, and bookkeeping). Four hundred pounds of gain will cost you $196, exclusive of interest, and personal property taxes.

If you bought a 700 lb. yearling at 30¢ per pound, you would have a cost of $210. If you put 450 pounds on him in a feed lot at 49¢ per pound you would have $220 more in him for a total of $430 in a 1,150 lb. steer. To break even on this animal, you would need about 38¢ per pound. After transportation, shrink, marketing, taxes, interest, and administration, you would need 40¢.

This is a rapidly fluctuating market and no game for amateurs. Remember the ancient Scottish proverb: "There are three ways of losing money—race horses, women, and fattening cattle. The first is the quickest, the second is the pleasantest, but the third is the surest."

B. Market Play
Mechanics of Marketing

In the old days when all large cattle movements were by rail, cattle would come into a central market consigned to a commission house known and friendly to a given rancher. The commission house would sell to a packing house, to a registered trader at the yards who would buy for his own account, or to feeders or other commission men who had been authorized to buy for their account.

The traders at the stockyards were normally men who would buy for their own account in rather large wholesale quantities and then sort and "shape" the herd for retail sales to the small farmers and feeders. Their average profit over a year would run from 25¢ to 50¢ per hundred pounds. Obviously, on some days, if they caught a rising market they could do very well; on other days, they might take substantial losses.

The commission houses would take a commission on the sale from the selling client, as well as from the purchasing client. All of these intermediate middleman charges would normally run from $2.00 to $5.00 per head on the overall transaction between the seller and buyer.

The stockyards themselves make their profits from the rather high price of feed sold while the cattle are in the pens and from various "yardage" fees. Other fees are charged commission houses and the traders for the use of the pens, which normally belong to the stockyards company and are rented out. In most cases, the stockyards also own the central office building associated with the yards and charge rent to all the users.

"Order buyers" could be commission men, traders, or regular salaried employees of associations or packing house groups who have been given firm orders to buy a certain number of cattle at specified weights and grades. When the cattle are purchased, the order buyers are authorized to write drafts on the buyers' accounts. As a rule, in most central yards, all of these people are bonded.

Until about 20 years ago, probably about 80% of the cattle changing hands in the United States followed a pattern of something similar to the preceding. The big change in all of this was occasioned by the development of the trucking industry and the large national highways. This caused the rise of the "country auction." In this situation, usually on a given day of the week, cattle over a given neighborhood are brought into a local sales barn and are auctioned off in various sized lots by professional auctioneers. A fee is paid on a per head basis to the auction house and usually additional profit is made by the auction house by the sale of hay and feed on which it has a monopoly.

At these auctions, the seller is permitted to put in a bid and buy back his cattle if he feels that he is not getting the proper price. In some cases the auctioneer has been directed by the seller to "take a bid off the back of the tent" if he does not feel there is enough action and if the cattle are going to be "given away." In recent years, these auctions have acquired enough volume so that direct representatives of the major packing houses usually attend them and buy for their own firm's accounts, and traders and order buyers come in from the major feeders so as to completely circumvent the central market.

Many of these markets are located in areas not serviced by railroads, and cattle come in by truck and go out by truck.

For a considerable time in history, most of the registered pedigreed business was conducted by "private treaty." This means that the buyer and the seller directly meet and work out a price without an intervening agent. In recent years, with the return of the large scale operation—particularly as regards feeders—many of the major feed operators in Missouri, Iowa, and Illinois send their own salaried employees directly into the ranch country to contract for the delivery of large quantities of a given class of animal to be weighed off the ranch under certain conditions, three, four, six, and even as much as eight months later. It is customary to put $5 to $10 per head as earnest money on these contracts and to go into great detail as to the conditions of weighing; whether or not the cattle are to be watered or fed on the day of weighing; who is responsible for the truck bills to the scales; how the cattle are to be worked before and during the day of weighing and as to what treatment should be given to any cattle that do not come up to the "normal specifications" or are "un-merchantable."

"Shrink" is the amount of actual weight that an animal will lose while it is being jostled around the pens, driven to the scales, or trucked to the nearest public scales. In some cases, where the weighing conditions are extremely favorable to the seller and the cattle are now actually going to receive much "physical shrink," the buyer often demands that 2% or 3% be subtracted from the final weight of the cattle to compensate him for these unfavorable weighing conditions. This is known as "pencil shrink."

The annual net profit of many a cattle trader is based on "shrink". If a 700 pound yearling steer is shipped 600 miles from a grass pasture in Oklahoma on a hot August day after he has been jostled around in a corral and the trucker overcrowds him and takes two days on the drive, the animal may shrink 50 pounds or 7%, by his arrival at a Kansas City scale. At 40¢ per pound this is worth $20. The steer will recover half of this weight after he has been fed, watered, and rested. However it will take 10 days on pasture to recover the initial weight. Newly weaned calves might take three weeks to start feeding and recover initial weight. Eight hundred pound steers

off a grain feed, shipped on a cold day, and carefully handled might shrink only 2% or 16 pounds.

A trader who buys shrunk-out animals even at a premium, puts them in a feedlot near the yard for a week, and sells them at 1¢ per pound discount will still make a profit from the shrink recovery. Often with the improvement in the animal's appearance from the rest and a "fill," the trader will not have to give a price discount and can make the full shrink recovery.

Geographic Differential

On a given day, due to local weather conditions preventing buyers or sellers from arriving, it would not be at all unusual for there to be a 2¢ per pound differential in prices in Kansas City, Omaha, Sioux City and Chicago. This could amount to as much as 10% to 15% of the selling price of an animal. It would be unlikely that anything greater than this would persist because it would then become economically worthwhile to move animals physically from one area to another.

Beyond the daily fluctuation due to local conditions, the general trend is that the closer you are to big centers of consumption, such as New York, Chicago, and Los Angeles, prices ought to be higher by at

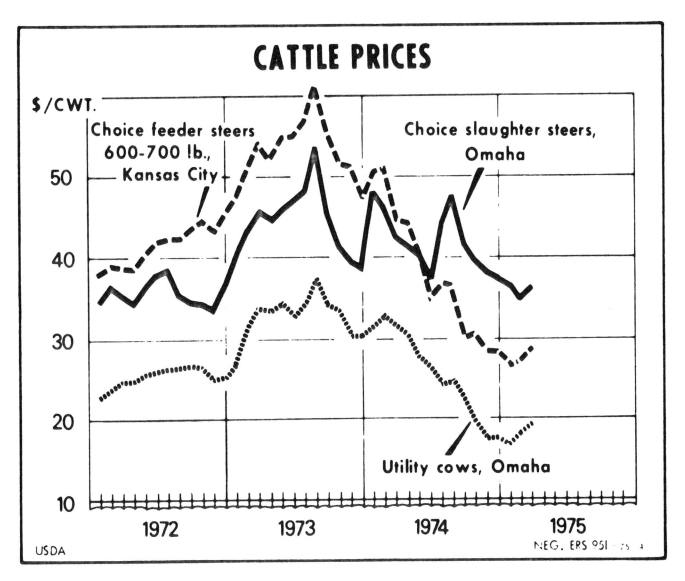

CATTLE PRICES

$/CWT.

Choice feeder steers 600-700 lb., Kansas City

Choice slaughter steers, Omaha

Utility cows, Omaha

1972   1973   1974   1975

USDA

NEG. ERS 951-75 4

15

least the amount of the transportation. A country auction in a small town on the northern border of Western Montana should certainly average out $5 to $10 per head cheaper than the Kansas City market. However, even this is not an absolute rule. For example, if this section of Montana had droughts for a couple of years and a greater part of the herd had been liquidated, the ranches would start to restock their ranges after a rain came. In this case, they could very well pay over Kansas City prices locally to get cattle moved in from more distant areas.

Totally unrelated to any of the preceding is a separate phenomenon due to seasonal variations between one section of the country and another. For example, in California rains start in September and the good cheap grass conditions occur during the "winter." June, July, and August are the months of dry pasture, drought, and the feeding of expensive hay. Consequently, it is cutomary to breed cows to drop calves in September and to be prepared to wean them off and sell all yearlings by June of the following year, when the heavy expenses start.

Beyond this, you have the physical factors that cattle from widely different geographic areas might take as much as one year to adapt themselves to new climatic conditions before starting to put on the normal growth. This acts as somewhat of a bar to free movement between widely separated areas regardless of the transportation costs. For example, it would probably be an extremely bad practice to move cattle from South Dakota to Florida even if the transportation were free.

Daily Market Play

At the time at which this article is being written, early in 1975, the Dow Jones industrial average of common stock had been fluctuating near the 650 level. A 5% change in the cattle at the central markets, at the country auctions, or on futures contracts is a daily occurrence that hardly occasions the lifting of an eyebrow. In fact, on the same day it is quite possible for prices in South Dakota to go up 5% and prices in Northern Arizona to go down 5%, again without more than a passing glance from the industry. A 5% fluctuation in the Dow Jones average would make headlines all over the world.

It is obvious that with this type of wide daily fluctuation as a matter of almost routine, considerable money can be made or lost by traders and speculators who buy and sell for their own account within a 48 hour period.

One of the principal fortunes in the cattle business has been made on a very simple device by a man we

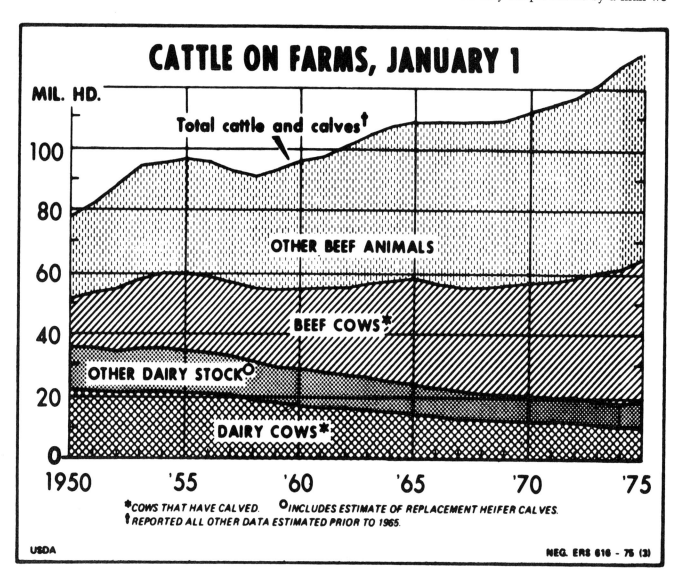

shall fictitiously call Mr. Tom Smith. Mr. Smith owns one of the large trading houses in one of the principal stockyards and is also in partnership with several of the major ranchers and feedlots at distances running from 100 to 300 miles from the location of the stockyards.

For years he has cultivated the friendship of the freight agents of the principal railroads serving his city. Every Friday night he has been in the habit of calling them to find out what cattle shipments are scheduled to arrive at his stockyards on the following Monday morning. He finds out what major class of cattle is coming in, what the cattles' weights are, and what their general quality and condition are.

If it looks as if 1,000 lb. two year old steers are going to arrive in volume, he directs all of his own people to hold off shipping anything in this category. If, at the same time, he finds nothing substantial is coming in on dry utility cows, that is the moment he sells the drys which he already has sorted off in special close in pastures for just this kind of play. On annual sales in excess of $10,000,000 this freight agent intelligence system cannot have failed to give him an increase of 3% in his annual net which amounts to around $300,000 per year. Besides this, he has built up a substantial customer clientele that knows he always has the particular class of cattle in his pens on which the market seems to be short that day.

Monthly Trends

The great bulk of U.S. fed cattle come from the feed grain areas of the Midwest. At the November harvest, feed is the cheapest, and the heaviest volume of cattle go on feed at this time. Later in April and May they should be coming out of the feedlots and be available for the slaughter market, and the increased sales volume should mean a lower market.

C. Background of Futures Trading in Cattle

Futures trading in calves, range yearlings, and even feedlot cattle has been going on in volume for a quarter of a century. It just has not been done on an organized basis on a major exchange.

Large Western ranchers dealing in 1,000 head units of calves or yearlings have never wanted to be at the mercy of the buyers at a central auction on a given day. A sudden snow storm might give adverse weighing conditions, and this many cattle might swamp the few buyers who had braved the snow storm to come.

Consequently, four or five months ahead of delivery these ranchers customarily negotiate sales via "private treaty." In such a sale, the buyer comes out, inspects the cattle, estimates what the grass conditions are, guesses the weights four months hence, and enters into a contract with a cash earnest money deposit to buy at a fixed price per pound and under given weighing conditions.

When the seller has a good reputation and a "name brand" and the buyer knows the quality of the cattle, the purchaser may enter into a contract without looking at the animals. In this case, you might put in a sliding price scale if they are over certain specified weights. Futures contracts are also negotiable merchandise. They might be bought and sold by three "traders" before they actually end up with the feedlot that is going to take the final delivery.

The same type of thing has been going on for years between packing houses and feeders with regard to slaughter cattle. Generally the time lag is only a month or two. The packer buyer, usually a salaried employee with the packing house, inspects a pen of cattle that are on full feed and have three to ten days on contract delivery time before they are "ready." He puts in a bid at a price per pound, with a 4% shrink, for the cattle to be weighed in at a local scales three to ten days hence.

The feeder may shop this bid around, attempt to get the buyer up a quarter of a cent, and then decide to accept the bid. A written future delivery contract is then entered into. Exceptions may be for "unmerchantables" with arrangements for arbitration on arguments. In this type of contract, it is unusual for the future grade of the animals on slaughter to be specified or for weight restrictions to be put in. Both the feeder and the packer buyer are professionals and they can estimate the future grade, dressing percentage, and weights on delivery date within a few points. If the feeder cannot do this, he will go broke. If the packing house buyer cannot do it, he will get fired.

D. Actual Mechanics
Rules and Regulations on Chicago
Mercantile Exchange

The firm of which I am Chairman of the Board, has in recent years been the largest in the United States in the management of ranch herds, and we have been fairly substantial in feedlot cattle. A major portion of our business has been the buying and selling of cattle by future delivery contract. I can say without qualification that in the thousands of contracts I have seen, I have never seen specifications pinned down so tightly as in the contract unit of the Beef Futures Division of the Chicago Mercantile Exchange. Prior to seeing this, I somewhat shared the view of the big packers that it would be hard to work out an interchangeable contract unit.

I now believe that I was wrong. I further believe that the unit has been accepted as a yardstick throughout the industry on other trading in addition to futures trading.

The following are only selected highlights:

1. The par unit will be 40,000 pounds of choice grade or better live steers.

2. Steers will be within the range 1,050 to 1,150 pounds; estimated yield requirements will be 61%.

3. Alternative: Steers will each be within the weight range of 1,151 to 1,250 pounds; estimated yield requirements will be 62%.

4. Delivery units with estimated yield under par will be acceptable with an allowance of one-fourth cent per pound for each one-half percent or less by which the estimated yield is under par.

5. Steers weighing from 100–200 pounds over or under the average weight of the steers in the delivery unit shall be deliverable at an allowance of 2¢ per pound.

6. Delivery units containing not more than 8 head of the top half of U.S.D.A. good grade steers may be substituted at 2¢ per pound under par price (computed on average weight of delivered unit).

7. The judgment of the grader (U.S.D.A.) as to such over-weight or under-weight cattle shall be final and shall be so certified on the grading certificate.

8. The cattle shall be choice by U.S.D.A. detailed specifications.

9. All unhealthy or unmerchantable animals are to be taken off.

10. All shipments must be to a licensed, registered, bonded livestock commission firm.

11. Weighing is to be done within one hour following completion of grading and estimated yield of exchange delivery.

12. Minimum initial margin shall be $1,200 per contract.

13. Contracts are to be delivered in April, June, August, October, February and December.

14. Delivery points: Joliet and Peoria, Illinois; Sioux City, Iowa; and Omaha, Nebraska; all at par. Delivery can also be made at Guymon, Oklahoma, with an allowance of 75¢ per 100 weight.

E. Operations

In wheat, which is an easily transported, easily stored commodity, less than 3% of the futures contracts ever result in a physical delivery of the actual grain contracted for and only when both parties want it that way. Live cattle, which have to be fed, are difficult to transport and cannot be stored, result in less than 1% physical delivery.

These are typical transactions:

1. Mr. A. is a Kansas feedlot operator with 2,000 steers on feed for his own account who is nervous about the June market. He sells June futures short in Chicago for 26 contracts, or approximately 1,000 head, at approximately 42¢ per pound. It is now January. Mr. B, a speculator, buys the contracts. Mr. A has these alternative courses of action:

a. Sometime before June he physically sorts off 1,000 head of cattle that meet the specifications and ships them to Omaha to fulfill his contracts.

b. He has an agent or commission man buy 1,000 head of cattle from feedlots around Omaha and delivers them to fulfill his contracts.

c. Several months before delivery time, he has his broker on the Exchange contact Mr. B and settle his contracts. If the price of June futures is now 43¢ per pound, he pays Mr. B 1¢ per pound in cash and settles the contracts. If the price is 41¢ per pound, Mr. B owes him 1¢ per pound.

d. If Mr. B does not want to settle and close out the contracts, Mr. A has his broker go to the market and buy someone else's June contracts. He then hands these to Mr. B and calls it quits. What he has to pay for these "covering contracts" determines whether he makes or loses money on the trade.

e. Unless Mr. B is actually a packer with a plant in Kansas, it is unlikely that he wants actual physical delivery. If he does, the last holder of the contracts can buy the cattle on the cash market around Omaha and deliver them to Mr. B's pen in the designated Omaha yards.

f. While this may never occur, the fact that it could, keeps the futures market near delivery date pretty close to the cash market.

g. Back in Kansas, Mr. A never intended to ship to sell any of his 2,000 head to anywhere but Amarillo. However, he figured that if the Amarillo market fell 3¢ between January and June the Omaha market would too. By selling short on the market, he could make 3¢ per pound on covering his sale with a "paper" transaction in a commodity transaction (Omaha June futures contract). This would break him even on the 3¢ he lost on his own live cattle in Amarillo.

h. It should be noted that Mr. A hedged only on 1,000 head of the 2,000 he had on feed. On the remaining he felt that he was in a financial position to gamble and could sustain a 3¢ drop.

II. Mr. C is a small packing plant owner. He cannot afford a large buying staff. He also has a very unfavorable union contract through which he will get stuck with an extra day's wages if his plant has to be shut down temporarily because he runs out of animals. His sales and delivery commitments are at fixed prices 30 days ahead. He is fearful of a temporary upswing in June which will put him in an intolerable squeeze. His plant is in Arkansas. He buys Omaha June futures at 42¢. He has these alternatives:

a. He takes delivery in Omaha and ships the animals to Arkansas.

b. He takes delivery in Omaha, sells the cattle on the Omaha cash market, and buys what he wants in Arkansas.

c. He settles or covers his Omaha contracts with cash given or received depending upon whether the market has gone up or down.

d. If the market over the country has gone up sharply, he has made enough on his Omaha contracts to cover the extra price he has to pay at home and he does not have to absorb the operating loss of a plant shut down.

e. It is theoretically possible that Mr. C actually bought the contracts sold by Mr. A in Kansas. One man was worried about a price decline; one was worried about a price increase. Physically, Mr. A could have shipped his cattle to Mr. C's plant in Arkansas. That was not necessary, as both were able to hedge themselves against a price fluctuation by a "paper" transaction in Omaha.

III. Mr. D is a small Missouri farmer with a nervous banker. He has taken a beating in the last two years and has borrowed to the hilt. He has plenty of feed on hand and has a proven record of competence as a cattle feeder but cannot convince his banker that cattle prices are not about to go down to the 1934 level.

a. If he could sell choice animals on the Kansas City market at 40¢ per pound, he would make a profit, sell his feed converted into beef, and pay off all of his bank loans.

b. It is November and he cannot convince his banker that June prices will not be down to 32¢. At that price he would get nothing for his feed and would default on his bank loans.

c. Omaha futures for June are going at 42¢. He tells his banker that this means that sophisticated people are willing to "put their money where their mouths are" and bet that cattle prices will be 42¢ in June.

d. That does not convince his banker, who says, "those people in Omaha are just a bunch of rich city boys who want to gamble with beef instead of playing roulette in Las Vegas."

e. Mr. D finally gets his loan by selling short on the Omaha futures market and assigning his short contracts to the banker.

f. The banker was finally convinced that if he had to foreclose on the cattle mortgage he could ship the collateral to Omaha, and demand payment at 42¢.

April Live Beef Cattle Futures Delivery
1972-73 to 1974-75

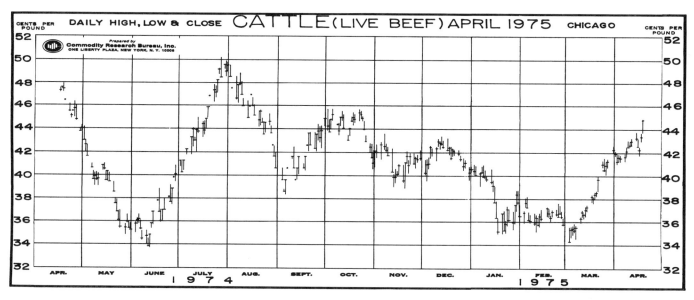

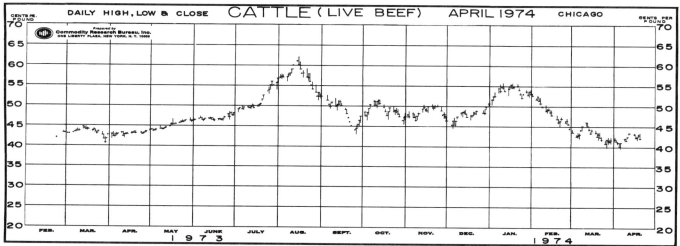

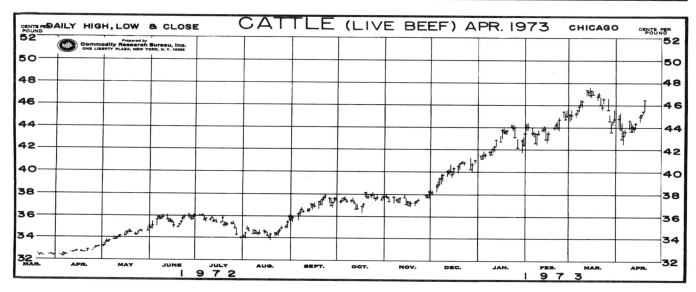

April Live Beef Cattle Futures Delivery
1969-70 to 1971-72

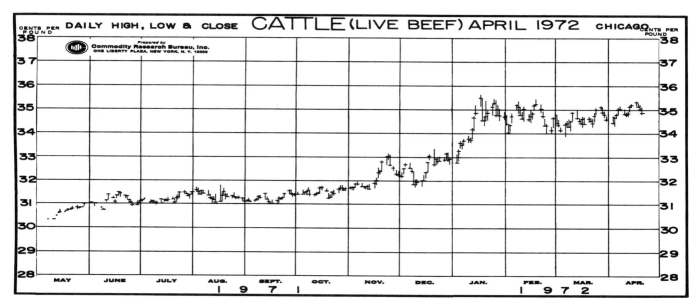

DAILY HIGH, LOW & CLOSE CATTLE (LIVE BEEF) APRIL 1972 CHICAGO

Prepared by
Commodity Research Bureau, Inc.
ONE LIBERTY PLAZA, NEW YORK, N.Y. 10006

MAY JUNE JULY AUG. SEPT. OCT. NOV. DEC. JAN. FEB. MAR. APR.
1 9 7 1   1 9 7 2

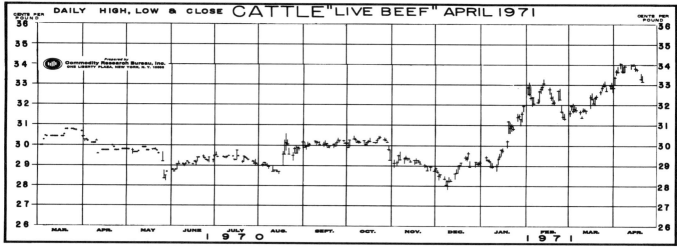

DAILY HIGH, LOW & CLOSE CATTLE "LIVE BEEF" APRIL 1971

Prepared by
Commodity Research Bureau, Inc.
ONE LIBERTY PLAZA, NEW YORK, N.Y. 10006

MAR. APR. MAY JUNE JULY AUG. SEPT. OCT. NOV. DEC. JAN. FEB. MAR. APR.
1 9 7 0   1 9 7 1

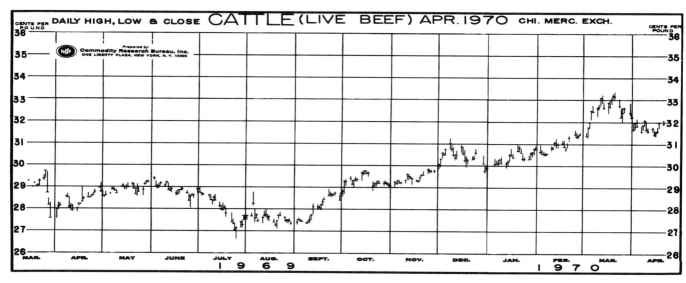

DAILY HIGH, LOW & CLOSE CATTLE (LIVE BEEF) APR. 1970 CHI. MERC. EXCH.

Prepared by
Commodity Research Bureau, Inc.
ONE LIBERTY PLAZA, NEW YORK, N.Y. 10006

MAR. APR. MAY JUNE JULY AUG. SEPT. OCT. NOV. DEC. JAN. FEB. MAR. APR.
1 9 6 9   1 9 7 0

April Live Beef Cattle Futures Delivery
1966-67 to 1968-69

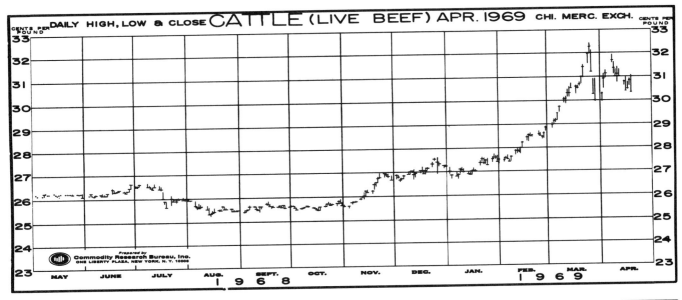

DAILY HIGH, LOW & CLOSE CATTLE (LIVE BEEF) APR. 1969 CHI. MERC. EXCH.

Prepared by Commodity Research Bureau, Inc. ONE LIBERTY PLAZA, NEW YORK, N.Y. 10006

MAY JUNE JULY AUG. SEPT. OCT. NOV. DEC. JAN. FEB. MAR. APR.
1 9 6 8   1 9 6 9

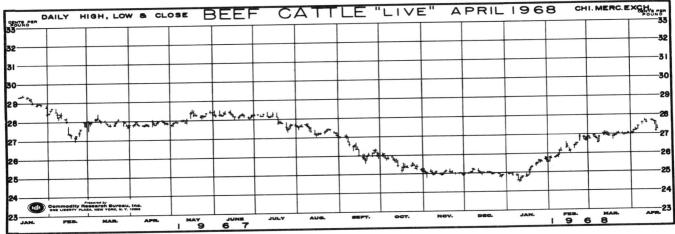

DAILY HIGH, LOW & CLOSE BEEF CATTLE "LIVE" APRIL 1968 CHI. MERC. EXCH.

Commodity Research Bureau, Inc. ONE LIBERTY PLAZA, NEW YORK, N.Y. 10006

JAN. FEB. MAR. APR. MAY JUNE JULY AUG. SEPT. OCT. NOV. DEC. JAN. FEB. MAR. APR.
1 9 6 7   1 9 6 8

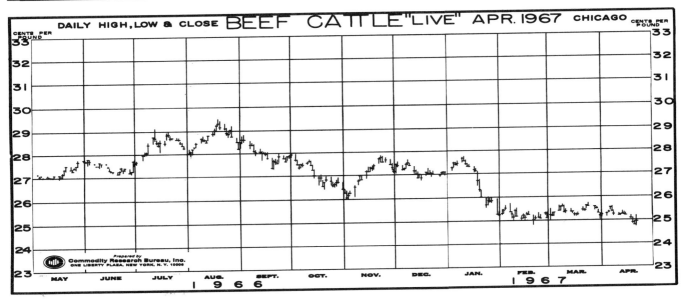

DAILY HIGH, LOW & CLOSE BEEF CATTLE "LIVE" APR. 1967 CHICAGO

Prepared by Commodity Research Bureau, Inc. ONE LIBERTY PLAZA, NEW YORK, N.Y. 10006

MAY JUNE JULY AUG. SEPT. OCT. NOV. DEC. JAN. FEB. MAR. APR.
1 9 6 6   1 9 6 7

21

A METHOD OF FORECASTING COCOA PRICES

BY WILLIAM STERN

Once upon a time, as all fairy tales begin, we wrote an article in the 1972 Commodity Year Book entitled "A Method of Forecasting Cocoa Prices." The basic concept of that article, and the method referred to, was to determine the end-year carryover stocks of cocoa in the world in terms of months' supply, and relate that stock position to the FOB value for cocoa in previous years where a similar supply situation existed. Based on the conclusions at that time a carryover of 4.7 months' supply was projected, which suggested an average price of 23¢ per lb. FOB for cocoa in 1972. Actually, the carryover turned out to be slightly less, and the average price for cocoa in 1972 was 24¢ per lb. FOB. At a glance, therefore, it appeared the method was a practical one for forecasting cocoa prices.

New Factors in Cocoa Price Analysis

However, that article was written before the days of double-digit inflation, $11 per barrel oil, $200 per oz. gold, 70¢ per lb. refined sugar, deepening world recessionary tendencies, and wildly fluctuating international currency markets, all of which have since had an enormous impact on the commodity world. In this article we will attempt to inter-relate these new developments on the commodity scene with the basic fundamental supply/demand approach referred to above, and attempt to come up with a new approach to forecasting cocoa prices. In the age of the computer, it would appear that a more scientific technical approach could be discovered to arrive at a new method for forecasting cocoa prices. There is—toss a coin in the air—if it turns up "heads" the market is headed higher; and if it turns up "tails" the market is going lower. But only if the coin lands on its end standing up should you speculate in cocoa!

Now let us go deeper into the cocoa picture and explore the fundamental statistical situation and outlook before attempting to evaluate the importance of many other factors which influence not only the day to day fluctuations of the cocoa market, but those that have more long range impact on the price of cocoa.

Factors That Influence Production

Initially, a brief agricultural history might prove helpful. Cocoa is a tropical tree crop grown in areas 20 degrees above or below the Equator. The five largest producers in the world are Ghana, Nigeria, Ivory Coast, Brazil and the Cameroons. These countries represent approximately 80% of the total annual world production.

A cocoa tree normally reaches maturity after four to six years and commences bearing fruit at that time. However, some of the newer plants begin bearing fruit within two to three years. The average yield per tree is between three and five pounds of dry cocoabeans. Flowers and fruits in all stages of maturity can be found on cocoa trees at all times of the year, although only two crops are harvested each year.

The larger of the two crops is the "main crop," which is harvested between the months of October and March in the West African countries. The summer or "mid crop" is usually harvested from May to August. In Brazil, however, the winter crop or the main crop, as it is called, is usually the smaller of the two crops, and the summer crop or the mid crop, called the "Temporao" crop, is the larger one.

Critical factors which seriously affect cocoa production in these countries, of course, include weather, prices paid to the farmers, government subsidies for spraying for effective pest control, and farm care and husbandry. In view of the volatility of crop outturns, these can change drastically from year to year depending on the above factors. One of the most important developments weatherwise in recent years has been the prolonged drought in Northern Africa which has drifted southward to affect the cocoa belt in West Africa, resulting in smaller crop outturns than expected. On the other hand, crop prospects in Brazil have improved in recent years.

The following table illustrates the highest and lowest crop outturns (in long tons) in each of the five major producing countries during the past fifteen years. The large discrepancies between the high and low production figures clearly point out the difficulties in forecasting crop outturns in these countries:

Origin	High	Year	Low	Year
Ghana	557,000 l.t.	1964/65	334,000 l.t.	1968/69
Nigeria	303,000 l.t.	1970/71	176,000 l.t.	1962/63
Ivory Coast	221,000 l.t.	1971/72	97,000 l.t.	1963/64
Cameroons	121,000 l.t.	1971/72	75,000 l.t.	1962/63
Brazil	242,000 l.t.	1973/74	111,000 l.t.	1962/63

From the above one can see that, with the exception of Ghana, the higher yields have come in recent years, indicating an upward production trend in most of the leading producing countries. The main reasons for this have been high world market prices and government attempts to revive and expand the cocoa industry. Certainly, current high world cocoa prices should prove a further stimulant for increasing production in the coming years, as prices to farmers have been raised and government subsidies for spraying have been liberally granted.

Trends in Production and Consumption

The long term trend of production and consumption in cocoa has been up, as the cocoa economy has expanded dynamically during the past 30 years from a world crop of 614,000 long tons in 1946/47 to 1,562,000 long tons in 1971/72. With recent high cocoa prices and the determination of the various producing countries to revitalize and expand the cocoa industry, it would not surprise us to see production within the next five years approach 2,000,000 long tons. World grindings have also dramatically improved from about 600,000 tons in 1947 to 1,546,000 tons in 1972. Consumption in the Western world has remained static during the past decade, and with increased use of substitutes in the Western consuming countries it is doubtful whether there is sufficient room for increasing grindings in this part of the world unless prices drop to levels that existed several years ago. On the other hand, an increasing trend in consumption in the Soviet Union and Eastern Europe makes it quite possible that world grindings may also approach 2,000,000 long tons by 1980.

One of the most interesting statistics and recent developments in the consuming picture has been the change in the trend of consumption in the past decade. There has been a very definite shift in emphasis in grindings from the Western countries to the Eastern countries. The same is true of an increased trend toward industrialization at origin. Grindings in the Western consuming world have remained static and, in fact, have declined during this period while grindings in the Soviet Union and Eastern Europe have increased significantly. The following table clearly illustrates this shift in emphasis in grindings:

	1962	1974
Western Europe	515,000 l.t.	519,000 l.t.
Eastern Europe	51,000 l.t.	107,000 l.t.
Soviet Union	43,000 l.t.	138,000 l.t.
West Africa	29,000 l.t.	137,000 l.t.
Brazil	52,000 l.t.	100,000 l.t.
United States	251,000 l.t.	230,000 l.t.

This has made projecting trends in consumption and grindings more difficult, inasmuch as accurate and current statistical information from many of these areas is not readily available to the market.

Cocoa is a cheap food and should become the food of the common man. China, Russia and India are potentially large consumers of cheap chocolate. To enable chocolate to reach parts of the world where it is unknown, producers must perfect agricultural techniques to reduce the cost of production so that farmers can produce more cocoa for less money and with less effort. In most of the leading producing countries of the world, old trees yield approximately two to five pounds of cocoa per tree, and 200 pounds of dry cocoa per acre. At experimental stations in the Ivory Coast under the most ideal conditions, yields as high as 1,000 to 2,000 pounds of dry cocoa per acre have been realized. While it is possible the farmer and the exporting country may receive a lower unit price for each pound of cocoa if production increases significantly, the farmer should be able to grow more cocoa and simultaneously diversify his farm economy to make better use of additional land to grow other crops, and ultimately increase his income.

Available Statistical Data

The accessibility and credibility of statistical data is still one of the major obstacles confronting analysts in cocoa in attempting to assess the information at hand. Official weekly purchase figures from farmers are reported from Ghana and Brazil on a regular basis, while similar information from Nigeria, Ivory Coast and Cameroons is usually semi-officially reported by trade or government sources from time to time. These figures are most important inasmuch as they are used as a guide in determining the eventual outturn of the crop in the respective countries. On the other side of the equation, grindings or consumption data is regularly reported by most of the major Western consuming countries. However, grinding data from the Soviet Union and other Eastern European countries is normally not available currently. Thus the fundamental approach to analyzing the supply/demand picture in cocoa is determined by evaluating all the production and grinding statistics available to arrive at a net addition to, or subtraction from, the previous year's stock position.

The Importance of End-Season Stocks

At this point we will update the table illustrating end-season stocks in terms of months' supply in relation to the FOB price for cocoa. The cocoa crop year runs from October 1 to the following September 30, and grindings are normally published on a calendar year basis. In the table on the following page grindings have been adjusted to a seasonal basis to coincide with the production figures.

It may be noted that two sets of possible fundamental situations which may arise in 1975 have been listed. The source of this table (Gill & Duffus Ltd.) in their report, dated December, 1974, forecast a slight surplus of 22,000 tons, while the author's own estimate is for a modest surplus of 50,000 tons. In either case, there should be an increase in the carryover stocks at the end of the season.

From the following table it can be seen that end season stocks in 1974 were the lowest in the post-war years, and, therefore, naturally cocoa prices reached historically high levels. It also appeared to the author (early in 1975) that a modest surplus of about 50,000 tons would be realized in 1975. Thus, end-season stocks in 1975 were expected to be increased slightly, but nevertheless would remain at a relatively low level, and supplies should remain tight. It does suggest, however, that the average FOB price for cocoa in 1975 should be lower than the estimated FOB price of 63¢ per lb. that existed in 1974. It follows, therefore, that premiums for actual cocoa, which were extraordinarily high early in 1975, had ample room to decline in 1975 while futures could decline, but to a lesser degree. This assumption was based strictly on the fundamental supply/demand position and did not take into consideration various other factors which were deemed likely to exert tremendous influence on prices in 1975.

How Sugar Influences Cocoa Consumption

The most important of these factors would be the course of sugar prices in 1975. As 50% of every chocolate bar consists of sugar it is easy to see why the role of sugar prices is so crucial to the candy and confectionery industry. The 1974 sugar market was the greatest bull market in commodity history. The full impact of 1974 sugar prices was not felt by the entire cocoa consuming world, as many European nations are insulated against price increases by Government subsidies. Whereas American manufacturers in 1974 were paying historical high prices for sugar, as high as 70¢ per lb., members of the European Economic Community were receiving sugar at prices as low as 18¢ per lb. It is doubtful that this type of government support will continue in 1975, and even more questionable is whether the actual sugar will be available in some nations to supply the industry. Thus consumption in 1975 is a bigger question mark than ever. If high sugar prices persist, it is quite conceivable that cocoa consumption may suffer a greater loss and, therefore, the estimated surplus in 1975 could be larger than the 50,000 tons currently projected.

How Inflation Affects Cocoa Price Forecasts

The effects of double-digit inflation have also upset the method of forecasting cocoa prices based on carryover in terms of months' supply compared to similar situations in previous years. One must now take into consideration the devaluation of the dollar during this period, and this makes it exceedingly difficult to accurately make comparisons with previous seasons. For example, a 2.5 months' carryover in 1953 or 1954 may have resulted in a 30¢ per lb. FOB price for cocoa whereas a similar carry-over in 1973 or 1974 could well result in a 60¢ per lb. FOB price. From a look at the effect of inflation and the devaluation of the dollar with the long term chart of cocoa on the next page, it appears price levels have approximately doubled in similar supply situations. Whereas 20¢ per lb. for futures was a historical support level for cocoa, it now appears to us that 40¢ per lb. for futures may well become a new support level in view of inflation and currency modifications. A side effect of inflation has been the increased use of commodity futures markets by "currency-type" speculators who have used international commodities like cocoa, sugar, copper, coffee, silver, and gold in a flight from paper currencies. In many instances this has resulted in wide distortions of price levels as fundamentals in a specific market have been largely ignored.

International Cocoa Agreement

An International Cocoa Agreement was finally implemented in 1973, although the United States is not a member of the Agreement. It has always been the contention of the American trade that cocoa is not a burdensome surplus commodity and, therefore, an international agreement is unnecessary. Certainly, events of the past few years have proven this position was correct. In fact, it has been difficult for production to maintain pace with consumption. The price range in the Agreement was 23¢ to 32¢ per lb. as originally drafted. These figures represent the average price of the first three active trading months in New York and London combined. The mechanism of the agreement does not go into effect until prices reach the lower end of that range. However, prices have been well above the maximum of the range since the agreement was put in force and, therefore, it has not been operative. A levy of 1¢ per lb. on cocoabean exports, however, has been collected by producers for

Cocoa Post-war Supply and Demand   (Thousand Long Tons)

Crop Season	Opening Stocks	Net World Crop	Seasonal Grindings	End Season Stock	Months' Supply	FOB Price
1946/1947	200	608	650	158	2.9	25¢
1947/1948	158	587	617	128	2.5	35
1948/1949	128	765	678	215	3.8	20
1949/1950	215	748	760	203	3.2	25
1950/1951	203	795	757	241	3.8	32
1951/1952	241	636	725	152	2.5	31
1952/1953	152	790	777	165	2.5	30
1953/1954	165	768	752	181	2.9	49
1954/1955	181	794	725	250	4.1	37
1955/1956	250	835	798	287	4.3	26
1956/1957	287	889	887	289	3.9	26
1957/1958	289	765	865	189	2.6	39
1958/1959	189	899	860	228	3.2	34
1959/1960	228	1029	907	350	4.6	26
1960/1961	350	1161	988	523	6.4	21
1961/1962	523	1113	1083	553	6.1	21
1962/1963	553	1152	1133	572	6.1	21
1963/1964	572	1204	1170	606	6.2	22
1964/1965	606	1467	1280	788	7.4	15
1965/1966	788	1193	1354	627	5.6	17
1966/1967	627	1320	1366	581	5.1	23
1967/1968	581	1320	1384	517	4.5	27
1968/1969	517	1209	1347	379	3.4	34
1969/1970	379	1404	1335	448	4.0	32
1970/1971	448	1464	1398	514	4.4	26
1971/1972	514	1546	1497	563	4.5	24
1972/1973	563	1359	1589	333	2.5	38
1973/1974	333	1408	1451	290	2.4	63 (EST)
1974/1975	290 (EST)	1392 (EST)	1370 (EST)	312 (EST)	2.7 (EST)	60 (EST)
1974/1975	290 (EST)	1400 (EST)	1350 (EST)	240 (EST)	3.0 (EST)	57 (EST)

Source: Gill & Duffus Ltd.   Estimated figures are our own.

eventual possible purchase of a "buffer stock" should prices fall below the lower end of the range in the agreement. In view of currency devaluations and re-valuations, producers and consumers have agreed to increase the price range in the agreement by 6½¢ per lb. The new range, therefore, is 29½¢ to 38½¢ per lb. It would appear that for the foreseeable future the International Cocoa Agreement is not a factor to be considered in determining a price level unless we see prices fall sharply to the low 30¢ range.

New Producer Marketing Techniques

New techniques in marketing by producers have strengthened the position of the major cocoa pro-ducers. Since 1962 there has been a Cocoa Pro-ducers' Alliance in existence where marketing and sales executives of the leading producers have peri-odic meetings to coordinate their sales policies. As a result of this cooperation among producers, selling pressure from origin sales has been well controlled and disciplined, preventing excessive pressure from hedge selling by competing producer selling. It has also been suspected that some producers are using the futures market at times for secret hedging opera-tions. Several origins continue to sell substantial quantities of cocoa and/or products on a price-fixa-tion basis against futures; thus using the futures market to greater advantage, and maintaining con-trol of their own hedging. This is particularly true in Brazil, where exporters and manufacturers have sold increasingly large quantities of cocoabeans and prod-ucts on a price-fixation basis against futures. Other origins, notably the Ivory Coast and Cameroons, have consistently used the futures market to sell cocoa forward.

Changing Speculative Patterns

The pattern of speculative participation in com-modities has changed drastically in the past several years. The most significant change has been the willingness of speculators to sell "short." In recent years speculators could normally be relied upon to absorb dealer hedge selling which made it easier for producers to dispose of their crops. Currently, specu-lators are equally willing to be short or long. In fact, for the first time in our recollection, there was recently a sizable "net" short speculative position in cocoa. Computerized technical trading has now made it more difficult to predict speculative behavior. Another innovation has been the so-called "guided commodity accounts" system which is a form of mutual fund for commodity speculating. This has created much more concerted speculative action instead of the former scattered rank and file type speculative activity. This has often led to wider fluctuations in prices, and what normally is considered a technical reaction in com-modities has now often become a major price move-ment. It has not been uncommon for cocoa futures to move 10¢ to 15¢ per pound in a two-week span without any basic fundamental change in the supply/demand outlook. These managed accounts have also often resulted in mass similar movement in com-modity prices which are not necessarily related to developments in a specific commodity. For example, we have in the past year or so witnessed violent cocoa price movements in sympathy with price action in grains, metals, sugar or other commodities. This, of course, makes trying to formulate a method for

forecasting cocoa prices based solely on end-year carry-over stocks an impossible task.

The Use of Substitutes

Burdened by high raw material costs of cocoa and sugar, the candy and confectionery industry has turned to extended use of compound coatings and substitutes. Technical improvements and techniques in modern laboratories have vastly improved the quality of these substitutes since the industry first turned in this direction due to high cocoabean prices in 1954. Many chocolate and candy manufacturers have resorted to increased use of substitute fats for cocoabutter, and this trend is likely to continue in 1975. Inasmuch as many products made with a substitute oil for cocoabutter have gained consumer acceptance, it is expected that continuing efforts will be exerted in this direction and it is more than likely that compound coatings will play a still greater role in the confectionery industry in the coming years. The 10¢ chocolate bar has disappeared from the cocoa scene and most manufacturers have adopted a 15¢ bar. In view of the recent high costs of the major ingredients of cocoa and sugar in the manufacture of chocolate bars, another increase to a 20¢ bar is not unlikely. With rising unemployment and difficult economic conditions in the United States and many Western European countries, it will be interesting to see consumer reaction to still higher prices for chocolate products. There are two schools of thought on this subject. One is that candy is a luxury item, unlike other staples, and is therefore bound to en-counter increased consumer resistance to higher prices. The other is that chocolate, being a high energy food, is still a relatively better buy for the consumer's money and, therefore, demand may re-main steadfastly high. While dollar sales have held up well in 1974 due to the increased prices of most chocolate items, it is believed poundage sales have suffered greatly because of the price increases, par-ticularly in the USA. In any event, it would certainly appear that 1975 should provide an answer to which of these schools of thought is correct.

Price Forecasting in the Late 1970's

From a preliminary view of the current statistical position in cocoa, it would appear that 1975 should be a year of lower prices than the estimated FOB price of 63¢ per lb. which prevailed in 1974. This is basically due to an anticipated surplus of 50,000 tons for the current season which suggests a build-up in carry-over stocks by the end of the season to about 3.0 months' supply. As explained previously, it is now (early in 1975) impossible to compare an end-season carryover to a previous year where a similar carryover existed, and forecast that futures in 1975 will average the same as they did in that year. Too many other variables, particularly the price of sugar and world economic conditions, must be considered. In addition, in view of the exceptionally high premiums for actual cocoa above Exchange levels, it is hopeless to try and forecast a price for cocoa in 1975. But it does appear to us that prices will average lower than 1974, at least by several cents. The danger in attempting to forecast cocoa prices, or for that matter the price of any commodity, is that the present deflationary aspects of our economy may exert greater downward pressure on prices than seems justified based on the estimated supply/demand statistical position, just as the inflationary aspects of our economy recently exerted greater upward pressure on prices than appeared warranted based on the fundamental situation in a specific commodity. In view of all these insurmountable problems and enigmatic questions, we would like to close this article with the advice offered by "Adam Smith" in his book entitled *The Money Game* wherein the author advises that "when you are tempted to speculate in cocoa, lie down until the feeling goes away."

March Cocoa Futures Delivery
1972-73 to 1974-75

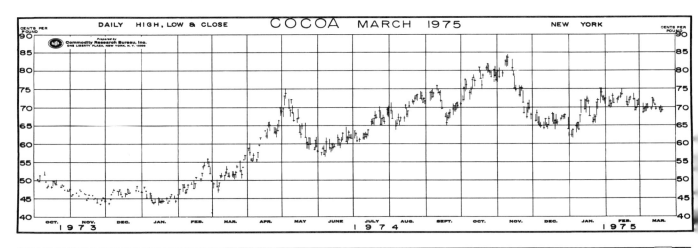

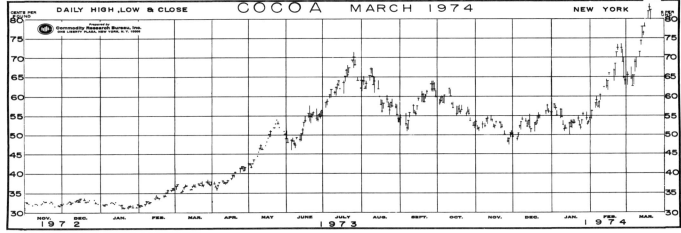

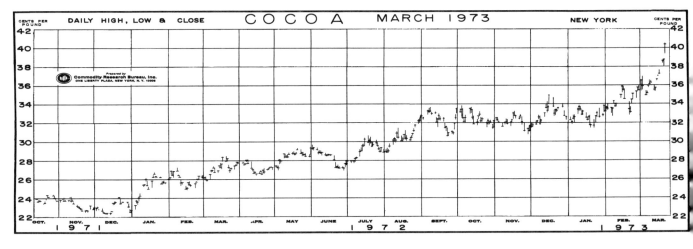

March Cocoa Futures Delivery
1969-70 to 1971-72

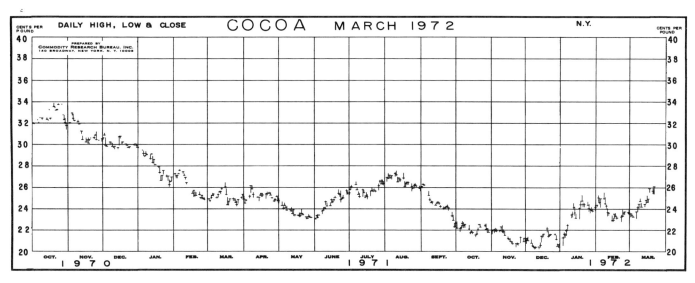

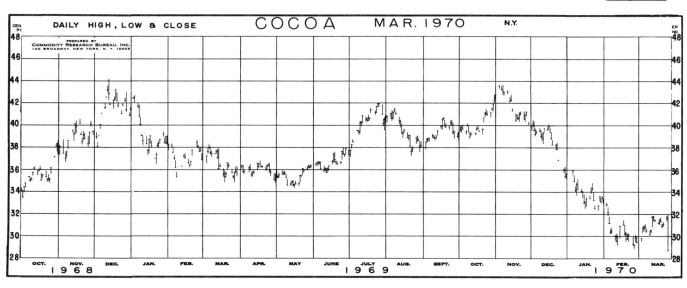

March Cocoa Futures Delivery
1966-67 to 1968-69

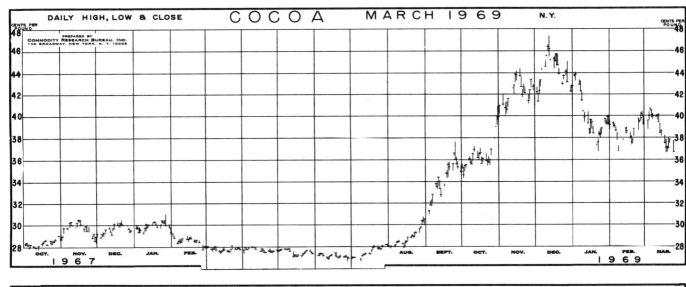

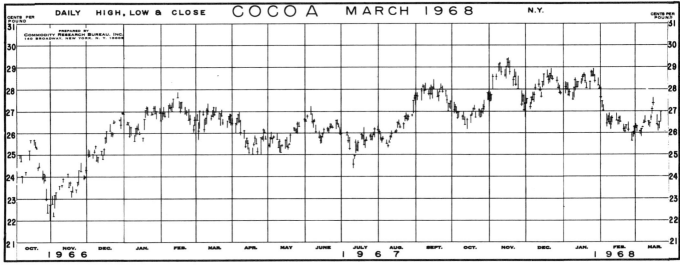

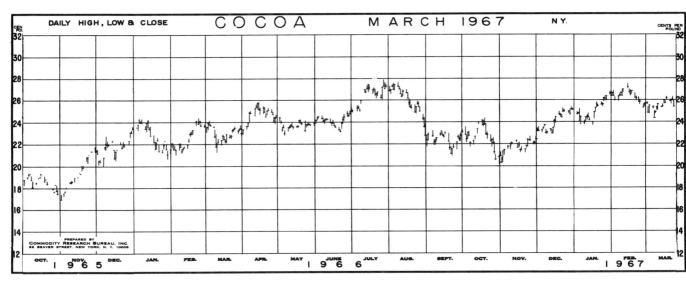

UNDERSTANDING THE COFFEE MARKET

BY DR. WILLIAM C. STRUNING

Supply of Coffee

The coffee tree thrives best in a tropical highland climate. Thus, the major coffee growing countries of the world are located, roughly speaking, within a wide belt, encircling the Equator, between 20° North and 20° South latitude.

Although some 60 nations produce green coffee in commercial quantities, Brazil alone accounts for roughly 30 percent of world exports, and the 14 major producing countries[1] listed in the accompanying table ship almost 90 percent of the world total. Therefore, the world supply of coffee depends, in a large measure, on the output of a relatively few countries.

It should not be assumed that all coffee is alike. Differences in tree species, climate, agricultural practices and bean processing are among the most significant variables creating distinct characteristics among green coffee beans. It is quite possible for one growth to be in short supply, while other types are in excess.

Although many species of coffee trees are found, two of them account for the vast majority of global outturn—*arabicas* and *robustas*. The International Coffee Organization has popularized a somewhat finer segmentation of coffee growths: Colombian Mild Arabicas, Other Mild Arabicas, Unwashed Arabicas, Robustas. *Arabica* coffees are the most important. They are grown mainly in the tropical highlands of the western hemisphere, and are not considered very tolerant of either frost or drought. The flavor of *arabica* coffees is typically softer and milder than other species. *Robusta* coffees are produced largely in low, hot areas of Africa and Asia. The trees are sturdier than *arabica* coffee trees, and the flavor of the fruit is characteristically pungent. They possess a technical superiority for processing into soluble (instant) coffee.

As can be noted in the table on the next page, the supply of coffee is not uniform throughout the year. As in the case of most agricultural products, coffee shows definite seasonality of production. In some countries, coffee output traces a two-year cycle due to the trees' need for rejuvenation in alternate years following seasons of heavy production. Some observers believe that longer cycles also exist, roughly five years from peak to trough, which is the approximate time for a new seedling to come into bearing. Depending upon the variety, climate and cultivation practices, the productive life of mature coffee trees varies from 15 to 30 years or more. Thus, it takes several years for coffee production to respond to changes in demand and price.

[1] The former French colonies in Africa, OAMCAF, will be treated as a single political unit in this presentation.

[2] Most producing countries measure time by coffee years, usually October 1–September 30. Therefore, the current crop year would extend from October 1, 1974 to September 30, 1975.

[3] Although the weight of bags varies by country, in order to provide uniformity, it is customary to specify trade in coffee in 60 kilo bags (132.276 pounds each).

Basically, the amount of coffee beans produced is dependent on the number of coffee trees planted. Since planting is influenced, in varying degrees, by government policies in the producing countries, much depends on the encouragement or discouragement given planters—especially in a financial sense.

The International Coffee Organization, through its Diversification Fund, attempted over the past decade to help individual countries to bring their national coffee outturns into line with anticipated world levels of consumption. Ultimately, it was hoped to bring about a better balance between global supply and demand. At the present time, those efforts have been discontinued and the Diversification Fund has been dissolved.

In the final analysis, an individual planter will cultivate coffee if he feels that the necessary investment is preferable to alternative applications of his efforts, talents and resources. In a large measure, he will be guided by his opportunities for maximizing profit; although habit, custom and lack of knowledge of alternatives are also influential.

Other potential influences on exportable output are weather, diseases of the coffee tree, methods of culture, harvesting practices, processing procedures and standards of grading.

Thus, many variables affect the supply of coffee; consequently, the trend of world outturn has taken numerous changes in direction. The volatility of coffee output has earned it the descriptive appellation, "boom and bust cycle."

Attempts have been made to ease the hardships caused by severe fluctuations between excess and scarcity. Initiative has stemmed largely from the producing countries in periods characterized by excessive stocks, and has taken the form of export quotas in order to keep surplus availabilities from depressing market prices.

The most sophisticated quota system was developed by the International Coffee Organization. Flexible quotas were featured that reacted to changes in price. Those quotas are not in operation at the present time (early in 1975).

Other factors also act as short-term restrictions to the supply of coffee: labor strikes, shortage of transportation facilities, and foreign-exchange difficulties.

For the current coffee year,[2] the United States Department of Agriculture estimates world exportable outturn of green coffee at 58.1 million bags.[3] That quantity is 34 percent above the abnormally low outturn in the preceding year (which was due primarily to frost damage in Brazil and, to a lesser degree, to drought in the Ivory Coast and plant exhaustion in Mexico). The figure for 1974/75 would represent the third highest world exportable crop in recent decades, exceeded only by the 66.4 million bags recorded for 1959/60 and the 66.1 million bags for 1965/66. The International Coffee Organization has estimated world demand in 1974/75 at 59.5 million bags; however, that figure is likely to be somewhat overstated.

It appears that availabilities will just exceed de-

MAJOR COFFEE EXPORTING COUNTRIES OF THE WORLD

Country	Principal Type of Coffee	Primary Coffee Growing Regions	Main Harvesting Season	Main Exporting Season	Growths Commonly Traded in New York Market	Primary Ports of Exports	Green Coffee Exports in 1973 (thousands of bags)
Brazil	Unwashed Arabicas	Paraná, Sao Paulo, Minas Gerais, Espirito Santo	April–September	Throughout the year	Santos 2/3, Santos 4, Paraná 4	Paranagua, Santos, Rio de Janeiro, Angra Dos Reis, Niteroi, Victoria	19,640
Colombia	Colombian Mild Arabicas	Caldas, Risaralda, Quindio, Tolima, Antioquia, Valle, Cundinamarea	Throughout the year. Peak: October–March	Throughout the year	MAMS	Cartagena, Barranquilla, Santa Marta, Buenaventura, Tumaco	6,766
OAMCAF	Robustas						6,513
Ivory Coast		Sassandra	Nov–April	Dec–March	Superior	Abidjan, Sassandra	
Cameroun		Mungo, Bamileke	Nov–January	Dec–March	Superior	Douala, Tiko, Victoria	
Malagasy		Tamatave, Mananjary	May–October	July–November		Tamatave, Majunga	
Togo		Palime	Nov–February	Jan–April		Lome	
Central Af. Republic		Obo, Bangui	Nov–March	Jan–April		(Cameroun ports)	
Dahomey		Ouidal, Cotonou	Nov–February	Jan–April		Cotonou	
Congo		Dolisie, Kibangou	Sept–October	Nov–December		Point Noire	
Gabon		Ogooue, Ivindo	May–September	June–October		Libreville	
Uganda	Robustas	Lake Victoria	Throughout the year. Peak: Nov–February	Throughout the year	Washed, Cleaned, Native Standard	(Kenya port)	3,339
Angola	Robustas	Ambriz, Amboin	May–September	July–November	Ambriz AA, Ambriz BB	Lobito, Luanda	3,298
El Salvador	Other Mild Arabicas	Santa Ana, La Libertad, Usulutan	Nov–March	Dec–March	High Grown, Central Standard	Acajutla, Cutuco, La Libertad	2,488
Guatemala	Other Mild Arabicas	San Marcos, Suchitepequez, Quetzaltenango	Aug–March	Oct–April	Prime Washed, Good Washed	Puerto Barrios, Santo Tomás de Castilla, Champerico, San José	1,927
México	Other Mild Arabicas	Chiapas, Veracruz, Oaxaca, Puebla	Oct–March	Dec–May	High Grown, Prime Washed	Veracruz, Coatzacoalcos,	2,320
Indonesia	Robustas	Java, Sumatra, Celebes, Bali, Timor	May–December	July–February	EK 20/25	Belawan Deli, Surabaya, Palembang, Pandjang	1,506
Ethiopia	Unwashed Arabicas	Limmu, Arbagugu, Djimma, Sidamo, Harar	Oct–December	Dec–March	Djimmas UGQ	Assab	1,403
Zaire	Robustas	Equateur, Orientale, Kivu	Throughout the year. Peak: Dec–February	Throughout the year	Robusta N2B	Matadi	1,097
Costa Rica	Other Mild Arabicas	Meseta Central, San Carlos, San Vito de Java	Sept–February	Nov–March	Hard Bean, Good Atlantic	Puerto Limón, Puntarenas	1,394
Kenya	Colombian Mild Arabicas	Nucri, Kiambu, Thika, Ruiru	Oct–March	Nov–April		Mombassa	1,242
Ecuador	Other Mild Arabicas	Manabí, Enayas, Los Ríos, El Río, Loja, Cumbaya	June–October	Sept–December	Washed, Extra Sup. Nat.	Guayaquil, Manta, Puerto Bolivar	1,166

Source: Pan-American Coffee Bureau, Annual Coffee Statistics 1973; Pan-American Coffee Bureau, Handbook of Green Coffee Price Differentials.

mand in the current coffee year. The shortfall or excess, if either occurs, will have to be drawn from or stored in producing countries who already hold more than 30 million bags—some sources believe that the amount of green coffee stocks could run to 40 million or more bags. At the same time, stocks of green coffee in the importing countries are melting away and could be headed for a recent-year's lowpoint —in the neighborhood of about six million bags (not including working stocks of, perhaps, another six million bags).

If the amount of total world stocks seems quite large, it should be remembered that demand for the remaining years of the 1970's is expected to average somewhere near 60 million bags of green coffee per year. Thus, another year like those of 1970/71 and 1973/74 when exportable production fell to some 40 to 44 million bags, could reduce world stocks by one-half, and two such years could completely exhaust world reserves. However, should favorable weather persist through the remainder of the 1970's, an increasingly large surplus could accumulate.

Estimates of world coffee production are prepared four times a year by the Foreign Agricultural Service of the U.S. Department of Commerce. The estimates —issued in June, September, December and March— are the most comprehensive available. Other projections are made, from time to time, by some of the coffee producing countries themselves, as well as by independent trade sources. These forecasts appear in the coffee trade press. In recent years, projections have been prepared by the International Coffee Organization as well.

Demand for Coffee

The world demand for green coffee, as indicated by imports, amounted to 58.4 million bags in 1973.[4] Of that quantity 37 percent was imported into the United States and another 34 percent into the nine countries of the European Economic Community. Thus, the bulk of world offtake of green coffee is accounted for by a relatively few of the 70 or more countries that import that commodity (the U.S.A. and West Germany together take almost one-half of world outturn).

Since most of the large coffee importing countries are industrialized nations of the temperate zones, the trade in coffee is largely from developing countries in the tropics to developed nations located in temperate zones.

Ultimately the quantity of coffee demanded depends upon the purchases of consumers. It is somewhat easier to estimate demand in terms of consumption than in terms of imports. That is because consumers tend to make gradual changes in their coffee drinking habits, while imports are subject to aberrations due to inventory fluctuations as persons concerned with coffee react to real or threatened changes in market conditions.

While prices affect coffee consumption patterns, the related changes in demand are quite modest; i.e., in most of the larger importing countries coffee demand is relatively price inelastic, except in the case of large price increases. A likely reason for this behavior is the consumers' dislike of altering their usual number of cups per day. Thus, if prices rise,

<hr>

[4] Importing countries traditionally report in calendar rather than coffee years.

they may drink their usual number of cups but use weaker coffee beverage. Or they may switch from regular to instant coffee in an attempt to continue their normal rate of consumption at a lower cost. Should prices decline, consumers who are already heavy coffee drinkers are unlikely to increase their rate of consumption; perhaps, a few drinkers may then feel that they can afford additional coffee intake, but coffee is already comparatively inexpensive in many importing countries.

Changes in disposable personal income are more apt to encourage or to discourage coffee drinking, but again the elasticity is quite low in many countries, especially the United States. However, cross elasticity is a viable concept—that is, significant changes in the prices of competitive beverages could affect the amount of coffee consumed.

One important element in stimulating coffee consumption in the past few decades has been increased availability of coffee. Notable examples are coffee vending machines and the availability of coffee at work.

Perhaps the most important influence on coffee consumption is life-style pattern. In the United States, for example, young persons have turned to cold drinks as the tempo of living has made it inconvenient to wait for hot drinks to cool. Moreover, cold drinks go well with spicy, salty snacks, more in vogue than sweet snacks which are better complemented by hot coffee. Furthermore, in the United States coffee is regarded as the drink of the "Establishment," i.e., an older person's drink—hardly conducive to encouraging young adults to choose coffee.

Other factors that affect coffee consumption include climate (although central heating, air conditioning, relatively more sedentary occupations and travel via automobile have done much to blunt the full thrust of this factor), the extent and effectiveness of generic coffee promotional campaigns, and publicity regarding the health hazards of drinking coffee.

One element in the demand for coffee has been a shift in recent years to instant from regular coffee, as consumers seek more convenience in the preparation of coffee beverage. That, in turn, has caused a shift in the demand for certain growths of coffee, largely robustas, whose low cost encourages their use in instant coffee where their rather strong flavor is not as obvious as in regular coffee.

Just as constraints on coffee exports can be found, so are there constraints on the importation of that product. In most importing countries these take the form of taxes and duties. Foreign exchange regulations also play a role in encouraging more "essential" imports than coffee into some countries.

World imports of green coffee reached an historic highpoint of 58.4 million bags in 1973. Data for 1974 was not complete early in 1975, but estimates placed the figure at a somewhat lower level.

Although the trend of green coffee imports into the United States has been easing downward since 1962, the shrinkage has been filled in a large measure by larger volumes of roasted and soluble intake. Thus, on balance, aggregate coffee imports into the United States, when adjusted for re-exports and inventory changes, have been quite static, despite per capita declines.

Increased intake into Europe has been the primary force in maintaining an increasing trend for global imports of green coffee. It is expected that this influence will continue, although at a decreasing rate of growth. However, the retail price of coffee is quite high in many European countries and, therefore, coffee is more vulnerable to declines in consumption (from higher prices, lower personal income or restrictions on imports) than it is in the United States. Future growth could come from areas such as Eastern Europe rather than from the traditional areas of heavy coffee consumption, *e.g.*, West Germany and Scandinavia.

The International Coffee Organization projects world demand at 66.6 million bags per year by 1980, reaching that level by average annual increments of 1.2 million bags from the present. Those estimates are not widely different from the projections of the U.S. Department of Agriculture which places world offtake in 1980 between 65.2 (low estimate) and 73.6 (high estimate) million bags. Forecasts of other observers fall somewhat short of those projections.

Inventories of Green Coffee

Green coffee can be stored for several years without much deterioration (mainly the loss of flavor and color) under favorable conditions.

Current production is expected to just about meet current demand. However, inventories of green coffee in producing countries probably exceed 30 million bags. Therefore, a shortage with respect to the consumer is not likely.

Many roasters, particularly in the United States, prefer fresh-crop coffee, which may be barely adequate to meet demand. Moreover, questions have been raised as to the quality of coffee stocks. Furthermore, inventories may not be balanced for all types of coffee. At the present time (early in 1975) the balance between supply/demand can be considered to be quite close and is thus, highly vulnerable to such influence as weather, disease, stock building, etc.

Nevertheless, it appears that current production plus stocks will be in excess of the amount of green coffee demanded—at least in the short run—and may, thus, act as a depressant on coffee prices. Over the longer term, the supply/demand balance is less clear since it is all but impossible to predict the occurrence and influence of frost, drought, disease, etc. Projections of supply and demand have been prepared by the International Coffee Organization and are shown below.

The International Coffee Organization projections assume that supply will increase by roughly 2.5 million bags per year, while demand will rise by 1.2 million bags per year. Should those estimates prove to be correct, the net result would be an increase of 27.6 million bags over the seven-year period.

The U.S. Department of Agriculture has also made projections of demand. Applying the International Coffee Organization estimates of supply against those projections yield a seven-year inventory build-up of about the same amount resulting from the use of International Coffee Organization's figures for estimated low demand to no appreciable build-up in the event of high demand.

Marketing Methods

Coffee is grown, for the most part, on plantations, but sizable quantities originate in family farms or are collected from non-cultivated coffee trees. When harvested, coffee is in the form of red cherries, each containing two coffee beans. The cherries must be depulped and parchment covering the beans removed. That processing is either performed at the plantation or, in the case of small farmers, at a local cooperative.

The beans then move to a central warehouse (private or government) where they are sorted and graded. Coffee is taken at that point by exporters or agents from consuming countries (frequently roasters and importers who also buy, in some instances, directly from plantations).

In the importing countries, coffee received via exporters is handled by exporters' agents or importer-jobbers. Further distribution can be made by importers to port coffee trade brokers, inland coffee trade brokers and roasters.

In the United States, following processing by roasters, the bulk of roasted and soluble coffee (a little more than 60 percent) moves through retail outlets to ultimate consumers for conversion to coffee beverage in households. En route, the coffee may pass through wholesalers or central distributing centers of retailers.

Another portion of processed coffee (35 percent) moves to eating places (restaurants, hotels, motels, airlines, in-plant and in-office feeding, caterers, etc.) and is served to consumers in beverage form. A small percentage is taken by institutions (hospitals, prisons, the military, etc.), some is exported, and a little is purchased by manufacturers for use in the preparation of flavorings and extracts.

In recent years increasing amounts of coffee in regular and soluble form have been imported into the United States but, although the trend is up, the amount is still relatively small (eight percent).

In the United States the total amount of coffee taken by consumers has remained quite constant for the past decade, indicating declines in per capita consumption. Also, an increasingly larger proportion is consumed out-of-home. It is too early to predict the effects of the energy crisis on these trends as well as other patterns of demand, *e.g.*, increased consumption of decaffeinated coffee and the tendency of housewives to buy larger size packages. Of interest, too, is the growing trend by housewives to prepare coffee beverage by the use of drip makers rather than the traditional percolator.

Coffee Industry in the United States

As late as 1964, coffee was the most valuable import into the United States next to petroleum. Although it is probably the tenth most important import in recent years, the value of green coffee imports amounted to $1.6 billion in 1973—still a sizable amount.

The value of shipments of soluble and regular

(Millions of 60 Kilo Bags)

Coffee Year	Supply	Demand	Inventory Accumulation
1974/75	60.3	59.5	+0.8
1975/76	61.8	60.6	+1.2
1976/77	64.4	61.8	+2.6
1977/78	66.9	63.0	+3.9
1978/79	69.3	64.2	+5.1
1979/80	71.8	65.4	+6.4
1980/81	74.2	66.6	+7.6

coffee from processing plants are currently approaching $2.7 billion. That would certainly not make the coffee industry a primary one in the United States; nevertheless, it is estimated that consumers' expenditures for coffee in retail stores and eating places exceed four billion dollars. Moreover, coffee generates other expenditures, *e.g.*, coffee makers, cups, spoons, cream, sugar, etc. The grand total could test the six billion dollar mark.

According to data gathered by the U.S. Department of Commerce, there were 208 establishments in the roasted coffee industry of the United States in 1972. That indicates a contraction from the 380 such establishments a decade earlier. Between those years, the number of bags of green coffee processed remained at roughly the same level, 20 million bags, indicating that the smaller number of establishments were processing a greater volume of coffee on the average.

Furthermore, only about 50 percent of the establishments have 20 employees or more; thus, most processing plants are comparatively small. Most of the establishments produce regular coffee, but only about 20 are believed to produce instant coffee. Very few new firms have entered the field in recent years, the contraction being caused by acquisitions and retirements.

Coffee production is a relatively concentrated industry. It is estimated that the two largest producers of regular coffee control almost one-half of that market, while the two largest soluble coffee producers account for more than three-fourths of the soluble market. Thus, the purchasing policies and promotional campaigns of those few companies can have significant effects on coffee prices.

In the United States, a major portion of roaster advertising expenditures for specific brands is directed toward television spot commercials. For regular coffee, the messages generally stress good taste or non-bitterness. In the case of soluble coffee, the messages frequently indicate that a particular brand tastes as good as regular coffee or emphasize convenience in preparation. Decaffeinated coffee vendors usually remind viewers that the caffein-less product will not keep them awake or make them nervous. Unfortunately, some of the messages noted earlier reflect in a negative sort of way on over-all coffee drinking.

Another promotional tool widely used is the cents-off campaign, frequently via a coupon toward the next purchase. Retailers use coffee on numerous occasions as a loss leader. Thus, housewives are conditioned to considering price when selecting a brand and have tended in the past to overreact when faced with price increases.

Prices of Coffee

As coffee moves through channels of distribution from grower to consumer, prices or values are established at points where the product either changes title and/or possession. The prices most frequently observed are f.o.b. (import), spot, futures, wholesale and retail.

The f.o.b. price is often estimated from import values, since importers or importing agents are required to include f.o.b. values on their declarations. However, the values and quantities from each declaration are aggregated by country of origin over periods of one month; thus, import (f.o.b.) prices

reflect a variety of prices and qualities. For some origins f.o.b. prices are reported directly through trade sources and there is no need to make estimates from import values. F.o.b. prices indicate price at the port of origin of coffee placed safely aboard the buyer's carrier.

Spot prices indicate the market value of green coffee at the port of destination. Spot prices are of several types, designated by the location of the coffee at the time of exchange. The most common type is the ex-dock price which reflects the seller's costs in placing coffee on a dock in the port of destination. Thus, the difference between f.o.b. and ex-dock prices could include charges for ocean freight, customs entry, sampling, insurance, interest and brokerage. Such costs from f.o.b. point to New York recently ranged from 3.2 cents per pound (Maracaibo, Venezuela) to 7.4 cents per pound (Palembang, Indonesia).

Trading in coffee futures on one of the organized exchanges (New York, London or Paris/Le Havre) establishes a value of coffee at some future delivery date. Futures trading will be covered in more detail in a later section of this paper.

Wholesale prices represent charges by a packer or roaster to a wholesaler or jobber for roasted or instant coffee in the United States. Prices are reported on a monthly basis by the Bureau of Labor Statistics. Wholesale prices normally remain quite constant since they are list prices from which discounts are made. Listed wholesale prices are frequently higher than retail prices, again due to the discounts applied as well as to services rendered by the seller. Another type of wholesale price is that charged by roasters or packers to restaurants, schools, hospitals and other institutions. Such prices are known as institutional prices and are not normally reported, although changes, *i.e.* the amount of change only, are frequently announced in the trade press.[5]

F.o.b. and spot prices tend to move closely together. Listed wholesale prices follow the same general direction, but with considerable time lag in their response to changes in raw product costs. Retail prices also follow the trend of green coffee prices, but lag behind them and show less variation. The lag is to be expected in view of the processing, packaging and distribution time required before the processed coffee is made available to the consumer. As is true of other agricultural products, coffee prices tend to be less volatile and to demonstrate reduced variability as the product moves closer to the ultimate consumer. Both wholesale and retail price changes result from alterations in processing and marketing costs as well as from increases or decreases in the cost of green coffee. Retail prices are also reported by the U.S. Bureau of Labor Statistics.

Factors that Influence Price Trends

The two basic determinants of price are supply and demand. Since, as it was noted earlier, those two factors are currently in fairly close balance, one would expect that prices of green coffee will remain firm. However, adequate stocks and easing importer demand have softened prices despite the threat of curtailment of supply due to disease, weather or

[5] *Some of the materials in this and in the following paragraph have been drawn from Pan-American Coffee Bureau, Annual Coffee Statistics 1973.*

greater-than-anticipated demand due, say, to a threatened strike.

In recent years, weather in Brazil has caused significant shortfalls in world output of coffee. This is largely because Brazil produces the largest share of world exportable outturn, almost 30 percent in "normal" years of the 1960's and early 1970's. Frost in that country—usually occurring in the period of June–August, if it happens at all—can reduce the next year's crop or even, in severe and prolonged frosts, kill the trees. Frost caused a reduction in Brazil to 1.5 million bags in 1970/71 from 10.3 million in 1969/70 and to 6.4 million bags in 1973/74 from 15.0 million in 1972/73—in terms of exportable production. Weather during the most important "flowering" period is an important determinant of coffee yields. A major frost or extended drought at this time can seriously reduce yields. The fruit of the coffee tree ripens about 7 to 9 months after blossoming. Even distribution of rainfall followed by sun when the berries are maturing, and dry harvest weather, are conducive to favorable yields. It is estimated that, on the average, a coffee tree will yield about 10 pounds of cherries, equal to about 2 pounds of green coffee. In Brazil, the September–October flowerings are the most important of the three or four flowerings which occur in a year, with harvesting active in the following July/October period.

Almost all coffee producing areas have some disease problems. Leaf rust is considered the most important disease, with leaf spot of secondary importance. Probably the most important pest is the coffee berry borer. Latin American coffee producing areas are considered largely free of the more seriously damaging insects, other than the coffee berry borer. Africa is particularly affected by a large number of pests which can cause serious damage.

Brazil, along with a few other Latin American countries, has also been troubled by a disease of the coffee trees, known as "coffee rust." However, the producing countries affected claim to have halted the advance of the "rust" and to have eradicated diseased trees.

Another factor affecting the price of coffee is change in the value of the dollar, since it is quoted largely in that currency. Theoretically, coffee becomes slightly cheaper to non-dollar customers during periods of dollar devaluation and a bit more expensive when the dollar appreciates. However, in practice, it is necessary for the exporting countries to increase prices a little, if they can, during dollar devaluations to make up for lost purchasing power.

At the green coffee level, the trend of prices turned upward in early 1972 and continued into the late Spring of 1974. Following a decline, prices firmed and rose in the last two months of that year.

At the wholesale and retail levels, trends also veered upward, but with most of the increases beginning in 1973. Those two series continued to show rising tendencies as roasters faced higher quotations for green coffee and as costs of manufacture and marketing continued upward well into 1974. The major roasters in the United States announced price reductions at the wholesale level in October 1974.

The Futures Market for Coffee

Trading in green coffee futures takes place on the floors of the New York Coffee and Sugar Exchange, the London Terminal Market and the Le Havre/Paris Exchange. A small number of contracts changed hands during 1973 at the West Coast Commodity Exchange in Los Angeles, California. Until recently some trading in coffee futures was conducted in Amsterdam. The possibility of establishing an exchange in Hamburg, West Germany is being discussed.

Robustas are traded in London and Le Havre/ Paris; during 1973 trading in mild coffees was initiated in London. The New York Coffee and Sugar Exchange offers trading in Brazilian coffee (B Contract), Central American and Colombian mild coffees (C Contract), and any coffee including *robustas* (U Contract). The discussion that follows will deal largely with the New York Coffee and Sugar Exchange.

All of the activity in recent years has been in the C Contract, with no trading reported in either the B or U Contracts. Apparently those interested in *robustas* prefer the London Terminal Market which provides an active market for that growth.

During 1973, the number of lots changing hands on the New York Coffee and Sugar Exchange reached an all-time high, 182,605. No other year in the post World War II period has approached that level, the nearest being 67,304 lots in 1955. (In the C Contract each lot consists of 37,500 pounds packed in approximately 250 bags.) Following that year, trading eased down (aside from a brief rally in 1964) and reached an average of only 100 or so lots each year in the 1968–1971 period. In 1974 trading activity amounted to 151,917 lots.

One reason for the loss of interest in futures trading in New York in the 1960's has been given as the general price stability created by the International Coffee Agreement together with heavy world surplus stocks. As the volume of trading declined, the fewer potential buyers and sellers made access to and exit from the market less fluid and discouraged many who might otherwise hedge or speculate. Some of those traders turned to the London Terminal Market which offered an active and broad market that enabled participants to avoid the risks inherent in a thin market.

However, in August 1972 activity on the New York Coffee and Sugar Exchange suddenly revived as 7,660 lots changed hands before the end of that year. All of the activity was in the "C" Contract. In that year the March position was as low as 45.60 cents per pound on February 28. On the same date of 1973, the March position was quoted at 80.20 cents per pound. However, the market broke sharply and March coffee sold at 62.25 cents per pound on March 12. By early January 1974 March coffee was testing the 75 cent level and was showing firmness. In February, the March position sold at close to 80 cents before falling back to around 70 cents. Thus substantial opportunity for speculation exists in the C Contract from the price aspect. But, another condition for exciting trader interest, open interest or liquidity, fell to a low level—fewer than 3,000 contracts outstanding at the close of 1974.

The Coffee Market in 1975

It is difficult to determine and project the trend of futures prices in the current year in view of the varied forces at work, with influences that are mutually offsetting on occasion. The following points must be considered.

(1) Supply of and demand for current-crop green coffee appears to be roughly in balance in the present coffee year.

(2) Modest annual excesses of supply over demand are projected for the remainder of this decade, subject to the vagaries of drought, frost and disease.

(3) A slower rate of gain in world demand for green coffee over the next seven or so years.

(4) World stocks of green coffee seem adequate to meet most contingencies in the short run with small annual accumulations projected over the long run; stocks in consuming countries have returned to roughly normal levels, thus yielding control of inventories to the producing countries.

(5) Prices of green coffee have eased down from their 1974 high points, but those decreases have not yet (early in 1975) been translated into price declines at the retail level (the 1974 peaks were relatively lower than for many other commodities).

(6) The coffee producing countries have announced their intentions to take steps to control the amount of green coffee released on the world market, thus keeping excess supply from weighing heavily on prices.

(7) Negotiations are in progress to restore some form of export quotas and, possibly, buffer stocks through the International Coffee Organization-decision may not be forthcoming until 1976.

(8) There is a current low level of liquidity in the *arabica* futures markets in New York and London: liquidity appears more favorable in the *robusta* futures market of London.

In summary, general availability of green coffee together with sluggish demand (as consuming countries draw down their inventories) have acted to soften prices. However, the market is considering the influence that controlled releases of green coffee by the producing countries might have; this has acted to blunt the downward thrust on prices of excess supply over demand. Thus, to a large extent, the trend of prices depends on actions taken by the producing countries. Investors must also watch the possibility of technical or temporary shortages as stocks in importing countries decline, as well as potential shortages due to unfavorable weather and disease. While the rather thin market may reduce liquidity, it also offers possibilities for rapid price changes.

SPOT COFFEE PRICES FOR THE NEW YORK MARKET

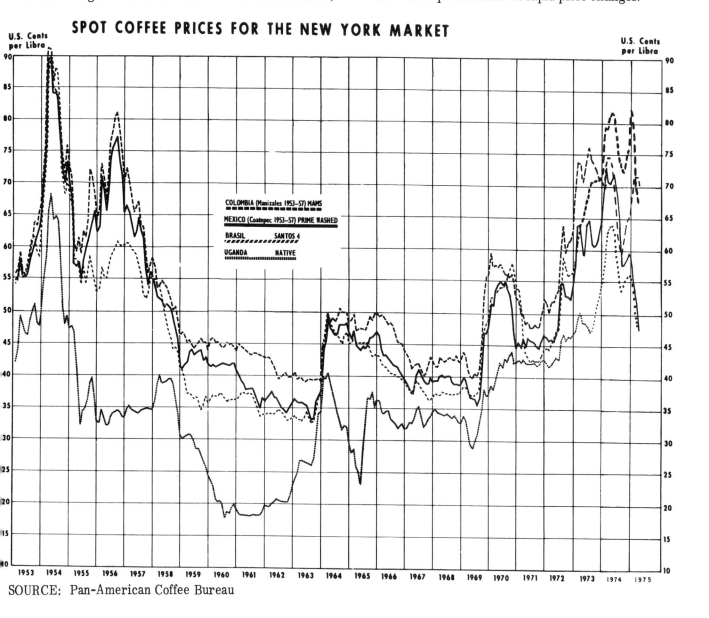

COLOMBIA (Manizales 1953–57) MAMS
MEXICO (Coatepec 1953–57) PRIME WASHED
BRASIL   SANTOS 4
UGANDA   NATIVE

SOURCE: Pan-American Coffee Bureau

35

March Coffee "C" Futures Delivery
1972-73 to 1974-75

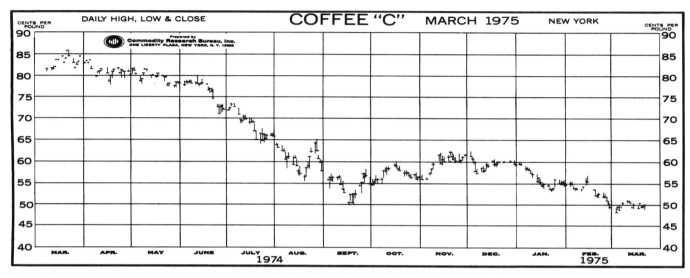

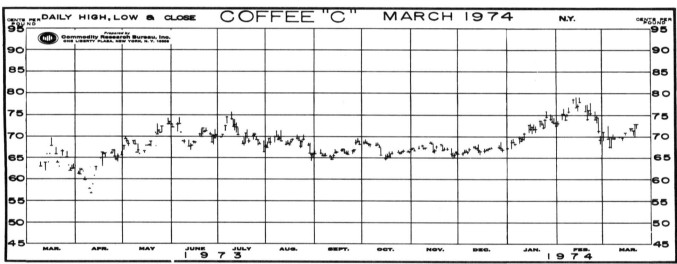

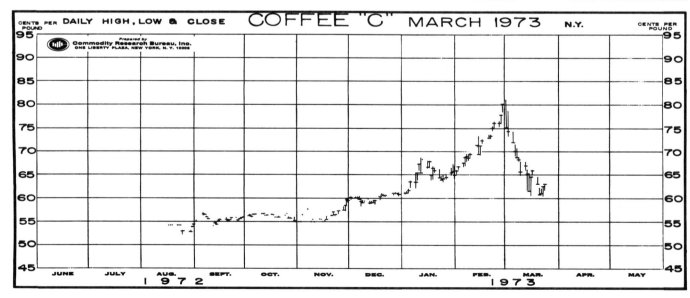

UNDERSTANDING THE COPPER FUTURES MARKET

BY ROBERT T. KECK

From Antiquity to the Twentieth Century

One of the oldest metals known to man, copper has played an invaluable role in the development of civilization. The first known use of copper dates back to around 4500 B.C., although its actual discovery may have occurred 1500 years earlier. The discovery and use of copper made possible the transition from the stone age to the metal age, as its extreme workability, durability and general availability made the metal an ideal substitute for stone in the making of weapons, tools and utensils. Copper's value was further enhanced after the discovery of tin, which made possible the magnificent bronze age. However, it was not until the mid-1800's and the inventions of the telegraph, the electric generator, the telephone and the incandescent light that the importance of the copper industry approached the proportions that it now enjoys. Today, copper is one of the most important and valuable of all metals.

The tremendous growth of the economic importance of copper through the years has presented the copper producer with many problems, not the least of which has been to assure the continued flow of raw material to the consumer at relatively stable prices. This has not been particularly easy in the face of rapidly changing political and economic conditions, the emergence of a rather militant and unstable labor force in many areas of the world and the appearance of more economical and, at times, more readily available substitutes.

Consequently, the historical pattern of copper prices has not been one of stability, but rather one of unusual and often extreme volatility. Yet, it is this erratic behavior of prices which makes the study of the copper market and the innumerable and often unpredictable factors which affect the forces of supply and demand so fascinating.

Production

Unlike many agricultural commodities for which production depends primarily upon the number of acres planted and the vagaries of Mother Nature from the planting to the harvest, the copper "crop" has always existed. World reserves have been estimated by the U.S. Bureau of Mines at over 200 million short tons, all of which was considered mineable under the technological and cost-price conditions prevailing in 1960. In comparison, world copper production in 1973 totaled an estimated 7.5 million short tons.

The responsibility for meeting the world's expanding copper requirements lies with the United States, Chile, Zambia, Canada, Zaire, the U.S.S.R. and Peru, which together produce about 80 percent of total world output. Of these seven countries, only one is a net importer: the United States, the world's largest copper producer. The U.S.S.R., for which accurate statistics are lacking, appears to be self-sufficient and is not considered a factor in foreign trade.

Through the years, world copper production has risen steadily with the rate of increase primarily dependent upon prices. Throughout history, high prices have usually spurred the undertaking of large-scale production expansion programs, while periods of depressed prices have resulted in the formation of cartels on the part of some major producer/exporters. These cartels, most of them unsuccessful, have tried to restrict output in an effort to force prices higher. During the long bear market of 1970, Chile, Zambia, Peru and Zaire, who aside from controlling about 33 percent of the world's production and being the major exporting nations of the world, formed a group known as the Intergovernmental Council of Copper Exporting Countries (C.I.P.E.C.). C.I.P.E.C. again became a factor in 1974/75 when the dramatic fall in prices from $1.40 per pound in London to around the 50–55¢ area spurred participating countries to curtail output by 15%.

Aside from the long range economic factors such as the level of copper prices and the availability of profitably recoverable reserves, copper production can also be affected by changing political situations, particularly in the emerging nations of Chile, Zambia, Peru and Zaire. The socio-economic demands placed upon these countries have led their respective governments to want an increased share of the copper industry's profits. Consequently, there has been a marked trend towards the "nationalization" of the copper industries which were, for the most part, owned and operated by international corporations with headquarters outside the country. Precisely what the ultimate effects of nationalization will be remains to be seen, but several observations can be made.

First of all, these nations depend heavily upon the foreign exchange acquired from copper exports to finance domestic programs. Therefore, there would seem to be a vested interest on the part of these nations to keep production running smoothly and labor unrest to a minimum. However, the political instability of some of these countries, highlighted by the fall of the Allende government in Chile, threaten to offset the expected beneficial effects of nationalization. There might also be a trend toward the development of new markets, particularly in the Communist countries. On the other hand, there is some question as to whether or not the new state controlled management companies will have the technical expertise or the access to capital financing necessary for the successful operation of the copper facilities and the full development of the exploitable reserves.

The Importance of Labor Developments

Probably the most important factor affecting copper production is the labor force which, in these South African and South American countries, might best be described as "volatile". Demands for a 70 percent wage boost, for example, are not uncommon in Chile and often workers have walked off the job over the lack of adequate housing, schools or medical facilities, low wages or just because the workers at a sister mine have gone on strike. These strikes, which are also used as political protests, can occur without warning and may last from a few hours to a few months. The instability of the labor force in these nations and its effect upon production has become one of the more important factors contributing to the erratic behavior of copper prices.

Of course, the United States and other more developed nations of the world are not immune to labor problems. In recent years, the U.S. labor force has become increasingly militant in its quest for a higher standard of living in the face of high taxes, periodic inflation and unemployment and has used the strike as a means to seek increased wages and fringe benefits. When a strike is threatened, consumers tend to build up their inventories to protect themselves against the lack of supplies that would result if a strike materialized. This "hedge" buying can place an additional burden on supplies prior to the expiration of the labor contract, but if a strike does not develop, consumer demand will usually decline until these stocks are reduced to normal levels. In mid 1967, domestic copper workers walked off the job and did not return for almost eight and one-half months. With the United States being the world's largest copper producer as well as consumer, the strike had a tremendous impact upon prices, forcing them upwards from 42¢ per pound to a high of over 75¢ per pound in March, 1968. The failure of an expected strike to materialize can have an equally great impact on prices. In mid-1974, a contract settlement averted a long strike and the lackluster demand that immediately followed as the industry utilized its "strike inventories" contributed to the sharp fall in values during the last half of 1974.

Even though copper production might be running normally, the availability of these new supplies is often hampered by transportation difficulties. When Britain imposed economic sanctions against Rhodesia in the mid 1960's, Zambian copper shipments were unable to reach the world market because the railroad through Rhodesia was the traditional shipping route to the coast for Zambian copper. Dock strikes, maritime strikes, rail strikes, a shortage of coal for the smelters, mechanical breakdowns, air pollution controls imposed by governing agencies and natural disasters, such as the cave-in at a large Zambian mine in 1970, can also interfere with the production and marketing of copper and have a significant effect upon prices.

"Force Majeure"

Whenever the flow of copper supplies to market is curtailed for a reason above and beyond the control of the producer, a "force majeure" is often declared. This "force majeure" may affect all production or a percentage of it and usually applies to a specified period during which shipments will be suspended or reduced. During 1973, there were over 20 "force majeures" declared, the highest number since 1945, and the resulting reduction in supply was a major factor contributing to the dynamic bull market of 1973/74.

The high prices during the last half of the 1960's and during 1973/74 encouraged most major producing countries to initiate programs to expand their copper output. Exploration for new deposits is always encouraged by high prices and new discoveries are continually reported. However, 3 to 4 years, often longer, is necessary before new deposits are developed and actual production begins. The copper analyst should be forewarned not to place too much emphasis on expected production entering the pipeline from these new sources as historically, the expectations are never fully fulfilled.

From Mine to Market

Depending upon the copper content of the ore, there are two basic methods of copper mining. The open-pit method is usually reserved for lower grade deposits, while underground mining, requiring the rather expensive construction of underground tunnels, is used in cases where the copper content of the ore is high enough to justify the additional expense. Generally speaking, the copper content of the ore can vary from as little as 4 percent to over 10 percent.

Once mined, the ore is taken to a concentrating mill where it undergoes the first in a series of steps designed to separate the copper from the other materials in the ore. When the copper concentrate leaves the mill, it contains about 20 to 30 percent copper. In the next step at the smelter, other base metals are removed from the concentrate, leaving what is known as "blister" copper which is about 98 to 99 percent pure copper. After smelting, the copper is refined by an electrolytic process to a large plate-like cathode of a minimum purity of 99.9 percent. The cathode may then be cast into shapes such as wirebars, ingots, cakes and billets or sold "as is" for remelting.

Most U.S. copper mines are located in the western part of the country, while the refineries are found in the major consuming and transportation centers along the East coast. Usually, however, both the concentrating mills and smelters are placed in close proximity to the mine since the relatively low copper content of ore before smelting would make transporting it to the East rather expensive.

After being refined, the copper is now ready for the copper fabricators, which include the wire mills, brass mills and foundries, who convert it into the basic shapes required by the major consuming industries.

Copper Scrap: An Important Source of Supply

Most of our discussion up to this point has centered upon the mine production of copper and the way in which it moves from the mine to the consuming industries. However, in the United States, and the same is thought to hold true to some extent for the other countries as well, refined copper produced from mined ore only accounts for about two-thirds of the total amount of copper consumed with the other third coming from copper scrap. Copper scrap is usually broken down into two categories: old scrap and new scrap. Old scrap is generated from metal articles which may be worn out, damaged or obsolete such as a junked automobile. Much of this old scrap is collected and returned to the secondary refineries, brass and bronze ingot makers and the brass mills, where it is reprocessed and emerges as an addition to overall supplies.

New scrap is for the most part generated in the fabricator and milling processes and is not really considered part of the overall supply in that it was already taken into consideration in refined production statistics. Further, new scrap is usually reprocessed by the custom smelter on toll from the fabricator or mill and thus, rarely re-enters the marketing system. If both old and new scrap were taken into consideration, they would probably amount to about one-half of total copper consumption.

Since copper is virtually indestructible and the usage pattern is such that it can be reclaimed, the reservoir of potential copper scrap is quite large, especially in the United States, due to a high rate of obsolescence. The amount recovered, however, will depend in large measure upon prices and the availability of regular producer copper.

Copper Consumption

Between the superior physical properties of copper, its versatility and the rapid technological advances that have characterized the past fifty years, it is no wonder that copper consumption has grown rapidly through the years. Copper is an excellent conductor of heat and electricity, resists corrosion, is durable, ductile and malleable and is easily alloyed with other metals, all of which are in part responsible for the prevalent use of copper today.

Demand for copper and its various alloys comes from five major areas: electrical and electronic products, consumer and general products, building construction, industrial machinery and equipment, and transportation. There is some overlapping of these categories in that nearly one-half of all copper consumed is used for its electrical properties even though the wiring in a refrigerator might fall into the consumption classification of "consumer products". Copper is found in many household appliances, such as radios and heaters; in automobiles, airplanes and missiles; in computers, telephones and other sophisticated communications equipment; in scientific instruments, coins, utensils, jewelry; and in a host of other products.

A brief glance at the many areas of copper use points up the obvious: the demand for copper must be the greatest in a highly developed, industrial nation. Not surprising, then, is the fact that the United States is by far and away the world's largest copper consumer, accounting for over 25 percent of overall world use. The other more industrial nations of the world such as Japan, the U.S.S.R., Germany and Great Britain account for almost 50 percent of total world consumption. Significantly, all, with the exception of the U.S.S.R., are net importers along with the United States.

The most important factor affecting the year to year level of copper consumption is the general level of economic and business activity, both in the U.S. and abroad. With the heavy concentration of copper usage in consumer appliances, automobiles and housing, periods of recession or stagnant economic growth can materially affect copper consumption. As our illustration of this impact, refer to the periods 1970/71 and 1974 during which tight money, inflation, reduced defense budgets, slashed corporate capital expenditures and sharply curtailed new construction joined forces to reduce copper usage and contributed to the dramatic price declines during those periods.

In periods of high economic activity, copper consumption has grown by leaps and bounds, growth which has often been accentuated by heavy military needs in time of war. Used in the manufacture of munitions, airplanes, helicopters, jeeps and ships, copper is a strategic metal. Substantial amounts of copper were used in both the Korean and Vietnam wars and to insure sufficient supplies of copper during the Vietnam conflict, the U.S. Government required producers to "set-aside" a certain percentage of their output for military needs. The importance of copper in this area of use explains the historical sensitivity of copper prices to threats of hostility such as the periodic fighting in the Middle East.

Copper Substitutes

Threatening a continuation of the growth in copper consumption is substitution. For the most part, fears of substitution abound when copper supplies are short and prices are high. And, while there have been some instances in which traditional copper outlets have been partially captured by other materials, the change-over from copper to another metal is often costly and before massive substitution has had a chance to occur, copper prices have usually receded, lessening the need. The major substitutes are aluminum in the electrical field and plastics and cast iron in the tubing industry.

While the vulnerability of copper to substitutes should not be taken lightly, particularly in periods of high prices, there are many areas of copper usage for which there are no substitutes, such as in the heating, air-conditioning and refrigeration industries where the unique properties of copper make it nonpareil. More importantly, however, it may well be that substitution will be quite necessary over the long run to make sufficient copper available to meet the growing needs in those areas of use for which only copper is suited. Furthermore, as technology advances, new uses such as in the desalinization process are bound to materialize, possibly more than offsetting the supplies freed by substitution.

With the level of copper consumption almost directly commensurate with the degree of technological advancement and economic activity, there would seem to be on the horizon tremendous growth in copper consumption as the emerging nations of the world advance economically. The People's Republic of China, for example, throughout the past several years has apparently been forced to rely on the rest of the world for an increasing amount of its copper requirements due to expanding internal needs. China's presence in the market during 1969 and again in 1973 contributed to the sharp upward price movements during those years.

The Influence of Refined Copper Stocks

As with any commodity, the level of stocks can either accentuate or buffer the effects upon price of an imbalanced production/consumption ratio. There are two basic stock series that should be examined before attempting to gauge the probable effects that changes in either production and/or consumption might have upon the market. The first series is released by the American Bureau of Metal Statistics, Inc., and provides data on refined copper stocks on a monthly basis for the United States and for most of the Free World countries as a bloc. Changes in the level of these stocks when viewed in the light of monthly refined copper production can help determine whether or not production is moving into consuming channels.

The second series, also released on a monthly basis by the American Bureau of Metal Statistics, Inc., shows the level of refined stocks at the U.S. fabricating plants. From this stock level, the Bureau subtracts the fabricators' working stocks, adds to the result the undelivered purchases of refined copper and from that total, subtracts the unfilled orders. If the result is positive, the fabricators have a surplus of refined copper, but if the result is negative, known as the "theoretical deficit", the fabricators will need more copper to fulfill their existing sales contracts.

Historically, U.S. fabricators "run in the red", so to speak, by not having sufficient copper on hand to meet existing orders. Periodically, however, the fabricators will show a small surplus such as in mid-1970, mid-1972 and again in late 1974. As it is normal industry practice to operate at a "theoretical deficit", the appearance of a surplus is indicative of excess supplies or reduced demand, or a combination of both.

Refined copper stocks which have been approved for delivery against futures contracts traded on the London Metal Exchange (reported weekly), the New York Commodity Exchange (reported daily), and the International Monetary Market (reported daily), should be taken into consideration. Although futures markets were designed as a means of price protection and not as an outlet for unwanted supplies or as a source of supply, a rising stock level in the warehouses is often indicative of a surplus condition and conversely, a falling stock level could be indicative of a tightening of supply.

Another source of supply has been the strategic stockpile maintained by the U.S. Government. Originally intended to provide copper for defense needs in time of war, the stockpile, in recent years, has been used primarily to provide the domestic copper industry with supplies in times of extreme shortages. As of early 1975, however, the stockpile had been depleted by such sales and as the amount of copper required in a nuclear war is estimated to be substantially less than in a conventional war, it is doubtful that in the future, the U.S. Government will be as significant a factor in the copper market as it was in the 1960's and early 1970's.

Copper Prices: What Do They Mean?

In the United States, the four basic markets for copper are the producer market, the merchant or dealer market, the scrap market and the futures market. The goal of the copper producers has been to assure the consuming sector of the industry of raw material at a reasonable and relatively stable price. Consequently, domestic copper producer prices are determined after taking into consideration producing and refining costs, profit margins and the price of competing substitutes and do not fluctuate in accordance with the day to day changes in the overall supply/demand situation. This is not to say, however, that there has never been any movement in producer prices. During the copper shortage of the 1960's, domestic producer prices almost doubled, from slightly over 30¢ per pound early in the decade to 60¢ per pound in early 1970, before dropping 10¢ in late 1970 through early 1971 as a result of the improvement in the supply situation. By mid-1974, however, producer prices had risen to the 85¢ per pound level during the great bull market when futures reached $1.40 per pound, but early 1975 found producer prices under 70¢. Obviously, producer prices do respond to changing supply/demand conditions, but not to the extent that futures or dealer prices do.

Although domestic producers supply the fabricators and mills with the bulk of their copper requirements, copper consumers must also rely on other sources, primarily dealer and scrap copper. The prices of both refined dealer copper and No. 2 heavy scrap copper, which usually trades at a discount of about 6¢ per pound to refined copper, do tend to fluctuate in accordance with the immediate supply/demand situation. When shipments or deliveries of producer copper are disrupted, consumer dependency upon the dealer and scrap markets increases and tends to force prices upwards. Often, both dealer copper and scrap copper command substantial premiums to producer prices when supplies are tight and, on occasion, substantial discounts when supplies are large. Usually, the producer price will be the last to be raised in a bull market and the last to be lowered in a bear market. (The U.S. government in 1970 completed an in-depth study of domestic copper prices, and although the general conclusion of the report was that a one-price system would benefit both the producer and the consumer, no steps in this direction have, as yet, been taken.)

Since the same factors which affect prices in the dealer and scrap markets also affect prices in the futures markets, the price changes in one tend to mirror the price changes in the other. Futures markets in copper, therefore, are constantly adjusting and readjusting to the changes in the fundamental supply/demand situation, providing a fairly accurate appraisal of the worth of copper at any given moment. Possibly because of this sensitivity, most major foreign producers including Chile, Zambia, Zaire and Peru base their daily selling prices on the futures market in London, i.e., the London Metal Exchange.

The Futures Markets

Aiding in the marketing and pricing of copper and providing a speculative medium for the public are the three copper futures markets, the London Metal Exchange (LME), the N.Y. Commodity Exchange (Comex) and the International Monetary Market (IMM) of the Chicago Mercantile Exchange.

There are two 25 metric ton contracts on the LME; one for copper wirebars (either electrolytic or high conductivity fire refined, with the latter deliverable at a discount of £20 per ton), and one for electrolytic copper cathodes. Trading on the LME takes place during two sessions, the morning or first session from 12:00 to 12:05 and the afternoon or the second session from 3:40 to 3:45 (London time). At the end of each session trading is permitted for approximately a twenty minute period, known as the "kerb". Trading is conducted either for immediate delivery ("Cash") the following day or for delivery in exactly three months. Delivery is made from Exchange approved warehouses located in England, in Hamburg or in Rotterdam. Stocks of copper in the warehouses are reported weekly and represent potentially deliverable supplies.

The LME is a "principals" market in that there is no clearing house as there is on Comex, and margins and commissions are established by individual agreement between the member and the customer. Significantly, there is no "force majeure" clause in either the LME contract or the one traded on Comex. (A "force majeure" is a suspension of contractual obligations due to circumstances beyond the control of the parties involved. Copper producers have often declared a "force majeure" whenever a strike or natural disaster has prevented them from fulfilling their shipping or delivery schedules.)

On the Comex, the copper futures contract calls for delivery of 12½ short tons (25,000 pounds) of either electrolytic copper, high conductivity fire refined copper or Lake copper, so named because it comes from the native copper mines of the Lake Superior district. Copper cathodes are deliverable at a ⅛¢ per pound discount and fire refined copper, at a ¼¢ per pound discount. Unlike the LME, trading on the Comex is continuous, running from 9:50 A.M. until 2:00 P.M. (New York time) and the delivery months, rather than being restricted to cash and three months, extend for 14 months and include January, March, May, July, September, October and December. An important point to remember is that the exact day of delivery is specified on the LME, where only the month is designated on the Comex, with the specific day of delivery at the option of the delivering seller. Delivery is permitted from any one of the Exchange licensed warehouses located in cities scattered from New York City to Tacoma, Washington, here again at the option of the seller.

Prices on the Comex are quoted in cents and tenths of a cent per pound, while prices on the LME are quoted in pounds sterling and tenths of a pound per ton. Prices on the Comex are not permitted to fluctuate more than 5¢ per pound above or below the previous session's settlement price, a regulation designed to minimize the response of the market to dynamic pieces of news which, on the next day, may not seem quite so important. No such daily price limits exist on the LME.

On Comex, minimum margins and commissions are established by the Exchange and all trading must be handled through members of the Exchange, who usually deal through a floor broker. All trades must be reported by the member to the Clearing Association which records the net positions of his customers. Since the LME morning session takes place well before Comex opens, any analyst is definitely aided in anticipating how Comex will probably open after taking into consideration the normal difference between the two and the change in prices in London from the previous Comex close.

In 1974, the International Monetary Market of the Chicago Mercantile Exchange began trading in a 12,500 pound copper contract (half the size of Comex). Although the contract specifications differ somewhat from the Comex contract, the mechanics of trading are very similar. Trading activity, however, for the most part remains centered in New York and London.

Carrying Charges

Carrying charges are those costs, i.e., storage, interest and sometimes insurance, inherent in owning copper from one month until the next. Usually, when the available supply of copper appears sufficient for future demand, the premium that the price of the more distant December contract, for example, will command over the price of the nearby March contract tends to approximate the cost of storing and financing copper from March to December. This situation, when each succeeding month carries a premium to the month immediately preceding it, is known as a "normal" or carrying charge market or, in the industry, as a "contango."

The premium that the more distant deliveries will command over the nearbys is governed almost entirely by carrying charges. If the difference between the two was greater than the cost of owning copper during the period, it would be profitable to buy the nearby delivery, say March, and sell the December contract, take delivery of the March, hold it until December and retender it against the December contract. The profit would be equal to the original premium for the December over March minus the actual cost of carrying from March to December. When a situation such as this arises, the buying of March and the selling of December would keep the difference limited to carrying charges.

When present supplies do not appear adequate for future needs, there is usually a greater demand for whatever nearby supplies do exist. This tends to cause the price of the nearby futures contract to gain on the price of the more distant month as the buyer is willing to pay more to assure himself of adequate supplies. When the nearby contract does trade at a premium to the more distant contracts, the market is said to be, "inverted" or, in the industry, when "cash" is above three months, a "backwardation" exists.

While there is a limit to the premium a distant contract can command over the nearby, i.e., carrying charges, there is theoretically no limit to the premium that the nearby contract can reach over the distant deliveries in times of shortage.

On the Comex, storage charges, without insurance which is arranged for by the actual owner, run about 10 to 20 points per month per pound or, for a 25 thousand pound contract, about $12.50 to $25.00 per month. Added to this must be the interest on the moneys tied up during the holding period.

Changes in the differences between months can often be a harbinger of changes in the fundamental supply/demand situation. During times of surplus, the differences may approximate full carrying charges, while a narrowing of the differences or an inversion could be indicative of a developing shortage.

Futures and the Industry

Futures markets were established primarily to serve as a hedging medium for producers, consumers, dealers, etc., who were vulnerable to rapid and sometimes devastating price movements. Hedging, simply defined, is taking a position in the futures market that is the opposite of the position held in the actual commodity. A sell hedge, for example, would protect the dealer against a decline in the value of his inventory, whereas a buy hedge would protect against a price rise betwen the fabricator's forward sale and his receipt of his raw material from the producer. Futures markets offer the industry benefits other than those afforded by hedging, such as price-fixing and inventory management. The advantages and mechanics of hedging are too numerous and detailed for the scope of this study, but an excellent treatise on the subject entitled, "New Hedging Concepts in Commodity Futures", can be found in the 1970 Commodity Year Book.

Futures and the Speculator

The risks that the hedger wishes to avoid are, in reality, absorbed by the speculator, who, in search of profit, often isn't aware of the valuable economic function that he serves. Successful speculation in any commodity is dependent upon a number of factors, the most important of which is adhering to the old adage: "let your profits run and limit your losses." A thorough study of the commodity involved should be made, keeping an eye pealed for those often unexpected "happenings", particularly in copper, which can upset the supply/demand balance. Chart analysis, which has become a recognized aid in commodity price forecasting, should be utilized in timing the purchases or sales which will be dictated by fundamental analysis. Finally, while the leverage is tremendous and the possible return often great, never risk more than you can afford to lose.

Sources of Statistical Data and Current Market Information

There is a wealth of statistical data available on copper in its various stages of production and consumption, but unfortunately, most of it is several weeks, and sometimes months old before it is compiled and released to the public. This time lag puts the serious student of the copper market at a decided disadvantage. Furthermore, because of the various governmental and private sources of statistical information, it is a mammoth undertaking to reconcile the different series to arrive at a comprehensive picture. For this reason, the Copper Development Association is to be highly complimented for having organized the different sets of statistics available from the U.S. Bureau of Mines, the U.S. Bureau of the Census, the U.S. Business and Defense Services Administration and the Copper Development Association itself into a logical sequence, tracing "the flow of copper in the industrial economy of the United States from mining and scrap collection through smelting, refining and ingot making to the brass mills, wire

mills and foundries and then on to the final end-use markets" on an annual basis. All of this information is compiled in their annual report.

Monthly reports on U.S. production, consumption and stocks are available from the U.S. Bureau of Mines, as is more detailed data on an annual basis. Foreign trade statistics are available from the U.S. Department of Commerce. The Copper Institute, now part of the American Bureau of Metal Statistics, among other things, releases monthly statistics on crude and refined production, producer deliveries and stocks, both for the U.S. and most of the Free World, as well as a detailed statistical abstract of the U.S. fabricator position. The American Bureau of Metal Statistics compiles annual statistics on world blister and smelter production and world consumption by country. The Bureau, in its annual yearbook, also reports on the Free World copper refining capacity and the annual production of leading copper mines. Comprehensive statistical data are also contained in the American Metal Market's annual yearbook as well as the Commodity Year Book, published by the Commodity Research Bureau, Inc. Unfortunately, while information on the copper industry in the United States is plentiful, meaningful data for the world are rather scarce except for annual production and consumption statistics and the monthly reports issued by the Copper Institute which were mentioned earlier.

There are about five principal sources of current market information, four of which are available by subscription. They are the daily trade newspaper, *The American Metal Market;* a bi-weekly magazine published in London entitled, *Metal Bulletin;* a weekly McGraw-Hill publication, *Metals Week;* and the Commodity Research Bureau's *Futures Market Service.* Finally, most brokerage firms maintain research departments that specialize in commodities and futures trading and often issue weekly market letters and other statistical information.

December Copper Futures Delivery 1974-75

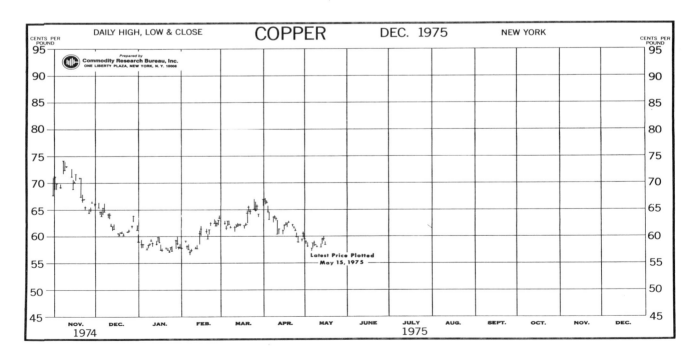

December Copper Futures Delivery
1971-72 to 1973-74

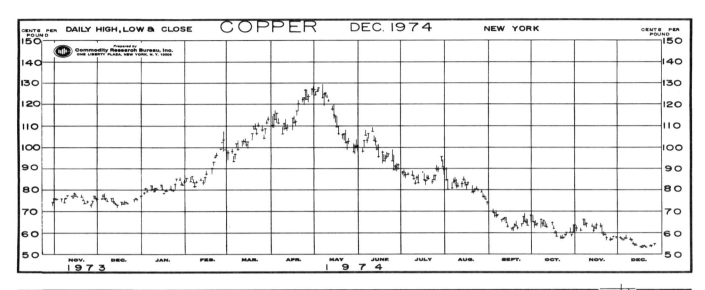

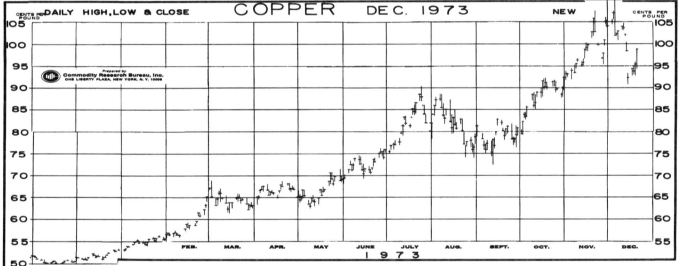

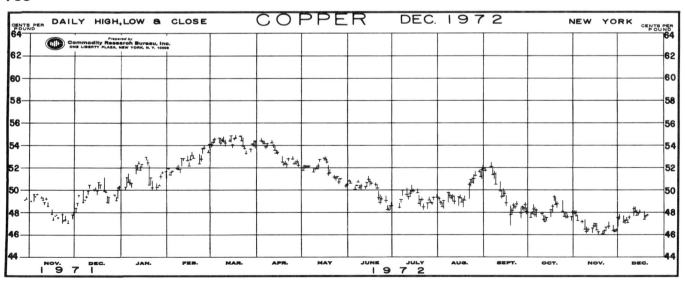

December Copper Futures Delivery
1968-69 to 1970-71

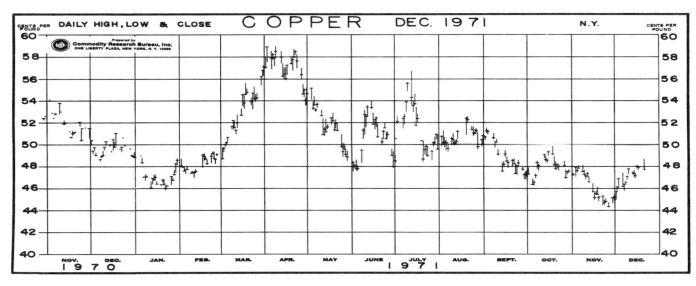

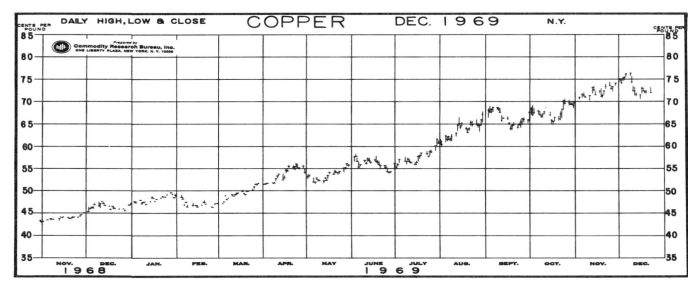

December Copper Futures Delivery
1965-66 to 1967-68

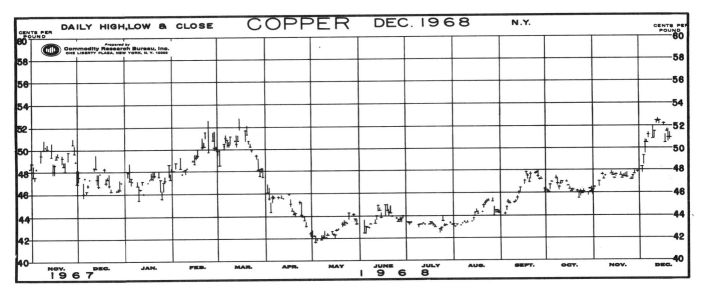

DAILY HIGH, LOW & CLOSE   COPPER   DEC. 1968   N.Y.

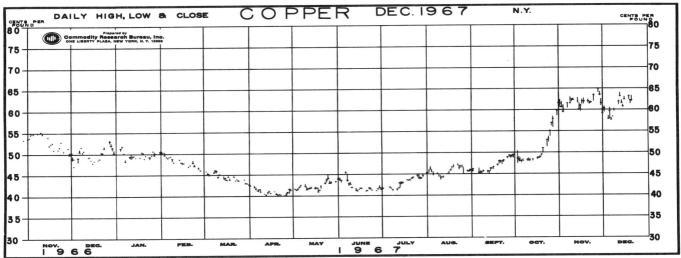

DAILY HIGH, LOW & CLOSE   COPPER   DEC. 1967   N.Y.

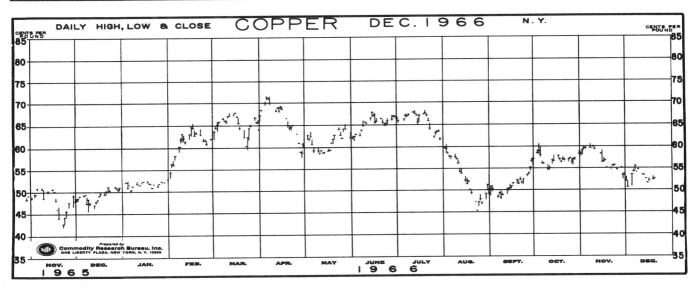

DAILY HIGH, LOW & CLOSE   COPPER   DEC. 1966   N.Y.

NEW GUIDELINES FOR FORECASTING CORN FUTURES

BY MALCOLM CLOUGH

The past 3 years have witnessed a phenomenal expansion in the demand for corn along with many other agricultural products. The rise in foreign demand has been especially pronounced due to grain shortages in a number of countries and expanding livestock and poultry production in others. But domestic demand also has shared in the sharp gain—with record or near record tonnages of corn fed in 1972/73 and 1973/74 at the highest prices in 20 years.

Unlike most past periods of sharply rising prices the dramatic gains in 1972/73 and 1973/74 occurred when we were neither in a war period nor a period of short supply. In fact, the sharp upsurge in demand came at a time when we were completing withdrawal from the Viet Nam war, rather than during a period of war escalation. Corn prices rose nearly 50% in 1972/73 over the preceding year, even though supplies increased 6% to a record 6.7 billion bushels. In 1973/74 the corn supply dropped 5% but was still the second largest of record—and prices increased another 62%.

Some other tangible factors in the changing demand for corn from 1971/72 to 1973/74 are as follows: Domestic use rose 6% even though corn prices rose 136%. The index of prices of livestock and livestock products was 33% higher in the 1973/74 feeding year than in 1971/72. Hog prices rose 46%, while cattle were only 20% higher and broilers were up 57%. With the increase in the demand for feed abroad, corn exports rose 56% from 1971/72 to 1973/74 and were more than double the 1965–70 average. The farm value of the corn exported rose from $860 million in 1971/72 to $3,170 million in

Table 1. Corn Acreage, Supply, Utilization, and Prices, United States 1958–74

Item	1958–59	1959–60	1960–61	1961–62	1962–63	1963–64	1964–65	1965–66	1966–67	1967–68	1968–69	1969–70	1970–71	1971–72	1972–73	1973–74	1974–75[1]
Acreage							Million Acres										
Planted	73.4	82.7	81.4	65.9	65.0	68.8	65.8	65.2	66.3	71.2	65.1	64.3	66.8	74.1	67.0	71.9	77.7
Harvested	63.5	72.1	71.4	57.6	55.7	59.2	55.4	55.4	57.0	60.7	56.0	54.6	57.4	64.0	57.4	61.9	65.2
							Bushels Per Acre										
Yield per acre	52.8	53.1	54.7	62.4	64.7	67.9	62.9	74.1	73.1	80.1	79.5	85.9	72.4	88.1	97.1	91.2	71.3
Supply							Million Bushels										
Carryover (Oct. 1)	1,469	1,524	1,787	2,016	1,653	1,365	1,537	1,147	842	826	1,169	1,118	1,005	667	1,126	709	483
Production	3,356	3,825	3,907	3,598	3,606	4,019	3,484	4,103	4,168	4,860	4,450	4,687	4,152	5,641	5,573	5,647	4,651
Imports	1	1	1	1	1	1	1	1	1	1	1	1	4	1	1	1	1
Total	4,826	5,350	5,695	5,615	5,260	5,385	5,022	5,251	5,011	5,687	5,620	5,806	5,161	6,309	6,700	6,357	5,135
Domestic use																	
Livestock feed	2,782	3,043	3,092	3,212	3,157	3,009	2,956	3,361	3,329	3,507	3,580	3,795	3,581	3,978	4,310	4,196	
Food, Ind. and seed	290	290	295	315	322	339	349	361	369	378	386	394	396	409	423	435	
Total	3,072	3,333	3,387	3,527	3,479	3,348	3,305	3,722	3,698	3,885	3,966	4,189	3,977	4,387	4,733	4,631	
Exports[2]	230	230	292	435	416	500	570	687	487	633	536	612	517	796	1,258	1,243	
Total use	3,302	3,563	3,679	3,962	3,895	3,848	3,875	4,409	4,185	4,518	4,502	4,801	4,494	5,183	5,991	5,874	
Carryover (Sept. 30)																	
Govt.[3]	1,400	1,675	1,890	1,535	1,275	1,300	924	437	374	714	736	543	330	718	172	12	
"Free"	124	112	126	118	90	237	223	405	452	455	382	462	337	408	537	471	
Total	1,524	1,787	2,016	1,653	1,365	1,537	1,147	842	826	1,169	1,118	1,005	667	1,126	709	483	
							Dollars Per Bushel										
Prices rec'd by farmers	1.12	1.05	1.00	1.10	1.12	1.11	1.17	1.16	1.24	1.03	1.08	1.16	1.33	1.08	1.57	2.55	
Chicago, No. 2 yellow	1.24	1.19	1.12	1.13	1.24	1.22	1.32	1.32	1.36	1.14	1.22	1.31	1.47	1.23	1.91	2.95	

[1] Preliminary. [2] Includes grain equivalent of products. [3] Owned by CCC or under loan.
Source: Economic Research Service, U.S.D.A.

1973/74. Following the big supplies in 1972 and 1973, a poor growing season in 1974 cut production 18% and the total supply dropped to only 5.1 billion bushels, the smallest since 1966. Prices again rose sharply, to a record $3.35 a bushel for October–December 1974, nearly 50% above the same quarter of 1973. The short supply was expected to bring a sharp reduction in domestic use and exports.

So dramatic was the change in the livestock-feed picture, as well as for other agricultural commodities in 1972 and 1973 that the Secretary of Agriculture in an address to the National Agricultural Outlook conference on Dec. 17, 1973, stated that "we have reached a significant turning point in American agriculture. We are in a new ball game, and this is clearly the overriding factor in the outlook for 1974.

"In the last eighteen months, we have shifted from concern over too much farm production to the question of potential food and fiber shortages both here and abroad.

"Realistically, there is no danger of food shortage in this country. The geography, climate, and resources of this nation make our crops virtually disaster proof. We need not fear having too little, nor do we need to wring our hands over means of disposing of too much."

Another agricultural economist observed that "American agriculture is riding the crest of a wave—the biggest wave any of us can remember." Whether we are in a new ball game or riding the crest of a high wave, the experience of the last 2 years would indicate that we need to take a fresh look at some of the factors which have been important in affecting corn prices during the past 2 decades.

The Corn Supply-Use Balance

The sharp upsurge in domestic use and exports of the past 2 years follows a longer term period of steadily rising corn supplies and consumption. While both domestic use and exports have increased, expansion in exports has been at a relatively faster pace.

Let us first turn our attention to domestic use, which may be broken down into two major categories; (1) livestock feed, (2) food, industry and seed. Livestock feed is by far the most important, accounting for a little over 90% of total U.S. consumption in recent years. The quantity consumed by livestock responds more readily to changes in corn prices and the corn supply while food and industrial usage has shown a steady upward trend—not influenced appreciably by corn prices.

Major factors which influence the quantities of corn consumed by livestock are (1) the price of corn, (2) the number of livestock to be fed and (3) prices of livestock and livestock products. Historically, a 10% change in corn prices has been associated with a 3% change (in the opposite direction) in the quantity consumed by livestock. This relationship, however, has not applied to the marked changes of the past 3 years. In other recent years it has worked reasonably well. In 1967/68 when corn prices dropped 17% from the preceding year, there was a 5% increase in corn consumed by livestock. In 1970/71 a 15% increase in the price of corn resulted in a 6% drop in the quantity fed. This was followed by a 19% drop in the price of corn in 1971/72 which brought an 11% increase in the amount of corn fed to livestock.

Table 2. Grain Consuming Animal Units, Feeding Rate, and Total Feed Consumed, U.S. 1964–73 (Year Beginning October)

Livestock Units	Unit	1964	1965	1966	1967	1968	1969	1970	1971	1972	1973[1]
Dairy cattle	Mil. units	19.2	18.1	17.3	16.4	15.8	13.2	13.0	13.0	12.8	12.5
Cattle on feed	do.	19.4	20.5	21.9	22.2	24.5	25.8	25.0	27.2	28.2	26.6
Other cattle	do.	5.8	5.9	5.9	6.0	6.0	6.7	6.9	7.0	7.4	8.0
Hogs	do.	32.3	31.2	34.4	35.5	35.5	35.7	39.3	36.5	34.6	33.6
Poultry	do.	27.2	28.6	29.9	29.3	29.7	31.2	31.4	31.5	30.7	31.0
Other livestock	do.	2.0	1.9	1.9	1.9	1.9	1.9	1.9	1.8	1.8	1.8
Total	Mil. units	105.9	106.2	111.3	111.3	113.4	114.5	117.5	117.0	115.5	113.5
Feeding rate per animal unit	Ton	1.37	1.52	1.46	1.48	1.53	1.61	1.54	1.65	1.69	1.66
Total concentrates fed	Mil. tons	145.3	161.5	162.1	164.6	173.9	184.1	180.4	192.5	194.7	188.7
Indexes of Feeding and Prices											
Animal units	1967–68 = 100	95	95	100	100	102	103	106	105	104	102
Feeding rate per animal unit	do.	93	103	99	100	103	109	104	111	114	112
Total concentrates fed		88	98	98	100	106	112	110	117	118	115
Feed grain prices	1967 = 100	100	101	104	90	93	97	110	96	141	222
Livestock prices	do.	90	105	101	102	113	120	114	129	168	171
Livestock prices divided by feed grain prices	Percent	90	104	97	113	122	124	104	134	119	77

[1] Preliminary.
Source: Economic Research Service and Statistical Reporting Service, U.S.D.A.

But the sharp increase in prices in 1972/73 and 1973/74 was entirely outside the experience of these earlier years. It came from rapidly expanding demand—both domestic and foreign—which caused not only higher prices but significantly larger domestic use and export. The price of corn rose about 50% from 1971/72 to 1972/73, domestic use was 8% larger, and exports were up 58%. Despite smaller supplies in 1973/74 and another sharp increase in prices, domestic use was only 2% below the 1972/73 record and exports were down only 1%.

Strong world demand, with short crops in some countries, was basic to the sharp upsurge in demand for feed. In the United States, higher prices for hogs, cattle, and broilers encouraged expansion in feeding even at substantially higher feed prices. Adverse harvesting weather and the resulting lower quality of the 1972 corn crop along with short supplies of protein feeds also contributed to heavier corn feeding. It is significant that livestock and poultry producers fed a record 4.3 billion bushels of corn in 1972/73 with a farm value of $6.7 billion. In 1973/74 the quantity fed dropped slightly to 4.2 billion bushels, but the farm value of the corn fed rose sharply to $10.7 billion. Never before has there been such a sharp rise in the value of corn fed. During the seven feeding years 1965/66 through 1971/72 the quantity fed ranged from 3.3 to 4.0 billion bushels with a farm value ranging from $3.6 to $4.8 billion. The quantity of corn fed was expected to drop 15 to 20% in 1974/75 due to short supplies, but with much higher prices the value was expected to exceed $11 billion.

While these figures are impressive, past experience would indicate that it is unlikely that corn and other feed grains will remain in such tight supply over the next several years as to maintain this level of prices and expenditures for feed. With the relaxation of the feed grain program, considering farmers' capacity to produce, it seems more likely that production will increase to levels that will substantially ease the feed grain supply situation and bring lower feed grain prices in the years ahead. Thus, farmers would be able to continue to expand total feed consumption, especially corn, but at prices and costs probably somewhat below those prevailing in 1973/74 and well below the 1974/75 level.

Feed Requirements Trending Upward

The combined tonnage of feed grains and other feed concentrates consumed by livestock has been trending upward for a number of years, averaging about 4% annually from 1964 to 1972. Corn is the basic ingredient in most livestock and poultry rations. It makes up about 60% of all concentrates fed and 75% of all feed grains. The uptrend in feeding—due both to increasing livestock numbers and heavier feeding per animal—is expected to continue in the future. In line with the longer term trend, total concentrate feeding rose about 35% from 1964 to 1972, but has dropped since then due to reduced feed grain supplies. The increase in feeding per animal unit accounted for about 2/3 of the overall increase and the increase in livestock and poultry numbers about 1/3. The upward trend in the feeding rate per animal has been due largely to the increase in the production of livestock products per animal and the tendency to rely more and more on feed concentrates and less on roughages.

The price of feed grains in relation to prices of livestock and livestock products also has had a bearing on the feeding rate. From 1964 to 1972 livestock prices, especially hog and cattle, rose at a faster pace than feed prices, encouraging more liberal feeding per animal. When the index of feed prices is low in relation to the livestock index there has been a tendency for the feeding rate to increase. It will be noted that in 1971/72 when the index of livestock and livestock products rose to 34% above the feed grain index (1967 equals 100) the rate of feeding rose sharply to a record 1.65 tons per animal unit. With livestock prices continuing high in relation to feed prices during most of 1972/73 the feeding rate rose again to slightly above the 1971/72 level.

From 1972/73 to 1973/74 feed grain prices rose 57%, while livestock prices rose only 2%. The index of livestock prices dropped to only 77% of feed grain prices (1967 = 100) much lower than in any of the past 10 years. The less favorable livestock-feed price relationship brought a slight drop in the feeding rate per animal and a 3% drop in the total tonnage of all concentrates fed. The sharp increase in feed grain prices has made this relationship even less favorable to livestock producers so far in 1974/75 (early in 1975). More substantial reductions in total concentrates fed and the feeding rate per animal unit are in prospect for the 1974/75 feeding season. Over the next several years it appears likely that the longer term upward trend will be resumed as farmers expand production of corn and other feeds and we return to more favorable livestock-feed price ratios.

The Importance of Corn in Livestock Feeding

Corn consumption rose sharply in 1972/73 as a percentage of total feed consumption. Corn has made up about 56 to 58% of total concentrates (grains and byproduct feeds) fed during most of the past 10 years. In 1971/72 corn accounted for about 58% of the total, then rose to 62% in 1972/73 and 1973/74. This increase reflects the large supply of corn available with limited supplies of other feeds. The change in the feed grain program permitting farmers more freedom to choose the crops they grow without acreage restrictions may turn out to be favorable for corn production as compared with other crops. In this event corn may continue to make up a larger share of livestock rations in the years ahead.

Cost of Feed Rises Faster than Other Production Costs

The overall cost of feed relative to other livestock production costs also has a bearing on the quantity of feed grains and other concentrates fed—both in total and per animal unit. Feed prices did not rise as rapidly during the calendar years 1964 through 1972 as farm machinery, buildings, fencing, wages, taxes and interest, and many other of the farmers' production costs. This tendency for feed to be relatively cheap has been important in contributing to heavier feeding per animal. As shown in Table 3, prices paid by farmers for feed rose only 8% from 1967 to 1972 while other major items in livestock and poultry production rose as much as 35 to 40%.

Table 3. Prices Paid by Farmers for Feed and Other Production Items, U.S. 1964–74

Calendar Year	Feed Purchased	Buildings and Fencing	Farm Machinery	Wage Rates	All Production Items Including Interest and Taxes
			1967 = 100		
1964	97	95	90	82	90
1965	98	96	92	86	94
1966	102	98	96	93	98
1967	100	100	100	100	100
1968	95	106	105	108	104
1969	97	114	110	119	110
1970	102	115	116	128	115
1971	106	124	124	134	121
1972	108	135	133	142	128
1973	164	154	144	155	150
1974	192	191	166	172	174

Source: Agricultural Prices, Statistical Reporting Service, U.S.D.A.

With the tight feed situation that developed in 1973/74, the price of feed grains rose sharply. Feed grain prices in the calendar year 1974 averaged 246% of the 1967 level and the price of all feeds purchased was 192% of 1967. Feed prices also were high in relation to other production items, most of which made much smaller gains than feed from 1972 to 1974.

With a very tight supply situation for feed in 1974/75, feed prices are unusually high in relation to other products going into livestock production in 1974, and early 1975. This will force a temporary reversal of the upward trend in the feed consumption as livestock producers will tend to be more saving on feed, the high cost item.

Corn Exports Take a More Important Role in the Corn Economy

Corn exports have been increasing in importance as an outlet for the U.S. corn during the past 20 years. Corn exports were generally below 200 million bushels until the late 1950's then ranged from 300 to 600 million during the 1960's and finally reached a record of 1,258 million in 1972/73. In the late 1950's exports accounted for only about 6 or 7% of total corn disappearance. During the 1960's exports tended to level off at about 12 to 15% of total disappearance. With the rapid expansion in foreign demand in the past 3 years, exports rose from 15% of the total in 1971/72 to 21% of total disappearance in 1972/73 and 1973/74.

Three factors appear to be largely responsible for the increasing importance of corn exports. (1) There has been a general tendency among many countries to expand livestock and poultry production to improve the protein content of the human diet. The increase in feed requirements to take care of the expanding demand for livestock and livestock products has made it necessary for these countries to increase imports of corn and other feed grains. Japan is a noteworthy example as U.S. exports of corn to Japan increased from only 21 million bushels in 1960/61 to 262 million in 1972/73, then receded slightly to 251 million in 1973/74.

Table 4. Corn Exports Relative to Total Disappearance, U.S. 1956–73

Year Beginning October	Total Disappearance[1]	Exports[2] Quantity	Exports[2] Percent of Disappearance
	Mil. bu.	Mil. bu.	Percent
1956/57	2,822	184	6.5
1957/58	2,997	200	6.7
1958/59	3,302	230	7.0
1959/60	3,563	230	6.5
1960/61	3,679	292	7.9
1961/62	3,962	435	11.0
1962/63	3,895	416	10.7
1963/64	3,848	500	13.0
1964/65	3,875	570	14.7
1965/66	4,409	687	15.6
1966/67	4,185	487	11.6
1967/68	4,518	633	14.0
1968/69	4,502	536	11.9
1969/70	4,801	612	12.7
1970/71	4,494	517	11.5
1971/72	5,183	796	15.4
1972/73	5,991	1,258	21.0
1973/74	5,874	1,243	21.2

[1] Domestic use and exports.   [2] Includes grain equivalent of products.

(2) The sharp increase in feed grain exports in the past 2 years may also be attributed in part to poor growing conditions in several important countries at a time when demand was unusually strong. Feed grain production was down substantially in South Africa, Australia, India, and China. A relatively poor crop also was produced in the USSR in 1972/73 leaving a substantial gap between supplies and requirements, which are increasing with expanding livestock production.

(3) Opening the door for sales of grain to Russia and China also contributed to increased feed grain exports. Corn exports to Russia ranged from 119 million to 136 million in the last 3 years. Exports to China began in 1972/73, totaling 48 million bushels and increased to 58 million in 1973/74. Corn exports to these two countries have accounted for 14 or 15% of our total exports in each of the last 3 years. Their importance may be more significant in terms of prospects for the future. The door is now opened to two major consuming countries with large populations and with a goal of expanding per capita consumption of livestock and poultry products.

The Role of Feed Grain Programs

Government programs have played a dominant role in the corn economy over the past 20 years. U.S. potential for corn production has consistently exceeded domestic and export requirements since the close of the Korean war. In the 1950's acreage was limited by the Corn Allotment program and also by acreage retired from production under the Soil Bank program.

Both of these programs proved ineffective in keeping corn production in line with total requirements. Production exceeded total use each year from 1952 through 1960. Carryover stocks rose consistently from the 487 million bushels October 1, 1952 to 2,016 million on October 1, 1961. Corn prices, which reached a high of $1.66 a bushel in 1951/52, at the close of the Korean war, fell steadily to a low of $1.00 a bushel in 1960/61. It was obvious that farmers' productive capacity was well in excess of domestic and export needs in the post-war years and a more effective program was needed to bring the two in balance.

The Feed Grain Program, included in the Agricultural Act of 1961, became effective with the 1961 crops. This program offered farmers the opportunity to divert acreage from corn, sorghums, and in some years, barley. In return they would qualify for loans on their feed grain crops and earn acreage diversion payments. In 1963 the price support phase of the program was changed, dividing the price support into the loan rate of $1.07 a bushel and the price support payment of 18¢ a bushel. This was an important change in the program in that it permitted setting the loan rate at a lower level so as to encourage increased corn consumption, and provided part of the compensation for participating in the program through direct payments.

The acreage diversion phase of the program was divided into two parts: (1) a minimum acreage diversion (usually 20% of the base) required for participation in the program and (2) a voluntary diversion usually an additional 0 to 30% for which farmers received payment based on the acreage diverted.

During the years 1961–70 acreage was diverted from the farmers' feed grain base (the average acreage planted in 1959 and 1960) putting limitations on the area farmers could plant to feed grains. Thus there was a firm ceiling on the acreage of feed grains (corn, grain sorghums and in some years barley) that the farmer could plant since the acreage diverted came from his feed grain base.

In 1971, the change to a Set-Aside Program gave farmers more freedom to plant feed grains or other crops after meeting the set-aside requirements under the program. For example, a farmer growing feed grains and other crops would be required to set aside 20% of his feed grain base in 1971 and then would be free to plant corn or other crops on the remainder of his crop acreage.

The reduction in feed grain stocks during the period 1961–65 was accomplished by diverting from 17 million to 24 million acres annually from corn production. With this large acreage taken out of corn, stocks were reduced from 2,016 million bushels on October 1, 1961 to 842 million by October 1, 1966. Corn prices rose from $1.00 in 1960/61 to $1.24 a bushel in 1966/67. In order to keep production in reasonably close balance with total requirements, it was necessary to maintain acreage diversion at a fairly high level through 1972. From 1961 to 1972 payments to corn producers averaged close to 1 billion dollars annually.

In only 2 years (1967 and 1971) of the 11 years from 1961–71 was the program relaxed to obtain larger plantings by offering farmers less incentive for acreage diversion or set-aside. In each of those years acreage increases were such as to boost production above total disappearance and stocks increased substantially. In 1967 the voluntary diversion provisions of the program were eliminated as stocks had been reduced to a low level. In that year only 16.2 million acres were diverted, 7½ million less than the preceding year. With the larger acreage of corn

planted in 1967, production jumped sharply and the carry-over at the close of the 1967–68 marketing year was 343 million bushels larger than at the beginning. In 1971 the program called for a reduced set-aside in view of the small 1970 crop due to corn blight. Again, corn production increased sharply to a record 5.6 billion bushels, exceeding total use by more than 400 million bushels. Thus, during these 11 years, our corn productive capacity was consistently above domestic and export requirements at prices considered satisfactory to producers.

The 1972/73 and 1973/74 seasons appear to have taken a rather sharp departure from the pattern of the previous 11 years. Although corn production in 1972 was only slightly below the record output of 1971, strong demand pushed total disappearance to 5,991 million bushels, 418 million above the crop. This brought the sharpest reduction in carryover during the 12-year period. Set-aside requirements were drastically reduced in 1973 so as to obtain larger corn production. Even though excessive rainfall interfered with planting the crop, another record crop was produced. Total disappearance of corn in 1973/74 dropped only 2% from the record 1972/73 level and exceeded the crop by 227 million bushels. Thus 1973 was the first year since the program began that disappearance exceeded production with such a small acreage of corn diverted (or set aside)— only 6 million acres.

Provisions of the 1974 and 1975 Feed Grain Programs

The Agriculture and Consumer Protection Act of 1973 carried feed grain program provisions for the 4 crop years 1974–77. The program is designed to permit expanded feed grain production and at the same time protect the farmers' income through guaranteed target prices.

Allotments—The feed grain base was eliminated under the new program and farmers were given instead feed grain allotments coinciding with the terminology used in the wheat and cotton programs. The feed grain allotments for 1974 and 1975 were set at 68% of the old feed grain base, or 89 million acres. If deficiency payments are needed to meet the target price they will be made on the basis of the entire allotment and not 50% of the base acreage as under the set-aside program. This has the effect of raising the feed grain price support payment 36% over the pay base under prior programs. Since the program provides for no acreage set-aside in 1975 the allotments for this year will be used solely for figuring payments, if any are due.

The 1975 loan rates—The loan rate for 1975 corn will be $1.10 a bushel, the same as in 1974. The loan for sorghum grain is $1.05 a bushel ($1.88 per CWT) and for barley, 90¢ a bushel.

Target prices—The target price for the 1974 and 1975 corn crops is established at $1.38 a bushel. The government will make payments to assure the target price only if the national weighted average price received by all corn growers for the first 5 months of the marketing year (October through February) is less than $1.38 per bushel. If the average price of corn for this period is below $1.38 per bushel target price, the participants will receive a payment. The per bushel payment rate will be the amount the target price exceeds the larger of: (1) the $1.10 loan rate or (2) the national average market price. This per bushel rate will be multiplied by the farm corn allotment times the established farm yield for corn to obtain the total program payment for the 1974 and 1975 crops. Because of the high price of corn in 1974/75 no payments were required on the 1974 crop.

Disaster payments—If natural disaster prevents farmers from planting their feed grain allotment to feed grains or other nonconserving crops, or who obtain total production of less than 2/3 the established farm yield times the allotment, producers may be considered as eligible for payment at a special rate to offset their crop loss.

Acreage limitations—There is no set-aside requirement for feed grains for 1974 or 1975. The set-aside provision is included in the Act of 1973, however, in case it is needed at some future date. Participating farmers are required to plant at least 90% of their allotment to either feed grains, or to crops designated by the Secretary as an eligible substitute, in order to retain their full allotment. Failure to plant at least 90% will result in the loss of allotment not to exceed 20% the following year. The allotment will not be reduced, however, if the producer elects not to receive payments on the portion not planted or if he is prevented from planting feed grains because of natural disaster.

Farmers Plant Larger Acreage Under 1974 Program

With a continuation of strong demand in 1974 all acreage limitations were removed for 1974 feed crops, for the first time since 1960. In response, farmers increased the 1974 corn acreage about 8% over 1973 or to 77.7 million acres—the largest acreage since 1960. The poor 1974 growing season resulted in a short corn crop and prospects for a further reduction in reserve stocks. With no acreage limitation again in 1975 farmers indicated their plans in March to reduce 1975 plantings 3% below 1974.

If we are at a new level of demand—both domestic and export—then it may be possible to maintain a balance between our production and requirements over the next several years with little if any acreage diversion from feed grain production. But considering the productive capacity of the U.S. corn farmer and the experience of the 1960's it appears more reasonable to anticipate a return to some form of acreage set-aside after reserve stocks are restored.

Reserve Stocks of Corn Contribute to Price Stability

The size of corn reserves over the past 2 decades has had an important bearing upon price stability. In the years when carryover stocks were large (usually accumulated under Government programs) corn prices have been much more stable than in years when reserves were low. Prices are stabilized at lower levels by the loan rate which acts as a floor under corn prices. On the upper side the government sale price (or the price at which farmers may redeem corn under loan) limits the level to which prices could rise.

The effect of the size of stocks is demonstrated by the experience of the last 16 years. During the 8 years 1958–65, feed grain stocks were at a high level ranging from 1.1 billion to 2.0 billion bushels. This period was marked by unusually stable prices both within the marketing year and from one marketing year to another. Year to year changes in prices for these years averaged only 4¢ a bushel and ranged from 1¢ to 10¢. The seasonal range in the monthly prices in these marketing years varied from a low of 6¢ a bushel in 1961/62 when record stocks were on hand to a high of 31¢ per bushel in 1965/66.

In the years 1966–73, carryover stocks were much lower, ranging from only 667 million bushels in 1971 to 1,169 million in 1968. In this period the year to year changes were significantly larger, ranging from 5¢ to 98¢ a bushel and averaging 29¢. The range in monthly prices during the marketing years also was

Table 5. Corn Price Support, Acreage Diversion and Production-use Balance, U.S. 1961–74

Crop Year	Price Support		Payments			Corn Acreage		Production	Total Disappearance	Surplus- or Deficit[3]	Carryover at Close of Year
	Loan Rate	Support Payment	Price Support[1]	Acreage Diversion[2]	Total	Diverted	Planted				
	Dol. per bu.		Million dollars			Million acres		Million bushels			
1961/62	1.20	.00	0	645	645	19.1	65.9	3,598	3,962	−364	1,653
1962/63	1.20	.00	0	684	684	20.3	65.0	3,606	3,895	−289	1,365
1963/64	1.07	.18	305	375	680	17.2	68.8	4,019	3,848	+171	1,537
1964/65	1.10	.15	224	703	927	22.2	65.8	3,484	3,875	−391	1,147
1965/66	1.05	.20	334	760	1,094	24.0	65.2	4,103	4,409	−306	842
1966/67	1.00	.30	449	579	1,028	23.7	66.3	4,168	4,185	−17	826
1967/68	1.05	.30	428	302	730	16.2	71.2	4,860	4,518	+342	1,169
1968/69	1.05	.30	514	652	1,166	25.4	65.1	4,450	4,502	−52	1,118
1969/70	1.05	.30	585	780	1,365	27.2	64.3	4,687	4,801	−114	1,005
1970/71	1.05	.30	583	645	1,228	26.1	66.8	4,152	4,494	−342	667
1971/72[4]	1.05	.32	893	0	893	14.1	74.1	5,641	5,183	+458	1,126
1972/73	1.05	.30	1,140	325	1,465	24.4	67.0	5,573	5,991	−418	709
1973/74[5]	1.05	.32	910	0	910	6.0	71.9	5,647	5,874	−227	483
1974/75	1.10	[6]	0	0	0	0	77.7	4,651			

[1] Price support payments for diverting the minimum acreage required for participating in the program. [2] Payments for voluntary acreage diversion above the minimum required. [3] Not adjusted for small quantities imported. [4] Set-aside Program beginning 1971. [5] Preliminary. [6] Deficiency payment, made if necessary to guarantee the target price of $1.38 a bushel on the allotment acreage. *Source: Compiled from reports of Agricultural Stabilization and Conservation Service and Economic Research Service, U.S.D.A.*

larger. In only two years was the range less than 20¢ and increased to a high of $1.49 a bushel in 1972–73.

Table 6. Size of the Corn Carryover and Variations in Corn Prices, 1958–74

| Year Beginning October | Carry-over | Range in Monthly Prices Received by Farmers | | | Season Average Price | Change from Preceding Year |
		High	Low	Range		
	Mil. bu.	Dollars per bushel				
1958/59	1,469	.94	1.16	.22	1.12	−.01
1959/60	1,524	.98	1.09	.11	1.05	−.07
1960/61	1,787	.90	1.05	.15	1.00	−.05
1961/62	2,016	.99	1.05	.06	1.10	+.10
1962/63	1,653	.99	1.12	.22	1.12	+.02
1963/64	1,365	1.05	1.17	.12	1.11	−.01
1964/65	1,537	1.07	1.26	.19	1.17	+.06
1965/66	1,147	1.04	1.35	.31	1.16	−.01
1966/67	842	1.11	1.29	.18	1.24	+.08
1967/68	826	.98	1.09	.11	1.03	−.21
1968/69	1,169	.96	1.19	.23	1.08	+.05
1969/70	1,118	1.07	1.38	.31	1.15	+.07
1970/71	1,005	1.11	1.43	.32	1.33	+.18
1971/72	667	.97	1.22	.25	1.08	−.25
1972/73	1,126	1.19	2.68	1.49	1.57	+.49
1973/74	709	2.17	3.37	1.20	2.55	+.98
1974/75	483				[1]3.51	+.96

[1] Preliminary estimate, Crop Values, January 16, 1975, SRS, U.S.D.A. *Source: Compiled from reports of Statistical Reporting Service, U.S.D.A.*

The experience of the past 3 years is indicative of what we may expect with small corn reserves and unusually strong domestic and export demand. Prices rise sharply above the loan rate when demand is strong and the crop is near, or below, domestic and export requirements. The season average price of the 1973 crop was $2.55 a bushel, 98¢ above 1972/73; the 1974 price was estimated at $3.51, up another 96¢.

A bumper crop in the future could bring prices down sharply, depending on the demand-supply balance. If the crop or a large part of the crop were consumed during the marketing year, prices would be expected to increase materially during the year, being particularly sensitive to prospects for the following crop and the prospective carryover at the end of the year. As long as production continues only about adequate to meet total needs, prices would remain well above the loan rate and would be subject to considerable variation as they were influenced by changes in supply and demand prospects.

Corn Production Trending Upward

Corn production has been trending upward since the 1930's. This long-term trend has been due entirely to the increase in yield per acre. The acreage planted in recent years has been much below the acreages of the 1930's and 1940's. During the period 1961–72, feed grain acreage was determined largely by the Government feed grain program. The acreage planted to corn was comparatively stable, ranging from 64 to 67 million acres in most of these years. Acreage went above 70 million acres in 1967, 1971, and 1973 when the program was relaxed to bring about an expansion in corn production.

The increase in production from 1961 to 1973 has averaged about 5% annually, about the same as the average increase in yield per acre. The sharpest increase in production in recent years occurred from 1970 to 1971. Following the blight year 1970, the program encouraged farmers to expand corn plantings and acreage rose 11%, yield rose 22% from the low level of the preceding year and production 36%.

The uptrend in yield over the past 20 years has been due to several factors: (1) the reduction in corn acreage has permitted a selection of higher yielding land; (2) a marked expansion in the use of nitrogen fertilizer, (3) improvement in machinery for planting and harvesting the crop, and (4) seed improvement. Current difficulties in expanding fertilizer production, and limitations on future supplies of fuel for operating planting, harvesting, and drying equipment make for some uncertainty as to the yield trend in the years ahead. But with no limitations on acreage, it appears likely that there will be ample capacity to produce sufficient corn to meet our total domestic and export requirements.

Corn Becoming More Important as a Cash Crop

Over the past 3 or 4 decades, the importance of corn in the market place has increased at a more rapid pace than corn production. Prior to World War II corn was grown largely as a feed grain to be used by the farmer in his livestock operations. But the past 25 years has seen a steady increase in the share of the crop moving to market. Only about a fourth of the crop was sold in the 1930's and early 1940's. Now over 60% of the crop moves to market. Farmers sold less than a billion bushels of corn during the 1940's but sold over 3 billion in 1971, 1972, and 1973.

Corn has become one of the leading cash crops of the nation with a value of sales exceeding cash returns from wheat, soybeans, or cotton in many of the past 10 years. In 1972/73 corn sold for export alone exceeded total sales in the years prior to 1957.

Table 7. Corn: Quantity Sold and Value of Sales, U.S. 1945–73

| Crop of | Quantity Sold by Farmers | Percent of Crop Sold | Value of Sales |
	Mil. bu.	Percent	Mil. doll.
1945	603	23	741
1950	789	29	1,202
1955	1,147	40	1,548
1960	1,777	45	1,785
1961	1,482	41	1,626
1962	1,562	43	1,745
1963	1,875	47	2,078
1964	1,703	49	1,988
1965	2,014	49	2,335
1966	2,105	50	2,613
1967	2,598	53	2,688
1968	2,355	53	2,553
1969	2,557	55	2,956
1970	2,264	55	3,007
1971	3,197	57	3,457
1972	3,248	58	5,095
1973[1]	3,439	61	8,193

[1] Preliminary.
Sources: Feed Situation, May 1973 and Feed Statistics, Stat. Bul. 410, E.R.S., U.S.D.A.; Crop Production Sales and Disposition Report, U.S.D.A.

The total value of corn sales from the 1972 crop exceeded $5 billion and rose to more than $8 billion in 1973–74. This was more than 4 times the value of sales in the early 1960's. Thus corn has become a leading cash crop as well as the most important feed basic to production of livestock and livestock products.

Major Factors Influencing Corn Prices

Of the many market forces that influence the price of corn in the United States, three appear to be most dominant: (1) corn supply (2) the number of livestock and poultry to be fed and (3) prices of livestock products. In addition to these factors in the domestic market, foreign demand, discussed in another section, is becoming increasingly important. Government programs have played a major role in influencing production, stocks and prices during the past 20 years.

There are many other factors which have a greater or lesser influence on corn prices, some of which are difficult to measure statistically. The speculative or storage demand for corn may have an important influence on corn prices for a short period of time or in some instances for a year or so. Weather is a major factor as it influences the size of the corn crop. But it also is important as it largely determines the condition of pastures and influences feed consumption by livestock. Supplies of other feeds which compete with corn in the market place also have a bearing on the level of corn prices.

Changes in the corn supply appear to have been dominant in the year to year changes in corn prices from 1960 to 1971. Of the various factors influencing price for this period there appears to be a closer relationship between corn production and price than for the other major factors. Demand, of course, had an important bearing on the level of corn prices, but changes in demand from one year to the next were not sufficient during this period to cause major price changes. During these years, a 1% change in production was associated with a 1 to 1.2% change in price. The response of price to changes in production was somewhat less than in earlier periods. This apparently was due to the role of the government program and the large stocks of corn on hand during the 1960's which had a stabilizing effect on corn prices.

While demand apparently did not account for much of the year to year variation in prices during 1960–71, the steady growth in demand was evident by rising production and consumption without price depression. To illustrate, in 1961 the 3.6 billion bushel crop brought a season average price of $1.10 a bushel. In 1965 a crop of 4.1 billion bushels averaged $1.16 a bushel. In 1971 corn production reached a record 5.6 billion bushels, with the price averaging about the same as 10 years earlier, or $1.08 a bushel.

Demand, which rose gradually during the 12 years 1960 to 1971, rose at an almost explosive rate from 1971 to 1973. The marked expansion in domestic and foreign demand in that 2-year period has overshadowed all other factors, bringing a sharp increase in prices despite record or near record supplies of corn and other feed grains for the 1972–73 and 1973–74 seasons. In 1974–75 when the corn supply dropped 19%, the farm price rose sharply to a record $3.35 a bushel in October–December 1974, 49% higher than a year earlier.

Changes in the government feed grain program in recent years should not be overlooked, since it will continue to be important in influencing the future course of feed grain prices. The recent sharp upturn in demand has minimized the role the feed grain program had in the supply-use-price balance. Government owned stocks of corn, which were the great stabilizer of prices in the early 1960's, have been disposed of in the last 3 years and are no longer a factor in the corn market. Government corn stocks (CCC owned and under loan), totaled nearly 1.9 billion bushels on October 1, 1961 amounting to about 1/3 of 5.6 billion bushels corn supply and over 90% of the total carryover. In contrast, the 5.1 billion bushel supply for 1974/75 contained only 7 million owned by CCC and 5 million under loan. Current prices are much above the loan rate and it is unlikely that any corn will be delivered to the government as was the case in the early 1960's. This situation permits much larger swings in corn prices than when large stocks are available to move into the market place.

The two major demand factors in the market were discussed earlier as they relate to total feed consumption. Both of these factors have a positive relationship to price. The more livestock and poultry to be fed, the stronger will be the demand for corn and other feeds. Also the higher the prices farmers receive for cattle, hogs, milk, and poultry, the more they can pay for feed. As pointed out earlier, higher livestock prices not only encourage increased livestock production but they also encourage heavier feeding per animal.

Despite these rather obvious relationships between the livestock sector and the feed sector, the correlation between the livestock production (or numbers), livestock prices and feed prices has not been especially close over the past 12 years or so. This may be due in part to the inverse correlation between livestock production and livestock prices which tends to overshadow the positive relation of each of these two factors to corn prices.

The Terminal Market Price and the Farm Price

Increasing demand, higher fuel costs, and transportation difficulties have brought a substantial widening of the spread between cash prices at terminal markets and prices received by farmers at local markets. The Chicago price of No. 2 Yellow corn generally ranged from around 10 to 15 cents a bushel above the average farm price prior to 1972/73. As shown in table 8, in the 1972/73 season this spread began at 13¢ in the fall but rose to 22¢ in the early spring and then up to a peak of 49¢ a bushel by July. In 1973/74 the spread dropped some from the wide range in the last half of the 1972/73 season, but continued well above 1971/72.

Importance of Corn Futures Enhanced by Recent Changes in the Corn Situation

While the above discussion has involved itself mainly with the effect of the demand-supply balance on cash prices, marked changes in the grain situation in the past 3 years have put increased emphasis on the futures market. During much of the period from 1960 to 1971, day to day, and week to week changes in futures prices, like cash prices, were comparatively small. But the very strong domestic demand of the last 3 years and the sharp upsurge in foreign demand and exports have brought sharp day to day and week to week variations in corn futures.

The charts which follow show changes in futures prices over the past several years. These charts show how much more sensitive futures prices have been to changing market conditions the past 2 or 3 years than they were a few years ago. The close demand-supply-balance which has developed since the harvest of the 1972 corn crop has made changes in prospects for corn acreage, corn production, domestic use and export much more important price factors than they were 5 to 10 years ago. Careful analyses of the supply and demand factors and cash and future prices are more important and much more rewarding than was the case when large feed grain stocks and more stable demand conditions kept prices at a lower and more stable level.

Table 8. Corn Prices: National Average and Chicago

	Oct.	Nov.	Dec.	Jan.	Feb.	Mar.	Apr.	May	June	July	Aug.	Sept.	Yearly Average
						Dollars per bushel							
1970–71													
Farm price	1.34	1.29	1.36	1.42	1.43	1.43	1.41	1.38	1.43	1.36	1.19	1.11	1.33
Chicago #2 Yellow	1.42	1.42	1.54	1.59	1.57	1.55	1.51	1.52	1.57	1.48	1.29	1.16	1.47
Difference	.08	.13	.18	.17	.14	.12	.10	.14	.14	.12	.10	.15	.14
1971–72													
Farm price	1.00	.97	1.08	1.09	1.09	1.10	1.13	1.15	1.13	1.14	1.15	1.22	1.08
Chicago #2 Yellow	1.10	1.07	1.22	1.22	1.21	1.22	1.26	1.28	1.25	1.29	1.29	1.40	1.23
Difference	.10	.10	.14	.13	.12	.12	.13	.13	.12	.15	.16	.18	.15
1972–73													
Farm price	1.19	1.20	1.42	1.39	1.35	1.37	1.42	1.61	1.99	2.03	2.68	2.15	1.57
Chicago #2 Yellow	1.32	1.33	1.57	1.58	1.59	1.59	1.65	2.01	2.42	2.52	2.91	2.47	1.91
Difference	.13	.13	.15	.19	.24	.22	.23	.40	.43	.49	.23	.32	.34
1973–74													
Farm price	2.17	2.18	2.39	2.59	2.76	2.68	2.41	2.45	2.57	2.91	3.37	3.30	2.55
Chicago #2 Yellow	2.37	2.50	2.68	2.90	3.13	3.00	2.69	2.70	2.93	3.35	3.63	3.55	2.95
Difference	.20	.32	.29	.31	.37	.32	.28	.25	.36	.44	.26	.25	.40

Source: Compiled from Feed Situation, E.R.S., U.S.D.A.

March Corn Futures Delivery
1972-73 to 1974-75

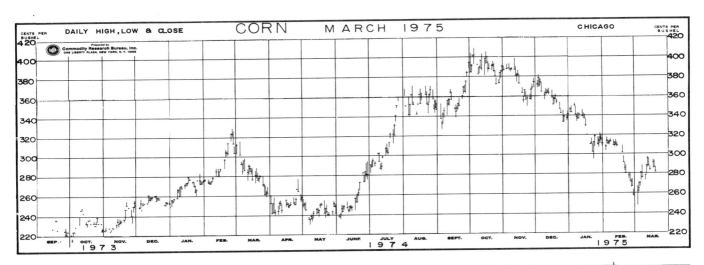

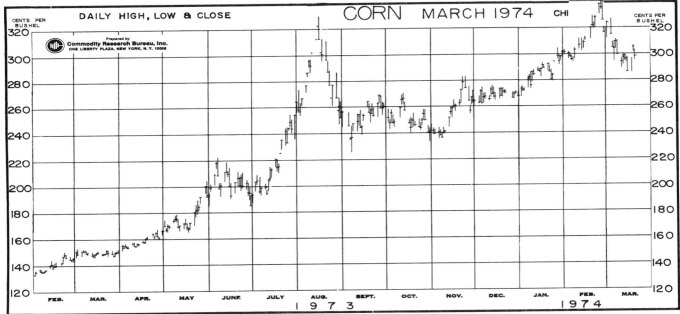

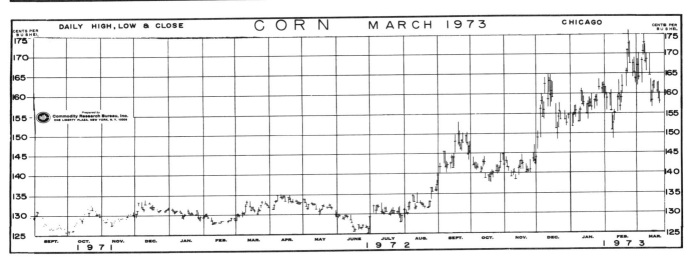

March Corn Futures Delivery
1969-70 to 1971-72

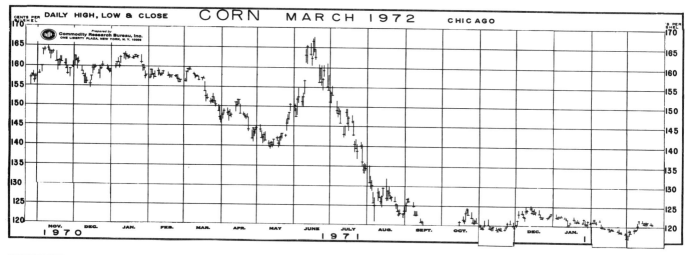

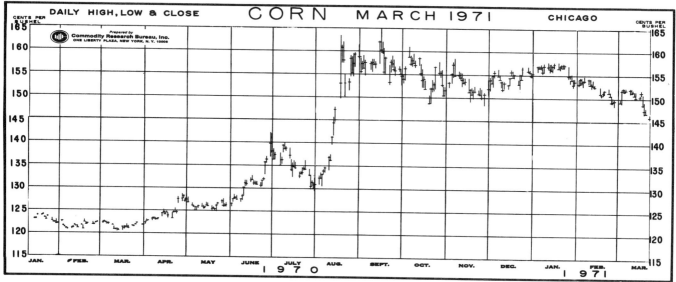

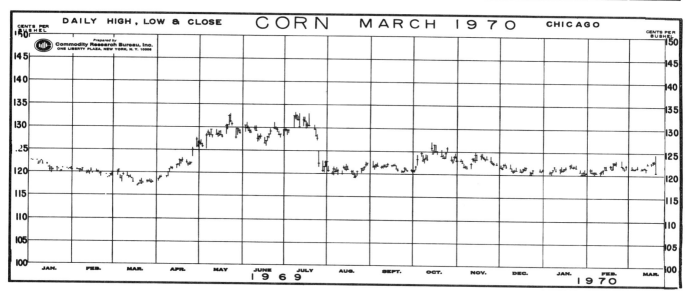

March Corn Futures Delivery 1963-64 to 1968-69

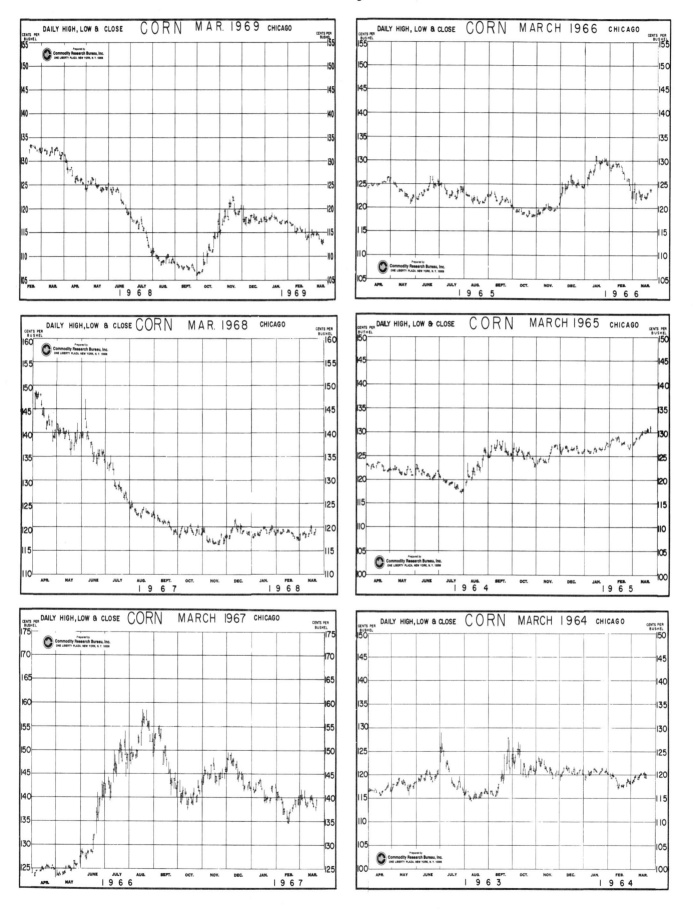

UNDERSTANDING THE COTTON FUTURES MARKET

BY WALTER L. EMERY

Cotton is so familiar to us in its apparel and household applications that its production and marketing are likely to be taken for granted. Yet changes within the industry even within the past few years have had far reaching effects upon the growing, merchandising, and consumption of this fiber, first used thousands of years ago. The purpose of this article is to provide a basic knowledge of the production, marketing, and use of cotton, and the factors affecting them, which helps to evaluate price making influences.

There are three principal species of cotton. By far the most important is "Gossypium hirsutum" which is native to Mexico and Central America, and from which American upland cotton was developed. Upland varieties account for more than 85% of world cotton production. This cotton varies in staple length from about ¾-inch to 1½ inches. It may be rain-grown or irrigated, depending upon area of growth and variety, and its use extends from coarse industrial fabrics to fine broadcloth. It is upland cotton with which this article is concerned: The second species is "G. barbadense" which includes the longer staple cottons such as Egyptian, American-Egyptian, Sea Island, Sealand, Sudanese, and some Peruvian and Brazilian varieties. This makes up the extra long staple group, mostly 1⅜ inches and longer, which is used primarily for very fine cloth and also for sewing thread. A third group, "G. herbaceum," comprises the Asiatic types native to India and China. These cottons tend to be of shorter staples—less than ¾ inch. Their main use is for wadding, padding, and blankets. There is some overlapping of upland cotton into both shorter staple and extra long staple types.

Marketing Changes

A number of changes in cotton marketing over the past few years have influenced cotton futures prices to some extent. They include: a shift in the basic spot and futures price quotations to a lower grade and longer staple cotton in order to be more representative of cotton production and mill demand—thus making the futures market a more viable hedging medium; a shift from gross weight to a net bale weight basis—permitting more flexibility in bale coverings and facilitating comparison with cotton of other countries; the growing importance of cotton knits—which tends to increase demand for high strength cotton grown in the Far West; a reduction in the number of designated spot markets—which is designed to improve the value of spot cotton quotations; a shift in the cotton loan program to a target price/loan price concept—the effect of which has yet to be tested; and new cotton spinning techniques—which may make cotton quality variations less important.

Forward Contracting

Probably the major change in cotton marketing which influences prices is the increased practice of farmers selling their crop (or a part of it) ahead of actual planting or harvesting, for a specified price. Crop contracting (forward sales contract) is the term given to an agreement between a cotton grower and either a merchant or mill which states that the grower will deliver, and the buyer will accept, at the time of harvest, all of the cotton produced on a specified number of acres at a specified price. The contract may or may not contain quality specifications, but usually contains a cut-off date (because the quality of cotton in a given area harvested after a certain date may decline rather sharply, and because the buyer may need the cotton to meet early season sales deadlines).

The presumed advantage of a forward sales contract to the grower is that it permits him to make production plans, knowing that he has established a selling price on the cotton produced from the acreage covered by the sales contract. It also is believed that crop contracting reduces price risks under a market-oriented price support program which allows for unlimited acreage. On the other hand, the grower does assume the risk that the buyer is financially responsible to take delivery.

The advantage (of crop contracting) to the merchant or mill is that it presumably assures supplies and fixes the cost of the cotton covered in the contract. In fact, crop contracting first became of significance when CCC stocks of desirable staple cotton were depleted in 1967. The buyer can fix prices for an extended period of time, but controlling the quality and quantity of cotton in acreage contracts has been a problem at times. Accordingly, a shift from acreage contracts to bale contracts (with premiums and discounts for quality) is anticipated.

As stated in testimony at House cotton sub-committee hearings in 1974, the merchant's problem in acreage contracts is as follows: "When we buy acres, we project bales and then hedge by spot sales to domestic or foreign customers, or cotton futures sales because we are merchants, not speculators, and to do a volume of business one cannot take the risk of severe market fluctuations." . . . On a nationwide basis (on 1973 contracts) we deleted 447,000 bales which was not delivered because of weather or default. As our company became aware of the bales we were losing off of our forward contracted acreage, we immediately purchased like numbers of bales in the New York Cotton Futures Market to hedge our projected bale loss."

As another witness at the House sub-committee hearings stated, "When the industry buys cotton on crop contract, at 30¢, one of two actions follows: either textile products are sold on the basis of 30¢ cotton or the textile company hedges these purchases by selling futures on the New York Cotton Exchange."

About 11% of the 1970/71 U.S. cotton crop was contracted, at an average price believed to be about 21¢ per lb. About 35% of the 1971/72 crop was contracted at around 23¢ average price. About 36%

of the 1972/73 crop was contracted at an average price believed to be about 26¢ per lb., and a huge 75% of the 1973/74 crop was reported contracted, at prices ranging from about 26¢ to 80¢ a pound, but mostly in the 30¢–40¢ area. It is believed that less than 25% of the 1974/75 cotton crop has been contracted.

There is some concern that if forward contracting of the U.S. cotton crop is to account for a consistently significant portion of cotton marketing, spot cotton market quotations will not be representative of the actual selling price of much cotton. The price of forward sales contracts is not included in the price quotations at the designated spot cotton markets (although it is included in the mid-month average price received for cotton by farmers). Since commercial differences at which cotton is delivered against the futures contract are based on quotations at certain of the designated spot markets, the maturing delivery in the cotton futures market may be affected.

Energy and Cotton

The high cost of, and concern over the availability of, petroleum-based inputs has exerted some impact on the cotton market, and is expected to remain a consideration in the foreseeable future. The reduced availability and high cost of petrochemical feedstocks needed for man-made fibers has bolstered the competitive position of cotton. On the other hand, almost all of the world's nitrogen fertilizer production depends directly on natural gas or petroleum products, and tight supplies and the high cost of this fertilizer may adversely affect cotton production (more so in less developed countries than the U.S.). Moreover, any extended period of reduced economic activity, accentuated by the "oil problem," would adversely affect world demand for textiles, including cotton.

The Plant and Its Growth

Market action frequently reflects evaluation by the trade and by traders of weather developments at different stages of cotton plant growth. Cotton emerges about 7–10 days after planting under normal conditions, followed about 45 days by "squaring" or formation of buds, and approximately 21 days later by the bloom. The boll maturation period or length of time between flowering and boll opening averages about 50 days. Approximately 180 days elapse between the time cotton is planted and a sufficient number of bolls are open to begin picking operations. The foregoing figures are averages and will vary with location, growing conditions, and variety of seed planted.

Cotton is a hot weather plant and thrives best under such conditions, given adequate and well-spaced moisture. Too little rainfall tends to hinder germination, stunt plant growth, reduce the number of blossoms, retard boll set, result in decreased boll size, and cause excessive shedding of bolls, depending upon the stage of growth. Too much moisture may result in reduced fruiting, excessive shedding, boll rot, and late maturity. Extremely high temperatures for an extended period of time may cause boll shedding, while low temperatures may halt germination, result in poor stands, slow plant growth, render the plant vulnerable to disease and insect infestation, and delay fruiting. A critical time for the fruiting plant is an approximate two-week period following the start of flowering.

While weather tends to exert the most influence on the grade of cotton, staple also can be adversely affected. Long continued dry, hot weather leaves fibers weak and brittle, and may result in an "immature" staple. Hot, moist weather is considered ideal for development of staple.

Harvesting

Virtually 100% of the crop is harvested by machine. The most important method is the machine-picker, which pulls cotton from the open boll. It accounts for about 66% of all cotton harvested belt-wide. The machine-stripper, which pulls the entire boll from the plant accounts for about 33% of the harvest and is the major method of harvest in areas of Texas and Oklahoma where yields tend to be low and this method is the most economical. A small amount of cotton is machine-scrapped each year. Plants are chemically defoliated prior to machine picking to ensure less trash (leaves, burrs, etc.), but it still requires much more seed cotton to produce a 500 pound bale of lint when cotton is machine-stripped or hand-snapped than when it is hand-picked or machine-picked. As a rule of thumb, it usually requires close to 1,500 pounds of seed cotton to produce a 500 lb. bale of cotton lint. As cotton bolls on a single plant do not all mature at the same time, more than one picking operation takes place over a period of time. The harvesting period has been shortened to about 4–6 weeks in any given area, and generally advanced to a later date with the increased use of mechanical harvesters.

Ginning of Cotton

Seed cotton moves rapidly from the field to one of the 3,300 gins in this country, although an increasing amount is being field-stored, which tends to extend the ginning period. Excessive moisture and trash is removed at the gin through such devices as the seed cotton drier and the cotton lint cleaner, and the lint separated from the seed in the ginning process. The cotton lint is pressed into so-called "flat" or gin bales, and wrapped in jute bagging fastened with six steel ties. Individual bales may vary in weight from as little as 300 pounds to as much as 700 pounds, but these "running" bales average out to about 493 pounds average for the U.S. (American cotton is now sold on a net weight basis.) It is at this stage of marketing that the individual cotton bale assumes an identity it will carry until it enters a mill bale-breaker and is blended with other cotton in the mill mix. Cotton varies in length, color, strength, fineness, trash content, and preparation by the gin. The suitability of a given bale of cotton for a particular yarn or fabric is determined by its grade, staple, micronaire and character. Almost all cotton today is classed under the Smith-Doxey Act which provides free U.S.D.A. classification to farmers who organize into a group to promote the improvement of cotton. The estimated percentage of cotton production sold by farmers within a marketing season tends to be heaviest, by far, in November–December–January.

Cotton Quality

Grade is composed of three factors: Color (ranging from White, which is the most important, down through Spotted, Tinged, Yellow Stained, and Gray);

Leaf, which is the dried and broken plant foliage, stems, and hulls; and Preparation, which refers to the smoothness of ginning. Grade names such as Good Middling, etc. provide a scale for variations in Color, Leaf, and Preparation.

Staple length of any cotton refers to the normal length by measurement of a typical portion of its fibers. Character is a measure of the quality of cotton for which there are no official standards. It includes such fiber properties as uniformity of fiber length, strength of fiber, and fineness, which are measurable in large degree by laboratory tests, but which have been in practice covered by reference to areas of growth and variety.

Despite the wide range of possible combinations of grade and staple, the major portion of any given year's crop generally falls into a relatively few grade and staple categories. For example 62% of the average production of cotton in the 1968–72 period graded White or Light Spotted Middling or Strict Low Middling. Cotton stapling $1\frac{1}{16}$″ or longer (mostly $1\frac{1}{16}$″ and $1\frac{3}{32}$″) accounted for 68% of all staples in the 1968–72 average ginnings. It is where an imbalance of indicated supply and demand of the more important grades and staples occurs that cotton prices, both spots and futures, reflect concern on the part of the trade over shifts in composition as well as size of the crop. The quality of cotton can vary in different areas of the same cotton field, from the top to the bottom of the cotton stalk, and within the boll itself.

As an oversimplification, weather, harvesting method, and preparation by the gin, play an important role in determining grade in that order. Staple is determined primarily by the variety planted, although weather does have some influence as indicated previously.

Area of growth is a major factor affecting quality of cotton and its spinning performance. For example, Middling $1\frac{1}{16}$″ of a new desirable variety in the Southeast early in the 1967/68 season sold at premiums of 300 points (3¢ per lb.) or more over other cotton grading Middling with a staple of $1\frac{1}{16}$″ in the same market. Even some characteristics of the same variety of cotton will vary by location of planting; in one area the same variety may be stronger in fiber than in another, and in another area the staple may not be as long. The speculator who is aware of these possible variations in cotton price quotations for a specific grade and staple at a given market is less likely to be insistent upon a hard and fast relationship between observed spot market quotations and futures prices. Changes in relationships are more significant for trading purposes than absolute price quotations themselves.

Spot Market Quotations

Spot cotton quotations at the designated 10 spot cotton markets receive considerable attention from all members of the cotton trade as a guide in their buying and selling operations, and from bankers handling cotton financing. These markets have been chosen by the USDA as representative markets in which spot cotton is sold in sufficient volume and under such conditions as to accurately reflect prices for a possible 500 grade and staple combinations. (In recent years, no cotton has been produced in about 200 of these combinations.) Each market maintains a quotations committee comprised of active members of the cotton trade whose duty is to ascertain and publish each business day the price or value of Strict Low Middling $1\frac{1}{16}$ inch and the differences between this price or value and other grades and staple lengths represented by the official U.S. cotton standards. Quotations reflect the value of spot cotton in the market for both tenderable (against futures contracts) and untenderable qualities delivered in warehouses uncompressed in mixed lots, though other types of transactions such as sales of even running lots may be used in arriving at such prices or values with appropriate adjustments.

Spot cotton quotations have a significance to cotton traders beyond their use as a grade to current spot prices, for average official spot cotton quotations at certain designated markets on the sixth business day prior to delivery against a futures contract are used to determine premiums and discounts at which grade and staple combinations may be settled. Trade shorts in maturing futures contracts watch spot quotations to determine the relative profitability of delivering cotton against their short futures position.

Major Growing Areas

There are four major upland cotton growing areas in the United States (the Southwest, Delta, West, and Southeast). The Southeast, including North Carolina, South Carolina, Georgia, and Alabama, is the oldest cotton growing area in the country, but its production accounts for less than one-eighth of total U.S. production. Planting in this area is usually underway in earlier sections by mid to late March and is mostly finished by late April or early May. About one-half to three-quarters of this crop is usually picked and ginned by November 1 and close to seven-eighths by December 1. The principal quality produced is Strict Low Middling $1\frac{1}{16}$″.

The major growing area called variously, the Delta, Mid-South, or South Central area, includes Mississippi, Arkansas, Tennessee, Louisiana, and Missouri. This area usually produces more than one-third of the cotton grown in this country. Production is concentrated in the Yazoo Basin section of the Mississippi delta region from around Jackson, Miss. to Memphis, Tenn., and across the River from this area in Arkansas. Planting is usually completed by late May, and the harvest is generally 50% or more complete by the end of October and close to 90% finished by the end of November. The principal quality produced is Strict Low Middling $1\frac{1}{16}$″.

The Southwest includes Texas (the leading producing state), and Oklahoma. This area usually produces about one-third of our production. There are a number of important growing areas in Texas. The lower Rio Grande Valley centering in the Harlingen area is the earliest producing section of the country. Cotton is sometimes planted as early as late February but usually into mid-March, with the harvest extending from July into or beyond late August. A second producing area is the Coastal Bend centering around Corpus Christi, and a third producing area, the Black lands, extends from around Austin northeast to beyond Dallas. Planting in this area is usually active in April with the harvest extending into and beyond September.

Major producing areas in Texas are centered in the High Plains in the vicinity of Lubbock and in the Low or Rolling Plains to the eastward. Planting here is usually well underway in early to mid-May and harvesting by mid-November. Statewide only about 30% of the Texas crop is ginned by the beginning of November, with 10–20% often still to be picked by mid-January. Both planting and harvesting of the Oklahoma crop tends to lag behind the late producing areas of Texas. Varieties of cotton produced in West Texas and Oklahoma range from short to long staple and grades can vary widely depending on weather and harvesting method. The principal quality produced is Middling Light Spot $15/16''$.

The final major group of cotton producing states is the West which includes California (one of the top 3 producers), Arizona, and New Mexico. A considerable portion of the western crop is grown on irrigated acreage and yields tend to be high and quality consistent in this area, which produces about 20% of the U.S. crop. The most important growing areas in the West are the San Joaquin Valley between Fresno and Bakersfield, California, and to a lesser degree the Imperial Valley centering around El Centro, California. Most Arizona upland cotton is produced between Tucson and Phoenix. Seeding of cotton in the Western belt usually starts by mid-March in early sections and is usually completed by mid-May. Harvesting usually starts in September and is nearly complete by early December. Cotton production in the Western belt averages higher in grade and longer in staple than any other area. The principal quality produced is Middling White $1 3/32''$.

Planting and picking operations in these major producing areas will vary with the weather, with the location within the area, and to some degree with the variety planted. The importance of weather to planting and harvesting operations can be illustrated by the fact that even within the past few years, ginnings to November 1 in Mississippi—the second largest producing state—have varied between 33% and 79% of the indicated crop for that state.

Marketing

Once cotton is ginned, different price factors come into play as cotton moves through various marketing channels on its way to domestic or foreign mills. This is the period when the major marketing agencies accumulate cotton from the country or primary markets and assemble it into lots that are alike in grade, staple, and character (even running lots) for their mill clients. Most important from the trader's point of view, this is the period when the merchants and shippers assume the price risk on such cotton until it is acquired by the mills.

Cotton first moves into the marketing stream at the local market, often referred to as the country or primary market. The purchaser from one of the 250,000 growers in the country may be the ginner (who usually accounts for about 17% of sales by farmers beltwide, though the percentage varies widely by year and by area), a local merchant or F.O.B. buyer, a farmer cooperative, or, seasonally around peak picking operations, a mill or shipper representative. Sometimes when prices are unattractive the cotton at this point may be pledged to the CCC loan by the grower, in which case it is likely to be removed from marketing channels for some time.

In recent years farmers are estimated to have sold about 63% of their production in the November–January period, divided almost equally among these three months. About 75–80% of the crop has moved out of first hands by the end of January across the cotton belt. This corresponds roughly with the period of heaviest reported purchases at the 10 designated spot cotton markets. While weather and market conditions may cause variations from year to year, it is of value to have some guide as to when a significant amount of cotton has usually moved into hands ineligible for the CCC loan, and hence subject to adverse price fluctuations unless hedged.

In the Southeast, where distance to the major mill consuming area is relatively short, cotton often moves direct from the gin to the mill by trucker or by rail without first moving to a compress. Increased direct mill buying in some areas in recent years has brought about a decline in the importance of the ginner, the F.O.B. buyer and commission broker as marketing agencies in the country markets, while the increased role played by grower cooperatives appears to have exerted much the same influence in other areas. The end result of this trend in central markets as well as in local markets may well be greater recourse to the cotton futures markets for hedging operations by both mills and cooperatives, now that commercial supplies are once again more important than government stocks.

PHYSICAL FLOW OF U. S. COTTON

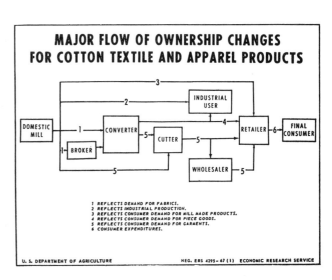

MAJOR FLOW OF OWNERSHIP CHANGES FOR COTTON TEXTILE AND APPAREL PRODUCTS

1 REFLECTS DEMAND FOR FABRICS.
2 REFLECTS INDUSTRIAL PRODUCTION.
3 REFLECTS CONSUMER DEMAND FOR MILL MADE PRODUCTS.
4 REFLECTS CONSUMER DEMAND FOR PIECE GOODS.
5 REFLECTS CONSUMER DEMAND FOR GARMENTS.
6 CONSUMER EXPENDITURES.

The Cotton Shipper

The importance of the various types of markets and marketing firms varies to some degree with the season and the stage of marketing, but by and large the major factor marketwise is the widely operating merchant or shipper who operates throughout the cotton belt, acquiring cotton in mixed lots from the country markets, concentrating this cotton at warehouses and compresses into even running lots. A good illustration of the number of firms operating in these major markets is provided by the list of more than 260 buyers of over 7.8 million bales of CCC cotton during the 1966/67 season. One widely operating shipper accounted for close to 10% of the total, followed closely by another large cotton merchant. The top 5 shippers acquired almost 3.0 million bales, while a dozen firms bought 100,000 bales or more, including a major cooperative. There are approximately 700 merchants (including small country buyers) in the U.S.

The shipper usually buys cotton in mixed lots as close to producer points as feasible, frequently from a ginner or local buyer, moving this cotton to a warehouse or compress where it is assembled and classed into even running lots of a specific grade and staple and area of growth. Much of the cotton handled by shippers as well as other marketing agencies in the central markets is not stored in these markets, being shipped from the warehouse or compress point direct to mill or port. The shipper assumes the costs of assembling, classing, storing, insuring, financing, compression to standard or high density bales, and usually transportation to mills. The shipper assumes the risk of adverse price changes from the time he pays for the cotton bought in the interior until it is purchased by the mill or sold to a foreign buyer.

Although spot cotton may be sold for Immediate, Prompt, or Forward shipment, the bulk of sales are made well in advance of the shipment date, permitting mills to contract for cotton many months in advance. Sales may be made at "Fixed" prices with price established at the time of sale, or "On Call" with price established at a later date based on the futures market, with the option of fixing the price usually assigned to the buyer. An example of these two methods of buying cotton is provided in a later section on hedging.

Consumption

The mill is the final destination in the marketing of raw cotton. There are about 400 textile mills using cotton in the U.S. It is estimated that mills usually acquire about 75% of their cotton needs from merchants; about 24% from co-operatives; and only 1% direct from producers and ginners through their own buyers. (This may be changing as crop contracting comes into greater use.)

A number of large integrated companies which spin cotton into yarn, weave the yarn into cloth, and also finish (bleach, dye, print, etc.) the cloth account for much of the raw cotton purchased. Most spinning and weaving plants are located in the South Atlantic states of North Carolina, South Carolina, and Georgia, while most finishing plants are located in the Middle Atlantic or New England states near the apparel manufacturing and household furnishing market for finished fabrics.

The converter, who buys gray goods from mill sources, and carries it in inventory through the finishing process to the manufacturer of apparel or household furnishings, occupies a strategic position in the trade whether he is independent or a division of one of the large integrated firms, for it is at this level that cloth inventories are held whether they are physically located at mills or finishing plants. Changes in inventory at this level, usually with a lag of some months, find reflection in the level of mill use and purchase of raw cotton. A measure of this relationship may be found in the ratio of mill cloth inventories to unfilled orders, based on statistics released by the Census Bureau monthly. A low or declining ratio tends to indicate continued favorable mill demand, or improving mill demand for raw cotton in coming months, while a rising ratio tends to indicate the reverse situation.

About 60% of the cotton consumed by domestic mills each year, has a staple length of $1\frac{1}{16}''$ or $1\frac{3}{32}''$. Increased use of this cotton has, in part, reflected technological changes in mill machinery, with high speed equipment requiring longer staple cotton for higher yarn strength and to maintain quality. In addition, in recent years there has been a distinct shift from the use of higher grades to the lower grades of cotton. The apparel industry accounts for slightly over 50% of the cotton consumed by mills in this country with the remainder divided between household and industrial uses. Although a myriad of articles are manufactured from cotton yarn and cloth, they are produced from a relatively small number of fabric constructions. Printcloth and sheetings are by far the most important of these constructions.

The most important end user of cotton is the apparel industry, mainly in men's and boy's clothing. The household market, which includes sheets, pillowcases, towels, drapery and upholstery fabrics is the second largest market for cotton. Industrial use is the third major market, consisting of sewing thread, coated fabrics, etc. Cotton's share in all the above categories has declined in recent years reflecting increased competition from non-cellulosic fibers and larger imports of both cotton and man-made fiber textiles. However, cotton has held its share of the towel market (virtually 100%) very well, and has increased its share of the drapery and upholstery market. In addition, cotton has held its ground in the important underwear and work clothing markets.

Within the limits imposed by machinery requirements and quality of fabric produced, mills do have some leeway in the choice of grade and staple of cotton which they purchase. However, beyond this range cost and efficiency of mill operations and quality of product suffer. At times shifts in mill buying policies on raw cotton within these limits will exert an impact only on the premiums and discounts for the different grade and staple combinations, and at times the impact will be on the market itself.

Cotton is no longer king, its share of the total textile fiber market has declined from about 60% in 1962 to 29% in 1973, primarily as a result of sharply increased production of non-cellulosic fibers. The per capita use of cotton in the United States has declined to around 17.4 pounds, and although the total market has expanded as a result of population growth, the number of bales consumed has declined also to around 7.0 million bales a season.

The term "Cotton Consumption" has two meanings. "Mill Consumption" refers to the amount of cotton processed by consuming establishments, whereas "Domestic Consumption" refers to mill consumption plus the cotton fiber equivalent of imported fabrics and manufactured products less the cotton equivalent of cloth and manufactured products exported.

The consumption figure which receives most trade attention is the daily rate of mill use monthly reported by the Census Bureau about three weeks after the close of the reporting period. This report provides a figure on mill consumption of cotton, stocks of cotton at consuming establishments, and stocks of cotton at public warehouses and compresses. Monthly data actually covers a 4 or 5 week period approximating the calendar month.

The cotton statistical year runs from August through the following July, approximating the harvest and distribution of cotton planted in the spring. There are moderate seasonals in monthly mill consumption of cotton. November, February, March and May, are usually relatively active months while August, September, December, and July, tend to be months of relatively low use on a daily rate basis.

An additional consideration in consumption of cotton is the cotton textile trade balance referred to above. On balance in recent years the cotton equivalent of U.S. imports of fabric and manufactured products has exceeded the cotton equivalent of fabric and manufactured products exported by the U.S. by about 500,000 to 600,000 bales. Although this number of bales may not appear large relative to total consumption, the impact of certain fabrics or types of wearing apparel imports upon mill production of such fabrics or apparel in this country can be sizable, with an eventual reduction in mill demand for the quality of U.S. raw cotton used in such fabric constructions, or apparel.

Foreign Cotton

The United States probably produces the widest range of cotton qualities of any country in the world, thus providing cotton suitable for a wide range of textile requirements. Although the U.S. is the largest exporter of cotton in the world, some foreign growths provide intense competition for U.S. cotton, both in price and quality.

Major foreign exporters of upland cotton are the USSR and Brazil. However, Turkey, Mexico, Syria and Iran also produce and export cotton of a quality comparable to that exported from the United States.

The USSR is second only to the U.S. in the export of cotton, and its crop often exceeds that of the United States. The USSR cotton crop is produced in Central Asia, most of it in the Republic of Uzbekistan. All USSR cotton is irrigated, and is planted in April–May and harvested in September/November. Peruyi–1 $^{31}\!/_{32}$ mm (average 1 $^1\!/_{16}$″) is the leading quality produced and exported.

Brazil is the third largest cotton exporter. About two-thirds of its production comes from South Brazil, and is rain-grown medium staple ($1^1\!/_{32}$″ to $1^3\!/_{32}$″). The crop is harvested in March/June—the South Brazil crop being the only large cotton crop that reaches the world market in the late spring. There is considerable variety in the grade of Brazilian cotton from year to year. North Brazil cotton is concentrated in the northeastern tip of the country and is harvested mostly in August/October. Most of North Brazil's cotton staples $1^1\!/_{32}$″ to $1^3\!/_{32}$″, but yields are low.

Most of Turkey's cotton production is upland, stapling 1″ to $1^1\!/_8$″. Most of the crop is irrigated, and

it is reported to be all hand picked. The harvest period runs from August to November, depending on the production area. The Cukurova region is the most important producing area.

Mexico is also an important exporter of cotton. Its major producing area is the Sinaloa-Sonora region on the West Coast. Mexican cotton is handpicked, with the harvest beginning in late June on the West Coast. The principal quality of cotton produced is Middling $1^1\!/_{16}$″.

Exports

Exports have always played an important role in the cotton market, averaging about 30% of total distribution in the 1968–72 period. The United States is the world's largest exporter, shipping 22% of the average 18.7 million bales of cotton which entered world trade in 1970–74. Our share of the world market has declined steadily, however, over a period of years, reflecting in part increased production in many foreign countries, some of whom shifted from a net import to a net export position.

World consumption of cotton has increased at an annual rate of slightly less than 2.5%, somewhat more than the rate of population growth, and equivalent to more than 1.1 million bales of cotton a year. Total world consumption of cotton in the past 10 years has ranged between a high of 59.2 million bales in 1973/74 (helped by a shortage of man-made fibers arising from the energy crisis), and a low of 50.7 million bales in the 1964/65 season. The United States used to carry the bulk of world stocks, accounting for one-half of the 1962/66 average of 25 million bales on hand August 1st, but now accounts for only about 25% of the 22 million bale carryover—which is smaller than the 5 months supply considered a minimum desirable world carryover. We are a residual supplier to areas which produce their own cotton in insufficient amount to supply their own needs. Demand from such areas, as well as from countries which are important consumers of cotton but produce none, is influenced by the degree to which their own normally modest stocks of raw cotton are affected by changes in economic activity and by the degree of competition from other fibers. U.S. cotton is usually preferred to other growths because of the wide range of qualities offered and because of the experience and financial responsibility of U.S. shippers.

Japan is the world's leading importer of cotton, and is by far our most important customer, taking about 22% of our total exports in recent years. Japan is experienced in the blending of short staple cotton with cotton of higher grade and staples, and for years much more than one-half of Japan's imports from the United States were of cotton stapling less than one-inch. More recently most imports have been 1″ to $1^1\!/_8$″ staple reflecting a switch to the production of finer count yarns requiring longer staple varieties than previously. Other major buyers of U.S. cotton include the Republic of Korea and Taiwan, both of which now buy less cotton stapling less than one-inch than medium staple cotton. A considerable portion of such cotton moves to these countries with the aid of the CCC export credit sales program. Canada, Italy, Indonesia, Thailand and Hong Kong are also important buyers of U.S. cotton, acquiring mostly cotton stapling 1″ to $1^1\!/_8$″.

Not all export sales are commercial sales. Some cotton is exported under PL480 programs. When each PL480 Title 1 agreement is signed, the USDA announces to the trade through issuance of Purchase Authorizations, the dollar amount of cotton to be financed, contracting and delivery period, and sales terms. The quantity of bales stated in the purchase authorizations is only an approximation, for the actual amount purchased depends upon the quality and price agreed upon by the exporter and the foreign buyer. Only cotton grown in the U.S. is eligible for PL480 financing, and unless otherwise specified the cotton must meet the Universal Standards for U.S. upland cotton and have a staple length of $13/16''$ or longer.

The basic factors influencing cotton exports are the level of cotton consumption abroad, and production in foreign countries. On this score consumption seems to have increased most in less developed countries which have produced some cotton and aim to produce more. In western Europe cotton has lost ground to man-made fibers. Within the limits imposed by the foregoing, our cotton exports are affected by the inventory position of foreign importing countries, which in turn reflect their economic conditions and prospective needs and supplies. Most foreign cotton producing countries tend to move cotton into commercial channels rather quickly each season, with carryover stocks usually modest. We are the major residual supplier. There have been occasions when foreign buyers, foreseeing a tightening supply situation in the U.S. have built up stocks to some degree, just as our own mills have done, with the result that exports have slackened off considerably within a season, or until foreign supplies have been depleted. USDA studies have indicated that free world mill consumption of cotton is affected primarily by changes in per capita income, by cotton prices, and by the use of non-cellulosic fibers.

There is a time lag in the interplay of the foregoing factors and cotton prices which can mislead the cotton analyst. The relative effect of these factors on price varies from time to time. Within any given season the price of U.S. cotton relative to other comparable growths such as Peruvian Tanguis, or Brazilian Type 6, and some Mexican and Turkish cottons exerts some influence on the volume of U.S. exports. Recently, competition from the USSR, which sometimes produces more cotton than the U.S., has been an increasingly important factor.

Exports tend to be heaviest in the December–March period coinciding with greater seasonal availability of U.S. cotton and with depletion of foreign stocks, and lightest in the July–September period when U.S. supplies tend to be seasonally lowest. However, this pattern can shift considerably on a year to year basis depending upon whether or not the crop is late or early and on the foreign mill inventory situation. Galveston has been the most important point of export, followed by New Orleans, Houston and Los Angeles. Most of the cotton shipped via Texas ports is destined for Japan and India. Favorable combined ocean-rail rates to the Orient are giving such West Coast ports as San Diego and Los Angeles a larger share of this business. Much of the cotton shipped through New Orleans is headed for Europe.

There is a tendency among cotton traders to compare exports at any given time during the season to shipments to the same date the previous season and to the USDA estimate of exports for the full season. Variations between early season export estimates and actual shipments have been rather large at times, with considerable effect on the size of the carryover, and also on prices. Market students should not overlook the tendency for relatively high U.S. cotton prices in one season to stimulate increased acreage abroad the following season within limits imposed by competition for acreage from food crops. If sizable speculative long positions have been built up on high distribution prospects early in the season, and an anticipated tight supply situation at the season's end, the market can prove quite vulnerable to liquidation as traders realize that actual shipments of cotton do not bear out expected tightness. It is not easy to learn whether or not lagging exports reflect high current U.S. prices, sizable inventories in importing countries, reduced consumption abroad, or competition from other cotton producers or from man-made fibers. Sometimes slow exports mean none of the foregoing, but merely that foreign buyers hope to obtain lower prices at a later date, knowing that they must enter the market at some point to meet commitments. Of course, the trader must make a judgment on the basis of imperfect knowledge, but then so does everyone else to a greater or lesser degree. However, being aware of the different possibilities, he is less likely to make a significantly wrong judgment.

The Loan Program

The amount of the cotton crop removed from commercial marketing channels by means of the loan program has at times accounted for as much as 8.1 million bales or 52.9% of the crop. The CCC held 12.3 million bales, or 73% of the record 16.9 million bale carryover on August 1, 1966. By the end of the 1973/74 season the CCC owned only 33 bales. The target (guaranteed) price on 1975 crop cotton allotted acres is 38¢ per lb. (basis Middling 1-inch). This means if the national average farm price for cotton during calendar 1975 averages less than 38¢, the grower will receive a deficiency payment equal to the difference between the target price and the higher of the farm price or the loan level. The preliminary national average cotton loan level for 1975 is 34.27¢ per lb., net weight, basis Middling 1-inch cotton, micronaire 3.5–4.9, at average location. CCC loans will be adjusted to Strict Low Middling $1\frac{1}{16}''$, the base quality now used for spot and futures price quotations.

The producer who complies with his acreage allotment may obtain a price support loan on cotton classed by the USDA Board of Examiners, presenting a loan agreement form and warehouse receipts to a lending agency or direct to the CCC. Producer members of cooperatives may obtain loans through their Association which may tender documents to the CCC covering the cotton acquired as collateral from producer members, and receive a loan on this cotton from the CCC. The producer has three choices in disposing of his loan cotton. He may repay his loan and sell his cotton in the open market, or he can sell his "Equity" in his cotton under loan. In practice most cotton is disposed of through the sale of equities. This equity represents the difference between the amount due on the cotton loan and the value of the cotton. Title to such cotton is transferred by means of a signed Equity Transfer. The third choice of the grower on his loan cotton, and one resorted to more frequently than not in some years, is to not repay the loan, permitting the CCC to take title at maturity, inasmuch as it is a non-recourse loan from the CCC.

The amount of cotton entered in the loan in any one year depends not only upon the basic loan rate for Strict Low Middling $1\frac{1}{16}''$ cotton, but also on the premiums and discounts for other grades and staples. The USDA establishes premiums and discounts on upland cotton for 15 different staple lengths and 40 grades plus 7 micronaire premium and discount categories. Differences ranged in the 1974 loan from a discount of about 1,150 points ($11\frac{1}{2}¢$ per lb.) for Low Middling Tinged $1\frac{3}{16}''$ cotton, to a premium of about 775 points ($7\frac{3}{4}¢$ per lb.) for Good Middling White $1\frac{1}{4}''$.

Disposal Program

The Commodity Credit Corporation owned cotton stocks totaling about 12.3 million bales at the start of the 1966/67 season. These stocks had been depleted by the end of the 1973/74 season. The U.S Department of Agriculture on November 29, 1974, announced the upland cotton sales policy for the 1975–76 marketing year. Beginning Aug. 1, 1975, any Commodity Credit Corporation stocks of upland cotton will be offered for sale for unrestricted use on a competitive bid basis at not less than the higher of: (1) the market price as determined by CCC, or (2) 43.70 cents per pound, basis Strict Low Middling one and one sixteenth inches (SLM $1\frac{1}{16}''$), at average U.S. location. The resale price for other qualities will be adjusted for current market differentials and location differentials applicable under the 1975 loan program, as determined by CCC. Carrying charges of 30 points (0.3 cents) per pound will be added each month from September through May.

The government holdings of cotton represent a secondary, but at times important, source of supply. Knowledge of the price level at which such supplies can enter the commercial market, and when sales are scheduled, can be of value to the cotton trader as an indication of potential hedge selling by the purchasers.

The Futures Contract

Trading in contract No. 1 (basis Middling $1\frac{5}{16}''$) is currently inactive. Trading in a new futures contract (No. 2) was initiated March 22, 1967 on the New York Cotton Exchange. The contract basis was Middling $1\frac{1}{16}''$ cotton, but has since been changed to Strict Low Middling $1\frac{1}{16}''$ cotton, which is considered to be most representative of both crop production and mill needs. The contract was strengthened further by the requirement that cotton must micronaire (measure of fiber fineness: fine fibers have low, and coarse fibers high "mike" reading) no lower than 3.5 or higher than 4.9 to be tenderable, and also by the inclusion of two interior delivery points, Memphis, Tennessee and Greenville, South Carolina in addition to the port delivery points of New Orleans, Houston, and Galveston. As a result of these contract changes, mill interest increased.

Compositon of the Futures Market

The total open interest (outstanding commitments) in cotton futures, in common with other futures markets, is made up the positions of different kinds of traders. There are three categories of traders; hedge, speculative, and straddle (spread). Much interest is centered in the share of the market accounted for by hedge positions. Straddle interest usually represents a minor portion of open interest and is assumed to exert little influence on prices. Speculative commitments tend to be a reciprocal of, or offset to, hedge commitments, and are generally considered to be more volatile in nature than hedge positions and therefore, at times, a considerable influence on prices. A knowledge of the current share of the market (as indicated by the latest monthly CEA report on traders' commitments in cotton futures) accounted for by hedge and speculative positions relative to that indicated in the preceding report, and by the average for the same month over a period of years, may reveal a "topheavy" position in one or another category of trader commitment.

In recent years, hedge long positions have averaged between approximately one-quarter and slightly more than one-third of the long side of the open interest in cotton futures. The percentage of open commitments accounted for by long hedges tends to be smallest in the February/May period, and largest in August/November. Short hedge positions have accounted for a little more than one-half to slightly over five-eighths of the short side of open interest. There tends to be a wider range in the share of the market represented by short hedges than by long hedges; the largest share occurring in the fall of the year—October/December, and the smallest in July/August.

It is apparent from the foregoing that short hedges invariably play a larger role than long hedges in cotton futures. On a "net" basis, the trade is always short, but tends to be less so in June/August than at other times.

Deliveries

The No. 2 futures contract basis grade is Strict Low Middling cotton, but Good Middling, Strict Middling, Middling Plus, and Low Middling can be delivered in the White grades. Good Middling Light Spotted, Strict Middling Light Spotted, and Middling Light Spotted can be delivered in the Light Spotted grades on the No. 2 contract. Only cotton stapling $1\frac{1}{32}''$ and longer may be delivered on this contract. Deliverable Grade differentials and Staple premiums and discounts for other than Strict Low Middling $1\frac{1}{16}''$ are based on the average of commercial differences quoted for the corresponding grades and staples on the 6th business day prior to the day of delivery by the USDA for Greenville, S.C., Greenwood, Miss., Memphis, Tenn., Dallas, Texas, and Phoenix, Arizona. These differences apply to cotton tendered for delivery at any one of the 6 delivery points for the No. 2 contract—Galveston, Texas; Houston, Texas; Greenville, South Carolina; Memphis, Tennessee; New Orleans, Louisiana; and Mobile, Alabama. Grade premiums and discounts are full averages, but cotton stapling $1\frac{1}{32}''$ is discounted 125% of the quoted difference between $1\frac{1}{32}''$ and $1\frac{1}{16}''$ staple. Cotton stapling above $1\frac{3}{32}''$ is deliverable at the same premium as $1\frac{3}{32}''$. Cotton must micronaire not less than 3.5 nor more than 4.9 to be tenderable on contract. Bales must weigh between 325 and 675 lbs. net to be deliverable.

The first day a short in futures can signify his intention of liquidating his position by a delivery is on the 5th business day prior to the day of delivery (prior to the opening of trading). Thus the trade short holding cotton which has been certificated (inspected, weighed, and sampled under New York Cotton Exchange supervision and determined deliverable against futures upon classification, review, and micronaire test under USDA regulations) pays close attention to grade and staple premiums and discounts at the aforementioned spot markets for the quality cotton he holds. USDA studies have indicated the difference between quoted and actual spot values at times has been of considerable significance. This relationship may influence a decision on the part of the trade short with respect to making delivery. Thus a large certificated stock does not necessarily mean heavy deliveries at any given time. The "ammunition" may be there, but whether or not it is used depends in part upon the relationship between quoted and actual spot values. Deliveries may also depend on the amount of the current discount for the maturing futures month under the next succeeding contract—it may be advantageous to switch a short hedge forward and permit the market to pay a portion of the carrying charges. Sometimes the price level itself may have declined to a low enough area to encourage lifting a short hedge rather than to deliver.

Hedging

It is probable that shifting of much of the carryover of cotton from government to trade hands will prompt increased use of the futures market by both shippers and mill interests for hedge purposes.

In the mid-sixties the CCC held as much as 73% of the large carryover, and there was little inducement for the trade to hold or hedge inventories. Prior to this period there was an active trade interest in the futures market and there has been an active trade interest since government stocks were depleted. Most business was based on futures prices. Typically the shipper purchased cotton from the interior at a fixed price, although occasionally on "Sellers call," and usually sold to mills on "Buyers call." An "On Call" transaction is one based on futures whereby the "Basis" or premium "On" or discount "Off" a futures month is established at the time of the sale, but the actual price is fixed (called) later. For example, a shipper sells to a mill 1,000 bales of Middling Plus $1\frac{1}{16}$" Memphis territory cotton at 75 (pts.) on March, buyer's call. The buyer normally must fix price before first notice day for the futures contract named.

The tendency generally has been for mills to purchase cotton on a fixed price basis when prices have been relatively low, and to buy on call when prices appeared relatively high and when the futures market was active. Increased direct mill buying has been a factor in the use of fixed price purchases by mills in recent years. Practice in past years varied to a degree on "fixations" when mills bought cotton on call, some mills fixing price on orders at times, and on the basis of what appeared to be a relatively low futures price at other times whether cloth orders were received or not, while other mills fixed price only against cloth orders.

The shipper is concerned initially with having a short position in futures to the extent of his "Overs" (the amount by which spot market purchases exceed fixed price sales), or a long position in futures when the reverse situation exists. Once hedged, the principal concern is that any "Basis" changes will be favorable rather than unfavorable. When an active representative hedge market is available and the merchant or shipper operates on a hedged basis, his main concern is the difference between his buying basis in the country for mixed lots, often bought "Hog-round" at an average price, and his selling basis for even running lots offered his mill clients.

Weather is a major factor affecting the basis. Ad-

Fixed Price

	Spot			Futures	
SHIPPER	Nov. 5 sells SM $1\frac{1}{16}$" to mill @ price of	38.50¢			
	(a) If long spots at fixed price and hedged		THEN	Buys in short March hedge @	38.00¢
	(b) if not long spots		THEN	Buys March futures @	38.00¢
	Jan. 5 acquires spot SM $1\frac{1}{16}$" @ ..	37.50¢	AND	Sells out long March hedge	37.00¢
		+1.00¢			−1.00¢

On Buyer's Call

	Spot			Futures	
SHIPPER	Nov. 5 sells to mill SM $1\frac{1}{16}$" @ 50 On March				
	(a) if long spots at fixed price and hedged		RETAINS	Short March hedge	
	(b) if not long spots		TAKES	No futures position	
	Jan. 5 acquires spot SM $1\frac{1}{16}$" @ ..	37.50¢	AND	Sells March futures @	37.00¢
	Feb. 15 Mill fixes price @	37.00¢	AND	Shipper buys in short	
	(March 36.50 plus 50 pts.)			March futures hedge @	36.50¢
		− .50¢			+ .50¢

Fixed Price

	Spot			Futures	
MILL	Nov. 5 buys SM 1¹/₁₆″ @ .... 38.50¢		AND	Sells March futures @	38.00¢
	Feb. 15 sells cloth based on				
	current spot price of .... 37.00¢		AND	Buys March futures @	36.50¢
	−1.50¢				−1.50¢

On Buyer's Call

	Spot			Futures	
MILL	Nov. 5 buys SM 1¹/₁₆″ @ 50 On March		BUT	Takes no futures position	
	Feb. 15 sells cloth based on		AND	Fixes price with March	36.50¢
	current spot price of .... 37.00¢			plus premium	50
					37.00¢

verse weather can tighten up the supply of desirable grades, especially when much high grade cotton has been sold ahead for forward shipment. On the other hand, there have been times when, owing to very open weather, a real scarcity of low grades existed with the result that premiums were paid over better grades where forward commitments had been made on low grades and not yet covered. Thus it is not just a question of weather affecting grades. The effect on the basis depends also on the forward sales commitments in a particular grade, or grade and staple combination, relative to the supply of that quality. As a matter of fact, the extent of any price move, in addition to basis changes, depends to no small degree upon the extent to which uncovered forward sales commitments have been made by the cotton trade.

The shipper or mill buyer has two choices in purchasing—at a fixed price, or on call. His subsequent use of the futures market will depend upon the course of action he takes. The following example illustrates action taken in the spot market and in the futures market when a sale is made on a fixed price basis, and on a call transaction . . . both arising from the same mill order:

Situation: A mill buyer on November 5, knowing that the mill will require 1,000 bales of SM 1¹/₁₆″ cotton sometime during late winter, but not having a cloth order for such, and noting from ginning and quality reports that the indicated supply of this quality cotton is likely to be much smaller than usual, decides now is the time to cover anticipated needs. The price quoted by a widely operating shipper is 38.50¢ per pound, or 50 "On" the March contract.

The shipper, receiving the foregoing order from the mill will operate in one of the ways illustrated on the preceding page depending upon the method of buying chosen by the mill, and on its own market position.

Sources of Cotton Information

United States Department of Agriculture studies on various aspects of the cotton situation provide a wealth of information on this subject, and good use has been made of them in this report. In addition there are a number of regular reports which are available, enabling the cotton trader to keep posted on factors affecting supply of and demand for cotton, such as:

—Daily 10 market average spot cotton prices released by the USDA the following morning.
—Weekly U.S. export sales report issued by the USDA.
—Weekly report on certificated stocks of cotton posted by the NYCE.
—Weekly Cotton Market Reviews issued by USDA, CMS-Cotton Division (Regional).
—Weekly report on loan entries and withdrawals released by CCC and posted by NYCE.
—Ginnings reports released twice monthly by the Census Bureau September 1 through mid-January, issued about the 8th day following the end of reporting period. Quality reports are also issued periodically.
—Monthly crop estimates in season, released around the 10th of the month giving production and yield estimates as of the 1st of the month, issued by the Crop Reporting Board (and usually preceded by private trade estimates).
—Monthly report of cotton consumption, stocks at mills, and in public storage and at compresses, issued by the Census Bureau about three weeks after close of the period.
—Monthly Current Industry Report of the Census Bureau providing gray goods production, inventory and unfilled order figures, released about 6 weeks after close of the period.
—Monthly official exports of raw cotton, by destination, released by the Census Bureau around the 28th of the month following the period covered.
—Bi-monthly "Cotton Situation" report issued by the Economic Research Service of the USDA.
—Planting intentions reports issued by the USDA around January 22 and March 17.
—July report of cotton in cultivation July 1, released about the 10th of July by the USDA.

In Summary

Basically, the supply side of the cotton equation is influenced by the size and quality of carryover; by the amount which is in commercial hands as opposed to CCC inventory; by indications of planting intentions relative to acreage allotments; by weather developments even before field preparation and continuing through the harvest; and by the growers' willingness to sell. These factors tend to exert an immediate and often short term effect on cotton prices.

The demand side of the cotton equation is influenced by less readily apparent considerations such as the relationship between cloth inventories and forward sales commitments for major cloth constructions; by the amount and quality of mill stocks of raw cotton; by the degree of competition between cotton and man-made fibers and blends; by competition from imports of cotton cloth or manufactured articles; and by mill margins. These factors take more time to exert an influence on raw cotton prices, but their effect is usually more lasting. A considerable time lag may be involved between increased demand for cloth and increased mill demand for raw cotton, depending upon the level of cloth inventories held at the converter or mill level and by the amount of raw cotton held by the mill. The demand side of the cotton equation insofar as exports are concerned depends partly upon much the same factors as outlined above for domestic mills, but also upon the supply and price of foreign growths of cotton.

March Cotton Futures Delivery 1972-73 to 1974-75

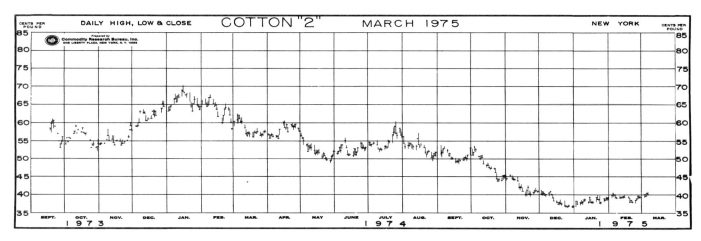

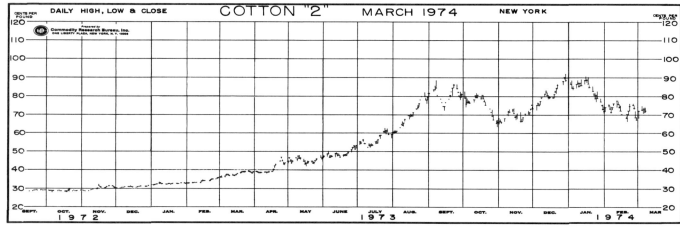

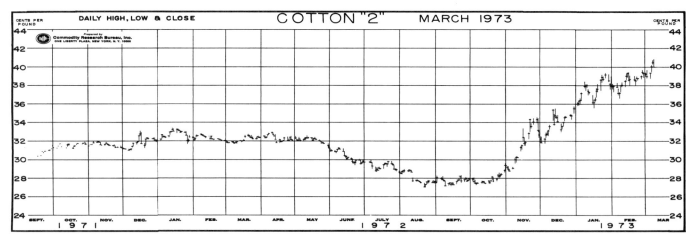

March Cotton Futures Delivery 1969-70 to 1971-72

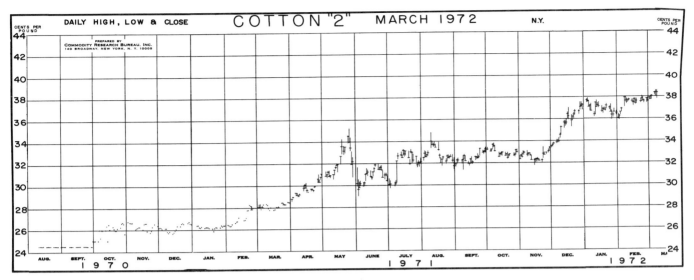

DAILY HIGH, LOW & CLOSE COTTON "2" MARCH 1972 N.Y.

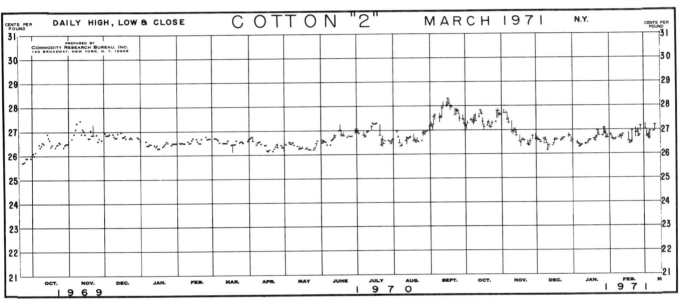

DAILY HIGH, LOW & CLOSE COTTON "2" MARCH 1971 N.Y.

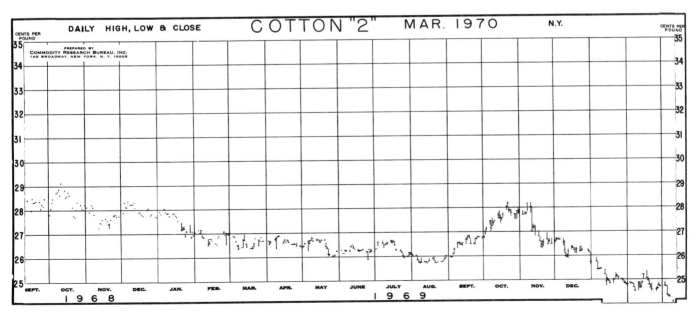

DAILY HIGH, LOW & CLOSE COTTON "2" MAR. 1970 N.Y.

March Cotton Futures Delivery 1966-67 to 1968-69

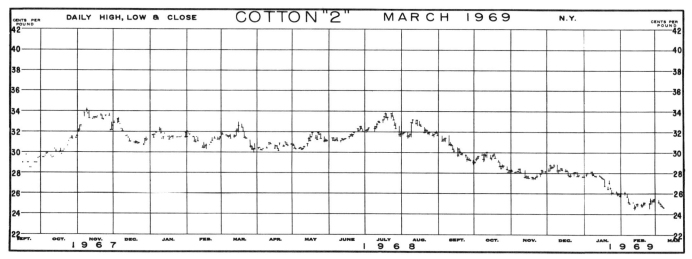

DAILY HIGH, LOW & CLOSE COTTON "2" MARCH 1969 N.Y.

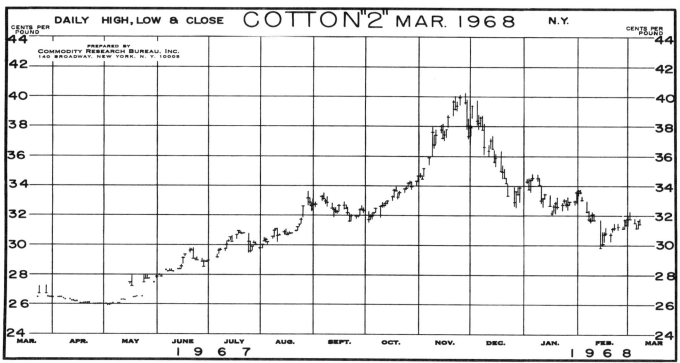

DAILY HIGH, LOW & CLOSE COTTON "2" MAR. 1968 N.Y.

PREPARED BY
COMMODITY RESEARCH BUREAU, INC.
140 BROADWAY, NEW YORK, N. Y. 10005

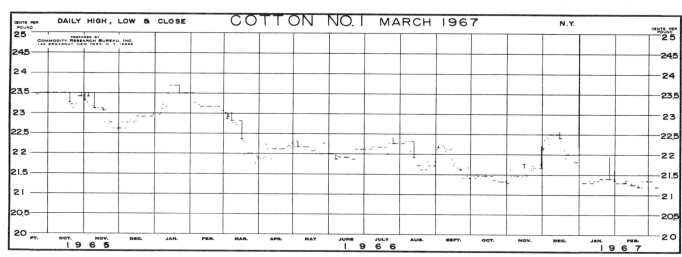

DAILY HIGH, LOW & CLOSE COTTON NO. 1 MARCH 1967 N.Y.

PREPARED BY
COMMODITY RESEARCH BUREAU, INC.
140 BROADWAY, NEW YORK, N. Y. 10005

UNDERSTANDING THE EGG FUTURES MARKET

BY DAVID M. INKELES

In the mid 1960's, trading of egg futures began a resurgence which again established it as a most lively and active commodity market. The rebirth was triggered by the switching from a storage egg to a fresh egg contract on the Chicago Mercantile Exchange. Storage eggs had been a major factor in the egg industry prior to World War II. Excess production in the spring was stored in warehouses and then sold profitably in the deficit periods of the fall and winter. After the war, new production techniques allowed for a more even production throughout the year. Storage eggs were shunned by supermarkets for reasons of quality. They were usually bought up by breakers at huge discounts. Their price no longer bore much relationship to actual supply and demand conditions in the fresh egg markets. As a result, storage egg futures lost their relevancy and trading dwindled to a point approaching extinction. In fact, by the mid 70's with less cyclical production and greater acceptance of frozen and dried eggs, there is virtually no speculative storing of fresh eggs being done anymore.

The new fresh egg contract has regained this lost relevancy and has been widely accepted by the producers, processors and speculators. Prices now have a closer correlation with the cash market and the futures contract is being used for both long and short hedges by members of the egg trade. This study is intended to be a review of the various economic factors that influence both the spot and futures prices for eggs. It is also a commentary on recent developments in the egg industry which may affect the trader in egg futures.

Structural Changes in the Egg Industry

Although virtually every farm in the country produces eggs for home consumption, severe cost pressures have made large scale efficient operations necessary for commercial survival. _Poultry Tribune_ estimates that 3% of farms now produce over 80% of the nation's eggs. Furthermore, they estimate that 82% of all layers are in controlled environment cages and they expect this number to reach 95% by 1979. The large producer may have all his birds in his own houses or he may contract their raising to local small farmers. The contractor supplies the bird and its feed, medication and overall supervision. He also markets the eggs. The contractee provides the hen house and labor. Remuneration is either on a flat rate per dozen or a percentage. 45.2% of all eggs are now produced on contract compared with only 27.4% in 1968.

Up until the early 1960's the West North Central region was the largest producer of eggs and exported to other sections of the country. By the 1970's this had shifted strongly in favor of the southern states because of cheaper labor, more small farms willing to contract, better weather and greater receptivity of the banks and feed companies that financed the operations. The large processors in Missouri, Nebraska and Minnesota now are constantly forced out of their areas to obtain sufficient supplies for their operations.

Other changes are affecting the markets in the 70's. These include: recent breakthroughs in the fight against poultry cancers, the continued drop in long term demand, the cholesterol question, the new nest run contract, the egg clearing house, and the increased power of the U.E.P. These will be discussed later in this article.

How Supply and Demand Influence Price Changes

The long term per capita demand for eggs is again falling. For many years it had increased in parallel with the nation's prosperity, going from 306 eggs per year in 1910 to 405 eggs in 1945. By the mid 60's it declined to around 320 where it seemed to hold steady. However, a spate of anti-cholesterol publicity has recently cut into demand with 1973 per capita usage down to 293 eggs.

The cholesterol question is not new. However, the medical profession now seems to be closing ranks. There is hardly a heart attack victim or sufferer of high blood pressure who has not been advised by his doctor to stop eating eggs; or at least to cut down his consumption. Furthermore, the national advertising by Fleishman's _Egg Beaters_ and Avoset Food's _Second Nature_ is focusing the problem on prime time T.V. rather than just in medical journals. Finally, there has been the establishment by the egg industry of the National Commission on Egg Nutrition as a watchdog on egg-cholesterol statements by physicians and columnists. The activities of this group were so vigorous as to bring on a restraining order by the F.T.C. Undoubtedly their activities only focused more attention on this problem and probably led to an even greater decline in consumption.

The short term demand for eggs is extremely inelastic in that a small percentage change in supply has a much greater inverse effect on price. As already mentioned, the long term consumption trend is down. However, this is a steady attrition and the rate is not likely to change drastically from month to month. Therefore, a major price swing lasting several months will not be attributable to significant changes in demand. Rather it will be due to supply changes in this arena of inelastic demand.

Demand changes due to holidays, weather, government purchases or sizable "long side" futures market commitments will affect prices. However, they tend not to disturb the overall trend which is based primarily on supply changes. These aberrations in demand will be examined later in this article since they flavor the overall trend. However, the place to begin any egg market analysis is with the projected supply. This is fortunate since it is in this area that we find most of the available statistics which can be brought to bear on an analysis.

Supply Components

The number of eggs produced each day is a function of the mature laying population of hens. This can be accurately estimated for any time within the next five months. We take the current population,

71

which is available monthly, and add the number of chicks hatched. These are added 5 months after they are hatched since this is when they begin to lay. We then subtract the number of hens that we expect will be slaughtered in the interval being examined. This figure must then be adjusted for prospective changes in the rate of lay based on the age of the flock and estimated molting. This supply statistic should then be compared with those of previous years with some adjustment made for long term demand attrition.

It must be emphatically stated that this simple statistical approach is only a starting point. In itself, it will not predict the price of eggs accurately enough to profit from the futures market. However, failure to make this calculation can be costly. In the spring of 1970 the hatch was between 15% and 20% above 1969. Therefore, it was generally assumed that by September the country would be inundated with eggs. In April, 1970 the price for September delivery was quite low.

The fallacy was that chickens are added to the laying flock only after five months. Thus, by September the spring hatch could only barely begin to affect supply. Even then its impact was to be mitigated by disease and aggressive culling. The full impact could not be expected until at least the year end. As it turned out, September, 1970 per capita production was less than 1% over 1969. The price of large eggs was over 40¢ and the market firm. On September 1, pullets not of laying age stood at 81.5 million, 12% above the preceding year. This clearly demonstrated the prematurity of the expected low prices.

Hatching

The first element in the production equation is the hatch. The number quoted for the monthly hatch only refers to the female chicks. The males are of no economic value and are destroyed shortly after birth. The hatch is both seasonal and cyclical. It is heaviest in the spring. It is also heaviest in a year following one of high prices and large profits for producers. A producer is more apt to expand with the blush of success around him than in lean years when many marginal producers are going out of business.

Since profitability affects the size of the hatch, we must be able to quickly assess the profitability of egg production. The cost per dozen at the farm 5 years ago was about 29¢ in an efficient operation. Today it is difficult to achieve an accurate estimate due to the general inflation in all costs, especially feed grains. The increased volatility in feed costs adds to this problem. A study by the University of California at San Diego is by far the most comprehensive ever done for this industry and is included here. It is computed as cost per dozen eggs produced and cost per layer on the farm.

A similar study by Dr. Howard Widely of the University of Georgia gives similar results but concludes even higher feed costs per dozen eggs produced.

Feed	29.25 cents
Hen dep.	9.00 cents
Contract payment	5.00 cents
Med. & sanitation	.45 cents
Overhead	1.00 cents
Total	39.70 cents

In addition to either calculation one must add 3¢ for processing plant costs, 2¢ for transportation to terminal markets and 2¢ for grade loss. Hence, non-cartoned eggs of a grade similar to that acceptable for futures delivery would have been produced for about 47¢ per dozen early in 1974. The U.S.D.A. egg-feed ratio can be used for a quick reference. It is the number of pounds of feed equal in value to a dozen eggs. However, this figure by itself can not be used as an indicator of profitability.

Average Results Per Dozen Eggs Produced

	1971	1972	1973
Feed layers only	15.4¢	17.1¢	26.9¢
Feed cost for replacements	3.2	1.8	2.7
Replacement chicks & started pullets	2.7	2.4	6.3
Supplies, taxes, utilities, misc.	1.4	1.2	1.5
Hired labor costs	1.9	2.0	2.1
Home chore labor	.1	.1	.1
Stock inventory + charge—credit	−.2	+1.3	−2.2
Cull sales—credit	−.4	−.4	−1.8
Net cash and labor cost	24.1¢	25.5¢	35.6¢
Depreciation 10% average value of buildings and equipment	1.2	1.1	1.2
Interest 8% on land stock and average value of building and equipment	1.4	1.2	1.4
Management	1.8	1.3	1.3
Net cost of production per dozen eggs	28.5¢	29.1¢	39.5¢
Income per dozen eggs	21.3¢	24.5¢	46.7¢

Average Results Per Layer (365 Hen-Days)

	1971	1972	1973
Feed layers only	$3.15	$3.31	$5.10
Feed for replacements	.65	.37	.51
Replacement chicks, started pullets	.54	.46	1.20
Supplies, taxes, utilities, misc.	.29	.23	.28
Hired labor	.38	.39	.39
Home chore labor	.03	.01	.01
Stock inventory + charge—credit	−0.3	+.25	−.42
Cull sales—credit	−.08	−.07	−.34
Net cash cost incl. home chore labor	$4.93	$4.95	$6.73
Depreciation 10% average value of buildings and equipment	.24	.22	.22
Interest 8% on land, stock, and average value of building and equipment	.28	.24	.26
Management (Including pullets raised)	.29	.25	.25
Total cost per hen	$5.74	$5.66	$7.47
Egg income per hen	$4.35	$4.76	$8.38

Source: Poultry Tribune.

Disease

In the past five years Marek's Disease (Avian Leukosis) has been virtually eliminated. By the late 1960's this virulent cancer of the young chick's lymphoid system had been killing from 7.3% to 32.3% of all egg type chicks hatched. The cause of this cancer was a virus and it is now controlled by an injectable vaccine. In 1972 there was an outbreak of

Newcastle's Disease in California and about 8 million birds were destroyed. This, too, is controlled by a vaccine and appears to be behind us. A new chick is now inoculated against Marek's, Newcastle's, bronchitis, laryngotracheitis, fowl pox and, in California, infectious coryza.

Molting

Once a hen has been laying for about 12 months its rate of lay falls to the point where it is no longer economical. It is then either slaughtered or molted. The latter is a six week process in which birds are first starved until they stop laying and their feathers fall out. They are then re-fed and begin to lay at a much higher rate for an additional six months. A producer who molts, has to amortize the feed and labor costs during the molting period. However, he has a bird whose original cost has been fully amortized. Molting is most aggressively practiced in periods of strong markets. Changes in the amount of molting can be deduced from inverse changes in the number of birds being slaughtered. In addition, the percent of hens and pullets of laying age being force molted and molt completed as of the first of each month, with year earlier comparisons, is now available for selected states in the monthly U.S.D.A. report on egg production and layer numbers.

Culling

Slaughter statistics for fowl are given weekly. However, only the cumulative total for a period of at least several months can be used to indicate a significant change in supply. The statistic most often used is for federally inspected packing plants. To obtain a more accurate approximation of total U.S. fowl slaughter, this should be doubled.

One must also consider the average age of the flock. This statistic appears monthly in a graph in *Poultry Tribune*. A period of high culling and low molting will bring the average age down. A younger flock has a higher rate of lay. This usually occurs during a period of low prices, or a period when low prices are expected.

Imports

Eggs are normally not imported in significant quantities. The major deterrents are high transportation costs plus duties. The latter amount to 3½¢ per dozen on fresh eggs and 10¢ per lb. on frozen eggs. The amount of eggs imported will depend on market conditions in other countries. These are difficult to keep track of since prices and statistics are not published here. When domestic egg prices move into higher ground, one should consult reliable trade people for import information and statistics. One must ignore rumors of large importations unless they can be verified. Too often in the past this route has been used unscrupulously by those wishing to lower the futures market.

Most shell eggs imported go to breakers and most frozen eggs are sold at discounts to the current cash price. However, they still replace the need for domestic eggs in these segments of the market. Hence they have a definite mitigating effect on any shortage.

Futures Market Affects the Supply

The futures market itself can dramatically affect the supply. If longs stand for delivery, eggs must be taken from channels of distribution and put aside. In a period of tight supplies this will aggravate the shortage. On the other hand, once trading for that month is completed the same eggs, not being deliverable in the succeeding month, go immediately into the channels of distribution. They represent a surplus added to current production and often sell at discounts of up to 15¢ per dozen below the cash price for large white eggs. They are no longer newly laid and may very well be out of position geographically.

The accumulation of these eggs at the beginning of the month can raise the cash market. Their release at the end of the month can depress it. In September 1970, longs stood for net delivery of over 250 cars of eggs. This represented 54 million eggs or about 25% of one day's production for the entire country. It caused an already tight cash market to advance still further. At the end of September, however, these same eggs became a "drug on the market" and many went to breakers at large discounts below the cash market.

Weather

A few days of very cold or very hot weather in the southern egg producing states can have a marked effect on prices. Usually this means temperatures consistently below 20 degrees or over 90 degrees. Severe weather in the Midwest can also affect prices but usually not as much since that area is more prepared for wide swings of the thermometer. Cold can put a bird entirely off lay for 2 weeks, once affected. Hot weather cuts the rate of lay in a more gradual manner. Older birds are more vulnerable to the vicissitudes of temperature.

Cold weather also causes birds to mature at a faster rate. For this reason in the fall there is a relative shortage of mediums. The new laying pullets quickly move up in size. Mediums which sell 10¢ per dozen under large in the spring may move to 3¢ under in the fall. A contraseasonal large discount for mediums often is the harbinger of weaker large egg prices. This is because those chickens laying mediums will move up in size in the weeks ahead.

The Effects of Holidays on Futures Prices

The fact that eggs are perishable prevents long term accumulation to satisfy holiday needs. Hence prices normally rise only in the three weeks before a major holiday. Thanksgiving, Christmas and Easter are the big egg consuming holidays. The Jewish high holidays in September and Passover in April have a smaller effect. Also a small increase in demand is traditionally attributed to Labor Day with the concomitant beginning of school and autumn weather.

Usually the big question in the egg trade is what will happen to prices after the holiday. For Thanksgiving this is not too important since post holiday surpluses are usually absorbed in pre-Christmas inventory build-up. After Christmas there is nothing to absorb the excess supplies. This is aggravated by the fact that many firms actively reduce inventories in the last week of the year so that their Dec. 31 financial statements will show extra heavy cash items.

A person short December eggs has until the end of the month to make delivery even though trading in that contract stops around the 21st of December. He can buy eggs in the week after Christmas when prices are somewhat softer. A long who gets delivery early in December can easily dispose of the eggs in the pre-Christmas shortage. However a long taking delivery in the post-Christmas week may have to accept a large discount in an already declining cash market.

The same principle applies to the pre- and post-Easter periods. Of course like everything else in commodity trading, neither the pre-holiday strength nor the post-holiday weakness occur every year. Extremely tight conditions can carry a rally past Christmas and right through January. This occurred in 1969–70. On the other hand, Christmas 1964 saw supplies so heavy and prices so depressed that a rally did not materialize.

U.S.D.A. Purchases

Each year, usually in the spring, the U.S.D.A. announces purchases of either dried eggs or scrambled egg mix. The latter consists of at least 51% dried whole egg with the remainder non-fat dried milk. These purchases are partially discounted by the futures market. However, the announcement causes at least a one day rise in prices. The purpose of the program is both to feed underprivileged people and to effect surplus removal. In 1974 there were no purchases at all. This was significant because it was the first time in over 10 years that the government was not a buyer. Purchases of mix for the preceding years were (in pounds):

1973—10,728,000
1972—12,348,000
1971—31,383,000
1970—16,587,000

When these purchases come in May and June they are well accommodated by the heavy production at that time. In 1966 the Defense Department made large scale purchases of dried eggs in November on top of an already firm market. The result of this was a temporary shortage which led to sharp rallies in cash and futures markets.

Breaker Demand

Breaker demand for eggs used to be quite seasonal with maximum activity in the spring during the heavy production period when prices were lowest. Today much less breaking is done by separate firms and most is done by large integrated firms that pack frozen, dried and fresh eggs. They are in some degree of operation all year and are quick to take advantage of price changes by switching from one product to another. Frozen egg and dried egg inventories are important statistics. Low inventories of both were a major contributor to the 1973 bull market.

Cash Markets

The wholesale price for all grades of eggs is quoted each day by the Urner Barry Publishing Co. based on its assessment of market conditions and on actual sales reported to them by many firms. Until March, 1970 it used the cash egg trading on the New York Mercantile Exchange as the most important factor for its price formulation. Urner Barry would usually quote the price eggs traded at on the close. However, if it felt that the sales had been made at prices artificially high or low in an attempt to influence the quoted price, Urner Barry would let the cash price differ from the last by as much as several cents.

The Urner Barry price is used as the basis for most of the eggs sold at wholesale throughout the nation. There are, of course, premiums or discounts depending on location, pack and quality. However, the base price is the Urner Barry quotation. For many years the U.S.D.A. has also quoted a market each day. Their price was rarely used as the basis for transactions since it was always quoted as a rather broad range. Undoubtedly the U.S.D.A. quoted it wide because it was describing the previous day's activity. Since the U.S.D.A. is a government agency it would prefer to not be in the controversial position of quoting the price on which transactions are based.

Since trades on the N.Y. Mercantile Exchange could be made in units as small as 50 cases many interested groups tried to maneuver this market. The object was to lose a little on a sacrifice trade and then recoup much larger profits in off the exchange transactions which were based on the exchange price. Dealers buying merchandise would try to lower the cash price by selling on the exchange. Producers would try to raise the New York price by buying. Since daily production throughout the nation totals over 500,000 cases, a sacrifice purchase of 500 cases at an inflated price could be recouped a thousand fold. Since the New York market also influenced the futures market, speculators would also try to move the market with small amounts of merchandise. There were many complaints of activities of this type and the C.E.A. finally eliminated cash egg trading on both the New York and Chicago Mercantile Exchanges.

Urner Barry no longer has exchange trading on which to base its market quotation. It is therefore much easier to second guess the Urner Barry quotation and many in the trade take the liberty of doing this. Nevertheless, it is agreed that the current situation is superior to not having a quoted cash market. In that case the supermarkets would negotiate the price of each load of eggs. Since the supermarkets are much larger and stronger companies than the typical egg producer they would undoubtedly force lower prices. Moreover, conditions would be more chaotic since there would be no accepted price for a given grade of eggs.

The Egg Clearing House is a new device by which car loads of fresh eggs may be offered or bid for anywhere in the nation. Mostly this is done by telephone. Prices of transactions consummated there are published daily. This is an excellent concept since it avails the producer of many more outlets for his product.

Some producers would like this organization to supplant Urner Barry and have its trades be the sole basis for the daily price at which most cash business is computed. However, the clearing house is mainly a producer's organization. There are many who feel that producers tend to put high priced trades through the clearing house while not publicizing their less favorable dispositions. Hence, it is doubtful that cash egg brokers or supermarkets would support this.

The pressure of producing groups to raise the cash price has had its effect. Ten years ago supermarkets in New York paid six to seven cents over New York for cartoned eggs warehouse delivery. Today (early in 1975) they pay only 1-2¢ over. Since packaging and transportation costs did not go down in this period, one can only conclude that the New York cash price has gradually worked itself higher. It is still a basis but it is now somewhat unrealistic. Trades of loose eggs are now made at a discount to this price. Trades of cartoned eggs are also at a discount since the premium of 1-2¢ does not reflect all of the inherent costs of packaging.

Army Prices

Army prices provide a level of reference determined by actual bid and offer. Therefore, they offer an excellent way of confirming that the Urner Barry price represents actual conditions. Each day the Department of Defense (called the Army in the trade) buys eggs for domestic installations and for overseas usage. The size of these purchases of course depends on the level of military activity. At the height of Viet Nam activity purchases through the Alameda, California shipping point ran 50-60 cars (700 cases per car) each week. Now they are considerably below this.

Army purchases are for delivery in 2 weeks at specific installation and in specific packaging. Each day they publish a range of prices for *sales transacted* for the various installations within each division. A trade house bidding low at one installation could easily drop the low price in the range. To drop the high price it would have to bid low at all the installations in the division. For this reason one should only use the high price in the range for reference.

When one hears that Army prices were up, down, or unchanged as an explanation of futures market activity, he should ask the following questions of his broker:

1. Was it the high end of the range that moved and how much?
2. Was one division or all divisions so affected?
3. How many cases of eggs were contracted in the divisions affected?

If either the number of divisions or the amount of eggs was low, one should wait until the next day's prices for confirmation. If only the low end of a range moved, it is of no consequence. A firm may have misjudged the market and bid low in error. Since Army prices call for delivery in two weeks, they are an indication of prospects for the near future. As such they are often used to predict short range price movements. Medium sized eggs can be delivered against Army commitments at a 12.2% discount. Hence any time the price of Mediums goes more than 12.2% below Large one can expect their demand to increase.

United Egg Producers

The United Egg Producers is the largest organization of independent egg producing companies. It is interested in the welfare of the producers and will do everything within reason to protect the price they receive for their commodity. Its main objective is to prevent periods of over-supply which in turn lead to severe financial losses or bankruptcies for their members. In the years before the integrated egg producer,

eggs were produced as a sideline on all the nation's farms. Since it was but a side line, low prices did not endanger the existence of the farm. Today a large producer with from 100,000 to over 1,000,000 hens has a very large investment in eggs. 1¢ per dozen change in the average price received for a year amounts to $15,000 per 100,000 hens. Large integrated producers are clearly a more efficient means of production. The U.E.P. by attempting to bring some stability to this heretofore violent market will encourage further capital improvements and efficiencies.

Each day the U.E.P. surveys its membership. It determines the tone of the market and so advises its membership so that they can adjust production and selling policies. It also aids its members in selling surplus eggs by informing dealers of their existence and whereabouts. In past years it used its market intelligence to influence prices on the New York Mercantile Exchange. Now that spot trading no longer exists, it publicizes its information in a legitimate attempt to influence dealers, consumers and most of all the Urner Barry price.

In addition to its direct efforts to affect the spot price, the U.E.P. has also used several more traditional methods to actually reduce supply. It strongly opposed increased hatching for flock replacement in 1970. It campaigned for no replacement chicks to be bought during August. The results were remarkable and attest to the strength of this group. In July 1970 the hatch was 10% over July 1969. However, in August it fell to 23% below 1969.

A trader in egg futures should bear in mind that the United Egg Producers wants to keep prices up. Any news item concerning this group should therefore be examined closely. Lest the trader be overly influenced, he should wring from the news item whatever enthusiasm he can find and accept only the hard facts that are apparent.

Futures Market Price Movements

It should be noted that almost every segment of the egg industry is involved in the futures market. Some trades are made as legitimate hedges. However, for the most part, their trading is purely speculative. In an industry of changing prices, the mere accumulation of a working inventory involves a speculation. Hence all the members are used to taking positions. The futures market offers another vehicle for testing the validity of their business judgment.

During the year futures prices tend to move parallel with the spot market. The degree of correlation increases as each contract approaches maturity. September generally sells above October. It still may be influenced by hot weather while October may get the benefit of increased production from spring hatch pullets. November sells above October and December because of Thanksgiving, Christmas accumulation. December sells below November because deliveries can be made in the week after Christmas. January through May sell at succeedingly lower prices reflecting increased supplies and lower demand. Easter can elevate March contracts and severe weather can play havoc with any winter or spring month. The summer is subject to supply deficits due to hot weather, so July and August sell at premiums to the spring months.

Deliveries

In the spot month delivered eggs are generally worth slightly less than the New York cash price. The eggs are deliverable in Chicago or in other cities with freight discounts to Chicago. However, eggs in Chicago usually sell 2¢ below New York reflecting the freight difference between the cities.

Delivered eggs are in warehouses in various parts of the country or they may be delivered at a discount in the producer's plant. The most popular today is the in-plant delivery. These eggs are not redeliverable unless taken to a warehouse and reinspected. They may have been accumulated in the seller's plant for several weeks, and they may be in a small town away from terminal markets and readily available transportation.

In any but the strongest markets they are considered tainted owing to this age and loss of quality. Thus we have a paradox. We have a fresh egg contract but the buyer who gets delivery late in the month gets eggs that are no longer recognized as "fresh." They sell at discounts of up to 15¢ below the cash market or the succeeding contract month.

In a bull market much of this is obscured by the scramble of the shorts to get eggs. There is a saying that, "money is in unlimited supply but eggs are not." When the chips are down one can buy as many contracts as one has money for. However, one needs eggs to satisfy short positions. Only a hen can lay eggs; a bank can not.

In a bull market most eggs are contracted ahead of time, even if this be just a few days. It may be extremely difficult, if not impossible, for shorts to accumulate 300 or 400 contracts of fresh eggs and take them out of circulation for up to one month. Hence the futures demand may drive the spot price sharply higher. The major difference between eggs and a storable commodity like wheat is that shorts can accumulate wheat for several months while deliverable eggs must be taken directly from current production. When there is already a shortage in the cash markets, this removal of eggs may be nearly impossible.

In a bear market buyers can be extremely choosy as to both quality and position. Most users have enough problems using eggs from normal suppliers. Hence surplus eggs go to bargain hunters who most of the time are breakers. The futures price can move considerably below the spot price in the spot month; perhaps as much as 15¢ per dozen.

The in-plant delivery can be particularly costly to the speculator taking delivery and equally profitable to those packers making delivery. Since the eggs are virtually not redeliverable and must be removed by the buyer in two days, the long is apt to offer them back to the owner of the plant. The plant owner who originally delivered the eggs usually will offer to buy back the same eggs at a substantial discount. Let the buyer beware! Some packers are alleged to have made consistent profits by this maneuver. It is usually little problem to the large integrated firm since the eggs can get lost in this fresh or broken output.

This quandry that the long may be in, causes the near month in weak markets to decline more than 10¢ below the succeeding delivery month as was the case with the November 1974 contract. Moreover, in December 1974 in relatively weak market conditions, prices were more than 15¢ below spot. This was in part due to the ability of shorts to deliver after Christmas but mainly because longs did not want delivery in out of the way locations. To meet the need of longs, a new breed of cash broker has arisen who specializes in handling in-plant deliveries and marketing them at terms usually better than those offered by the delivering short in whose plant the eggs reside.

We see that in the spot month the futures price can vary from a few cents above the spot price to 15¢ below it. All the while the spot price itself is extremely volatile. This explains the basis for the gyrations in futures prices one often finds during the last few days of trading.

Spot month price movements are most confusing in months when there is neither a clear cut bull or bear trend in the cash markets. Much of the eventual movement is due to the number of actual deliveries made early in the spot month. Who makes the deliveries and who stops them are equally important. Early large scale deliveries by well financed shorts may scare a great many longs into liquidation. On the other hand if trade longs take delivery of a substantial number of contracts early in the spot month and not redeliver, it may scare shorts into liquidating. They may fear a squeeze and the runaway prices brought on by such an operation.

Either long or short liquidation can feed on itself. In eggs, a perishable commodity, this is magnified for two reasons.

1. Eggs delivered this month in-plant can not be redelivered, causing the longs that eventually get the eggs to be prey of bargain hunting jobbers and breakers.
2. Since deliveries must be fresh eggs from current production it is difficult to accumulate sufficient eggs in tight markets to satisfy the short commitment. Shorts are in constant trepidation of squeezes, actual or imaginary; planned or accidental.

As a result of these two opposing factors, most traders hold contracts into the spot month and then run if price movements begin to go against them.

Despite some disadvantages associated with the deliveries, the fresh egg contract continues to thrive. For many reasons it is quite suitable to the trade and trade participation is necessary for the success of any futures contract. The dynamic interplay of short and long term supply and demand coupled with a liquid market continues to excite the interest of speculators.

Sept. Shell Eggs Futures Delivery 1968-69 to 1973-74

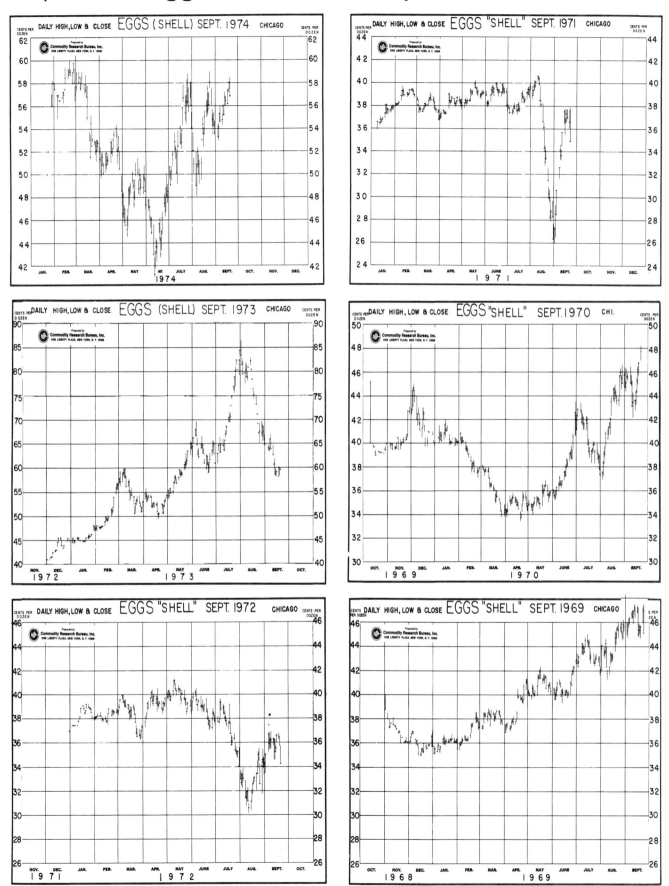

Sept. Shell Eggs Futures Delivery
1962-63 to 1967-68

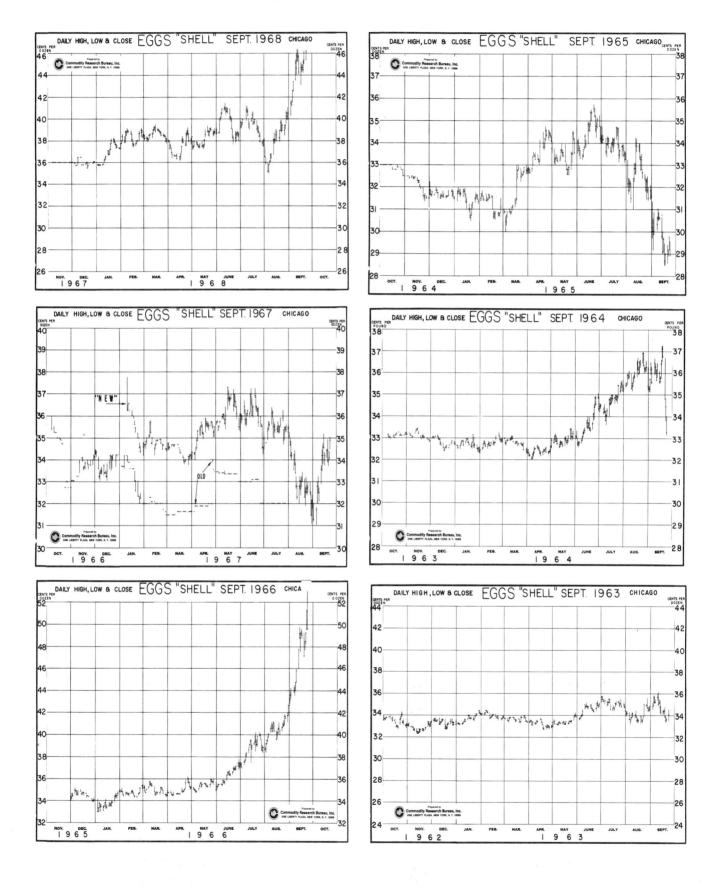

UNDERSTANDING GOLD AND WORLD GOLD MARKETS

BY VINCENT J. CONWAY

Gold has long been considered the king of precious metals. Its beauty, scarcity and imperishability have made this metal a symbol of wealth and excellence. For centuries, gold has been used as a medium of exchange, measure of value, and has been held in high esteem. Yet, despite its many favorable qualities, gold has also been surrounded with controversy. John Maynard Keynes referred to gold as a barbarous relic, though still recognizing man's strong attachment to it. Robert Triffin, a noted professor from Yale University, once commented on what he considered an absurd waste of human resources whereby gold is dug in distant corners of the earth for the sole purpose of transporting and re-burying it in some other well-guarded deep hole. Students of domestic political history must surely remember William Jennings Bryan's speech to the Democratic National Convention when he expressed his opposition to the gold standard by stating: ". . . You shall not crucify mankind upon a cross of gold."

Today, sparked by booming prices and the apparent interconnection between gold market activity and commodity prices, the gold debate rages on. The principal area of discussion concerns gold's role in the world monetary system. Many views have been expressed, ranging from those who would like to see a return to the gold standard and a sharp increase in the official price of gold to some who wish to do away with gold-currency ties altogether. Meanwhile, in the U.S. an increased cry for a lifting of the ban on private gold ownership resulted in a recent elimination of all ownership restrictions. On December 31, 1974, U.S. citizens were permitted to own gold without restrictions for the first time since April 5, 1933, when President Roosevelt issued an Executive Order prohibiting private ownership. The legalization of gold was accompanied by the inauguration of domestic gold futures trading and with it the beginning of a new era for commodity markets.

World Sources of Supply

Gold supplies are derived from three basic sources: (1) newly mined production, (2) scrap recovery operations including melted jewelry, and (3) disposal of either private hoards or government stocks. Mine production occurs in over 50 different countries. However, almost 90% of the world's gold production takes place in only 4 countries: South Africa, the Soviet Union, the United States and Canada.

From this grouping, South Africa emerges as the true giant of gold producers. South Africa accounts for about 65% of total world gold supplies despite a downturn in output over the past few years. The Soviet Union ranks second, producing about 17%, while Canada and the United States now account for 5% and 3%, respectively.

South Africa has dominated the gold production scene since the early 1900's. It has been suggested that perhaps 25% of all the gold that exists today came from South Africa. This position was attained because of several reasons. Firstly, the most abundant

gold-bearing ore is found in South Africa. Secondly, an availability of inexpensive labor has permitted large scale mining, even when gold prices were at low levels, whereas other producers were required to curtail output as working force and machinery costs increased. This advantage appears to have diminished somewhat in recent years. Finally, both the Government and banking community of South Africa have extended considerable financial support to the gold mining industry. For example, most South African gold mines are partially owned by mining finance houses. These are major investment banking firms that have access to the capital necessary for financing current operations or new workings. South African gold is sold to and marketed by the South African Reserve Bank.

South Africa has been the world's principal gold producer for about 70 years. However, the big leap in South African gold production was recorded during the twelve-year period between 1953 through 1965. Output almost tripled, rising from 11.9 million ounces in 1953 to 30.5 million ounces in 1965. This was influenced by the opening of several large mines in the Evander area. Thereafter, production growth slowed and, following a peak level of 32.2 million ounces recorded in 1970, output has trended lower. The 1974 estimated annual total of 25 million ounces represents a 22% drop from peak levels of 4 years ago. Labor problems, a shortage of skilled technicians, and occasional operational difficulties at some mines, have contributed to the lower outturn. In addition, the higher gold prices have encouraged the transfer of men and equipment to mining poorer quality ore that can now be recovered profitably.

Gold Mining in the United States

The United States was the world's leading gold producer throughout the entire second half of the 19th century. This leadership came about because of an event that occurred on a seemingly uneventful day in 1848, when a carpenter named James Marshall found specks of gold at John Sutter's mill in California. This find initiated the famous California gold rush. It proved to be one of the great gold discoveries of all time, second only to the South African discoveries of 1886.

Gold mining in the United States occurred well before the California discoveries. Mining operations can be traced back to the 1700's, when Spanish explorers mined gold in Arizona. Surprisingly, the first major gold discovery occurred in the East in the mountains of North Carolina in 1799. This state remained our principal gold producer for about 50 years, until the California discovery. United States gold coins, mintmarked "C" (Charlotte, North Carolina Mint) now are extremely rare objects. Today, a fair amount of gold still can be found in the Southern Appalachian area, although recovery costs are substantial.

Domestic gold production has fallen to less than a third of the amount yielded 35 years ago. Rising costs, the depletion of the higher quality gold bearing ore, and until recently, low gold prices were the principal reasons for the declining rate of output. Today, the bulk of domestic gold production is situated in a few Western states. South Dakota, Utah, and Nevada were the three largest gold-producing states last year, and they accounted for about 80% of total domestic outturn. The Homestake Mine in South Dakota is the largest domestic gold producer. This mine accounts for about 30% of total U.S. gold production. Meanwhile, California, the scene of last century's famous gold rush, now supplies only small quantities of gold.

About 30% of domestic gold mine production is recovered as a by-product of non-ferrous metals mining. This accounts for the fact that Kennecott Copper Co., the nation's largest copper producer, ranks second in the production of gold.

Mining Techniques

Gold has been mined for 6,000 years, and may well have been the first metal known to man. It occurs in nature in the form of nuggets or flakes. Early mining techniques were very simple. Miners used sheepskins and pans to capture deposits flowing in streams or rivers. On land, the pick and shovel was the principal method for digging gold ore from the ground. Today, methods of gold mining have become more complex. The particular approach now utilized is based upon such geological factors as the size and shape of the deposit, characteristics of the ore and surrounding rocks and depth of the deposit. Placer mining techniques are typically used for surface or near-surface deposits. This operation generally requires large quantities of water. Gold-bearing gravel is recovered by means of bucket line dredging. The gravel is then delivered to a washing plant for recovery of the gold. The ore, which at that point has been finely divided and suspended in water, is then passed over a surface of mercury to form an amalgam. The amalgam is subjected to a fire-refining process to separate the gold portion from the mercury alloy, or amalgam. Most of the gold recovered in California and Alaska utilizes placer mining techniques.

Lode or vein gold deposits are mined by first constructing deep shafts. When removed, the gold-containing ore is subjected to several steps during which rocks and other impurities are taken out. This operation includes the cyanidation process, which extracts gold in the form of a cyanide slime from the ore by treatment with a solution of potassium cyanide or sodium cyanide. Following some additional treatment, gold is finally smelted and then cast into bars.

Open pit mining is similar to the previous approach; the basic difference is that this method does not involve digging an extensive complex of tunnels or shafts, but instead uses an excavation process whereby ore is scooped up with large steam shovels, bulldozers, and other heavy construction equipment. By-product gold, i.e., gold recovered during the mining of copper and other non-ferrous metals can be obtained by either open pit or lode mining techniques. A major consideration here is that gold is not sought for its own sake, but instead, is considered an added benefit from base metal mining.

Gold is widely distributed in the natural state, but usually in very small quantities relative to the surrounding ore; a fair grade ore contains about **three** tenths of an ounce of gold per ton of ore. At any rate, areas where gold is found in sufficient quantities to warrant mining operations are limited. The richest and most abundant mines are located in South Africa. Yet, South African mines produce an average of only one half ounce of gold per ton of ore. Even their Free State Geduld, the world's richest gold mine, produces only slightly more than one ounce of gold per ton of ore.

World Production Trends

The trend of cumulative world gold production during the 20th century has been diverse. There have been periods of rapid gains in output, other times when production has fallen sharply, and years of stagnation. The most rapid growth occurred during the late stages of the 1930's depression years. This seemingly unusual phenomenon was not because of the business climate, but rather, a change in price. The official price of gold was raised sharply in 1934, when the U.S. dollar was devalued and gold officially changed from $20.63 to $35 an ounce. In response, annual world gold production rose from about 28 million ounces in 1934 to about 41 million ounces six years later. All major gold-producing nations posted significant increases during this period. The production gains recorded during the 1930's were retraced almost fully during World War II. Thereafter, the higher production costs evidenced during the postwar period slowed mining growth rates. The record output of 41 million ounces recorded in 1940 was not topped until 1962, more than twenty years later.

From the mid-1960's through year 1973, mine production tended to stagnate and then turn lower. This episode was caused by rising costs, the diminishing quality of ore in many regions, and, until recently, relatively low gold prices. From 1934 through early 1968, the price of gold remained at the $35 level, while mining costs rose sharply. The past few years have witnessed sharply higher gold prices. However, significant production gains might not be realized until the late 1970's because of the relatively long time period required to initiate new mines or to rehabilitate abandoned workings. Moreover, South Africa, the world's largest producer, apparently has not yet made major efforts towards expanding output. The United States, Canada, and the Soviet Union plan to step up gold production. Some observers suggest that Soviet production may have risen sharply during the past year or so. However, it must be remembered that Soviet gold is not sold on a regular basis. The Russians appear to be market-minded and conduct sales accordingly. Thus, increased production does not necessarily mean increased sales.

World Gold Resources

The level of gold production in the years ahead will depend upon many factors, including price level and South Africa's intentions. However, ample supplies of gold clearly can be made available. This assumes that the relatively high free market price levels in evidence during the middle seventies are generally maintained or that the essentially defunct official price is re-introduced well above the current $42.22/oz. level. Of course, if gold prices decline, mine output will not cease. The main point is simply that as gold prices advance, the amount of potentially mineable gold increases and vice versa.

A study of potential world gold resources conducted several years ago by the U.S. Government indicated the existence of substantial amounts of potentially mineable gold, although much of this ore requires relatively high gold prices before recovery is economically feasible. The survey indicated that U.S. resources mineable at a gold price of $145/ounce or less ($190/ounce or less at 1974 costs) approximated 237 million ounces. An additional 60 million ounces was estimated to be recoverable as a by-product of non-ferrous metal ores. In this instance, gold price level would not be a factor. The accompanying table depicts approximate domestic gold resources. Alaska has the largest quantity of potentially mineable gold, while California ranks second. However, the ore in both states is of low grade, and high prices are required before it can be mined profitably. In fact, only Nevada and South Dakota have what might be described as significant quantities of gold that can be recovered at low prices, or prices under $100/ounce.

Major U.S. Gold Resources
(In Thousand Troy Ounces)

State	Gold Potentially Producible at $35 Per Ounce or Less	Gold Potentially Producible at $35 to $145 Per Ounce*	Total Potentially Producible Gold Up to $145 Per Ounce*
Alaska	28	54,975	55,003
Arizona	3	4,658	4,661
California	35	41,394	41,429
Colorado	8	19,572	19,580
Idaho	3	11,501	11,504
Montana	3	22,166	22,169
Nevada	15,530	23,107	38,637
New Mexico	—	3,358	3,358
Oregon	—	6,923	6,923
South Dakota	5,400	10,466	15,866
Washington	868	12,801	13,669
Wyoming	—	1,566	1,566
Total United States	21,878	215,608	237,486

* The upper price level in 1974 dollars is approximately $190. *Source: U.S. Bureau of Mines.*

The quantity of gold potentially mineable at relatively high prices outside the United States is estimated at better than 900 million ounces. Most of this metal is located within the boundaries of a few countries including: South Africa, the Soviet Union, Canada, Australia, Colombia, and Rhodesia. Combined with U.S. totals, world resources approximate 1.2 billion ounces. However, this amount pales when compared with the quantities of gold contained in the oceans. Some studies suggest that perhaps 600 billion ounces of gold are estimated to be in the ocean waters of the earth. The major problem is that with current technology, only small quantities can be recovered, and the costs are substantial.

Scrap Recovery Operations Have Become an Important Supply Source

Because gold is practically indestructible, scrap recovery has become an important source of supply. Currently, about 25% of total gold supplies are derived from reclaiming operations.

There are two main classifications of gold scrap: high grade or "karat" scrap and low grade scrap. The former contains a high percentage of gold content relative to other components of the particular object. Sources of this type of scrap include discarded jewelry, rolled gold plate, brazing alloys, electronic contacts, dental alloys, gold grindings and gold fillings. Low grade gold scrap is measured by the ounces of gold per ton of metal. This type includes: gold brazed base metal components, plated jewelry, optical scrap and gold polishings or sweepings. Payment for scrap is usually based upon a 100% allowance for gold content, less a refining charge which depends largely upon the incoming weight and composition of the material.

In the United States, precious metal reclaiming operations have become a rapidly growing industry in recent years. In fact, domestic scrap production of gold has exceeded mine output since the mid-1960's.

Private Hoards and Central Bank Holdings

For most metals, mine production and scrap recovery usually comprise the bulk of available supplies. However, these two areas represent only a fraction of the total gold supply picture. The vast majority of gold supplies are found in the hoards of private citizens and in the vaults of Central Banks. There are no exact figures on the total amount of gold held throughout the world, although some estimates put holdings above the 3.5 billion ounce level. Theoretically, this is enough metal to fill all industrial needs for the next 100 years or longer.

On first consideration, the amount of gold stocks relative to annual usage rates suggests "the largest oversupply of any commodity since the dawn of time." Yet the existence of gold, and its availability, remain quite distinct. This potentially huge overhang failed to deter the booming prices in evidence during the past few years. The principal reason for this apparent inconsistency is simply that those holding gold are reluctant to part with it.

The United States was once the largest single holder of gold. Domestic gold stocks totaled a peak level of approximately 700 million ounces in 1949. Today, U.S. gold holdings are around the 276 million ounce level. They have held steady from August, 1971, when all dollar redemptions in gold were terminated until the recent sale of 750,000 ounces of Treasury gold from the 2 million ounce GSA offering. Gold held by non-government sources worldwide, including bars, coins, jewelry and so forth, is estimated at 2.5 billion ounces.

Europe's greatest gold hoarders are the French. It appears that the better than a dozen devaluations since 1915 have fostered a strong attraction for this metal. It has been estimated that the people of France hold 100 to 150 million ounces of gold. The upper estimate is equivalent to about four years of total world production. The wealthy citizens of oil-rich Mid-East nations are also believed to hold large amounts of gold, although no estimates of their holdings are available. Some observers have attributed part of the gold price gains scored in 1973–74 to buying encouraged by the belief that a percentage of the increased revenue received by Arab nations following sharp crude oil price increases would be put into gold.

Central Banks' gold stocks total about 1.2 billion ounces, according to data from the IMF. These holdings are perhaps the single greatest source of potential supplies. Most of this gold was acquired at $35/ounce or well below the seventies' free market prices. This suggests a possible growing temptation to take profits by selling part of their holdings. In fact, rumors of possible Central Bank gold sales have, on more than one occasion, exerted a negative impact upon gold prices. With the exception of the U.S. Treasury sale in January 1975, no Central Bank has openly sold large quantities of gold on the free market, although they are now permitted to do so.

1974 Official Gold Holdings*
(In Million Troy Ounces)

United States	275.9
West Germany	117.4
France	100.9
Switzerland	83.2
Italy	82.5
Holland	54.2
Belgium	42.2
Latin America	30.2
Middle East	28.3
Canada	21.9
Britain	21.3
Japan	21.1
South Africa	18.9
Other Europe	81.0
Other Asia	18.4
Other Africa	11.5
Rest of World	14.2
International Organizations	160.2
	1,183.3

* Does not include Soviet holdings or metal owned by private citizens throughout the world. Totals as of end June 1974.

Sources of Demand

The demand for gold can be broken down into three distinct categories: (1) the acquisition of gold because of its long-proven ability to retain value and/or appreciate in value; (2) the purchase of gold solely for industrial purposes; (3) purchases by the Central Banks. Industrial applications take advantage of gold's many unique properties. They include: high resistance to corrosion, malleability, ductility, electrical conductivity and the ability to adhere firmly to other metals. In fact, gold is the most malleable and ductile metal known. It can be hammered into sheets less than five one millionths of an inch thick; a single ounce of gold can be drawn into a wire 35 miles long, or used to plate a thread of copper wire a thousand miles long. Gold is such a superb reflector of heat that a thin film only millionths of an inch thick can protect delicate rocket instruments from the heat of their engines. A microscopic circuit of liquid gold printed on a strip of plastic can replace miles of wiring in a computer. Meanwhile, unlike silver, gold does not tarnish and is not corroded by most acids.

The Use of Gold in Jewelry

Despite these many unique properties, its principal area of industrial use—jewelry—takes advantage of only a few of them. Jewelry has long been the largest single source of industrial demand, presently account-

ing for an estimated 60% to 70% of total industrial usage. Of course, the very fact that jewelry is even considered an area of industrial demand is debatable; some might argue that jewelry purchases, especially in underdeveloped nations, are a source of hoarding. In any event, the jewelry industry consumed an estimated 20 to 25 million ounces of gold last year.

The term "karat" is associated with jewelry. This refers to the percentage of gold in a particular item. Twenty-four karats is pure gold, while 12 karats would be approximately half gold and half other substances.

Electrical and Electronic Industries Spark Industrial Demand

The percentage of gold used in jewelry applications relative to all others has slipped somewhat in recent years. This was prompted by the dawn of the electronic age and its many new discoveries utilizing gold. In fact, electrical and electronic applications now rank second among the various areas of gold usage accounting for about 25% of total industrialized demands.

The major area of gold usage in electric and electronic applications is in separable conductors and sockets. These devices are used to provide various types of electrical connections; for example, from circuit to circuit, from component to circuit or from sub-system to sub-system such as a magnetic tape unit to a digital computer. The basic reason for using gold as opposed to copper or some other lower-priced substitute is that most electronic equipment utilizes very low energy levels. Thus, it is essential that the already weak electrical flows be unimpaired by high resistance materials. Another reason for the extensive use of gold in semiconductors is this metal's ease of fusion bonding, solderability and, of course, its ability to withstand high processing temperatures. The recent trend towards a reduction in the average quantity of gold used per semiconductor has resulted from more efficient use by plating other less expensive metals with thin layers of gold.

Gold is also used for numerous other electronic applications, and is found in such devices as telephone set microphones, parts for specialty capacitors, slip rings, specialty component terminals. These and other miscellaneous applications are for specialty components associated with defense and space electronics. In addition, gold possesses excellent aging characteristics and components will retain their reliability over an extensive period of time, whether in use or storage. Gold consumed for dental equipment accounts for about 10% of industrial demand. Miscellaneous uses include the manufacture of certain types of glassware, gold powders and a colloidal suspension of radioactive gold for treatment of certain types of cancers.

The Hoarding Influence

At times, the strongest demand for gold is neither jewelry, electronics nor any other similar area, but rather purchases by private citizens. This source of demand, though immeasurable and subject to sudden and abrupt change, is capable of absorbing huge volumes of gold under certain conditions.

The basic motive underlying private demand for gold is fear. Gold, unlike currencies or some other commodities, has been able to retain value during both normal times and crisis periods. In fact, the instinct of millions of Europeans and countless other citizens of nations that permit private gold ownership is to reach for gold whenever a crisis appears to be unfolding. Until a few years ago, purchases made by a private citizen were a limited risk affair, since gold was both bought and sold at $35/ounce. Today, a different situation has unfolded. Gold is essentially a free commodity and can theoretically sell at whatever value supply/demand conditions warrant. Price, although trending higher, is no longer a one-way street. In fact, the period from mid-1973 to near year's end witnessed a fairly substantial overall drop in gold prices from better than $125/ounce to about $90/ounce, or more than 25% loss in value. The subsequent emerging of a serious world-wide economic crisis prompted a full retracing of these losses and movement to new highs. However, it did not change one obvious fact: gold prices are vulnerable under certain conditions. Whether or not this emerging condition dampens private demand for this metal cannot be determined at this time.

Gold and Inflation

During the past few years, the rate of inflation has accelerated rapidly. There has been an intense search for investment vehicles that retain or appreciate in value despite inflation. The price of gold has appreciated significantly during 1973 and 1974, while this same time span witnessed a considerable erosion in the purchasing power of many currencies. This action has contributed to a growing popular view that gold is a source of protection against inflation, i.e., an inflation hedge. However, recent price action suggests that gold prices do not correlate well with inflation rates, at least over the short run. The rate of inflation of all nations has moved steadily upward, while the price of gold has fluctuated over a broad range.

This sometimes divergent trend between inflation and gold prices leads to certain observations:

1. Gold apparently is not necessarily an inflation hedge over the short run, i.e., approximately one year or so. Instead, prices tend to fluctuate in response to a variety of considerations. This is not to say that inflation or expectations of inflation cannot influence gold market action over the near term. Gold prices react to numerous fundamental, psychological, and technical influences. A given instance might find price action influenced mostly by inflation fears. However, other factors have already demonstrated the ability to blunt momentarily what could appear the logical price direction if inflation were the sole gold market price criteria.

2. Gold might prove to be an inflation hedge over the long run. This particular view is supported by the sharply higher on balance price gains scored by gold during 1973 and 1974, when inflation became a paramount issue. However, this ability has not been fully proven yet because of the greater price appreciation scored by certain other commodities and a few currencies. Of course, one could argue that these price gains were in response to a temporary situation specific to that commodity or currency, which might be corrected at a later date, rather than to a reaction to inflation. If this proves correct, we could assume that, even though certain other investments out-performed gold in price appreciation, they are not neces-

sarily better inflation hedges. However, a viable study comparing gold versus other commodities and currencies would have to cover many years or even decades. The relatively short period of freely fluctuating gold prices (less than seven years) tends to limit the scope of such comparisons.

Gold and Deflation

There has been considerable discussion about the impact of a deflationary environment on the price of gold. Some observers point out that the price of gold rose substantially during the depression of the 1930's. This increase in the price of gold should be examined closely, however. Gold prices advanced during the 1930's primarily because of actions of the U.S. Government. From September 8, 1933, to January 16, 1934, the U.S. Reconstruction Finance Corporation announced frequent upward revisions in the price it would pay for all domestically mined gold. This action was taken because of the belief that higher gold prices would boost other commodity prices. Second, under the terms of the 1934 dollar devaluation, gold was pegged to the dollar at a 35 to 1 ratio, i.e. the official price of gold was established at $35 an ounce versus the previous official price of $20.63 an ounce. This action also required the U.S. Government to purchase all gold at $35 an ounce, effectively placing a floor on price substantially above the previous official price.

Deflation occurs when demand for goods and services is declining. Under these circumstances, the purchasing power of currencies increases and prices for many commodities decline. One might assume that the price of gold might also decline in a deflationary environment, since private holdings of gold might be reduced to pay for life's necessities. In addition, industrial firms holding gold might be forced to liquidate part of their inventories in order to raise needed working capital. These assumptions ignore, however, possible changes in the monetary role for gold, if any, and actions by the world's monetary authorities to boost the international monetary reserves. If taken, they could blunt the logical price impact of deflation on gold values. In addition, the apparent popular view of gold as an "insurance of last resort" suggests that the metal might perform better than most investments during serious deflation.

The sharply lower silver prices recorded in the 1930's also support the view that deflation could result in somewhat lower gold values. Indeed, the price of free market silver fell from a peak level of nearly $1.50/ounce in the 1920's to an all-time recorded low of about 24¢ in 1933, or about 1/6 of pre-depression levels.

The discussion on gold and deflation is highly conjectural. A prolonged deflationary period appears unlikely. What seems more likely is a recessionary period followed by an economic recovery. However, at this juncture, early in 1975, the extent of an expected economic slowdown, as well as its duration, is subject to considerable debate because of the apparent significant economic impact of one key but partially uncontrollable factor—crude oil prices.

Gold's Monetary Role

The connection between gold and money traces its beginnings several thousand years ago. Gold was used for money as early as 1900 B.C., while use of gold coins can be traced back to 550 B.C. King Croesus of Lydia, a short-lived kingdom in Asia Minor, was credited with minting the first coins of pure gold. Gold coins and bullion remained a medium of exchange for thousands of years. The introduction of paper currency in the 17th and 18th centuries was nothing more than a more sophisticated use of gold in a monetary sense. That is, gold was the backing for paper currency, which possessed value only because it could be redeemed for a certain quantity of gold. Under the now-defunct Gold Standard, used by many industrial nations during the 1800's through 1930's, governments issued paper money which was backed by and fully exchangeable for gold.

The Gold Standard

The gold standard was a monetary system developed during the 18th century. The ground rules involved a fixed price for gold, with paper currencies expressed in terms of and redeemable in gold. England is credited with becoming the first nation to adopt an official gold standard in 1816. Actually an unofficial gold standard had existed since 1717, when Sir Isaac Newton, acting as Master of the Mint, established a fixed price for gold. By the 1870's, most European countries were on some form of the gold standard. The United States was legally on a bimetallic standard (silver and gold) at a ratio of 15 to 1 from 1792 to 1834, and 16 to 1 from 1834 to 1900. However, for all practical purposes, this was a de facto gold standard. The real price of silver was well below its official price throughout much of this time period. The Gold Standard Act of 1900 put the U.S. on an official gold standard.

An attractive feature of the gold standard was that the paper currency of participating nations was readily acceptable both domestically and abroad, since it represented claims against a certain weight of gold. The gold standard played an additional theoretical role: It would serve as an economic disciplinarian, since all balance of payments were supposedly settled in gold rather than in credits. The procedure theoretically worked as follows: A nation with balance-of-payments deficits would incur an outflow of gold. This reduction would leave less gold available domestically. The attendant reduction in money supply then translated into less demand for goods and services and, of course, declining prices. The lower prices would make exports more competitive, and balance of payments would supposedly improve as exports increased. The opposite was also expected to occur. That is, a balance of payments surplus would cause increased gold imports, an increase in money supply, rising prices, and reduced exports.

In theory, the gold standard seemed like the perfect adjustment mechanism. In reality, it proved harsh, since it contributed to exaggerated fluctuations in the business cycle. The 19th century was featured by alternating booms and slumps in economic activity. Consequently, when the gold standard faced its first real test at the outbreak of World War I, it was almost universally suspended. Another problem was that the gold standard required a stable price for gold, since changes therein would cause a revaluation or devaluation of currencies whose par values were expressed in terms of gold.

The Gold Exchange Standard

The period following the end of World War I experienced sharply higher prices for goods and services without a comparable increase in gold supplies needed to expand money supply. This lack of metal made the gold standard essentially unworkable and led to a succeeding monetary system—the gold exchange standard. In later years, it was sometimes called the dollar exchange standard. At any rate, this system initially evolved spontaneously, as Central Banks held in reserve those currencies backed by gold. A meeting of monetary authorities in Genoa, Italy, in 1922 led to the "Genoa Agreement," which created the gold exchange standard. Under this system, Central Banks' reserves could consist of currencies backed by and pegged to gold, in lieu of gold. Balance-of-payment deficits could be settled with either these currencies or gold. This supposedly would economize gold, since a nation could theoretically participate in international trade on a large scale without owning a single ounce, provided they held adequate amounts of currencies backed by gold. The United States supported the Genoa Agreement but remained on the gold standard domestically until 1934.

The gold exchange standard collapsed during the depression of the 1930's. However, it was modified and re-introduced at a monetary conference at Bretton Woods, New Hampshire, in 1944. The "new" gold exchange standard, in principle, was the same as the one developed years earlier. However, it was considerably more specifically delineated. A major development at Bretton Woods was creation of the International Monetary Fund. Through this agency, the currency of each participating nation was tied, either directly or indirectly, to gold. That is, the value of the U.S. dollar was pegged to gold, while other currencies were also pegged to gold or pegged to the dollar. In addition, a specific range of fluctuation around parity for each currency was established before Central Bank intervention was required.

Despite its modification, the revised gold exchange standard still had certain weaknesses. One major problem was the likelihood of speculative attacks against currencies redeemable in gold, especially when doubts arose concerning the ability of a government to retain convertibility into gold. Such doubt was the crux of the dollar problem that was first evidenced when foreign holdings of dollars began to exceed total U.S. government gold stocks at the official value of $35/ounce.

The Gold Pool

In October, 1960, a burst of speculative buying on the belief of a possible change in U.S. gold policy briefly pushed the price on the London gold market to about the $40/ounce level. If maintained at this level or higher, the price change would have represented a de facto devaluation of the dollar and all currencies pegged to the dollar or to gold. In order to preserve monetary stability, U.S. and other Government officials decided to force a return to the $35 price level via sales from official stocks. This plan was implemented with the formation of the Gold Pool. Under that agreement, eight Central Banks proportionately shared the buying and selling of gold in any amount necessary to keep the free market price at $35.

The Gold Pool worked quite well until 1965, since purchases and sales were about equal. Thereafter, the international monetary climate began to change rapidly. Growing currency problems were initiated by serious U.S. and United Kingdom balance-of-payment problems, and worsened considerably when the pound sterling was devalued in 1967. This latter development sparked a huge speculative demand for gold that peaked in March, 1968. The heavy drain on official stocks necessary to meet this buying eventually led to the collapse of the Gold Pool. It was dissolved on March 14, 1968, when the two-tier gold market was established. This action represented the beginning of the end for the gold exchange standard.

The Two-Tier Market

Under the two-tier system, efforts at maintaining a single $35/ounce gold price were largely abandoned. That is, free market transactions were permitted to take place at whatever price supply/demand conditions warranted. Meanwhile, Central Bank transactions were kept at the then official price of $35/ounce. The net result was that foreigners holding dollars could no longer redeem them in gold. Central Banks could, however, turn in their dollar holding for gold if they so desired. This privilege, too, was terminated in August, 1971, when the U.S. closed its gold window to everyone and effectively initiated an era of freely floating exchange rates. Today, no major currency can be redeemed in gold at a pegged price.

The rapid growth of international trade and inadequate gold production led to the development of a supplement for gold in settling balance of payments differences. This new international reserve asset was officially inaugurated in August, 1967, and christened Special Drawing Rights or SDR's. The SDR plan is based upon the need for increased international liquidity by supplementing gold and reserve currencies in international transactions. Member nations of the IMF are allocated SDR's on a quota basis. SDR valuation is now based upon the market value of a "special basket" of sixteen different major currencies.

Gold Marketing

The marketing of gold became more complex following the establishing of the two-tier market in 1968. Until then, domestic producers sold their output to the U.S. government, which in turn supplied industrial users with needed metal. All transactions were at the then-prevailing $35 price. Following the dissolution of the gold pool and establishment of a dual gold price, both users and suppliers were required to use the free market for their gold sales and/or purchases. This resulted in expanded activities on existing gold markets and the development of new gold trading centers.

Currently, there are more than a dozen different centers where a significant amount of gold trading takes place. They are scattered throughout the world including the following places: Accra, Amsterdam, Beruit, Brussels, Dubai, Frankfurt, Geneva, Hong Kong, London, Macao, Manila, Paris, Singapore, Sydney, Toronto, Vienna, Winnipeg and Zurich. In the U.S., dealer markets for users and suppliers only are located in New York and San Francisco, while gold futures are traded in New York, Chicago, and elsewhere.

The London Gold Market

The London Gold Market is considered to be one of the world's major gold exchanges. Trading began on September 12, 1919, and continued until the outbreak of World War II. It reopened in 1954 and with a few brief exceptions has been in operation ever since. Trading is conducted by five member firms who act as Principals: Mocatta and Goldsmid; Sharps, Pixley and Company; N. M. Rothschild and Sons; Johnson Matthey; and Samuel Montagu and Company.

The London Gold Market conducts trading sessions twice daily at 10:30 A.M. and 3:00 P.M. London time on all business days. The prices established are referred to as fixings, while the standard unit of trading is usually a 400-ounce gold bar of .995 fineness. However, members are prepared to deal in smaller quantities. Most transactions are on spot basis and full payment is normally made two days later.

The procedure at each fixing (trading session) is as follows: a representative from each of the five member firms meet at the offices of N. M. Rothschild. They are in direct communication with their trading room, where the real buy or sell decisions are made. The Chairman begins the fixing with a suggested price, which is usually influenced by the previous price plus any fresh developments. At the opening price, each member declares his intention, i.e., either a buyer or seller, or no interest at all. If there is one tendency, such as all buyers or all sellers, another price is tried. This procedure continues until a level is found at which there are both willing buyers and sellers.

At that point, quantity figures are disclosed. If the amount offered does not equal the amount wanted, other prices are tried until the buying and selling quantities are equal. The official fixing is then announced.

Gold transactions that take place at other times than official fixings are normally called unofficial dealings. Indeed, it is possible to purchase gold from a member of the London Gold Market 24 hours a day, at his discretion. The quality of gold traded at the fixing prices can sometimes be compared with a tip of an iceberg. Substantial quantities of gold are sold before, in between, and after, the official fixings.

The Zurich Gold Market

The Zurich Gold Market has rivaled London in recent years. Here, three major banks in Zurich—Swiss Bank Corporation, The Union Bank of Switzerland, and Credit Suisse—operate a pool. They trade from 9:30 A.M. until 12:30 P.M. and from 2:00 P.M. until 4:00 P.M. All business which these three banks handle goes into a pool. Unlike London, the Swiss banks do not compete with each other on price, but on customer service. In recent years, a major portion of South African gold has been sold on the Zurich market.

Gold Futures

The gold price gyrations in evidence since the dual price was established in 1968 have created serious problems for both users and suppliers alike. The gold consumer never really knows what prices he will be paying in the months ahead. At the same time, a producer who introduces new workings at a given gold price level can never really be sure that gold values will be at these levels when the metal is available for sale. This situation led to the formation of gold futures markets.

The Winnipeg Commodity Exchange of Canada began trading in gold futures in November, 1972. This event was somewhat of a milestone, since it represented the only real international gold futures market in operation, until the recent inauguration of domestic gold futures trading that accompanied the lifting of the 41-year-old gold ban.

Currently, early in 1975, gold futures are traded on several major domestic commodity exchanges including: The New York Commodity Exchange, The New York Mercantile Exchange, the Chicago Board of Trade, and the International Monetary Market of Chicago.

The New York Mercantile Exchange conducts futures trading in a one kilogram contract (32.15 troy ounces). The others mentioned trade contracts approximating either 100 troy ounces (The New York Commodity Exchange and The International Monetary Market); or three kilograms—Chicago Board of Trade. The mechanics of gold futures trading will be similar to the basic procedures evidenced on all domestic commodity exchanges. That is, trading is conducted during market hours by the members of the exchange in a specified area sometimes referred to as a trading ring or pit. Various delivery months are traded, usually up to a year forward or longer. However, in order to assure greater liquidity, not every calendar month is traded on any one exchange. Prices are determined by open outcry, and the procedure is not too unlike trading on The New York Stock Exchange. Additional information on trading techniques as well as a more detailed breakdown of contract specifications can usually be obtained from either the respective exchanges or their member firms.

What Are Gold Futures?

The term "futures" or "futures contracts" refers to the unit of trading on commodity exchanges. By definition, futures are a written agreement to deliver or receive a given quantity of a particular commodity during a certain time or time period. Specific contract characteristics such as deliverable grade, contract size, delivery points, etc. are contained in the by-laws of the exchange which trades the particular commodity. A buyer of futures, then, agrees to receive the amount stated in the contract when it matures. A seller, on the other hand, agrees to deliver the amount stated during maturity. This course of events assumes that the buyer or seller actually chooses to make or take delivery. Such action is not required if the position is closed out before maturity via an offsetting transaction. That is, a buyer of a futures contract can eliminate delivery obligations by selling that same month anytime before the delivery period and vice versa. Liquidation via offset is the usual manner of completing transactions in the market; futures are essentially a pricing medium rather than an area of acquisition or disposal of product. About 98% of the time, contracts are liquidated without taking delivery.

Hedging Is the Main Purpose of Gold Futures

The principal role of gold futures lies in providing a mechanism for forward pricing. This permits both a user, or one who supplies this metal, to confront more realistically the problems caused by sharp price changes. The use of futures to forward price is referred to as hedging. Basically, it involves the assumption of a futures market position opposite to that held or anticipated to be held in "actuals." For example, a consumer needing gold requires a certain amount of metal over a given time period. In this instance, hedging could involve the purchase of futures contracts equivalent to all or part of expected needs over a certain period of time up to about 18 months ahead. This action establishes a price for his gold requirements and thus protects the user from the adverse impact of rising prices. A gold supplier could hedge, i.e., protect the value of his production, by selling futures against part or all of anticipated production over a given period, or against his inventories. This would protect the supplier from the adverse impact of falling prices. In both instances, the use of futures enables the hedger to determine selling or buying prices well in advance of the current date.

Gold futures are not limited to members of the trade. Private citizens can and indeed have traded gold futures daily since legalization. Their reasons are, of course, different from members of the gold consuming or supplying industry. Monetary and economic uncertainty has caused increased interest in precious metals, especially gold. Consequently, some investors and speculators prefer to have a percentage of their assets in gold or some other precious metal. Many favor futures rather than actuals because of the ease of entry and exit, as well as the leverage factor. At the time of this writing, futures can be purchased on margin, approximating about 10% of the value of the metal.

Conclusion

Gold has and probably will continue to remain unique among metals. This characteristic includes not only its monetary ties and various specialized applications but also extends to price and those factors that influence price. For most commodities, the level of production, rates of industrial usage and prevailing stocks levels are the major components of price; gold appears to be the exception to this observation. An evaluation of gold market action since 1968, when non-Central Bank transactions were permitted to seek their own price level, indicates a different situation.

It seems that the basic supply/demand factors cited do not usually affect price moves over the short run. Instead, psychology and emotion, with particular emphasis on inflation and diminishing purchasing power of currencies, seem to be the ruling near term factors. That is, those numerous outside events which encourage the purchase or sale of gold by speculators and hoarders are often the principal reason underlying gold price changes. For example, a sudden economic or political crisis almost invariably results in higher gold prices, while improved conditions tend to put downward pressure on gold values. In recent years, the periods of crisis and doubts about currencies have apparently outweighed calmer conditions, with the resultant higher overall gold prices.

In the long run, those fundamentals more directly connected with the basic picture (production, industrial usage, etc.) could prove to also hold much price significance. However, the relatively short period of freely fluctuating gold prices (seven years) and the even shorter period of high gold prices (two years) tends to limit the scope of long term fundamental price studies. Thus, market observers seeking to formulate price studies will probably have to place significant emphasis on the many events that influence the overall economic and political climate worldwide.

Those willing to meet the challenge of attempting to formulate a price outlook with limited data must also consider two possible additional components to the gold price picture. The first involves an uncertain demand picture now that the ban on U.S. citizen gold ownership has been lifted. The second must focus on the very real possiblity of additional sales of gold from either U.S. or foreign government holdings. Both hold tremendous price significance and, if nothing else, these possible developments make the outlook for gold quite exciting.

Daily United States Futures Delivery

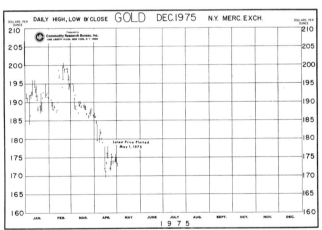

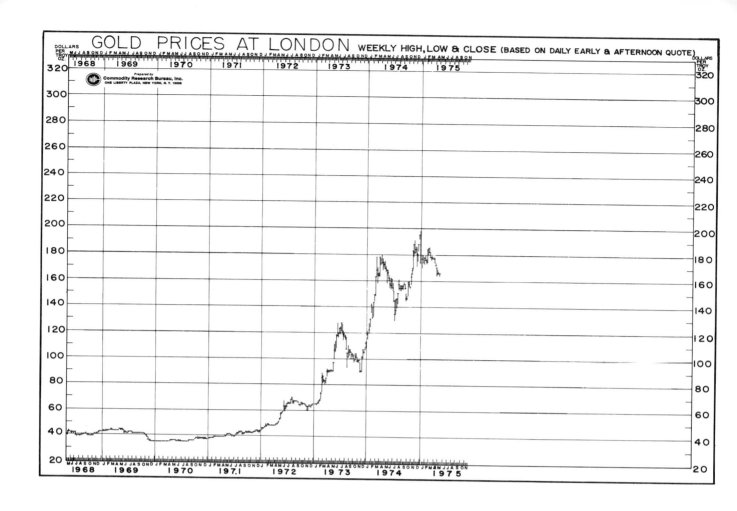

GOLD PRICES AT LONDON WEEKLY HIGH, LOW & CLOSE (BASED ON DAILY EARLY & AFTERNOON QUOTE)

Prepared by
Commodity Research Bureau, Inc.
ONE LIBERTY PLAZA, NEW YORK, N.Y. 10006

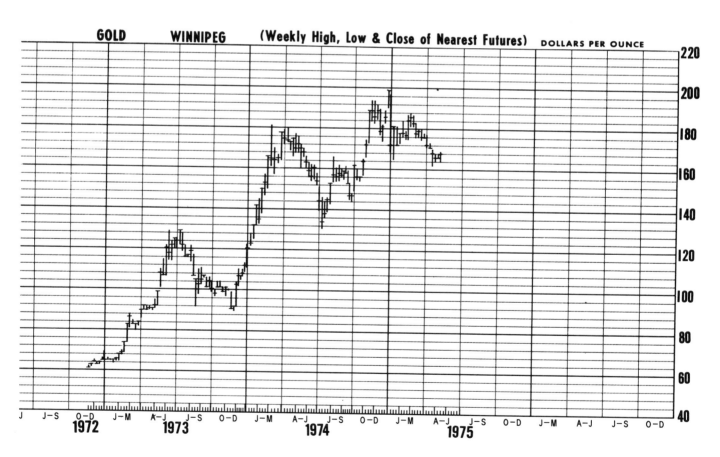

GOLD   WINNIPEG   (Weekly High, Low & Close of Nearest Futures)   DOLLARS PER OUNCE

Daily London Spot Gold 1970 to 1975

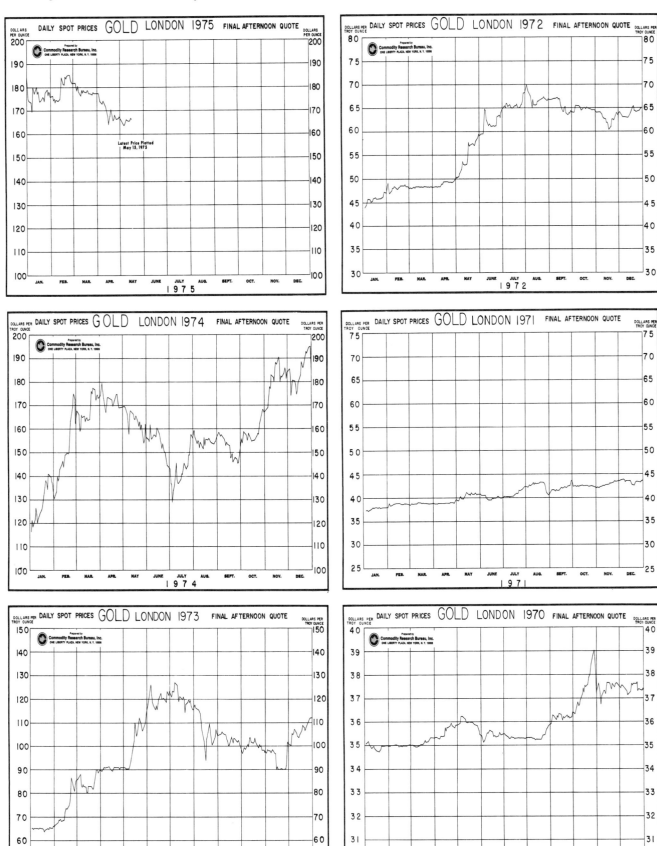

FORECASTING HOG FUTURES PRICES

BY FRANK LESSITER

In any discussion of hog futures contracts, confusion can exist for the inexperienced trader since there are three contracts for various parts of the hog.

The live hog futures contract refers to trading the entire hog on a live basis. Two separate live hog contracts are traded on both the Chicago Mercantile Exchange and the MidAmerica Commodity Exchange.

The pork belly contract deals only with the meat and fat coming from the underside of the hog. When cured and smoked, it becomes bacon. This contract is traded on the Chicago Mercantile Exchange.

Finally, there is the ham futures contract which deals with meat coming from the rear of the hog. While fairly inactive at this point, this contract is traded on the Chicago Mercantile Exchange.

The live hog futures contracts are among the newest futures contracts for livestock. The contracts started on February 28, 1966 at the Chicago Mercantile Exchange and on June 3, 1974 at the Mid-America Commodity Exchange.

While the MidAmerica live hog futures contract traded 34,352 contracts during its seven months of existence in 1974, most of the live hog trading takes place on the Chicago Mercantile Exchange. After three slow years with less than 10,000 contracts traded, the Chicago Mercantile Exchange live hog contract started to catch fire.

Some 262,358 contracts were traded in 1971. This increased to 542,599 contracts in 1972; 1,061,440 contracts in 1973 and 1,083,512 contracts in 1974. It now ranks ahead of the pork belly futures contract since only 735,246 pork belly contracts were traded in 1974.

The Changing Scene in the Hog Industry

Changes are coming fast in the hog business. Since 1950, the number of hog producers in the United States has dropped by more than 50 percent. At the same time, hog production has increased by more than 25 percent.

Specialization has been the cause. Today's hog producer is a better manager and accepts new ideas faster than ever before. This includes the use of live hog futures as a hedging tool for price protection.

A "top doing" hog today should gain about 2.4 pounds per day. It should take about 225 pounds of feed to put on 100 pounds of gain. The carcass from this hog should be 32.5 inches long, there should be about .85 inches backfat, an 8.1 square inch loin eye and 17.8 percent ham. The hog should be about 180 days of age when he reaches a slaughter weight of 220 pounds.

The live hog futures contract has given the swine producer a new marketing tool. No longer must he take whatever price is offered by a packer on the day his animals are marketed. He can now utilize the option of setting his selling price months in advance of his actual marketing date. Using the live hog futures contract enables him to share the risk of changing hog prices by hedging his hog production.

To hedge, a hog producer sells futures to cover the hogs in his feedlot. This establishes a known selling price. At market time, he buys back the contract, or in rare instances delivers the hogs.

But hedging does not guarantee the hog producer a profit. His profit depends on placing the hedge at a price that exceeds all of his costs. So he must know his costs accurately to make a safe hedge.

Before we go any further, we should define several of the more common hog terms:

A barrow is a castrated male hog. Barrows give more valuable pork and gain more efficiently than do boars. Besides, pork from boars gives off an undesirable male odor. A barrow is the equal of a steer in beef cattle or a wether in the sheep business.

Farrowing is a sow or gilt giving birth. The offspring are called a litter. Estimated average litter size was 7.09 pigs in the United States during 1974, although it can range from 5 to 15 pigs. This pigs per litter average was the lowest in a number of years.

Gilts are female hogs that have not yet given birth to a litter of pigs; either young females who have not yet reached puberty or bred gilts waiting to farrow.

Sows are female swine which have given birth to a litter of pigs. They would likely be rebred for another farrowing to come an average of 112 days following breeding.

Boars are male hogs used for breeding purposes. A boar castrated after sexual maturity is a stag.

The Hog Futures Contract

Trading in live hog futures on the Chicago Mercantile Exchange is for the delivery months of February, April, June, July, August, October and December. Each contract calls for 30,000 pounds of live hogs, the equivalent of 130 to 150 hogs marketed in the usual weight range of 200 pounds to 230 pounds. At least 90 hogs in each delivery unit must fall within the 200 to 230 pound weight range. No hogs under 190 pounds or over 240 pounds are deliverable.

The futures contract calls for live hogs falling into the United States Department of Agriculture (USDA) grades of No. 1, No. 2, No. 3 and No. 4 hogs. These can be either barrows or gilts.

Changes in delivery points were made in 1970 on the live hogs futures contract. This change was necessary as the Chicago Stock Yards quit handling hogs (and it went out of business entirely in 1971). Deliveries are made at Peoria, Illinois. For an allowance of 25¢ per hundredweight, deliveries can also be made from approved livestock yards in Omaha, Nebraska, East St. Louis, Illinois, Sioux City, Iowa, or St. Paul, Minnesota. Deliveries can be made at Kansas City, Missouri for an allowance of 50¢ per cwt. (That 25¢ allowance would amount to $75 per contract. The 50¢ allowance equals $150 for each 30,000 pound contract.)

Discounts are also given for too many No. 3 and No. 4 hogs in a deliverable load. Grading and delivery regulations are supervised by USDA Consumer Marketing Service Livestock Division graders.

Differences between various hog grades depend on the amount of lean meat, backfat and degree of muscling. For example, a U.S. No. 1 hog might have 1.4 inches of fat on its back, a carcass measuring 30 inches long and be thick muscled at a hot carcass weight of 165 pounds. By comparison, a U.S. No. 4 hog at the same 165 pound hot carcass weight could have 2 inches of backfat, be 30 inches long and show only slightly thin muscling.

A second live hog futures contract was started during the summer of 1974 on Chicago's MidAmerica Commodity Exchange. The main difference between this contract and the live hog contract at the Chicago Mercantile Exchange is the number of pounds in the trading unit. While the Chicago Mercantile Exchange contract is for 30,000 pounds or about 150 hogs, the MidAmerica Commodity Exchange contract is for 15,000 pounds or only about 75 hogs.

As open interest in the new contract develops, it may prove valuable for hedging by smaller hog producers and meat firms.

Delivery months for the MidAmerica Commodity Exchange contract are February, April, June, July, August, October and December.

The minimum price fluctuation for this contract is .02½¢ per pound. While there is a 1½¢ per pound daily price movement limit on the contract, it has a unique feature since these limits do not apply to bona-fide hedging positions.

The contract is based on USDA hog grades No. 1, No. 2, No. 3, and No. 4. Discounts are based on both grade and weight. Hogs must weigh between 190 and 240 pounds. Discounts are made for hogs weighing under 200 pounds and over 230 pounds. Inspection of the livestock is done by the Livestock Division of USDA.

Live hog deliveries against the MidAmerica hog futures contract can be made without any discount at stockyards in Peoria. Hogs are discounted 25¢ per 100 pounds when delivered at Omaha, East St. Louis, Sioux City or St. Paul. The discount for delivery at Kansas City or St. Joseph is 50¢ per 100 pounds.

Prices for hogs are the most variable of all livestock prices. Hogs go to slaughter within a narrow weight and age span. So the hog man does not have the feeding and marketing flexibility that the cattleman enjoys.

Factors that Influence Price Trends

Prices and price trends for both live hogs and pork products are generally determined by two basic factors, the number of hogs raised on farms and the consumer demand for pork and pork products.

Production of live hogs is concentrated primarily in the Corn Belt area. The four states of Iowa, Illinois, Indiana and Missouri accounted for 51 percent of the total United States hog production late in 1974. The 14 Corn Belt states featured in the quarterly Hogs and Pigs Report from USDA accounted for 85½ percent of the total United States hog production during 1974.

Yet other states outside the Corn Belt have greatly increased their production of hogs in recent years. With more specialization in hog production, other areas are likely to produce an even larger share of the hogs in the future.

The number of hogs moving to market at any given time is dependent upon decisions made by hog producers many months earlier. First off, the hog producer must decide whether to breed sows and gilts. Given a month for breeding, 3½ months for the sow or gilt gestation period and six months to finish pigs for market, you can see that it is about a 10½ month process to get pigs to market.

How does a hog producer decide on the size of his hog herd? Basically, he considers previous hog prices, his own management ability, facilities available for farrowing and/or feeding plus the availability of grains and other essential swine feeds. His decisions along these lines determine how many hogs he will be marketing in the months ahead.

Previous hog prices are very important to the producer in determining the size of his breeding herd—often more so than they probably should be. When prices have been low and are starting to go up, he likely will increase the scale of hog production. When prices are falling, he may reduce the size of his breeding herd.

Unfortunately, many producers fail to make the right move when considering the previous or present hog price situations. They tend to make decisions based on what they feel they should do in terms of today's market rather than considering what the market may be like 10 or 12 months in the future.

The producer must also consider his own management ability and the number of hogs he can effectively handle by himself or with his crew of hired hands. With the move toward more hog specialization and complete confinement facilities, one man now handles many more hogs than he could five or ten years ago.

Availability of feed and its price plays an important role. Cost of feed can greatly affect production costs for feeding pigs to marketweights. In fact, feed makes up about three quarters of the cost of producing a marketweight hog.

Hog profits during 1973 were excellent for most producers. But in 1974, there was a tremendous squeeze on hog profits as feed costs sky-rocketed with a shortage of corn and soybean oil meal for both hog and beef cattle feeding. With corn selling as high as $3.50 per bushel instead of the more normal $1 to $1.50 per bushel, many hog producers considered cash grain sales being more attractive than feeding corn to hogs.

Hog producers who normally buy corn for feeding hogs also felt corn prices were too high. So many got out of the hog business or cut back on hog numbers since they saw little profit in finishing hogs for market.

Adding to the squeeze were lower hog prices. Corn, the major hog ration ingredient, was going up in price while hog prices were sinking lower. The result was a tremendous squeeze on hog profits during 1974.

Feed prices also affect the weight at which hogs are sold. With low feed prices, hog producers tend to feed hogs to heavier weights, which leads to lower prices. When feed prices are high, hogs tend to be marketed at lighter weights.

Besides knowing his feed costs, the hog producer must be able to figure his "basis"—the difference between the live hog futures market price for Peoria delivery and his local hog price. This spread between futures and local prices includes transportation, shrink and other marketing costs. Supply and demand factors can also be included in some instances.

To determine a "basis," you need to compare your

local cash price with the Peoria live hog price over a period of time.

The Hog Cycle

Any explanation of how hog prices are determined must begin with an understanding of the hog cycle. Fifty years ago, most hog producers farrowed once a year—either in the fall or the spring with more pigs coming during the fall months. By World War II, many producers were farrowing both in the spring and fall.

Then came confinement of hogs in the late 1950's and early 1960's. Producers were soon farrowing three, four, six or more times a year to pay off expensive farrowing and hog finishing facilities more rapidly. Today, it is not uncommon to find some hog producers farrowing continuously the year around.

However, there is a long run pattern for hog production and hog prices called the hog cycle. While it may be three to six years from one high to the next, the normal cycle has averaged about four years in length over the past 80 years.

This cycle is normally divided into alternate major and minor cycles. High peaks are usually followed by a lesser peak.

During the 55 years from 1890 to 1945, there were 14 hog cycles. Eight were considered as major cycles while six were listed as minor cycles. While World War II interrupted the cyclical movement, it had reestablished itself by 1950.

Since 1960, there have been four severe roller coaster swings in hog prices. The 1970 adjustment period resulted in one of the sharpest hog price drops in history. Between February and December of 1970, barrow and gilt prices at the seven (there are only six today since Chicago is no longer represented) major midwestern markets dropped from $28.25 to $16.65 per cwt. This amounted to a drop in income of $25.52 per head for producers marketing an average 220 pound hog during this period.

While the trend toward more frequent farrowings and more specialized pork production has leveled out the pork cycle, we still need to flatten out hog production over the long run if we are to avoid costly sharp ups and downs in hog prices.

A high price for hogs one year stimulates overproduction during the next year or two. Larger pig crops generally show up at market about ten months later. The high level of pork production then depresses the price of hogs. This results in a decrease in the size of the next few pig crops during the next year or so. This decreases hog slaughter and raises hog prices—resulting in the start of another hog cycle which just continues to roll along.

Whether the regular four-year hog cycle pattern that we have had during the 1950's and 1960's stays with us remains to be seen. Government price supports and storage programs for corn controlled most of the cycles to some extent during the past 25 years. But if we do not have similar programs in the future, hog production will respond primarily to changes in the supply of corn as it did before 1950.

The Hog-Corn Ratio

You can't spend much time analyzing hog prices without hearing the term "hog-corn ratio" come up. As you could guess, this is the ratio between the price of hogs and the corn price. Corn is the chief feed ingredient used to finish hogs in the United States today. The hog-corn ratio is the number of bushels of corn it would take to buy 100 pounds of live pork.

The hog-corn ratio can have an impact on the hog cycle. When the hog-corn ratio is higher than normal, hog feeding is more profitable. This is when farmers generally respond by breeding and feeding more hogs. The opposite holds true if the hog-corn ratio is lower than usual. The best indicator of the effect of the hog-corn ratio is the change in the number of sows farrowed from one year to the next.

But remember that the hog-corn ratio is not an accurate indicator of the amount of change in hog production. It merely shows the direction in which hog production is heading—either upward or downward.

Either a change in corn prices or hog prices—sometimes even both—brings a change in the hog-corn ratio. Corn prices change from year to year with changes in corn production and demand. They also change during the year due to demand, crop prospects for the next year, storage costs and other reasons.

Being realistic, the hog-corn ratio is no longer as important as it once was in measuring the profitability of hog production. Nor is it necessarily a good clue to future hog production trends. Considerably higher protein supplement costs have thrown the hog-corn ratio "out of whack" in many instances. What is needed is a formula that includes all feed and other costs, but an accurate one has not yet been developed.

Seasonal Factors in Price Movements

Although seasonal trends are decreasing in the hog business, they are still with us. The largest number of sows generally farrow during March, April and May. The smallest number of sows farrow in December, January and February.

This seasonality factor brings a definite seasonal pattern to both hog slaughter and hog prices. Hog prices tend to hit their low for the year from August through December. This is the time when the large number of pigs farrowed in March through May are coming on the market. It is also the time of year when hog slaughter is at its highest.

Hog prices tend to be highest during early summer when hog slaughter is at its lowest point of the year.

The seasonal trend has leveled off in recent years as producers have gone to complete confinement and specialization in hogs. When you have $100,000 or more invested in hog facilities, you want to produce hogs the year around to make the payments and earn a good profit.

More producers are also planning production to take advantage of the low price periods in the early hog cycle.

Yet we still have a number of producers who only farrow once a year during late spring on pasture. This is likely to continue for some time, although the total proportion of spring pigs continues to drop.

How to Calculate Pork Production

As hogs reach a 210 to 240 pound market weight, they are slaughtered at packing plants. Thus the live hog is turned into pork and pork products for consumption by the consumer.

On the average, a 220 pound U.S. No. 2 grade hog

will produce 153 pounds of pork, pork trimmings and lard. From January through November of 1971, hogs slaughtered in federally-inspected plants had an average 77.1 percent dressing yield.

Wholesale pork cuts from a 220 pound hog would average: 20 percent ham, 17 percent loin, 15 percent belly, 8 percent picnic, 7 percent boston butt and 3 percent spareribs. Other parts would include jowls, front feet, neck bones, tail, lean trimmings and lard. Lard alone would make up about 13 percent (21 pounds) of this carcass.

Let's say we expect 32.3 million hogs to come to market during a four month period. Actual figures will be less due to death losses and retention of some female hogs for breeding purposes.

By multiplying the estimated slaughter by the pounds of pork produced from each hog (153 pounds each), you have 4.94 billion pounds of pork available for sale.

You could go a step farther and figure the amount of pork bellies or hams available for sale. Since the average hog produces 23 pounds of bellies per head, you would have 742.9 million pounds of pork bellies available for sale from your four month projected hog slaughter.

But this would not give you the entire story on pork available for sale during a given period. Pork products can also be stored as either chilled or frozen meats. So you would have to consider the amount of pork or pork products in storage to get the true picture.

There is also a definite seasonal pattern for the storage and movement of stored pork products, such as bellies. This is tied in with the seasonality of hog production, slaughter and demand.

Consumer Demand for Pork Products

The live market for hogs is dependent on the consumer demand for fresh pork and pork products. Whether the lady of the house is buying large amounts of pork chops, pork loins, hams, bacon, sausage or other processed pork products can have an impact on live hog prices.

Consumer demand depends on the price of various pork products, level of income, age of the purchaser, religion, tastes, preferences and the price of various substitutes for pork.

Yet pork consumption is increasing during most years. During 1971, pork consumption reached 73 pounds per capita, an increase of nearly seven pounds over 1970. This was the highest per capita consumption of pork since 1944. But the decision of hog producers to raise fewer pigs in 1972 caused per capita consumption to drop back to around the 68 pound level.

With more pork being produced, consumption increased to nearly 70 pounds in 1973. But then we had less hogs produced in 1974 and pork consumption fell off to 66½ pounds per capita. It will likely be around 58½ pounds per capita in 1975, as fewer hogs are produced.

During 1974, American consumers ate a record 117 pounds of beef, 2.4 pounds of lamb and 2.1 pounds of veal in addition to 66½ pounds of pork.

Prices for pork and pork products play an important role in the demand for pork. For each 1 percent decrease in the price of pork, the amount of pork demanded by consumers increases by .75 percent.

Income level also has a big impact on the amount of pork demanded by consumers. For each 1 percent increase in income, the amount of pork demanded increases by .32 percent.

With consumption of pork at the present level of 58½ pounds per person, an increase in income levels of 1 percent would increase per capita consumption by .18 pounds. With our current population of slightly over 213 million, it would result in a nationwide increase in pork demand of about 40 million pounds per year.

Primary substitutes for pork are beef, poultry and to some extent fish. As the price of these substitutes goes up relative to pork, consumers purchase more pork and pork products.

If the price of beef should increase by 1 percent, the demand for pork would increase by about .13 percent. If the price of chicken would increase by 16 percent, the amount of pork demanded would increase by about 1 percent.

Demand for pork loins, hams, picnic hams and butts has increased on a per capita basis in recent years. Much of the increased demand for these leaner types and cuts of pork and pork products has been brought about by the concern by consumers over weight. Demand for the fatter pork during the same period has remained about steady or decreased slightly.

Producers themselves have helped by producing leaner type hogs. Today's average modern meat hog should have about 1.6 inches of backfat compared to 2.5 inches for the hog of 50 years ago. During that same time span, the percentage of ham and loin has gone from 32 percent up to 39 percent. The average loin eye size has gone from 3 square inches up to 4.1 square inches.

Demand for bacon, the cured end product of pork bellies, has increased slightly in recent years. This has been chiefly due to our increasing population, although per capita consumption of bacon has also moved slightly ahead. With few substitutes available, bacon demand remains fairly stable. But if prices move extremely high or low, consumption can change by as much as 15 to 20 percent.

Consumer demand for hams has changed in recent years due to regard for both fat content and waste. Demand for sliced hams and canned hams is up since fat and bone do not have to be removed. This is convenience the housewife is willing to pay extra for.

The demand for pork tends to reach its peak during the summer and early fall months. This is partly due to the large number of people taking vacations during this time of the year and also due to lower prices at the time of peak hog production. Vacationers tend to consume more processed luncheon meats and bacon on the road than at home.

Pork demand tends to be lowest during the winter and early spring. This is due to a lower demand for luncheon-type meat products and higher hog prices.

Ham consumption soars during the Thanksgiving to Christmas period and at Easter time. Its demand hits its low point during the winter and again in summer to early fall.

Factors that Influence Variations in Daily Hog Receipts

Hog producers are always trying to decide on the best time to sell their hogs. Many producers continually wonder whether to sell this week or wait for better prices next week.

But feeding to heavier weights can be costly. First, next week's hog prices may be lower. Second, the cost of putting on extra gain will go up since it costs more to put on gain after hogs reach 210 to 220 pound weights than it does at lighter weights. Third, feeding to heavier weights could mean hogs will be down graded, resulting in a lower price per hundredweight. Fourth, hogs may also be discounted by packers due to heavier weights. So it is not easy to try and outguess the hog market.

Daily receipts of live hogs for slaughter at the various markets are also important in evaluating futures contract possibilities. Once again, supply and demand factors enter the picture.

Bad weather may mean many hog producers will decide not to market hogs on a given day. This could be ice, snow, below zero temperatures, or temperatures in the 90's during the summer. Producers know both hot and cold temperatures can bring stress on pigs and result in death losses. Frozen hams can be a problem on cold winter days if caution is not observed.

Other factors also enter into whether there will be a big run of hogs on any given market day. During the spring crop planting rush, farmers may hold hogs to finish corn or soybean planting. They may figure they will be done planting in a week and can then send hogs to market. A rainstorm may bring a deluge of hogs the next day during April or early May when farmers can't work in wet fields. The same thinking holds true during fall harvesting of corn and soybeans.

If income has been good during the year, hog producers may delay marketing hogs that should go to market during the tail end of December. They may push hog income into the next year to avoid paying excess income tax for the preceding year.

Packers, on the other hand, may have considerable demand for hogs on a day when hog numbers are light. They are then willing to pay more to get the hogs they need.

During a recent summer month, daily arrivals of hogs at the Peoria, Illinois, stockyards varied from a low of 3,200 head to a high of 5,400 hogs.

During the same month, the lowest daily number of hogs marketed on the six major markets was 23,000 head. The high volume for the month on these six markets was 39,000 head.

For the 11 major hog markets, the daily low was 32,600 head during the same month. The high for the month on these 11 major markets was 53,100 head in a single day.

How to Analyze Hog Reports

Keeping up with the hog market is not a difficult task as you can take advantage of many reports available from USDA and other sources.

Success in the futures market depends on getting information and accurately evaluating that information. Fortunately, agriculture is well supplied with a large number of crop and livestock reporting services.

Besides the usual information available on the hog market from brokers and magazines, you can take full advantage of governmental reports. Most state universities put out a number of economic reports during the year on changes in the hog market and expected changes—particularly in the major hog producing states.

In addition, you can subscribe to a number of free reports available from USDA to help you keep abreast of the hog market.

The market page of your daily newspaper probably contains quotations on both cash and futures markets for hogs. Follow these prices daily to get a good understanding of both the cash and futures market for hogs. A good way to learn more about the market is to start keeping daily charts on both cash and futures prices for hogs. It is difficult to follow price trends unless you keep some kind of daily record.

Contacts with meat packing officials, farmers and other people in the livestock and meat business are also good sources of information.

The major hog report is the Hogs and Pigs report issued quarterly by the Statistical Reporting Service branch of USDA. This publication shows the number of sows farrowing for four periods, pigs per litter, actual and estimated pig crops, number of animals kept for breeding purposes and the number of animals intended for market broken down into five different weight classifications.

For 1975, there will not likely be any changes in the Hogs and Pigs Report that is issued to show the hog situation as of March 1 and September 1 in the 14 major hog producing states—Georgia, Illinois, Indiana, Iowa, Kansas, Kentucky, Minnesota, Missouri, Nebraska, North Carolina, Ohio, South Dakota, Texas and Wisconsin. These reports will be issued on March 21 and September 19.

The June 1 report gives individual estimates for 23 states plus combined estimates for the 27 remaining states. These 27 combined estimate states normally account for only around 5 percent of the total United States hog inventory or production. This report will be released by USDA on June 23.

The December report (issued on December 22) will continue to provide state estimates for the 50 states on an individual basis. This report presents the United States situation as of December 1 for number of hogs on hand, various weight groups, sows farrowed and pig crops for the December to May and June to November periods. Individual state estimates will be provided for only 23 states for the December to May intentions to farrow. A combined estimate of intended farrowings will be made for the 27 other states.

The Importance of USDA Reports and Aids to Their Interpretation

You can expect the USDA reports on number of hogs on hand to be accurate within about 2 percent. Actual farrowings during the three months ahead of the reporting date may differ 3 percent or 4 percent from the intentions reported by farmers. Farrowings up to six months ahead can differ considerably.

Remember the data in these reports is only an estimate by hog producers themselves. They may change their minds or market conditions can force changes.

The USDA reports tend to keep salesmen and hog buyers honest. Many feed companies and hog processors have large organizations operating throughout the country. They would have some knowledge of changes in prospective market prices even if there were no USDA reports. So farmers would probably suffer most if USDA ever got out of the livestock estimating business.

Use these reports to see how hog production compares with a year earlier at the current time and up to six months ahead. The reports also help packers and retailers get set to process and sell whatever amount of pork will be marketed.

The reports are primarily useful in projecting future supply prospects. While the data is given by individual states, the most useful information is from the aggregate figures. In making projections, comparisons of both supplies and prices can be made with year earlier figures.

The information is useful both to indicate near term and long term market supplies and prices. It provides producer guidelines on how fast to push hogs already on hand to marketweights.

Quarterly pig crop reports are important in indicating changes in the hog cycle. The cycle often distorts the increasingly mild seasonal patterns in marketing and prices. In some cases, marketing might be delayed a week or two (or advanced a similar amount) to take advantage of indicated changes in market supplies.

Estimates of farrowing intentions provide an early indication of year to year hog changes. Indications of a sharp buildup in farrowings may be a signal for producers to hold the line or cut back since lower prices and profits may be ahead. Evidence that farrowings are being reduced may indicate more expansion could be profitable.

The data also help producers decide whether to contract hogs into future months. It is also valuable in preparing hog producer estimates of cash flow. Farmers might postpone large capital expenditures for farm improvements or family living when the report points to substantial increases in hogs and a consequent reduction in hog prices.

Use the hog report estimates to indicate probable marketings in the months ahead. To do this, figure most hogs go to market at six months of age. Most hogs will gain around 1.55 lbs. per day from 75 lbs. to 125 lbs. and 1.65 lbs. daily after 125 lbs. Now you can project the inventory and farrowing data ahead to get an estimate of the year to year change in marketing.

Let's say you are analyzing the March 1 Hogs and Pigs Report from USDA. By the time the report was released on March 21, those pigs in the 220 pound and over category and the 180 to 219 pound group would already have been sold. A 180 pound pig on March 1 should reach 220 pounds by March 25.

Hogs in the 120 to 179 pound group should be marketed from March 22 to April 30. Hogs in the 60 to 119 pound group should hit the market from April 30 to June 10. Market dates for pigs under 60 pounds would be June 10 to July 18.

Sow farrowing numbers can be projected in the same way. With most hogs going to market at an average six months of age, pigs farrowed from March 1 to May 1 would be marketed from August 1 to October 1. Figure when pigs will be marketed from other sow farrowing groups in the same way.

The reports also show turning points in hog production cycles. For example, let's assume the quarterly report indicates hog slaughter will be 8 percent above a year earlier three to five months from now.

Prospects for 8 percent more pork than a year earlier would suggest a 16 percent to 20 percent lower price than a year earlier. However, you should probably reduce this estimate by 1 percent. You also need to consider year to year changes in beef prices, broiler prices, consumer income and any other significant influence on hog prices.

This 8 percent expected increase might suggest that producers try to market prior to the period of expected larger volume. For hogs destined for sale during the particular period, it would probably suggest marketing at the minimum weight acceptable without a discount. Producers also use this information to estimate the profit potential in buying feeder pigs.

The main pitfall to watch is basing your decisions entirely on this report. It is just one of several reports. Many other things also influence hog prices.

Other reports of interest include the Livestock and Meat Situation Report. A publication of USDA's Economic Research Service branch, it contains historical summaries of market data and professional analysis on general economic conditions affecting the various livestock and meat markets. During 1975, it will be issued during February, May, July, August, October and November.

The monthly Livestock Slaughter and Meat Production Report from USDA's Statistical Reporting Service can provide you with the number of hogs slaughtered in commercial packing plants. It also gives an indication of average slaughter weights for the previous month for hogs, cattle, calves, sheep and lambs.

A weekly report, available through the Livestock Division of USDA's Consumer and Marketing Service, is Livestock, Meat and Wool Market News. This report serves as an up-to-date source of information on hog marketing receipts and slaughter. Besides covering all species of livestock, it includes weekly bacon slicings. Its price and slaughter weight charts are updated weekly throughout the year and provide a good analysis of the current and historical hog situation.

These USDA reports are available free of charge. Simply write to the branch of USDA mentioned above and ask to be put on the mailing list. The basic USDA address is United States Department of Agriculture, Washington, D.C. 20250.

April Hog Futures Delivery 1972-73 to 1974-75

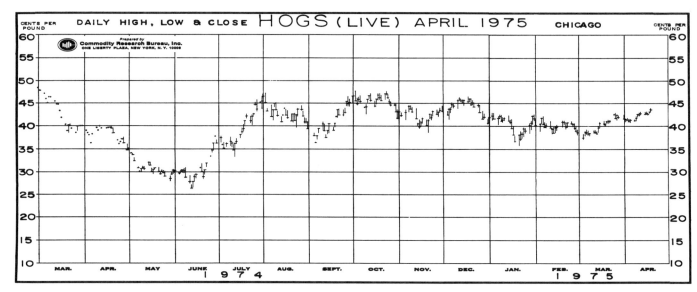

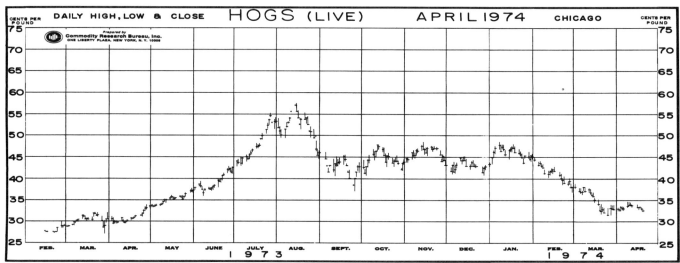

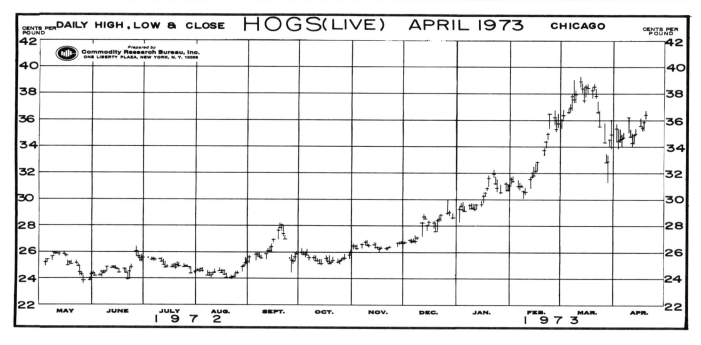

April Hog Futures Delivery 1966-67 to 1971-72

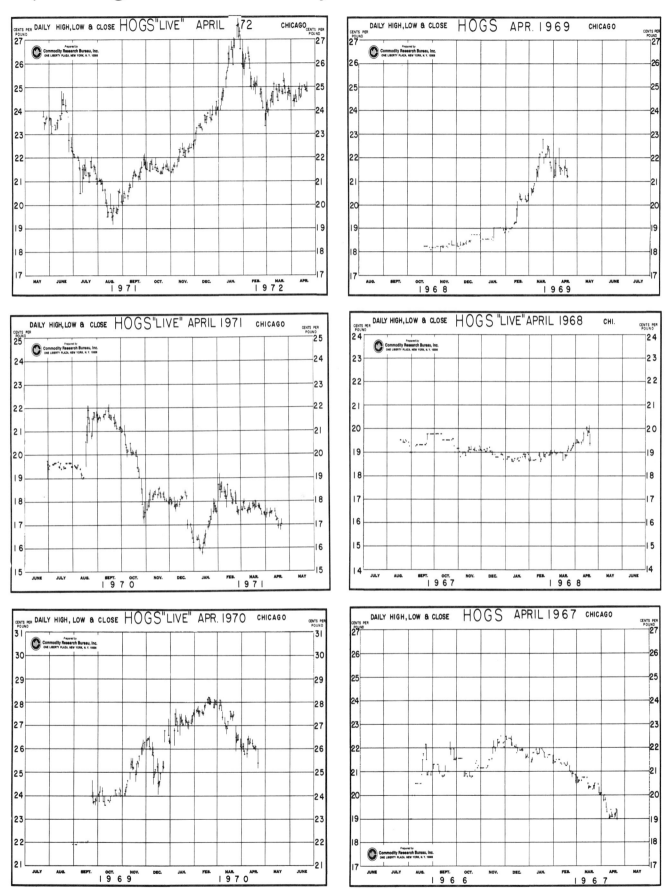

UNDERSTANDING THE LUMBER AND PLYWOOD FUTURES MARKETS

BY JAMES P. OLMEDO, JR.

The lumber and plywood futures markets began trading in late 1969 and have been a glowing success. They have afforded the forest products industry a pricing mechanism that could be employed in overall marketing strategy, and offered the speculator a market that exhibited much volatility, characterized by price moves four or five times that of initial margin outlays. The remarkable success of these markets was foreseen as their historical price path reflected a market characterized by large seasonal price swings and inherent volatility when short term constraints on either supply or demand became acute.

The Futures Contracts

Two plywood contracts and a lumber contract commenced trading late in 1969. Each of the initial plywood contracts specified the same basic product, i.e. one-half inch exterior sheathing of Group 1 species, but other specifications differed. New York Mercantile Exchange plywood called for on track delivery and a unit size of 70,000 square feet. In contrast, the Chicago Board of Trade contract stipulated 69,120 square feet of plywood per contract, and a shipping certificate, which is a call on a seller's production, to be utilized in delivery proceedings. The original lumber contract designated 40,000 board feet of kiln dried 2″ x 4″ dimension white fir in random lengths ranging from eight to twenty feet.

Original contract specifications of all forest products futures were altered significantly to encourage more speculative trading and further tailor the contract base to commercial needs. The Chicago Mercantile Exchange lumber contract, for instance, was expanded to include western hemlock and the unit size was increased to 100,000 board feet. These modifications increased the contract value two and one half times that of the previous contract, which proved attractive to speculators, and incorporated a new species, which broadened commercial interest. The New York plywood contract was amended to include changes in delivery procedure, and the Chicago contract was modified to allow producers to issue additional shipping certificates and enable plywood wholesalers to make their warehouses regular for delivery upon meeting contract material and financial qualifications. Presently only the Chicago based plywood and lumber futures contracts are actively traded.

Trading History

Early trading activity was relatively dull. Commercials attempting to familiarize themselves with the markets and the mechanics of trading were the dominant participants. The desired speculative component consisting of both local and general public traders was conspicuously absent because the forecasted economic scenario for the balance of 1969 and most of 1970 suggested that a mild recession was imminent. A weakened economy precluded extended wood usage and dispelled visions of dramatic price moves comparable to the meteoric surge in late 1968 and early 1969. Cash lumber and plywood prices and futures drifted lower in late 1969 following seasonal fourth quarter weakness.

Futures prices for lumber and plywood were contained in a narrow range between $70–80 during most of 1970. Price swings, moderate as they were, followed regular seasonal patterns, rising into the spring and summer, followed by weakness in the fall. Activity was mixed; volume in New York plywood slowed to zero by June of that year, Chicago's volume averaged over 300 units daily by late fall, and lumber volume remained erratic, spurting occasionally to daily levels of 2,000 or more in late fall when tax straddles were executed.

The pace of trading picked up early in the first quarter of 1971, abetted by a favorable economic outlook and a short term restriction of supply flow due to inclement weather in major producing regions. A notable scarcity of shipping certificates applicable for delivery of plywood in Chicago, coupled with a relatively large open interest in the nearby contract, also prompted a price advance when shorts were forced to cover their positions upon expiration of trading in spot contracts. Volume and open interest improved steadily by mid-March in both plywood and lumber futures. After weakening in the second quarter, futures again worked upward fueled by transportation strikes, and an excellent forecast for both near and long term wood utilization. Futures followed cash early in the fourth quarter and strengthened when concentrated inventory buying for spring needs developed later in the quarter. A roller-coaster pattern in futures and cash markets was evidenced during the turbulent 1972–74 period. Two major price peaks and successive troughs were witnessed. A record boom in housing and related construction that began in 1971 and continued into 1973, coupled with a tight supply situation for lumber and plywood, fostered in part by price controls, carried futures and cash prices to historic highs which persisted until early 1973. The resumption of a free competitive market and a reversal in housing trends in the spring of 1973 exerted severe pressure on futures and cash values that continued into the fall of that year. Supply constraints including propane gas, glue, and railcar shortages sparked an intermediate price advance in the fourth quarter of 1973 and set the stage for substantial price improvement in the first half of 1974. Again prices reversed as an excess supply situation developed and economic indicators pointed to a recession.

Factors Influencing the Supply of Softwood Lumber and Plywood

The supply of softwood lumber and plywood is a function of several variables including availability of timber and its cost, domestic production capacity, economic factors associated with manufacturing costs such as labor rates, raw material costs and capital expenditures, international trade, and ultimate product sales price. Especially pertinent to timber and its costs is government policy because the largest portion of softwood saw timber inventory, about 63%, is located in the national forests and other public lands. Only 17% of total inventory, which serves as the primary base of softwood plywood and lumber output, is owned by the forest industry with another 20% being held by private sources. Figures for 1970 timber allocation indicated that only 36% of the timber utilized that year originated from public lands while the bulk of the resource came from forest industry and other private lands.

Major Production Costs

The cost of wood is in most cases the major cost of manufacture and therefore has a tremendous influence on planned production expansion or contraction. The cost as a percentage of total manufacturing cost varies. Forest products companies obtaining their wood from their own holdings would generally have lower cost inputs than those companies dependent on outside sources. Wood costs have represented more than 50% of all manufacturing plywood and lumber costs during a tight stumpage market. Stumpage prices, which represent the cost of standing timber, have advanced steadily since 1959. For example, western hemlock stumpage prices in current dollars sold from National Forests have increased from $6.30 per thousand board feet in 1959 to $101.60 in the first quarter of 1973. Douglas fir prices from the same location rose from $16.40 to $109.80 during the same time span. Prices for stumpage obtained from non-public lands not owned by the particular company have exhibited greater advances than those realized from public lands.

Another significant cost consideration is labor. Labor rates are variable across the nation. They tend to be higher in the West and lower in the South. In the state of Washington, a leading producer of lumber and plywood, hourly rates increased from $2.00 in 1951 to $4.99 in 1973. Hourly earnings in Arkansas, a representative of Southern production, rose from $0.98 to $2.82 from 1951 to 1973. As a component of total plywood manufacturing costs labor represented over 30% while it accounted for 40–45% of total lumber manufacturing costs.

Lumber Production

Domestic softwood lumber production capacity is very difficult to gauge since the industry is fragmented, consisting of more than 10,000 mills—none of which produces more than 5% of total annual output. Furthermore, initial entry into the industry is relatively inexpensive when compared to other manufacturing operations. Over the long run supply has tended to be elastic. When prices become attractive, operating mills increase the number of shifts and place shut down mills into operation. If prices remain at a profitable level for an extended period of time, new operations and/or additions are installed. During the past two decades, lumber production has ranged between a low of 26.1 billion board feet in 1961 to an outturn of 32.2 billion board feet in 1972.

Despite recent advances in production, the United States is a net importer of softwood lumber, the bulk of which comes from Canada. In 1972 imports totaled 8.9 billion board feet (22% of domestic production), while exports, primarily to Japan, totaled about 1.2 billion board feet.

Plywood Production

Potential plywood operating capacity is less difficult to evaluate than lumber in that only 192 mills are in operation and reported production data is quite reliable. The industry has exhibited rapid growth in both production output and geographical distribution. From 1950, when production totaled 2.6 billion square feet annually, outturn soared to 18.3 billion square feet in 1973. Operating capacity has been projected to reach over 20 billion square feet within the next few years. Initially plywood production was confined principally to the West Coast where large diameter Douglas Fir logs of peeler quality were readily available. However, as these logs became less abundant and more costly, new innovations were derived to make plywood from other species, and smaller diameter logs, profitable. The result has been a marked increase in southern pine plywood production, which now represents over 30% of annual national production. Unlike lumber, international trade in softwood plywood is relatively insignificant, with net exports averaging less than 300 million square feet per year.

Supply Factors in Contract Grades of Futures Markets

The general overview presented of the supply sector in the softwood lumber and plywood markets is applicable with modification to the supply and production of hem-fir 2 x 4 dimension, the contract grade of lumber futures, and one-half inch exterior sheathing, the contract grade of plywood futures. Hem-fir, which is a combination of western hemlock and white fir is produced in the Inland and Coast regions. In 1973 about 25% of Coast production was composed of western hemlock and 3% white fir. The Inland region, on the other hand, produced an insignificant amount of western hemlock, but 18.1% of total production was white fir.

The total volume of contract species produced was 4.5 billion board feet, or 14.4% of total national softwood lumber production. An additional 1.5 billion board feet of the contract species was imported from Canada and represented almost a fifth of total imports. About 18.3 billion square feet of plywood was produced in 1973. Half-inch western exterior sheathing, the futures contract grade, accounted for 14.2% of that year's outturn. A similar southern pine plywood grade that is hedgeable, but not feasibly deliverable, represented an additional 16.9% of the total.

Production of the futures contract grades tends to be seasonal: lumber production has normally been high in mid-spring and early fall and low from November through February. Plywood production shows nearly the same seasonal configuration as lumber with the exception of a sharp downturn in July. The factors which create these seasonal patterns include cold weather during the winter season, which retards woods and mill work; the reluctance of mills to build inventories at the end of a tax year; an abatement in construction usage in the colder months; and shut downs for maintenance and vacations.

Size and Composition of Demand, and Factors Influencing Consumption

The demand for lumber and plywood is closely related to the general economic health of the United States and is geared especially to the construction and production sectors of the economy, as well as the availability of wood fiber and non-wood substitutes. Per capita consumption of lumber has ranged between 156–219 board feet and totaled 192 feet in 1972. Plywood consumption has grown at the expense of lumber, increasing from 18 square feet per capita in the mid-1950's to 87 square feet in 1972. The following tables show the estimated consumption of all lumber and plywood consumed in major end use categories.

TABLE 1
Estimated Softwood Lumber Consumption by Major Uses 1967–1971 (Millions of Board Feet)

Markets	1967	1968	1969	1970	1971	1972	1973
Residential Construction	12,434	14,184	13,377	12,848	17,175	20,025	17,945
Other New Construction	7,051	7,225	7,070	6,972	6,600	6,424	6,302
Repair and Remodeling	5,385	5,608	5,687	6,001	6,315	6,430	6,456
Materials Handling	2,563	2,717	2,829	2,255	2,300	3,184	3,325
All Others	3,589	4,161	3,728	4,145	4,635	3,759	4,011
U.S. CONSUMPTION	31,022	33,895	32,691	32,228	37,025	39,822	38,039

Source: Western Wood Products Association

TABLE 2
Plywood Estimated Consumption by End-Use Market (Billions of square feet—⅜ inch Basis)

Market	1970	1971	1972	1973
Residential Construction	7.3	8.8	9.4	9.7
General Construction	2.0	2.1	2.2	2.4
Industrial	3.1	3.2	3.3	3.3
Other	2.3	2.3	2.3	2.3

Source: American Plywood Association

Housing the Major Consumption Sector

It is evident that the single most important market for plywood and lumber is the residential housing market. Wood utilization in this area is dependent on the housing mix, size of unit, type of unit, and geographic location. Table 3 indicates the average amount of lumber and plywood consumed per unit type.

As can be inferred from Table 3, a significant change in the housing mix could have a dramatic effect on wood usage. That is, an increase in the proportion of multiple unit dwellings could dilute wood use even though total housing start numbers might be relatively high. In the early 1950's as an illustration, single conventional units represented 78% of all housing construction. This proportion has declined steadily with less than sixty percent of housing production in the early seventy's consisting of single units. Assuming constant lumber and plywood use per unit, a change in the housing mix from 51% single family, 33% multi-family and 16% mobile homes to one containing 43% single family, 41% multi-family and 16% mobile homes, the required amount of plywood and lumber would fall 9% and 8%, respectively.

The size and location of the housing unit is also important in determining potential plywood and lumber usage. Compared with 1959, when single units averaged 1,143 square feet, the average square footage increased to 1,660 square feet in 1973. The location of a home also affects the materials utilized, and substitution of wood and nonwood products. In the South, for instance, more concrete and particleboard is used than plywood, which is employed extensively in the more Northern regions.

Factors Affecting Housing

Because housing is a major barometer of lumber and plywood usage, an understanding of the variables affecting the supply and demand is invaluable. History has shown that housing flourishes during a soft economy and weakens with prosperity. The main reasons for this somewhat unexpected phenomenon are more availability of equipment and labor and reduced competition for credit.

The major considerations attuned to housing demand include demographic material detailing vacancy rates, and the number of households headed by individuals 25–34 years of age. Financial considerations, depending on what housing type is being projected, include mortgage yields, the discount rate, money flow into savings and loan institutions, yields on three-month Treasury bills and long-term government bond yields. Demographic variables

TABLE 3
Lumber and Plywood Use in Housing, by Type of Unit, 1969

Type of unit	Use Per Unit		Total Use	
	Lumber	Plywood	Lumber	Plywood
	Board Feet	Square Feet (⅜-inch basis)	Thousand Board Feet	Thousand Square Feet (⅜-inch basis)
One- and two-family	11,850	5,430	10,190	4,670
Multi-family	4,260	1,910	2,730	1,220
Mobile homes	1,910	1,330	790	550
All types	7,170	3,370	13,710	6,440

Source: U.S. Department of Agriculture, Forest Service

are correlated positively with housing demand, while the discount and mortgage rates relate negatively to housing production. Costs and profitability are also significant in determining if, and what type of structure will be built. An immediate change in most of the financial variables has no effect on the near term housing outlook. For example, any change in the discount rate would not be significant until three quarters into the future.

Subsidized units and mobile homes, which use less wood than conventional units, have recently become significant elements in the whole housing picture. Mobile homes have encroached on the output of single unit construction and account for more than 90% of the homes built costing less than $15,000. Shipments of mobile homes increased from slightly under 200,000 units in 1964 to 600,000 (seasonally adjusted) in mid-1972. Government subsidized living quarters for low middle income groups have played a major role in housing at various times. However, their influence is directly dependent on government policies.

Other Wood Using Sectors

Non-residential construction, which includes the building of highways, churches, office buildings, and other commercial buildings, is another major end use for lumber, and to a lesser degree, for plywood. Wood usage in these areas is extremely variable, being dependent on building codes, location, and size of project. In general, as a proportion of total materials cost, less wood is used in the Northeast and North Central region than in the South and West. In approximating wood use in this very diverse segment of consumption the value of non-residential construction is the key economic indicator.

The utilization of wood in other areas such as transportation, manufacturing, materials handling, railroad repair, general home remodeling and construction, and agriculture has been extremely variable and is subject to changes in structural design, material substitutes, and consumer trends over a relatively short period of time. In ascertaining the direction or trend of wood usage in these areas, historic usage is associated with trends in such exogenous variables as disposable income, indices of industrial production, outlays for alterations and addition and relative price relationships with other structural materials. Production indices in major wood using markets such as furniture, containers, and transportation equipment manufacture also must be considered. Leading associations such as the American Plywood Association and National Forest Products Association present annual forecasts in these areas. However, trends and deviations in wood utilization expectations during the course of the year could be evaluated following the preceding indicators and up-to-date trade news.

Major Uses of Lumber and Plywood Futures Contract Grades

The contract grades of lumber and plywood futures are not normally utilized in all of the economic wood consuming sectors described. The foregoing discussion is pertinent, though, because of the substitutability of the contract grades in the production and demand mix. Dimension 2 x 4 hem-fir and one-half inch sheathing exterior plywood are utilized primarily in the residential housing and general construction markets. Dimension lumber is used mainly for framing, while sheathing is used for walls, roofs, and floors.

How Interaction of Supply/Demand Has Affected Price: An Historical Overview

An analysis of the forest products economic system should begin with an historical appraisal of how supply and demand have interacted over long and short time spans and how this interaction has affected price. The most notable characteristic of supply for both lumber and plywood is that it is elastic over the long run, thus a prolonged period of profitable operation can encourage added production. Supply over the short term period (less than a year) is inelastic; therefore, any temporary advance or retreat of price generally has a negligible effect on output. Demand for lumber and plywood is derived and subject to large fluctuations depending on the strength or weakness in the wood using sectors of the national economy. Any sharp advance or decline in demand coupled with the inelastic nature of supply over the short term, has had a tremendous bearing on price level.

Two featured developments clearly illustrate the short term interaction of inelastic supply and derived demand and their effect on price.

The Boom Bust of 1968–1969

A forecast in 1968 of an excellent wood consumption year to follow encouraged wholesalers, who were holding moderate inventories, to place multiple orders. When the order flow exceeded the near term production represented by mill order file levels, the mills raised their prices. The rise in prices was accompanied by additional waves of distributor buying, which reached virtually panic proportions. As demand was reaching abnormally high levels, supply was curtailed due to poor producing weather in major regions of production. If that were not enough, interruptions in supply flow were aggravated by an inadequate supply of box cars for transcontinental shipment and an East Coast dock strike. Additional timber supplies were not available, and logs needed domestically were being exported to Japan at an unprecedented rate.

In conjunction with the surge in demand and paucity of supply, prices for lumber and plywood attained record levels by February 1969, as mentioned previously. However, as quickly as the market had advanced, it retreated. Wholesalers had increased their inventories to record levels in anticipation of a good wood using year; but, new fiscal policies presaged a slackening in housing, the major market for plywood and lumber. Buyer resistance by distributors formed and mills were forced to lower prices. Thus, in a two month period prices broke to levels which had prevailed in mid-1968.

Record Heights in 1972–1973

Prices surpassed the record levels of 1969 in 1972 and 1973. The impetus was the same as in past years when derived demand outpaced supply;

but, the situation was unlike 1969. Economic forecasts for housing and other significant wood using markets again foresaw a record wood using year. However, the additional influence of a price control policy sparked advances to record heights rather than perform the contrary. The control policy was rather broad and general to pertain to the freely competitive, auction type, and fragmented forest products industry. Enforcement was difficult and the regulations porous enough to permit many exceptions. The results in sum were less than satisfactory. Normal buying patterns were disrupted, production (despite unparalleled demand) was curtailed, non uniform prices for the same products were prevalent and imports at prices well above domestic ceilings were booming. Despite prospects of a favorable business year, wholesalers and other wood buyers were reluctant to build inventories at prices near government ceilings, and well above five-year average prices. They feared large losses comparable to those of 1969 when they were left high and dry with high priced inventories. Most buyers were also assuming that they could always obtain the wood at ceiling prices, "a guaranteed price," and therefore could successfully impose a hand-to-mouth inventory policy until prices declined to attractive levels for inventory replenishment.

Demand became very persistent throughout the year, and, because most distributors were buying hand-to-mouth, premiums developed for immediate delivery. In order to realize more profitable levels, producers formulated a strategy of manufacturing products that had more profit potential than those based on lower imposed ceilings. In several cases such a strategy thwarted the production of key demand items since their production was not conducive to maximization of profits. Interspersed in this chain of events were the pricing policies of smaller organizations, not yet under controls at the time, which could sell and resell a commodity until the maximum price the market would bear was attained. For example, plywood sheathing which sold at a mill ceiling of $123.00 per thousand square feet could eventually be purchased by the final user at $200.00 or more. It is evident that the short term surge in demand plus the short term inelastic character of supply fueled the record price advance in 1972. Price control considerations appeared as a secondary issue.

Analysis of Long Term and Short Term Fundamentals

The diverse economic nature of the lumber and plywood markets over a long and short span of time necessitates a two-stage approach to fundamental analysis. First, the long term outlook must be evaluated to ascertain overall trends in supply, demand and price. Then a short term analysis is required, which is especially relevant to futures trading and contract grade economic systems to depict whether or not the previously forecasted long term trends are following anticipated routes. The question of how any deviations from these initial trends could interact and affect overall price direction also is explored.

Evaluating Long Term Supply

The broad overview of potential supply is dependent on several considerations including availability and cost of public and private timber, industry capacity, previous selling prices for forest products, trends in international trade and mill stocks on hand at the beginning of the period. The interaction is complex and requires detailed mathematical analysis. Some investigators have found that the annual supply of softwood lumber is negatively correlated with the price of labor and stumpage and positively correlated with productivity and the price of lumber during the previous quarter. The supply of plywood was found to be negatively correlated with the price of veneer logs and labor costs, while positively correlated with the price of the preceding year and productivity. Trends in such exogenous variables as Gross National Product have been included in some models as well as time trends.

Annual projections are made by major trade associations, government organizations, and private economic services. The most notable are the American Plywood Association, Western Wood Products Association, and National Forest Product Association.

Projecting Long Term Consumption

The projection of long term demand generally begins with a model of the national economy emphasizing housing starts, industrial production, disposable income, expenditures for plant repair and maintenance, furniture index, new construction put in place, and transportation indices. The international situation should be appraised, especially an analysis of the major import source, Canada, and export outlet Japan. Monetary exchange rates should also be studied. Normally a general consumption forecast can be made extrapolating past trends of usage in major wood use areas relative to changes in each end use variable. Subjectivity, with special reference to encroachment of substitute materials, expected levels of promotional efforts, and cost differential ratios should also be focused upon in these general projections.

Mathematical approaches in approximating consumption have ranged from graphical analysis and extrapolation of trends to multiple regression analysis. In the latter case, annual demand for lumber has been found to be a function of disposable income, gross national product, value of total construction, the price of substitute products and lumber the previous year, and the wages of construction workers the previous year. Each approach entailed a combination of general economic shifts, substitution of products, and costs of the material the year before. Besides estimating plywood demand via a graphical technique, regression analysis studies have indicated that demand is related to the price of competing materials, the price of plywood, disposable income, gross national product and changes in other major economic indicators.

Deviations from Long Term Projections

Long term trends are subject to seasonal and short term aberrations caused by previously unforeseen or unassumed influences. It historically has been the "unforeseen or unassumed" that have thrust prices beyond normal bounds. The unknown elements include new or revised government policies, strikes, changes in consumer trends, emergence of substitute materials, among others. Rather than attempt to analyze the interaction of all these variables, upon a change of a variable or combination of variables from an assumed path one can observe the net effect via a myriad of available trade statistics. These statistics, which differ in measuring units for lumber and plywood, indicate the quantities being produced, mills' operating capacity, the flow of new orders, and the quantity of unfilled orders, and distributor inventory levels and current price levels.

Seasonal Characteristics

The seasonal tendencies of these variables and some of the chief use indicators gauged to the use of the contract grade of lumber and plywood are presented in Table 4.

struction activity, and the simultaneous abatement of plywood production in July and the drawdown of stocks when construction activity is strong. These underlying relationships, including a lagging of variables, affect price. Normally an expected advance in construction coupled with low distributor stocks early in the year provokes a flow of new orders and a spring price rise. The opposite situation occurs in late fall, when a decline in construction, and reduced concern to build inventories because of tax considerations, and storage costs weakens prices.

How to Analyze Futures Price Trends

The theory and principles pertaining to the national softwood and lumber markets can be applied with

TABLE 4
Average Monthly Seasonal Indices of Major Supply, Consumption and Economic Factors Related to Lumber and Plywood Markets

Variable	Average Seasonal Index											
	Jan.	Feb.	Mar.	Apr.	May	June	July	Aug.	Sep.	Oct.	Nov.	Dec.
Lumber Production	.900	.933	1.06	1.04	1.07	1.01	0.95	1.07	1.06	1.06	.938	.895
New Orders	.955	.938	1.07	1.06	1.04	1.02	1.01	1.03	.990	1.04	.903	.948
Unfilled Orders	1.08	1.08	1.11	1.09	1.01	.970	1.00	.956	.918	.917	.892	.976
Gross Stocks	1.00	1.01	1.02	1.01	1.02	1.01	.970	.976	.990	.994	1.00	.998
Imports	.712	.867	1.08	1.02	1.08	1.14	1.10	1.14	1.05	1.03	.928	.848
Exports	.945	.878	1.04	.936	1.16	1.00	1.11	.948	.857	1.08	1.01	1.04
Plywood Production	.946	.935	1.06	1.03	1.02	1.01	.915	1.03	1.04	1.07	.982	.960
New Orders	1.03	.924	.968	1.05	1.04	1.00	.968	1.06	.993	1.06	.963	.946
Shipments	.946	.925	1.01	1.05	1.08	.993	.923	1.03	1.03	1.07	.973	.970
Mill Inventory	.960	1.03	1.09	1.09	1.08	1.05	.937	.947	.959	.981	.960	.918
Economic Factors Actual Housing	.682	.680	1.01	1.21	1.20	1.18	1.11	1.09	1.03	1.08	.937	.790
New Construction Put in Place	.797	.749	.845	.946	1.02	1.09	1.12	1.14	1.13	1.11	1.07	.981
Non-residential Construction	.830	.812	.886	.959	.991	1.03	1.04	1.08	1.11	1.12	1.09	1.04
Mobile Home Production	.684	.771	.960	1.05	1.05	1.12	1.03	1.17	1.19	1.19	.971	.805

Note: Lumber indices calculated for period 1961–1971.
Plywood indices calculated for period 1964–1971.
Economic indices calculated for period 1964–1971.

The calculated average index for monthly data for an historical period is a base for seasonal analysis. The index shows the weight of each monthly observation relative to an average calendar year. An index number less than 1.0 indicates weakness in the variable, and, conversely, an index greater than 1.0 suggests strength.

The index table shows that lumber production has normally peaked in March and early fall and declines in late fall and winter. The same general pattern, with the exception of a production decline in July due to vacation shutdowns, is witnessed in plywood. The overall production scheme has appeared to be affected by weather in the past, but has become less seasonal with added production emanating from the southern region. Inventories at the mill and distributor level tend to increase early in the year and decline in late summer. Order flow and shipments increase in the spring and deteriorate later in the year. It is worthy to note the relationship between the flow of orders and the increased levels of con-

some modification to the analysis of forest products futures and contract grade pricing. The figures analyzed are regional and related particularly to the supply and demand of the contract grades. On the supply side, the quantity of timber available from the Western national forests is significant because about half of the production emanating from the Inland and Coast regions, where the major portion of contract grade material evolves, is dependent on this raw resource. Lumber production, stocks, new orders, and unfilled orders in the Inland and Coast regions can be studied to evaluate near term supply and fresh demand. Statistics showing the operating capacity, flow of orders, and stocks on hand for unsanded plywood are also available for analysis. Broad economic data especially relevant to the contract grade are housing and construction figures.

The futures markets have tended to react to the unfolding of the above statistics which, with the exception of housing and construction data, are released weekly. An indication of market strength and possibly higher prices is the inflow of new orders over operating production levels. This event would be a very strong factor when mill order files have been extended for three weeks or more. The rate of shipments is an indication of the immediate needs of the consumer. The proportion of unfilled orders relative to mill inventories shows how strong or weak orders files are. The monthly data for housing and new construction put in place, plus the level of inventories held by wholesalers must be interpolated and combined with weekly data, to evaluate price direction. Building permit numbers are better indicators of future wood needs than seasonally-adjusted housing starts or actual units constructed because these figures point only to past use. Some lumber traders use past price levels or competing material prices to ascertain the short term price environment. White spruce lumber, a major import material from Canada, which is used in framing applications and competes often with hem-fir lumber has been used as a guide for near term price analysis. It appears to be a logical choice in that net imports from Canada serve as a balance between domestic U.S. production and potential and active consumption. A number of plywood traders have used southern yellow pine plywood in the same manner that white spruce is used in lumber trading. Another measure used as an indicator of the pace of forest products activity is the level of transit business. Transits are unsold cars of lumber and plywood on track which are sold by distributors en route. A scarcity of transits infers brisk business, while an abundance signals that final consumer needs might be flagging. The summation of all these variables is price, which is negotiated daily and serves as a basic point to depart from for futures strategy.

The above discussion centered on the normal or regular factors one can assess on a periodic basis. Each, of course, has some type of a seasonal, whether strong or weak, and must be evaluated accordingly. Besides these normal and seasonal considerations the implication of strikes, abnormal weather and government activity must be analyzed. The type of strikes which have historically affected forest product prices include rail, dock, truck, wood workers and mill workers. Abnormal weather patterns which curtail production in major producing regions when good construction weather occurs in another, normally advances prices. Government activity; whether increasing or reducing timber flow, initiating new monetary policies, expanding or contracting government purchases of wood products, or accentuating the building of low income housing, has a long term effect on forest products prices. In applying these various considerations to a trading strategy, a long term and seasonal evaluation should first be determined, then impending abnormalities can be assessed.

Hedging Forest Products

Hedging is a marketing instrument enabling one, who sells or purchases lumber or plywood, to transfer or shift undesirable price risks. Essentially one takes a position in futures opposite to that held in the cash market, thus, an owner or producer of lumber and plywood would sell a futures position and one who expects to use lumber or plywood would hedge by buying futures contracts. The theory underlying the hedging mechanism is that cash and futures price movements tend to parallel each other and upon expiration of a futures position cash and futures converge. Over a span of time and barring outside influences and contract technicalities the theory would apply.

Cash/Futures Price Relationships

In the early stages of trading, cash and futures moved parallel to each other in both lumber and plywood. By late 1970 plywood futures began trading at abnormal premiums to cash and upon expiration futures closed $20.00 or more above prevailing cash levels. Contributing to the premiums of futures over cash were the delivery provisions of the plywood contract. The contract stipulated that only mills could issue shipping certificates (which are a call on their production by the buyer) for a portion of their production. The buyer could delay shipment as long as a year paying a nominal fee for daily storage in the interim. Since only a small number of certificates were allocated and these certificates were closely held, a shortage of certificates developed. Thus, those holding short positions in an expiring plywood contract were forced to cover their futures positions at large premiums to cash. A modification of the contract shortly thereafter allowing mills to issue a number of shipping certificates for a larger portion of their production and enabling wholesalers to become "regular" for delivery and issue certificates has resolved the possibility of such technical tightness developing again.

The imposition of price ceilings late in 1971 set the stage for an artificial spur of futures above cash for a prolonged period of time. Price ceilings for lumber and plywood were established, but in several instances the real trading market or "free" market price was reflected by futures. It has been observed that when the high trading cash prices (which reflected the immediate demand of the cash commodity) were compared with the futures expiration price rather than government ceiling prices, reasonable parallelism was evident. Since the lifting of price controls a favorable convergence pattern of cash to nearby futures has generally been realized during the final days of trading prior to the futures contract expiration.

A Method for Hedging Non-Deliverable Grades

The mechanics of hedging the contract grade are relatively straightforward. However, the contract grades of lumber and plywood represent less than 15% of the total supply of softwood lumber and plywood. A satisfactory approach which has been used in evaluating the feasibility of hedging the myriad of other products is correlation analysis. The procedure is mathematical and attempts to describe the historical relationship between the contract grade and the potential hedge item. A correlation coefficient (which ranges from -1.0 to 1.0) is a measure of how one price series variation is associated with variation of another. Also determined is the standard deviation of the variation. The closer the correlation approaches $+1.0$ the more positively the one variable is associated with the other, i.e., high values associated with high values, assuming a sound economic relationship exists. Remember, correlation does not imply causation. Normally, a correlation of a 0.90 or better is desired for potential hedging. The standard deviation of the estimate indicates there is a 68% probability, under certain statistical assumptions, that an observation in one price series would correspond with an observation in the other series ± the standard deviation, with a greater proportion of observations falling at the midpoint of that range on the line of regression. If the boundary were extended to ± two standard deviations the probability would be increased to 95%.

Practical application of the method is based on the assumptions that contract grade cash and futures parallel each other, and that if the correlation between the contract grade and the product to be hedged is greater than 0.90, the product's price movement would also parallel futures. An example of how a wholesaler could forward price a non-specified grade serves as an illustration. The product selected is kiln dried 2″ x 8″ Douglas fir. An historical analysis for 1964–1970 indicates a correlation coefficient of 0.98 and a standard error of $3.14. Additional statistical figures show that the constant is 12.08 and the beta coefficient is 0.947.

Inserted in the linear equation $y = a + bx$ where y is the price to be calculated, a is a constant, b is the beta coefficient and x is the futures price of a particular month at a list base one can ascertain the value of the tested product relative to a futures quote. Thus the value of 2″ x 8″ kiln dried Douglas fir is calculated as follows:

$$y = a + bx$$

$$y = 12.08 + (.947) \ (\$150 \text{ futures price list})$$

$$y = \$143.50$$

Rather than settle on one estimate alone, it is more prudent to project a range by adding and subtracting one standard deviation from the single estimate calculated. In this case a range of $140.36–$146.44 can be projected. At this juncture the normal decisions made relative to hedging the contract grade are made to determine the profitability of the non-deliverable product hedge. Market views and anticipated price trends play an important role at this point.

Conclusion

Lumber and plywood futures have become significant members among the futures commodities group. They have demonstrated the volatility and vigor attractive to the speculator and at the same time have been successfully employed in the marketing strategy of forest industry concerns. The commodity exchanges are investigating new fiber contracts including logs, pulp, particleboard, and a variety of lumber and plywood items to expand the interest in forest products, and broaden trade participation. The establishment of a mortgage futures market should instill further interest on the part of home building industries. Virtually all the segments,

from providers of raw material, users, and the financial community might be afforded access to an invaluable pricing tool—commodity futures contracts.

SOURCES OF INFORMATION

Annual Data

1. U.S. Department of Agriculture—Forest Service: *Timber Trends in the U.S.* (Forest Resource Rep. 17) (Washington: Supt. of Documents, U.S. Government Printing Office, 1965).
2. U.S. Department of Commerce, Bureau of the Census. *Lumber Production and Mill Stocks.* (Cur. Indus. Reps. Ser. MA 24T) (Washington, U.S. Department of Commerce, Bureau of the Census, annual).
3. U.S. Department of Commerce, Bureau of the Census, *Softwood Plywood* (Cur. Indus. Reps. Ser. MA 24H). (Washington: U.S. Department of Commerce, Bureau of the Census).

Monthly Data

4. American Plywood Association
   Monthly Plywood Statistics
   Tacoma, Washington.
5. F. W. Dodge, Construction Bulletin. Division of McGraw-Hill, 1040 Merchandise Mart, Chicago, Illinois 60654.
6. National Forest Products Association
   Fingertip Facts and Figures (Washington National Forest Products Association).
7. Southern Pine Association
   Weekly Trade Barometer
   (New Orleans, La: Southern Pine Association.)
8. Destination of Lumber Shipments (WWPA) Western Woods Products Association, 1500 Yeon Building, Portland, Oregon.
9. Lumber Price Trends (Inland Index) (WWPA).
10. Western Lumber Facts (WWPA).
11. Monthly F.O.B. Price Summary Past Sales (Coast Mills) (WWPA).
12. U.S. Department of Commerce, Bureau of the Census. *Housing Starts.* (Construct. Reps. C20) (Washington: Supt. of Document, U.S. Government Printing Office.)
13. *C-40 Housing Authorized in Individual Permit— Issuing Places.* U.S. Department of Commerce, Bureau of the Census.
14. U.S. Department of Commerce.
    Construction Activity. (Construct. Reps. C30) (Washington: Supt. of Documents, U.S. Government Printing Office).

Weekly Data

15. *Barometer* (WWPA).
16. Weekly F.O.B. Price Summary Past Sales (Inland Mills) (WWPA).
17. *Random Lengths*, P.O. Box 867, Eugene, Oregon 97401.
18. *Crow's Weekly Letter.* C. C. Crow Publications, Inc., Terminal Sales Building, Portland, Oregon 97205.

March Lumber Futures Delivery 1969-70 to 1974-75

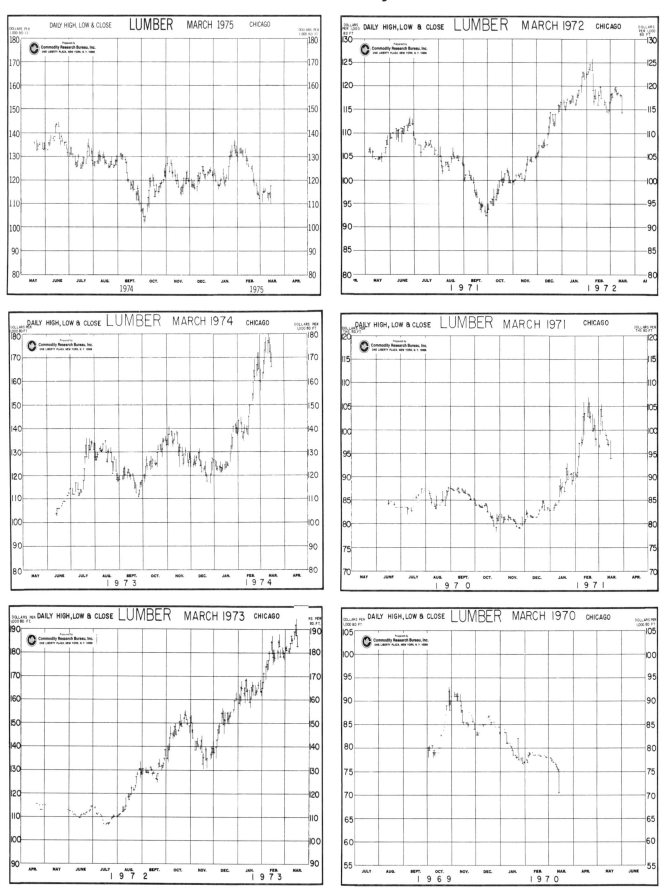

March Plywood Futures Delivery 1969-70 to 1974-75

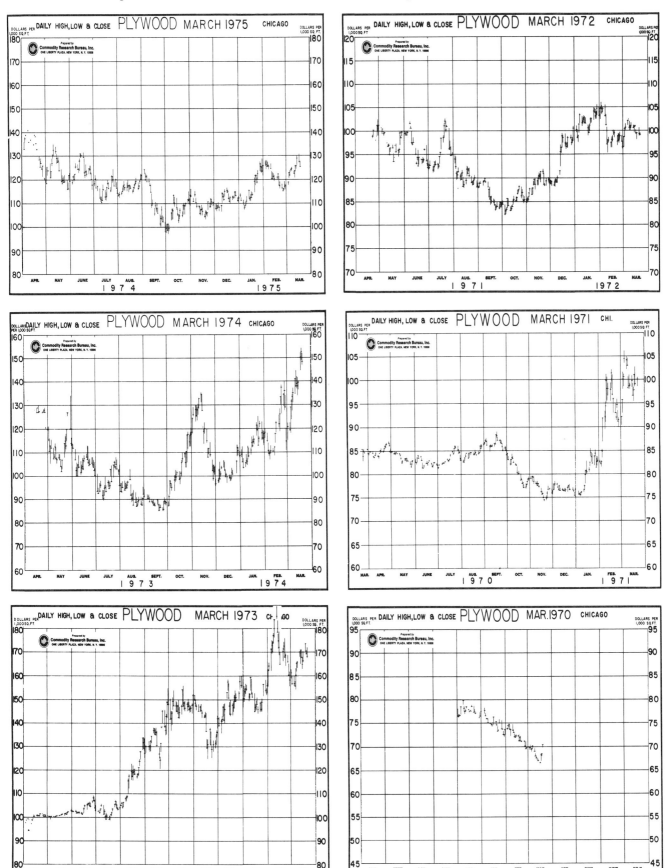

UNDERSTANDING THE OATS FUTURES MARKET

BY DAVID MYRON INKELES

A Gentleman Never Trades Oats

There used to be an old adage in commodity markets which had it that "a gentleman never trades oats." The implication therein was that a sporting man could find more lively areas for speculation in commodities like wheat, soybeans, sugar or pork bellies. Oats, with their history of narrow price movement had usually been the province of the neophyte or the timid soul. Yet like most generalizations, this one was filled with exceptions. Oats had an intriguing interrelationship with corn upon which are based historically significant seasonal straddles. A sharp movement in corn prices such as the 1970 blight scare, produced a sympathetic movement in oats. When this occurred, speculators were usually unfamiliar with oats and unsure of the extent of interchangeability. Oats futures were and still are a vehicle for both currency and freight arbitrages since they are traded in both the U.S. and Canada.

Oddly enough, many speculators first came into contact with the oats futures market through the acquisition of a short position in oats as the "dead" leg in a margin saving spread involving a long position in another grain on the Chicago Board of Trade. Generally, fluctuations in the price of oats futures tended to be smaller than, and unrelated to, fluctuations in the price of grains other than corn. Thus, the presumption was that in a rising market the long leg of a spread involving another grain would gain more than the short "dead" leg in oats futures. Traders have also sold oats against a losing long position in another grain prior to a margin call to avoid liquidating or adding capital. This was not a healthy trading practice, but it provided many speculators with their first positions in oats.

However, this may all be history. 1972 marked the beginning of a major bull market in feed grains, in which oats participated. In marked contradistinction from its normal 10¢–15¢ per bushel yearly range, the price of oats advanced nearly 200% from around 70¢ per bushel in early 1972 to over $2.00 in the summer of 1974. The rally was marked by increases of daily trading volume from under 2 million bushels to almost 10 million and at one point a three fold increase in open interest. While these changes were significant, the big daily volumes of oats futures still are only 7 or 8% of the 150 million bushels recorded in the corn pit on a busy day. Still, oats are no longer the same commodity; no longer the home of the neophyte or timid soul. In August 1974 we had two straight limit down days followed by 3 straight limit up days. The range of these five days was greater than the yearly range in typical years of the 1950s or 1960s.

What's more, the rally in oats has had its own identity rather than simply being a mirror of the corn market. It is true that corn prices were the major impetus for the rally. However, the long term decline in oats production from 1.4 billion bushels in 1955 to less than a billion in 1963 and to only 649 million bushels in 1974 may have finally had a positive effect on prices.

A comparison of oats and corn prices allowing 2 contracts of oats for 1 of corn to compensate roughly for the difference in weight and calories per bushel, showed a large variation in 1974. On May 24 March corn traded at $2.40 while March oats traded at $1.30. Therefore, 2 contracts of oats were worth 20¢ more than a contract of corn. On July 30 at the height of the first bull leg of 1974, corn reached $3.80 and oats $2.06. Two contracts of oats now exceeded corn by 32¢. So far the results were in line with the seasonal spread described later in this article. However the second bull leg which came with the September frost pushed corn to $4.04. The oats which had been harvested two months earlier only reached $2.06 and the spread narrowed to only 8¢. When the full effect of the frost was felt by the end of October the spread went completely contra-seasonally. Two contracts of March oats sold for 10¢ below March corn or 42¢ below the high point of the spread.

The oats crop is an enormous iceberg. It ranks 4th in total world acreage following wheat, corn and rice. In the U.S. it ranks 5th following wheat, corn, soybeans and just this year the increasingly popular grain sorghum. However, most of the oats harvested are consumed on the farm where they were produced. In fact about 25% of all acreage committed to oats is never harvested for grain but is committed either to silage or forage. Of the 661 million bushels actually harvested in 1973 only 102.2 million bushels, or less than 20%, ever reached the 13 primary markets for which statistics are kept by the U.S.D.A. This is significantly different from 1969 when 93.8 million bushels were marketed out of a crop of over 950 million bushels. This represents a large drop of on farm feeding since marketings increased despite a sizable decline in production.

U.S. Total Acreage 1973   Millions of Acres

Corn	71.6
Wheat	70.1
Soybeans	57.2
Oats	19.2
Grain Sorghum	19.3
Barley	9.3

Source: 1974 Commodity Year Book—Their source, USDA Agricultural Marketing Service.

The primary reason for the lack of crop movement is the bulkiness of oats. They weigh only 32* pounds per bushel compared with 56 pounds for corn. On a weight basis the feeding value of oats and corn are similar but due to oats' bulkiness, corn has almost double the economic and feeding value on a volume basis. With much of the cost of grain transportation, storage and commissions based on volume measurement, the handling of oats is at a disadvantage when compared with the heavier feed grains. However, while somewhat interchangeable, oats and corn are

* Minimum to be changed to 33 pounds.

quite different, with each having areas of specific advantage. Also, the stalk of the oats plant has a definite economic value in the raising of livestock. It will be seen that while the commercial value of oats is significant, it only explains part of the reason behind its production. The remainder deals with factors such as crop rotation, preferences of the animals, the health of the animals and the by-products of oats. Because of these non-commercial factors, the price and the supply of oats have reduced cross-elasticity with other feed grains.

Volume of Trading in Grain Futures at All "Contract" Markets in the U.S.
Millions of Bushels

Year	Corn	Wheat	Soybeans	Oats
1961–62	4,987	4,140	4,731	1,605
1962–63	3,880	5,151	14,231	883
1963–64	3,759	5,354	13,129	610
1964–65	3,506	2,826	17,827	483
1965–66	8,391	6,000	15,761	398
1966–67	11,012	10,425	5,525	569
1967–68	7,248	9,259	4,718	413
1968–69	9,067	6,930	5,004	693
1969–70	8,630	3,713	10,156	536
1970–71	12,425	4,235	15,565	385
1971–72	8,014	3,535	20,217	196
1972–73	20,012	9,764	13,712	441

Source: Commodity Year Book—1974—Their source, C.E.A.

Climate and Soil

With the exception of rice, it requires more moisture to produce a given weight of dry matter with oats than with any other grain. Oats are quite vulnerable to injury by hot, dry weather. This is especially true during the month preceding harvest when maximum kernel weight develops. Consequently, oats are best suited to cool, moist climates. Probably the best yields could be achieved in a maritime area with good soil. That production is centered in the plains states is more related to oats' value as a rotation crop than its yield as a grain. Except for rye, oats are the least selective grain as to soil. As long as temperatures and moisture are adequate, any reasonably fertile well drained soil is suitable. The center of oats production on this continent is in an area receiving at least 15 inches of rain from April to September. The crop is likely to be short when at least 10 inches of evenly distributed precipitation do not fall within the first half of this period. Owing to the early harvest, day length and day light are not factors as they are in soybean production. Generally, oats adapt better and give better yields in the northern as opposed to the southern areas of the great plains.

Spring and Winter Oats

Winter oats are planted in the fall and harvested in the late spring. They are generally preferred south of the Ohio River and in the Pacific Northwest, but do not account for more than 10% of the total domestic harvest. Spring oats are planted in the spring as soon as possible after the last frost. This usually means late March in the corn belt and middle May in the Canadian prairie provinces. They are harvested from mid-July to late August, requiring from 100 to 120 days from seeding to the harvest. Five states,

Minnesota, South Dakota, North Dakota, Iowa and Wisconsin account for over two-thirds of total U.S. production. These states grow only spring oats. Various experiments over the years have shown that early seeding in the spring produces the best yields. A delay of one month from the optimum date for a specific area can reduce yields by over 25%.

Wild Oats

The common wild oats (Avena Fatua L.) which are supposedly sown by every young man, are distinct from the cultivated spring oats (Avena Sativa L.) and the fall seeded winter oats (Avena Byzantina). For many years they have persisted as one of the most troublesome weeds and contaminants in domestic grain fields. They are segregated in the milling of spring wheat and sold in car lots as "feed oats." These have 90% of the feeding value of common oats and, of course, are not deliverable against futures contracts. Wild oats are commonly planted in Texas and California for hay.

World Production

The U.S.S.R. now accounts for 32% of total world production of 54.6 million metric tons. The U.S. with 19% is second followed by Canada, West Germany and Poland. By comparison, in 1963–1964 Russia produced only 8% of world production while the U.S. produced about 30%.

Major Oats Producing Countries
Thousand Metric Tons

	1963–4	1973–4
U.S.A.	14,014	10,194
U.S.S.R.	3,700	17,500
Canada	6,988	5,141
West Germany	3,444	4,129
Poland	2,830	2,850
Total World	47,725	54,659

Source: Commodity Year Book 1974—their source FAS, USDA.

World production has increased in the past decade after sharply declining in the 1950s. The initial decline was due to the reduction of the world horse population. The recent increase is due mainly to the rapid modernization and expansion of agriculture in the U.S.S.R.

International trade in oats is small except for intra-European trade and U.S.-Canadian trade. Longer distances than these are usually uneconomical due to the low value to volume of oats. U.S. exports usually total between 5 and 25 million bushels. However, in the 1973–74 season, due to the world-wide feed grain shortage, exports increased to a record 53 million bushels. This helped total disappearance for the year reach 800 million bushels. Since production was only 649 million bushels, we see the influence of both the disappearance and exports on price.

Of all the countries of the world, Scotland places the greatest importance on oats with over 50% of the cropped land devoted to it. As is the case with other grains, small producers such as the Netherlands, and Denmark have the highest yields per acre. The larger producers such as the U.S., Canada and Russia tend to sacrifice yield to mechanization. Overall, due to scientific farming and newer disease resistant strains, total yields per acre, worldwide, have virtually doubled since World War II.

Supply and Demand

The price of oats in the cash market in Minneapolis or the futures market in Chicago, has relatively little influence over the amount of oats planted each year. The reason is that harvesting oats for grain and selling the grain is clearly unprofitable. This is clearly illustrated by the decline in 1973–74 acreage despite a sharp increase in the price realized for the previous year's crop.

A farmer in Iowa growing oats may produce 70 bushels per acre. If he receives $1.00 per bushel at the farm he will gross $70 per acre. If he grows corn he can produce 100 bushels and receive about $3.00 per bushel giving him a gross return of $300.00 per acre. So the importance of oats lies in other areas than the gross return per acre for grain harvested. The value of oats lies in it being a component of a crop rotation which will increase corn, soybean or wheat yields on the same land in other years. Oats are a good nurse crop for grass and legumes. Also due to different harvest times, the labor requirement does not interfere with corn production on adjacent fields. Finally, since most oats produced are consumed on the same farm, they are actually sold in the form of pork, eggs, milk and meat. In these forms oats generally yield double what they yield as grain.

The price of oats as a grain is dependent on many factors. While important, current production and livestock numbers are secondary. The price of corn and the free supply of oats at terminal markets are more important. To the speculator, variances with the price of corn are of foremost interest. To the farmer, the price of oats is of secondary importance since his oats were not planted as an income crop.

Oats as Animal Feed

Oats, corn, barley and wheat are all principal animal feeds. In most areas, wheat is usually priced out of the market due to the great demand for human consumption. The others are only partially substitutable. Oats furnish the least expensive grain protein available, reducing the need for expensive protein supplements. However, they have certain peculiarities such as bulk, digestability and palatability which affect their substitutability. Also, the percentage of oats fed can vary the caloric value. When fed to milk cows, oats have an energy level of 80 therms per hundredweight in concentrations of less than 25%. When used as the principal feed, the value drops to 72 therms per hundredweight.

Feeding Components of Oats and Corn

	Oats Whole Average	Corn 13% Moisture
Protein	12.0%	9.7%
Fats	5.4%	4.0%
Crude Fibre	10.9%	2.0%
Moisture	9.3%	13.0%
Productive Energy (Poultry) Therms Per Cwt.	76	111.8

Source: OATS and OAT IMPROVEMENT, p. 564.

Dairy Cattle

The feed value of oats is about 10% more when fed to dairy cattle than when fed to beef cattle. Dairy cattle consume 34% of oats used for animal feed, and oats make up 5% of total feed consumed by these animals but 35% of all grain fed them. The principal feed is grass either living or as hay. Empirically, in feeding dairy cattle, oats have been found to be more nutritious than scientific analysis would indicate.

Poultry Consumption of Oats

The oat groat (hull removed) contains more protein and energy than sorghums, corn, or barley. However, since the hull is indigestible by poultry the whole grain is not as economical as corn. The hull has certain value which cannot be measured so readily. Its presence in feed, while non-nutritious, has the important quality of reducing feather picking and cannibalism in growing and laying flocks. Also, when pullets are raised on restricted feedings, oats have a special satiety value. The hulls fill the pullets up so they consume less corn. They don't get as fat and reach maturity in better laying condition.

One of the favorable aspects of feeding oats to hens is the tranquilizing effect of the hull. Oats are used in turkey production for similar reasons. The oat hull is felt to help the temperament of these birds, keeping them on feed despite excessive summer temperatures. Also, the main turkey intensive feeding begins in July and August which coincides with the principal oats harvest and the seasonal low point in prices. Many growers prefer to feed oats throughout the growing period and then finish the birds on rations high in corn and sorghums. Broiler production is essentially a 9 week finishing program from hatch to slaughter. Hence, oats are not used with feeds leaning to higher carbohydrate corn with protein supplements.

Feeding Oats to Hogs

Pigs do not like the taste of whole oats. However, if the hulls are removed they prefer the groat to corn. What seems to be the most desirable is to grind whole oats and use them as part of a balanced feed. The percentage of oats in the balance is increased during the gestation period to prevent the sow from gaining too much weight. Nursing pigs and starting pigs are fed rolled oats and groats, both of which are tasty. As a result of these varieties of preparation, pigs still manage to consume 19% of all oats fed to animals in spite of the fact that they do not like whole oats.

All of this points up the complexity of animal feeding. No feed is good if the animal will not eat it; if it doesn't gain enough weight; or if it causes temperament changes.

Horses and Mules

Horses and mules prefer oats to any other cereal. Oats make up 31% of their total diet.

Although other grains might be substituted, horse owners will pay considerably more to obtain high grade oats. Because of their hulls, they are considered to be the safest and easiest feed. Oats form a loose mass in the animal's stomach and are easily digested, while wheat, corn and barley tend to pack and induce colic. The only disadvantage is that when fed oats the diet may be too bulky and not give enough energy.

The horse and mule population declined from 27 million in 1920 to 3.7 million in 1960. The number is now steady. This attrition of horses has been partially compensated by increases in the populations and consumption of other animals.

To summarize, oats although inferior to corn in energy, are an excellent grain for the continued well being of an animal. Hence, they are prized in the growth of animals that must be maintained for long periods of time such as laying hens, milk cows and horses. They are not as good as corn as a fattener, so they are not used as much in the finishing of beef cattle, hogs and broilers. Perhaps in the future, safe pharmaceutical tranquilizers in feed concentrate will even displace oats from their entrenched preserves. Of course, the strong ecological movement for organic foods may delay this eventuality.

Oats for Human Food

The demand for oats as a breakfast food is extremely stable. In the early 1940s about 40 million bushels were used each year. Now about 50 million bushels are used. This represents about 6% of total production. Most of this production goes directly from the farm to the large processors with price relatively unimportant and quality paramount because the cost of the unfinished oats is a small fraction of the price of the finished product. Per capita production is about 4 lbs. per year although twice that weight is needed since the hull is undigestible by humans. By comparison, the per capita consumption of wheat is around 120 lbs. per year. The demand for oat breakfast products may increase gradually since oats are the major component of granola and other "natural cereals."

How Oats Price Movements Are Determined

The price of oats is the price for those oats that leave the farm and move to terminal markets. It may be claimed that a higher price would draw more oats off the farm. However, this is doubtful owing to the relative inflexibility of the feed structure.

Once off the farm, oats are very much dominated by corn. Since a U.S. bushel of oats weighs 32 lbs. and a bushel of corn weighs 56 lbs., a bushel of oats should cost 57% of the price of a bushel of corn. (As a result of revisions in the U.S. standards for oats, effective June 1, 1975, including an increase in the minimum test weight for U.S. No. 2 oats to 33 lbs. from 32 lbs., a bushel of oats then should cost 59% of the price of a bushel of corn.) This assumes equal feed values. In reality most of the feed uses are different. Yet there is enough substitutability in those oats which leave the farm for the price of corn to have a dominant role in the price of oats.

In his excellent article "The Demand and Price Structure for Oats, Barley, and Sorghum Grains" of September 1953, Kenneth Meinken showed that the average price ratio of oats to corn for November to May, 1910 to 1951, was 59.7%. This was only 2.7% above the theoretical level. November to May was used because it is after the corn harvest yet prior to the oats harvest. The extremes were a low of 45% and a high of 72%. These extremes in the price ratio came when the supply ratio of oats to corn was at an opposite extreme. This method can be followed today, except that adjustment need be made for the large

expansion of corn production and the simultaneous contraction of oats production. While the 1910–1950 supply ratio showed the average oats to corn production ratio to be 47.3%, in 1973 oats production by bushel amounted to only 11.8% of that of corn.

Another study by Malcolm Clough of the U.S.D.A. in August, 1970 brought this comparison up to date. This study used a ratio based on weight as opposed to bushels. Thus, 100% by weight is equal to 57% by volume.

The recent feed grain bull market as mentioned earlier was mainly due to production shortfalls in the corn market. The corn-oats spread moved in favor of corn after making the necessary allowance for weight. At the end of October 1974 using March futures as a basis, we find the ratio, based on Meinken's calculations was 48.4% and 85.1% based on Clough. Both of these are at the low end of their historic range.

Oats vs. Corn Production   Millions of Bushels

Year	Oats	Corn	Ratio Oats/Corn
1964	852.3	3,484	24.3
1965	929.5	4,103	22.7
1966	803.3	4,168	19.4
1967	793.8	4,860	16.6
1968	950.6	4,450	21.4
1969	965.8	4,687	20.7
1970	917.1	4,152	22.1
1971	881.2	5,641	15.6
1972	691.9	5,573	12.4
1973	666.9	5,647	11.8
1974	620.5	4,651	13.3

A year to year change in the oats/corn production ratio is significant in predicting the ratio of prices. This information is useful in spreads between oats and corn. The absolute figure is of no value since the ratio itself is in a long term downtrend. The 16.6 of 1967 was a sharp decline from the previous year, and oats were very strong relative to corn. The 13.3 of 1974 was a lower absolute ratio. However, it succeeded the even lower 11.8 of 1973. Oats in 1974 were very weak compared to corn.

The Classical Spring–Fall, Oats-Corn Spread

This spread involved the purchase of 2 contracts of December Oats and the sale of 1 contract of December Corn. The 2–1 ratio roughly accounted for the 56–32 pound difference in weight advantage of a bushel of corn. The spread was put on around mid-May and closed out in mid-November. The theory was that the oats harvest comes in July and August, creating a weak futures market from the spring through Labor Day. The corn harvest comes in October and November, creating a weak market from September through December. In the late spring corn should be firmer than oats while in the late fall the reverse should be true. For many years this was a reliable spread. In recent years, possibly owing to its past popularity, it has been less consistent. In 1974 due to the shortfall in the corn harvest and the resulting increased oats-corn ratio, the results of this spread were contraseasonal. Despite this result, the spread has historic basis and should be considered annually on its own fundamentals.

The Effects of Animal Numbers on Prices

The number of animals on farms is often used as a guide in estimating feed grain prices. This is probably justifiable in the case of corn inasmuch as beef cattle and hog numbers vary considerably from season to season. However, the number of horses, milk cows and laying hens do not fluctuate markedly from year to year. Also the use of oats is too widespread amongst the various animals for this tool to be useful. A more logical approach might be to use animal numbers to estimate the price of corn. Corn feeding centers predominantly on hogs, beef cattle and broilers. The oats price could then be inferred from this corn estimate according to the relative size of each crop.

Futures Market—Chicago

Oats are traded in round lots of 5,000 bushels on the Chicago Board of Trade. They enjoy both the lowest commission and margin of any Board of Trade commodity. Traditionally the oats pit is quiet and generally is dominated by a few men. The number of cash firms concentrating on oats is also relatively small. The futures market is quite thin and care must be exercised in entering large orders. Fluctuations are usually sympathetic with those of corn. However, in the delivery month Chicago and Minneapolis–St. Paul stocks and local growing conditions can play a more significant role. Deliveries are generally from crops grown near these terminals. Deliveries must be in Chicago, or in Minneapolis–St. Paul at a 7½¢ per bushel discount. Currently, No. 1 white and No. 2 heavy white may be delivered at par, with discounts scheduled for lesser grades. Daily trading limits are 6¢ per bushel above or below the previous day's settling price.

Futures Market—Winnipeg

A futures market for oats exists on the Winnipeg Commodity Exchange. Recent trading there has been even lighter than in Chicago. Much of this may be due to the dominating influence of the Canadian Wheat Board which supervises the marketing of Canadian oats. The quality of the delivery grades in Canada normally command a premium over the comparable grade in Chicago. This partially compensates for the duty if an arbitrage is considered. The minimum weight per bushel in Winnipeg is 34 pounds while Chicago allows 32 lbs. until June 1, 1975. Hence, the price of a Winnipeg bushel must be deflated by 6% to account for the extra 2 pounds.

In recent years, exports from Canada have declined sharply and as a result very little spreading goes on between Chicago and Winnipeg. This practice existed in past years and sufficient oats moved across the border to make it meaningful.

Both Canada and the U.S. are normally net exporters of oats. The U.S. is also an importer of Canadian oats mainly to satisfy feeding needs of areas near the border. Specifically, these areas are the northern New England States and northern New York State. Both of these areas are grain deficit areas with significant dairy herds. On rarer occasions, Canadian oats have moved into the south central and western states. However, in these areas they are at a definite competitive disadvantage to the domestic crop from Minnesota and the Dakotas.

In the East, Canadian oats are often quite competitive. Great Lake freight rates from Fort William (now Thunder Bay) to Chicago and Buffalo are about equal as is the rate between Chicago and Buffalo. If Canadian oats can be shipped to Buffalo duty paid at a price equal to the Chicago cash price, then they are at a competitive advantage to oats produced in the leading north central states. At these times Canadian oats can be hedged in either Winnipeg or Chicago and the threat of delivery will keep these markets from moving further out of line.

There are ample statistics available from the Canadian Wheat Board on production estimates, elevator stocks, terminal market stocks, shipments from major ports and railheads and bonded stocks in the U.S. Canada has few railroads and major ports. Hence reporting is both timely and accurate.

Outlook

The past 25 years have witnessed a 50% reduction in oats acreage. The 1975 crop appeared to end this trend. For 1975, farmers intended to plant 18.2 million acres in oats. This represents a slight gain over the 18.1 million acres in 1974 but 25.7% below the 24.5 million acres planted for harvest in 1970. Over the years, increases in yields have mitigated the fall in acreage somewhat. Still, total output fell from 1.5 billion bushels in 1954 to under 650 million bushels in 1974. Since the horse population had already been decimated by 1954, the decline in oats acreage must be attributed to changes in both feeding plans and land utilization.

It is questionable as to how much further oats acreage can contract. It remains a specialized feed for both animals and humans even if its use as a pure caloric feed grain is being curtailed. Hence it will remain a viable market. Should general feed grain acreage expand in the coming years we probably will see oats participating since it is a good rotation crop. Its expansion will not keep pace with corn and in all probability its price relationship with corn will assume a more normal relationship.

BIBLIOGRAPHY

Clough, Malcolm, Feed Price Variations—Past and Present, Fds-233 U.S.D.A.–Apr. 1970.

Coffman, Franklin A. ed., Oats and Oat Improvement, The American Society of Agronomy, Madison, Wisconsin, 1961.

Gann, W. D., How to Make Profits in Commodities, Lambert Gann Publishing Co., Miami, 1951.

Meinken, Kenneth W., The Demand and Price Structure for Oats, Barley and Sorghum Grains, Technical Bulletin No. 1080 U.S. Department of Agriculture, Sept. 1953.

Morrison, F. B., Feeds and Feeding, The Morrison Publishing Company, Ithaca, New York, 1945.

Canadian Grain Handbook 1973–1974, The Canadian Wheat Board, Winnipeg, Canada.

Various reports and statistics of the U.S.D.A.

Commodity Yearbook 1974, Commodity Research Bureau, Inc. N.Y., N.Y.

March Chicago Oats Futures Delivery
1969-70 to 1974-75

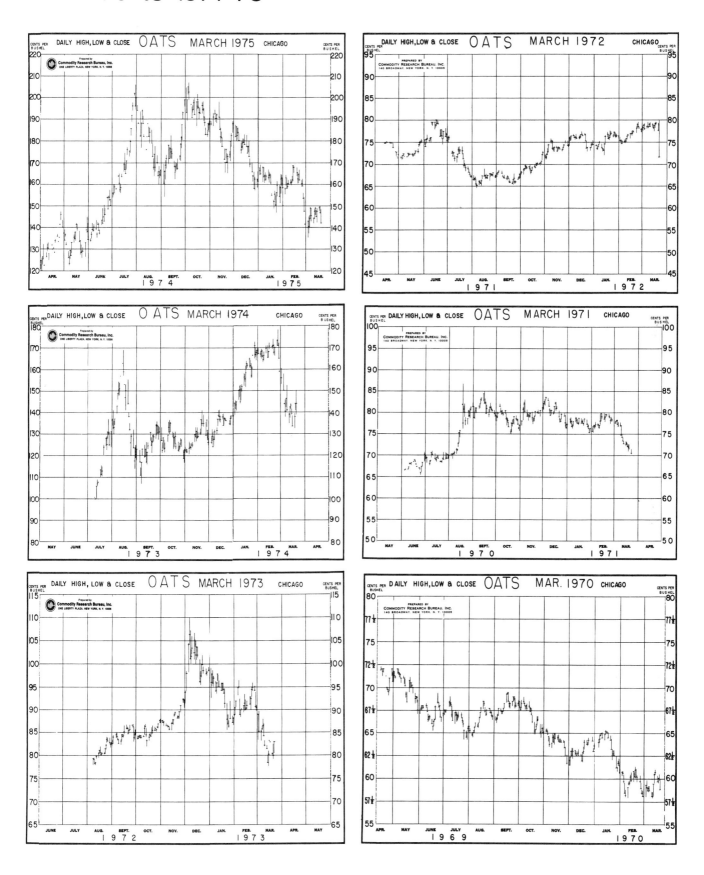

March Chicago Oats Futures Delivery
1963-64 to 1968-69

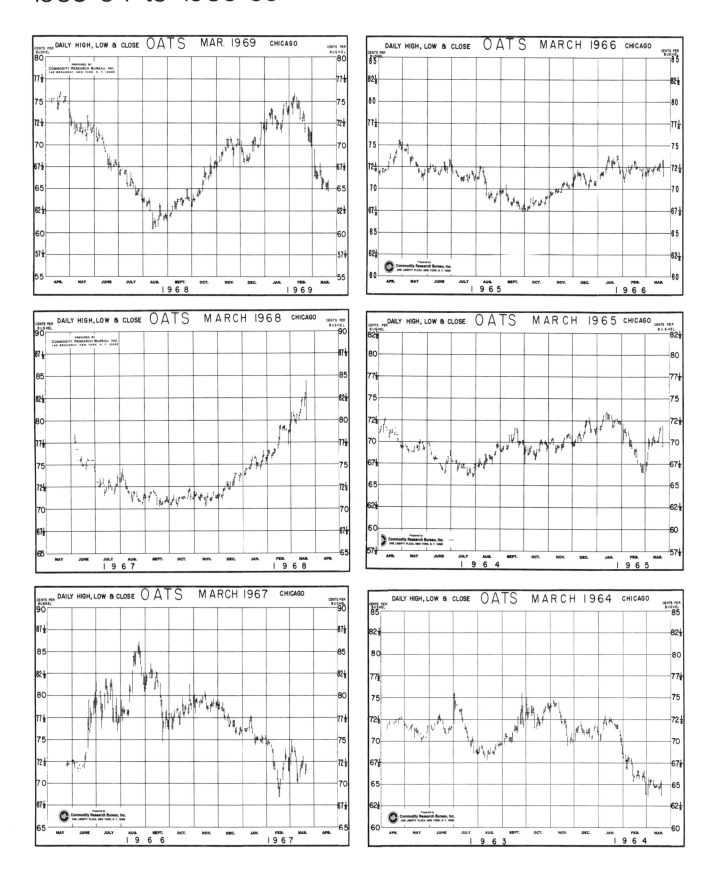

HOW TO ANALYZE THE ORANGE JUICE FUTURES MARKET

BY CLARENCE H. ROSENBAUM

The Frozen Concentrated Orange Juice (FCOJ) futures contract, traded on the New York Cotton Exchange only since 1966 represents the first fully processed food commodity to utilize the futures concept successfully. With delivery points at exchange licensed warehouses in Florida, this instrument gives the burgeoning Florida orange economy a valuable marketing tool for its grower, processor, and distributor components. Concurrently, the contract has proved most attractive as a speculative medium.

Orange Production in Florida Moves Ahead

If consistently expanding production of the subject commodity is any criterion for success in futures trading, the rapidly growing Florida orange production was a promising augury for the FCOJ contract. Of the total U.S. orange bearing acreage of 926.9 thousand acres in 1972–73, Florida accounted for 641.9 thousand, as contrasted to 429.8 thousand acres in 1961–62, and only 324.8 thousand in 1951–52. Orange acreage in that state is heaviest in the central and south central counties of Polk, Lake, Orange, Hardee, Hillsborough, Highlands, Pasco, and St. Lucie.

Florida production amounts to 26% of the global orange output. In the United States, Florida accounted for about 77% of the 1973–74 crops, with California producing 18%, and the remaining 5% grown in Texas and Arizona. Over 90% of the oranges used in U.S. frozen concentrated orange juice originate in Florida groves.

Average estimates for production of Florida oranges and Temples by the Florida Department of Citrus and the University of Florida range upward year by year to 211.0 million boxes by 1979–80 (from an estimated crop of 182.9 million boxes in 1974–75).

The key factor responsible for this expected burgeoning Florida orange output is the very low age of a great percentage of that state's existing acreage.

In addition to the youth of Florida orange groves, future production is certain to benefit from such technological considerations as improving cultural practices, more widespread irrigation, better fertilization, and more effective insect and disease control.

Other examples of the potential for enhanced productivity in orange culture include mechanical harvesting and the use of abscission chemicals. Now in its early stages in the Florida citrus industry, mechanical fruit picking is considered by many as indispensable for offsetting rapidly advancing labor costs in this industry.

Increasing Demand for Frozen Concentrated Orange Juice

So far, the Florida orange economy has been able to avoid extended periods of price depression because of the restricting effects of periodic adverse growing conditions on this weather sensitive crop; the rapidly increasing consumer offtake of frozen concentrated orange juice over the past quarter century; and the marketing of new products using FCOJ.

In 1973–74, 171.8 million gallons of 45 degree brix FCOJ were produced vs. the record 1972–73 output of 176.1 million gallons; 134.2 million in 1971–72; 125.2 million in 1970–71; and only 84.4 million in 1960–61.

The output of FCOJ, the principal processed orange end product (the others being canned single strength orange juice and chilled juice) has increased at an even more rapid rate than the raw fruit itself, due to the progressively increasing proportion of the total Florida orange production directed to that item.

The proportion of the total Florida orange crop (including Temples) utilized for concentrate was about 77.4% in 1973–74, 74.6% in 1972–73, 73.4%

Utilization of Florida Oranges   1,000,000 Boxes

	Frozen Concentrated Orange Juice	Fresh Oranges	Canned Single Strength Orange Juice	Chilled Orange Juice
1951–52	31.4	29.1	13.7	—
1956–57	49.2	22.0	10.0	5.6
1961–62	73.6	18.6	8.3	7.3
1966–67	96.8	17.1	8.8	16.5
1969–70	100.7	12.6	7.1	18.6
1970–71	103.5	12.0	7.7	19.8
1971–72	104.4	9.7	6.5	19.5
1972–73	132,2	12.1	8.0	20.5
1973–74	132.5	10.1	6.6	20.4

in 1971–72, 70.3% in 1970–71, 64.5% in 1960–61, and 54.0% in 1955–56.

The increasing distribution of Florida oranges into frozen concentrate channels has been in part at the expense of consumption of oranges in fresh form. In addition, the usage of Florida fruit for canned single

U.S. Per Capita Consumption, Fresh and Processed Oranges   (Pounds)

	Frozen Concentrated Orange Juice[1]	Fresh Oranges[2]	Canned Single Strength Orange Juice[3]	Chilled Orange Juice[3]
1952	10.76	27.9	3.58	—
1957	15.23	21.6	2.45	1.72
1962	17.98	15.6	1.92	2.19
1967	19.49	18.1	1.57	4.15
1970	20.69	16.2	1.75	4.35
1971	20.40	16.2	1.60	4.35
1972	20.20	14.6	1.47	4.58
1973	24.40	14.9	1.67	4.70

[1] Single strength basis [2] Fresh weight basis [3] Product weight basis

strength orange juice has substantially declined from that of the early 1950's.

On the other hand, boxes of Florida oranges directed to chilled orange juice, a relatively new, but rapidly growing segment of the orange complex, have soared.

Per person offtake of orange products discloses similar trends.

The steep upward trend in total offtake of FCOJ over the years is set forth in the following movement statistics (in terms of gallons, for that product), a result of both increasing per capita consumption and expanding population:

1962–63	69,997,967	1969–70	117,236,419
1964–65	77,933,509	1970–71	137,742,761
1966–67	117,758,215	1971–72	140,714,745
1967–68	101,680,777	1972–73	160,552,385
1968–69	103,527,758	1973–74	174,955,581

The enhanced popularity of FCOJ over the past quarter century stemmed from the consumer convenience which is inherent in the product, and the economy which results in great measure from the elimination of the necessity of paying for the transportation of water and waste in fresh fruit and single strength juice.

On the other hand, a certain amount of consumer disenchantment with FCOJ has been generated by the occasional quality deterioration of the product due to careless handling in distribution channels—a situation which is, in fact, the Achilles' heel of the entire frozen food industry. Although the product may well leave the processing plant in top quality condition, negligent supervision during transportation and at wholesale, retail, and consumer levels often manifests itself in permitting the frozen item to remain above optimum temperature ranges for inordinately long periods of time, thus adversely affecting the quality. Despite efforts to correct this situation, the industry has not yet achieved complete success.

Factors in Juice Production

In addition to the total volume of oranges produced, and the percentage of the crop utilized, the total production of FCOJ depends upon the yield of concentrate in terms of gallons per box of raw oranges, a factor dependent in great degree upon conditions prevailing during the growing season. In 1973–74, the yield was 1.30 gallons, as compared with 1.33 in 1972–73; in 1970–71, the yield was 1.21 gallons per box; in 1969–70 it was 1.24 gallons, and the 1966–67 season witnessed an extremely high 1.36 gallons.

Thus, a rule of thumb method for estimating the production of FCOJ for a given pack year in progress is to multiply the product of the latest USDA Florida orange estimate for that season and the proportion of the crop utilized for concentrate (recently about 77%), by the most recent USDA projected yield factor.

Accordingly, from the supply side of the price equation, the most pertinent basic data are the USDA crop and yield estimates, announced about the 10th of each month from October through July (excepting November), and reflecting conditions as of the first of the month in which the forecast is issued.

The Importance of Weekly Movement Statistics

The most accurate representation of running demand for FCOJ consists in the weekly figures compiled by the Florida Canners Association, indicating total movement for the previous week from processors into the hands of wholesale grocers, supermarket chain warehouses, institutional distributors, and manufacturers of products using FCOJ as an ingredient. These reports break down the total gallonage movement into retail sizes, institutional containers, and bulk product. In addition, the cumulative movement for the entire season is indicated for the marketing year to date, which begins on the nearest Sunday to the previous December 1.

Prices frequently fluctuate extremely sensitively to the weekly movement figure, especially when the impact of other influences, such as the Florida orange production outlook, is at an ebb. In fact, trading in futures is often transacted on Wednesdays (the day when the movement statistics for the previous week are released, following the close of the market) on the basis of conjecture as to the amount of the forthcoming figure. (These guesses, in some instances, prove wide of the mark.)

Experienced market students are most circumspect in interpreting these movement statistics. For example, the figures may be abnormally inflated during the weeks immediately following an end-product price advance, when processors permit their distributor customers to purchase quantities of merchandise at the old price for a short period of time following the effective date of the increased quotations. By the same token, movement in succeeding weeks may be inordinately low, when wholesale grocers and supermarkets are working down stocks acquired during the preceding "back-in" period.

How to Interpret Carryover Stocks

Cold storage stocks tabulations, issued monthly by the Bureau of the Census, include total inventories of FCOJ at all levels, including distributors as well as processors. Given in terms of pounds, these statistics can be converted into gallons by dividing them by a factor averaging about 10 (varying slightly with differences in average pounds solids). From the resulting gallonage figure one can subtract processors' inventories as designated by the Florida Canners Association report, thus obtaining an approximation of distributors' stocks. In turn, a comparison of distributors' inventories from month to month will provide some indication of the flow into the hands of final consumers. However, this procedure is subject to a considerable degree of error owing to the frequent difference in the date on which the cold storage figure was compiled, from that of the nearest weekly canners' stock taking.

The central role of the weekly canners' movement statistics as a price making factor is manifested in their indication of the extent of the carryover inventories which will remain at the close of the pack year around the following December 1.

Sequentially, carryover stocks, a key quantitative entity in dealing with almost all commodities, assume particular significance in the case of FCOJ. This circumstance stems from the fact that the inventories remaining at the end of the season usually consist predominantly of top quality concentrate from the preceding spring's Valencia orange crop. These stocks are required for mixing with new product from the lower quality oranges which are harvested in November and December of the new pack year, in order to make an acceptable end-product at the beginning of the season.

Carryover stocks at the end of the 1973–74 pack year were 48.9 million gallons; for 1972–73, they were 47.4 million gallons; in 1971–72 they came to 27.8 million; and at the end of the 1964–65 season they were 22.5 million gallons.

In recent years, the proportion of the end of year carryover to total movement during the season has varied from 29.5% in 1972–73, to 20.0% in 1971–72 to 16.4% in 1970–71, to 22.7% in 1969–70, and to 16.8% in 1968–69. The carryover at the end of the 1973–74 pack year was 48,861,211 gallons, as against the total movement for that season of 174,955,581 gallons, for a percentage of 27.9%.

The average proportion of carryover to movement for the eight years 1966–67 through 1973–74 was 21.1%, a figure that could be considered neutral pricewise for the following season, assuming an output in the next pack year of about 7% over that of the preceding season, an assumption that would, of course, not allow for excessive weather damage to the upcoming orange crop.

The Crop Scare Season in Florida

The orange producing season in Florida extends from October into early summer. Harvesting of early, mid-season, and navel varieties, which constitute approximately 50 to 55 per cent of the total crop, is generally completed by March 1. The remainder of the output consists largely of the later preferred Valencia oranges, noted for their high juice content.

An extremely weather sensitive crop, Florida oranges every year must run the gauntlet of the hurricane season during September and October, and the extremely dangerous freeze period from late November until March. In addition, drought conditions have been an important climatic influence, although crop damage from dryness has been alleviated to a great extent in recent years due to expanded irrigation facilities.

Despite the development over the years of more sophisticated methods for dealing with low temperatures, the danger from freezing remains a major threat, as manifested during the 1970–71 season, when inordinate coldness in mid-January resulted in a revision of the USDA Florida orange crop estimate from a huge 166.5 million boxes, including Temples, reflecting conditions on January 1, 1971, before the freeze, to 154.5 million boxes in April, and to an ultimate outturn of 147.3 million boxes for the season.

It is for this reason that FCOJ futures prices have tended to follow a seasonal upward trend from the middle of the fourth quarter to the end of January, with values subsequently trending downward in tandem with the progressive abatement of concern over additional freeze damage.

During the "freeze scare" period, the industry frequently exhibits reluctance to hedge a crop that might be severely damaged, while, for the same reason, professionals and speculators tend to buy more liberally. However, as the end of the cold weather season approaches, prices often have been subjected to sharp downward corrective action, a pattern which is intensified in those years when the crop has come through the winter largely unscathed.

Relationships of Futures to Spot Prices in the Orange Economy

FCOJ futures are quoted in terms of the price per pound of orange solids for concentrate packed in 55 gallon drums, with the contract unit 15,000 pounds of orange solids, 3% more or less. The quality must be U.S. Grade A, with a Brix value (the percentage by weight of natural soluble fruit solids in the concentrate) of not less than 51 degrees. Some time ago, the contract terms were amended to provide for a minimum quality score of 94 points, bringing the delivery specifications into greater conformity with industry practices, thus encouraging more participation from the trade.

Futures prices bear a relationship with other values in the orange economy. Consequently, astute market participants watch the latter quotations closely in the expectation that they will provide clues to the direction of moves in futures.

Thus, "delivered-in" prices for oranges are quoted for processors' purchases of open market fruit (as contrasted to payments for most oranges, which are made under long term participation plans), on the basis of cents per pound for solids delivered to the processing plant. The difference between the delivered-in price and the 55 gallon 58 degree Brix future contract quotation represents the processing cost, which averages about 10¢ per pound. Thus, for example, a delivered-in price of 47¢ per pound would equate to a board quotation of 57¢. However, caution is indicated against using this correlation inflexibly, as it does not apply rigidly, and other factors sometimes distort the margin.

To the trader who desires to relate the "on-tree" price of oranges with futures, a quotation one step further removed from that of the board product, the margin equivalent to the cost of picking and hauling a 90 pound box of oranges with a solids weight of 5.6 pounds per box is calculated at about 11¼¢ per pound. This differential, when added to the on-tree price, would theoretically equal the delivered-in quotation, to which reference has previously been made.

On the other side of the futures price is the end-product quotation, which is designated in terms of the price per dozen of 6 ounce cans (the most popular size) of non-advertised brands of concentrate quoted by the packer to the distributor. As a rule of thumb, a 1¢ per pound board price fluctuation is considered approximately equivalent to a 2½¢ per dozen change in the end product. For example, a quotation of $1.87½ per dozen 6 ounce cans is comparable with a 61¢ per pound futures price.

Here, again, it must be borne in mind that these price relationships are approximate, and are valid primarily as average correlations over the intermediate or long term. End-product prices change much less frequently and less sensitively than do futures quotations. However, the expectation of an alteration in end-product values often does influence a corresponding change in futures. Therefore, price changes in the consumer item constitute a significant benchmark in determining the trend of the futures market.

Factors That Influence Consumption

Although the demand for FCOJ exhibited relative elasticity during its earlier growth period, there has been some evidence in recent years of a tendency for its offtake at the consumer level to become a little less sensitive to price change. The well entrenched position of the product as a major American breakfast beverage has endowed it with certain inelastic characteristics at a given income level. For example, the movement in the 1970–71 season exceeded that of the previous year by 17.5%, despite wholesale price increases in the former marketing period.

At the same time, FCOJ has been marked by a rather positive income elasticity of demand, indicating a greater per capita consumption at higher income brackets, a factor which renders its offtake somewhat sensitive to the general economic cycle. However, as indicated above, within any given income range there have been signs of an increasing demand inelasticity.

This characteristic tends to stimulate relatively wide price fluctuations, inversely correlated with variations in the expectations for future supplies, and, correspondingly, to enhance the value of the futures market, both for industry hedging and speculative participation.

In the second half of 1974, offtake of FCOJ benefited from an extraneous factor attendant upon soaring sugar prices. Costs of carbonated soft drinks, in which sugar is the major ingredient, escalated to retail levels which substantially exceeded those of reconstituted frozen orange juice concentrate, a relationship which was not lost on inflation wracked household consumers, many of whom substituted the latter for the former. If, as, and when sugar values recede, it remains to be seen how much of this consumption windfall FCOJ will retain on a permanent basis.

However, it must not be assumed that FCOJ is without competition. Rivaling that product for the housewife's attention are other pure juices, such as canned single strength grapefruit juice, pineapple juice, and tomato juice. In addition, such synthetic orange juice substitutes as Awake and Tang have made inroads into FCOJ consumption as a result of advertising impact. Finally, the proliferation of non-carbonated fruit based canned drinks during the past decade and a half has been a thorn in the side of the FCOJ industry, although some of these beverages use FCOJ as an ingredient as evidenced by expanding sales of bulk orange concentrate for these products.

To a certain extent, the consumption of all of these items vis-a-vis FCOJ is influenced by the relative prices of the two categories at any given time, and is somewhat affected by tighter consumer budgets during recessionary periods of the business cycle.

Furthermore, the two other processed pure orange juice products, chilled and canned single strength, although of considerably lesser importance volumewise, must be considered in relation to FCOJ, as both of these varieties draw upon the same raw orange supplies.

Chilled orange juice has exhibited an amazing growth rate, with the net pack having been expanded from 41,856,890 gallons as recently as 1964–65 to 112,401,971 gallons in 1972–73. This orange juice type has an additional relationship to FCOJ in that sometimes chilled juice is processed by reconstitution of bulk FCOJ. In 1972–73, 13,194,764 gallons of FCOJ were used for this purpose, as compared with 11,251,272 gallons in 1971–72, and 7,502,110 gallons in 1964–65.

The pack of canned single strength orange juice in 1973–74 was 10,884,879 cases, basis 24/2's, a level near which it has stabilized over the past decade. Prior to the 1960's, the annual production of single strength orange juice had declined from a record output of 25,593,134 cases in 1947–48.

Sales of single strength canned orange juice have been maintained in recent years in part because of improved processing techniques, which have resulted in better retention of the natural orange flavor.

Despite the record movement of FCOJ in 1973–74, industry concern that the growth rate of the product may be moderating has been manifested in various proposals to stimulate consumption. Among these have been efforts to popularize the 16 ounce retailer size, as opposed to the 12 ounce container, a project that has met with some success.

Governmental Activities

In addition, various programs for expanding offtake of FCOJ under the school lunch program, along with increasing interest in exploiting the export potentialities of FCOJ have been noted. Substantial increases in overseas sales are being recorded, a growth that is likely to be maintained by the quality excellence of the Florida product, and because of the increasing availabilities of home freezer facilities in such developed areas as Western Europe and Australia.

Government sponsored price stabilization efforts have enjoyed a degree of success in some periods of anticipated over-supply. Chief among these plans have been the school lunch and poverty programs under which the USDA purchases from processors quantities of FCOJ or single strength canned orange juice on a bid basis.

Growers Co-operatives

In recent years, the Florida citrus industry has moved its raw oranges increasingly through grower cooperatives or under participation plans, as opposed to cash marketings. Well over 80% of all Florida raw fruit used in processing FCOJ is distributed under these arrangements, with the remainder sold under firm price contracts between processors and growers, and on a spot price basis to independent buyers who resell to processors.

Growers' cooperatives pool the receipts of raw oranges from their members, returning to them at the close of the period, pro rata, that portion of the cooperative's sales to processors remaining after sales expenses and other costs. Some cooperatives have incorporated FCOJ processing plants into their operations as well, thus assuring an affiliated market within their own organizations for a portion of their members' fruit.

Growers benefit from cooperatives in that a "home" for their fruit is assured under such arrangements, even though it is unpriced until the end of the season. At the same time, independent processors who affiliate with cooperatives can be reasonably certain of obtaining stated supplies of raw fruit.

There are many varieties of participation plans, but most incorporate agreements whereby a grower binds himself to make available to the processor all, or a designated portion of his crop. At the termination of the pack year, the processor pays the grower in accordance with a formula based on the average wholesale price of 6 ounce cans of concentrate as determined by the Florida Canners Association, converted into a delivered-in pounds solids basis, allowing for a processing margin to the canner.

Thus, the participation plan essentially is a consignment arrangement, with the processor paying only for the fruit used in the concentrate he sells over the pack year, as determined by his end-product selling price. Its advantage to the grower consists in a guaranteed market for a portion of his crop, and to the processor in assured supplies, so that he can plan his processing and marketing operations with a greater degree of accuracy, and can depend on a profit margin related to his processing costs.

In addition to raw fruit marketing through cooperatives and participation plans, a considerable quantity of Florida processing oranges is sold outright to intermediate handlers, sometimes called "bird dogs," who pay growers a flat price for their fruit on the tree, and, in turn, market the oranges to processors on the basis of "delivered-in" prices per pound of solids. Such transactions enable the trade to obtain a bearing on the trend of fresh fruit values at any given time, and to relate them to board quotations.

The Place of Futures Markets in the Marketing Scheme

Many processors initially opposed futures trading in FCOJ in the belief that such operations might interfere with good participation deals. However, most packers are now reconciled to futures trading, and there is evidence that some of them are making use of the exchange for hedging substantial one-shot cash raw fruit purchases from large growers or cooperatives. In this connection, it should be borne in mind that the cash market for raw oranges is still large enough to constitute a significant factor in the pricing of end-products by processors.

A stabilizing element in the distribution of FCOJ results from the activity of several firms which buy bulk concentrate in 55-gallon drums and resell it to processors, or deliver it on the futures market. These companies, functioning somewhat similarly to operators in the raw sugar trade, perform a useful role in serving as a balance wheel to the industry, often buying when there are few other purchasers, and selling when there is a dearth of offerings.

As might be expected, such organizations make extensive use of the futures market, although this aspect of their operations is made more difficult at such times as a normal carrying charge market does not exist, i.e. when current stocks are relatively scarce, resulting in a premium of nearby months over distant deliveries.

In this connection, average carrying charges are generally approximated at about 100 points per month including commissions, storage costs, insurance, and interest, although they may be a little higher in the months when product is placed in storage and in those when it is withdrawn, due to check-in and check-out charges at those times.

Hedging Orange Juice Futures

While industry hedging in the FCOJ market has been growing, there is potential for a considerable widening of trade participation. Clearly, FCOJ processors are the most logical industry element for making use of the hedging facilities inherent in futures. Moreover, growers, due to their intimate relationship with processors through participation plans, have a vital stake in processor hedging; it is these growers who bear the greatest burden of inventory risk because of the link between end-product prices and their own returns.

Also, there is opportunity for the orange grower, individually or through his cooperative to use the futures market to advantage by relating the "delivered-in" price of his product to the futures quotation. The latter, as has been pointed out, should bear a theoretical average premium of 10¢ per pound to the raw fruit delivered-in value, a differential representing the rough equivalent of processing costs.

However, so far, growers have accounted for very little hedging in futures. This situation has been attributed to their experience of frequently having been "rescued" from potential price depressing surpluses by freezes; the substantial growth of the FCOJ industry over the past two decades, which has tended to maintain demand for increasing orange production; and the reluctance of many growers to go short in futures in the face of the possibility of freeze damage to their crops.

Finally, distributors, such as large wholesale grocers and supermarket chains, constitute a vast potential for hedging in FCOJ futures. As FCOJ is one of the few processed food commodities for which active futures markets exist, grocery distributors are afforded a rare opportunity to hedge a major product in essentially the same form in which they sell it.

Operating on razor-thin net profit margins, food wholesalers and retailers depend upon rapid inventory turnover for earnings, a situation that dictates minimum stocks at any given time. Thus, these merchants are confronted with a dilemma, in that their rapid turnover policy, restricted warehouse space, and frequently limited capital availabilities, often preclude their taking advantage of periodic low prices to stockpile larger than normal quantities.

However, with access to the FCOJ futures market, they can use long positions to protect a low price situation over a period of time, and, at the same time, avoid the necessity of acquiring additional costly warehouse space and financial resources—this at a capital outlay of only a fraction of that which would be entailed in purchasing equivalent quantities of the actual commodity.

As a result, a grocery distributor so using FCOJ futures would be placed in an extremely advantageous competitive position in being able to offer merchandising specials on FCOJ over periods extending long after increased processors' end-product quotations would otherwise have rendered such special pricing impossible on a profitable basis.

To the extent that broadened distributor interest in utilizing the FCOJ futures market can be stimulated, some observers envisage the viability of futures markets in a number of other processed food products, such as, for example, certain large volume canned fruit and vegetable items. In view of the demonstrated success of FCOJ as a vehicle for futures trading, there would appear to be no logical impediment to similar experience with other processed food items using the same marketing channels.

In the marketing of the end-product, approximately one fourth of retail sales are accounted for by nationally advertised brands of such firms as the Coca-Cola Company and General Foods Corporation. (Some of these companies own a considerable amount of Florida orange acreage in their own right.) Another one third of the retail distribution is sold under wholesalers' and retailers' private labels, with the remainder marketed under non-advertised packers' brands.

As in the case of many other processed food products, the national brands seek to maintain a price premium over their private label counterparts by means of building an image of product differentiation through heavy advertising.

This is not to say, however, that the national advertising companies' pricing decisions have no competitive effect upon their private label rivals. For example, the practice of the national brand firms of occasionally granting substantial merchandising allowances from their list quotations often has had decided impact upon the private brand processors' pricing determinations, and, under some circumstances, even upon the futures market itself.

On the other hand, the f.o.b. cannery quotations of the private label packers undoubtedly constitute the most direct influence on the end-product pricing pattern. Known as "card" prices because of the form of the weekly lists issued by the larger non-advertised brand companies, these closely watched quotations impart a major impact upon the level of futures.

The Significance of Imports and Exports

Although the FCOJ citrus contract is oriented primarily to the Florida industry, cognizance should also be directed to the growing significance of foreign and domestic orange juice imports and exports, and the general international aspects of the citrus complex—all of which have had an increasingly important effect upon the economics of that commodity in recent years.

Foreign imports of FCOJ, of which Brazil is a major source, expanded to record proportions in 1971–72. Comparative imports in recent years, all on a single strength gallon basis, are as follows:

1963–64	9,036,000	1968–69	11,512,000
1964–65	6,584,000	1969–70	1,888,000
1965–66	1,956,000	1970–71	14,288,000
1966–67	3,248,000	1971–72	19,885,000
1967–68	9,612,000	1972–73	3,770,000

These imports are subject to a duty of 35¢ per gallon of single strength equivalent, equal to $1.40 per gallon of 42 degree Brix concentrate, or about 32¢ to 34¢ per pound of solids, a prohibitive rate, which precludes sales of the product in the domestic market.

However, under the terms of a drawback provision, any individual importer-processor can recover 99% of the duty for a like quantity of product which he re-exports within a period of three years. This procedure enables processors to market orange juice to foreign customers on a price basis fully competitive with such low cost exporters as Brazil.

Actually, Florida exports of orange juice are quite considerably higher than imports of concentrate, as set forth by the following tabulation in terms of gallons single strength equivalent:

1963–64	13,710,000	1968–69	26,189,000
1964–65	15,890,000	1969–70	35,397,000
1965–66	18,464,000	1970–71	41,763,000
1966–67	28,694,000	1971–72	28,190,000
1967–68	30,090,000	1972–73	37,720,000

Until recently, foreign concentrate imports did not exert a significant impact on domestic prices. In effect, they merely insured an export market to the U.S., which would be non-existent in the absence of the import-export drawback device. In later years, however, many sources have considered such imports as an increasingly important supplement to domestic production, especially in years of short packs.

The three-year period in which processors are permitted to offset foreign imports by exports in order to qualify for the drawback, provides some flexibility in sustaining supplies in periods of relatively low domestic production which might occur within that span.

"Domestic" imports refer to FCOJ shipped into Florida from other U.S. states, such as California. In 1970–71, a total of 15,288,000 gallons of FCOJ, single strength basis, from other states came into Florida contrasted to 2,935,000 gallons in 1969–70, and 4,108,000 gallons in 1968–69. At certain times of year, Florida processors require for blending purposes California juice, which possesses excellent color characteristics. By the same token, Florida juice is sometimes purchased by California processors for quality considerations.

The record foreign and domestic imports of 1970–71 were a welcome addition to total Florida supplies in that season. Without them the none too large carry-over of 22,567,578 gallons of FCOJ would have been pared to a most uncomfortably low level.

Long Term Trends in World Production and Trade

From a global standpoint, the outlook for the orange industry points increasingly to prospects of production outrunning demand, resulting in the probability of enhanced competitive price pressure for consuming markets. The 1970–71 world output of all citrus fruits was the third successive record crop, and considerable production increases in coming years are held likely.

This situation has resulted in depressed orange prices, especially in Western Europe, and has encouraged the proliferation of protectionist measures in various parts of the world. Among these are Common Market duties and reference prices, in addition to preferential terms benefiting Spanish, North African, and Israeli citrus imports into the European Economic Community. These restrictions and preferences have been opposed by the United States government as inimical to the American citrus industry. Moreover, the expanding world orange production has resulted in a larger proportion of fruit used for processing, thereby enhancing global competition for such important end-products as FCOJ.

As the leading exporter of FCOJ, the United States counts Canada as its number one customer, with other major buyers consisting of the United Kingdom, Sweden, West Germany, the Netherlands, Switzerland, and Belgium.

In view of the consistently expanding foreign sales of FCOJ by the United States in recent years, it is small wonder that the industry views with a jaundiced eye the favored terms accorded by the Common Market to citrus imports from Israel, Spain, and certain North African countries, a situation which bids fair to be exacerbated by the entry into the E.E.C. of the United Kingdom, the second largest export destination for U.S. orange concentrate.

Moreover, Brazil, the second largest exporter of FCOJ, looms as an increasingly powerful competitor in foreign sales.

Brazil's position as a major exporter of FCOJ stemmed from the destructive 1962 freeze in Florida, which sharply curtailed U.S. availabilities, and resulted in high prices for the American product. This encouraged Brazil to establish processing plants for the utilization of some of her surplus citrus.

Thus, in consideration of the possibility of a flattening in the rate of increase in U.S. per capita offtake of FCOJ in the years ahead, of surplus world production of oranges, of more intensive competition for export markets, and of increasingly restrictive protectionist measures in many important consuming areas, the U.S. orange industry is faced with potential market saturation, with only partial relief that could be expected from normal population growth.

That factor, in combination with the likelihood of periodic physical damage to this weather sensitive crop, could well result in a widening amplitude of FCOJ price fluctuations over the years ahead, rendering the futures market for that commodity an increasingly useful and interesting instrument for industry hedging and speculative participation.

BIBLIOGRAPHY

Weekly Processed Citrus Statistics, Florida Canners Association, Winter Haven, Florida

Yearly Statistical Summary, Florida Canners Association, Winter Haven, Florida

"Triangle", Weekly Bulletin of Florida Citrus Mutual, Lakeland, Florida

Futures Exchange Weekly Report, Citrus Service Bureau, New York Cotton Exchange, N.Y., N.Y.

Journal of Commerce, New York, N.Y.

Florida Citrus Reports, Florida Crop and Livestock Reporting Service, Orlando, Florida

The Fruit Situation, U.S. Department of Agriculture, Washington, D.C.

Florida Agricultural Statistics, Yearly Citrus Summary, Florida Department of Agriculture, Tallahassee, Fla.

Market Research Reports, Florida Department of Citrus, Lakeland, Florida

Estimated Florida Orange, Temple and Grapefruit Production, 1970–71 to 1979–80, Florida Department of Citrus, University of Florida, Gainesville, Florida

Costs of Processing, Warehousing and Selling Florida Citrus Products 1969–70 Season, by A. H. Spurlock, University of Florida, Gainesville, Florida

Agribusiness Coordination, by Ray A. Goldberg, Division of Research Graduate School of Business Administration, Harvard University, Boston, 1968

Commodity Futures as a Business Management Tool, by Henry B. Arthur, Division of Research, Graduate School of Business Administration, Harvard University, Boston, 1971

Futures Trading and the Florida Orange Industry, by B. A. Dominick, Jr. and F. W. Williams, Department of Agricultural Economics, Florida Agricultural Experiment Stations, Gainesville, Florida, 1965

Futures Trading in Frozen Concentrated Orange Juice, Commodity Exchange Authority, U.S. Department of Agriculture, Washington, D.C., 1970

Futures Trading and Hedging in Frozen Concentrated Orange Juice, by Roger W. Gray, 1970

Annual Statistical Report, 1973–74 Season, Florida Citrus Mutual, Lakeland, Florida

March Orange Juice Futures Delivery
1972-73 to 1974-75

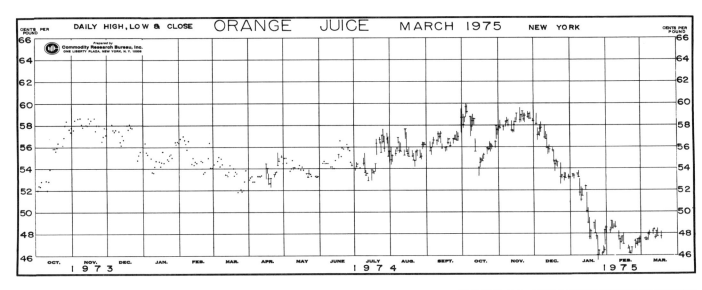

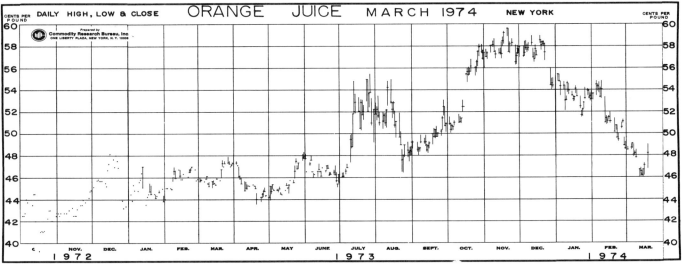

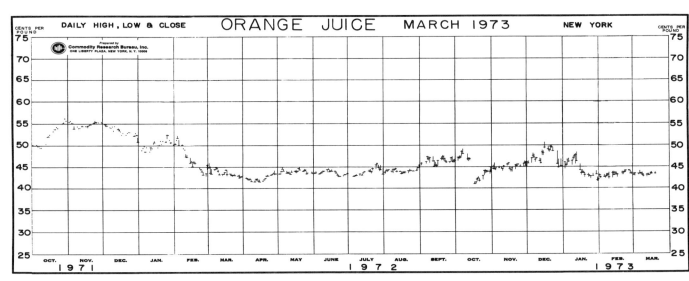

March Orange Juice Futures Delivery
1966-67 to 1971-72

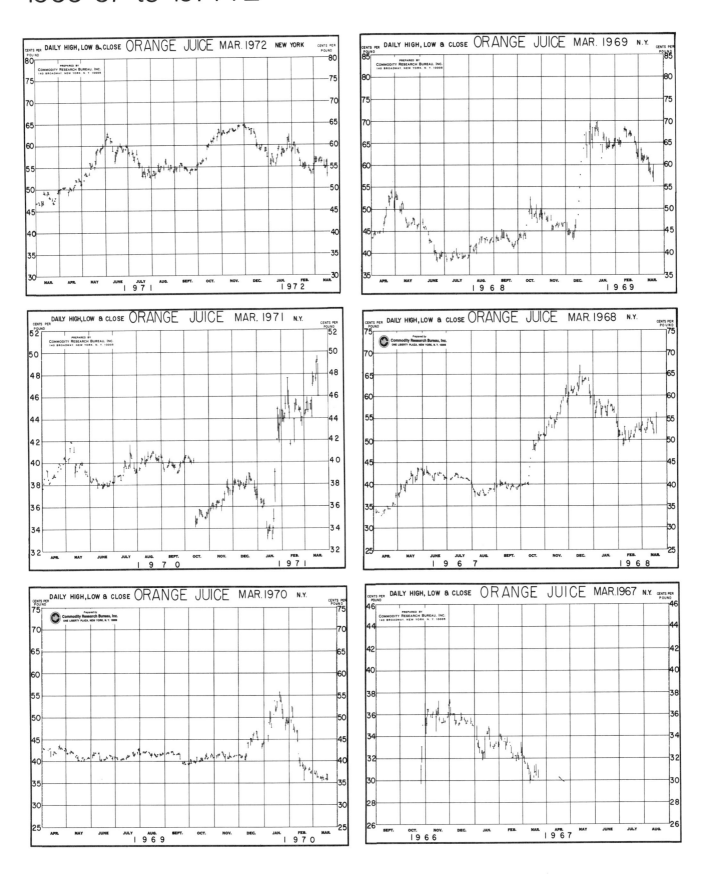

UNDERSTANDING THE MAINE POTATO FUTURES MARKET

BY DAVID INKELES

During the past twenty years, Maine potato futures traded on the New York Mercantile Exchange have matured into one of the consistently favorite speculative commodities.

Apparently, potato futures satisfy all of the requirements of an actively traded commodity. To begin with, the futures market is used by all branches of the potato industry either for outright hedges, or for speculative positions. At the same time, the size of the contract at normal price levels is the smallest of any actively traded commodity. At a price of $5.00 per cwt. the 50,000 lb. contract has a value of only $2,500. Broker's commissions at $30.00 per round trip including fees are amongst the highest of actively traded commodities when considered as a percentage of total contract value (1%–2%). These two factors enable many small speculators to freely enter this market and also provide the customer's man with reasonable incentives for servicing accounts.

However, it is the consistent fluctuations of great magnitude that are most responsible for the popularity of potato futures. Historically, the May contract has fluctuated from below $2.00 to above $19.00 per cwt. In more years than not, this contract will have its contract high exceeding its low by at least 100%. Other commodities can boast of greater fluctuations. However, dramatic movements in these commodities are often interspaced with long periods of hibernation. This has not been the case with potatoes, owing to its exceedingly low elasticity of demand taken together with its perishability and high fixed marketing costs. All of these contribute to a fairly rigid demand. A shortage of a few percent on an annual basis can cause price rises of over 50%. An excess of the same amount can lead to an intolerable glut, generally remediable only by governmental diversion programs.

In fact, the remarkable bull markets in virtually every traded commodity in the past 3 years have somewhat obscured the traditional volatility of the Maine Potato market. Potatoes nevertheless have remained consistently a leader in range of price movement and speculative activity. In 1974 the May contract high of $19.15 was more than twice as high as the $9.20 high of the 1973 May contract. It was more than 3 times higher than the previous contract high of just over $6.00 recorded in 1965.

This article will attempt to present factual information which can serve as background material for those who trade in the potato futures markets. The emphasis will center on the trading of Maine potatoes in New York. This does not ignore the contract for Idaho Russets traded in Chicago. However, it acknowledges the fact that activity in this contract has been relatively light. Most of the time, prices in New York and Chicago run parallel after considering the premium normally afforded the Idaho Russet. Nevertheless, in the recent bull market, New York actually went to a premium over Chicago since the major impetus for this sustained rally was a shortfall in eastern potato production.

1973–74 Bull Market

It was the unusual occurrence of back to back years of declining production in the eastern and central fall producing states which accounted for the bull markets in the 1973 and 1974 spring contracts. The 1971 harvest was heavy and total production of 319.3 million cwt. almost equalled the record 325.7 million cwt. of 1970. Two successive bumper crops left May 1972 stocks of frozen potatoes at the record level of 844.8 million pounds. Production in 1972 fell to 295.9 million cwt. on 10% less harvested acreage. Stocks of frozen potatoes declined sharply to 746.6 million cwt. by May 1973 and the May contract of that year reached $9.20 before expiration. The summer of 1973 was pre-recession and pre-gas shortage. French fry consumption was heavy with stocks falling to 245.6 million pounds by September. This was fully 40% below the previous year. At the same time the weather was terrible in the eastern and central states such that, despite increased acreage, the fall crops was a shortage of potatoes for delivery against the spring contracts in 1974, and prices reached their astronomical levels. Despite actual increases in production of western potatoes in both 1972 and 1973 prices of Idaho potatoes moved to over $18.00 in Chicago as the eastern demand easily overcame the freight differential.

Production Factors

The potato plant is a short dicotyledonous annual with long underground stems called rhizomes or stolons. The potato, a tuber, is formed generally at the end of the stolon but infrequently also along the stolon as well. The size of the tuber will depend on the degree of crowding in addition to other general conditions affecting photosynthesis.

Temperature

Potato plants grow best in areas where the temperature seldom exceeds 70 degrees. The optimum level for photosynthesis is 68 degrees. At temperatures between 68 and 85 degrees, there is a slight increase in photosynthesis but this is more than compensated by an increase in food utilization for respiration. Temperatures above 85 are detrimental to the well being of the plant.

Tuber development occurs when the plant is between 5 and 7 weeks old, and is between 6 and 8 inches high. At this time, the plant is most vulnerable to climatic variations. Tuber formation requires temperatures in the mid-60s for optimum development. Temperatures above 70 degrees lead to smaller numbers of poorly formed tubers. These rigid restrictions explain why the majority of potato production occurs in northern states and why production in southern states takes place during the winter and spring months when temperatures are well below their yearly maximums.

Moisture

Lack of moisture, especially during the period of tuber formation, can greatly reduce yields. The best natural areas for growing potatoes are those with humid climates and rainfall of 12 to 18 inches during the growing season. Drought at any time will slow or even stop tuber growth. This will seriously reduce yields, since potatoes will be smaller and misshapened, as the post-drought growth will be irregular. Today, the drought threat, while potentially great, is of smaller overall significance since a greater percentage of potato land is under irrigation.

Too much rain will usually not be a problem owing to the superior drainage of potato land. It can become extremely significant at planting or harvesting time. The problem here is in getting machinery into the fields. Delayed planting usually means a shorter growing season since the first frost in northern fields often is the major determinant at harvesting time. Heavy rains around harvest time can curtail yields due to rot and may cause a large loss of potatoes that are eventually frozen in the ground at the time of the first hard freeze.

Growing Season

The yield per acre is usually a direct function of the length of the growing season. Unlike the soybean or corn plant, the potato plant's maturation is not governed by the number of hours of sunlight per day. Planting should be done as early as possible and harvesting delayed. The level of sunlight, as determined by the number of days with full cloud cover, is not significant because the crop is capable of utilizing low light intensities for long durations.

Flowering of the plants is of little significance, since plants not permitted to flower still produce excellent tubers. However, it still can be used as a rough guide because the type of weather that reduces the quality of flowering also has a tendency to impinge on tuber quality.

In the northern states, planting and harvesting are controlled by fear of frost. Planting too early can result in severe stunting due to a May frost, while a delay in harvest can often lead to a complete loss if there is a premature hard freeze. The autumn frost makes for particularly treacherous market conditions. It is difficult to know if a reported frost in Maine or Idaho caused tuber damage.

The question, that must be answered, is how cold did it get and for how long. The potato is insulated by the 6 inches to 2 feet of soil on top of it. The depth of the frost penetration must be determined. In a quick overnight frost the soil layer will generally protect the crop, while in a hard freeze, it could permanently imprison it. In the first instance, the short overnight freeze will kill the potato vine which is the above ground portion of the plant. During the growing season this is serious. However, around harvest time, this is of benefit to the grower since the vine must be removed for mechanical harvesting.

In southern states, where a hard freeze is out of the question, a vine killing short freeze during the growing season before maturity can be extremely harmful. The crops in northern Florida (Hastings), Alabama and Mississippi have this to contend with in the early winter. Harvest in the southern states is not determined by the weather as in the North. Here, the vines can be cleared and the potatoes actually stored in the ground prior to harvest. The harvest to a large degree is at the discretion of the grower and he has fairly wide latitude in waiting for good selling terms.

Vine Killing

Vine killing is necessary for two reasons. First, vines must be removed to facilitate automated harvesting. Secondly, it is necessary to kill the vines to set the skins. This is a chemical change that takes place in the skin and makes it more resistant to bruising and skinning during the harvest operation. In addition to these, harvest without prior vine removal enhances the probability of disease transfer (late blight) from the vine to the tubers. The modern fungicides and insecticides tend to delay vine maturity. This necessitates killing by mechanical or chemical methods.

Structure of the Potato Industry

The Trend Towards Fewer and Larger Farms

Potatoes possess a value to weight ratio well below those of most widely consumed solid foods and almost equalling those of liquid foods such as beer, soda water and milk. For this reason transportation costs as a percentage of volume have always been high for this bulky food. Historically, farms were always close to cities for exactly the same reason that soft drink bottling plants were scattered throughout the country in even the smallest cities. Farms were generally small with potatoes only one of many vegetables grown. The failure of the grower price to rise materially in the last 30 or 40 years, along with the rising cost of land near the cities, caused more and more of this land to be taken from potato production. At the same time new mechanical methods for planting, cultivating and harvesting made production on large tracts much more economical. Lastly, although all areas of the country can produce an adequate yield of potatoes, clearly certain northern areas come much closer to meeting the rigorous moisture soil and temperature demands discussed in the preceeding section.

The advent of potato processing has brought on further concentration as manufacturers find it more economical to locate processing plants near the fields. This affords them the advantages of lower labor costs in the rural areas. They also have lower transportation costs derived from shipping dehydrated and frozen potatoes, as opposed to bulky fresh unprocessed varieties.

As a consequence of this relentless change, the number of farms reporting potato production dropped precipitously. The sharp drop is partly attributable to the fact that many farmers near big cities have sold out to suburban builders while the farms further away have tended to specialize.

It is usually felt that farmers are reluctant to radically change crop production in response to price changes except in areas of established rotation patterns. Recently, it was felt that increased wheat prices in 1972 caused acreage in the West to move out of potatoes which had poor markets that year and move into wheat. This was partially reversed by the higher prices for potatoes in the past two years.

Merchandising

Ideally, the grower will first remove a percentage of culls and either sell them to the starch factory or feed them to his livestock. He will then sell his potatoes to a packer who will assemble car load lots and send them to the terminal market. The grower might circumvent this route by selling under a contract directly to the local potato processor.

Unfortunately, the actual structure is not quite so simple due to vertical and horizontal integration. Potatoes, sold as fresh potatoes, are taken from the farm, washed, graded to size and quality and packed in various sized bags. Before this step (if they were fall potatoes), they might have been stored for several months. Nevertheless, once they are packaged they usually end up in a supermarket or roadside stand. The packaging may be done by the packer or by a special prepackager in the terminal market who buys loose potatoes shipped in carload lots. Supermarket chains have extended their operations into Maine, Idaho and Red River Valley producing areas to cut costs and insure adequate supplies. At the same time, independent growers and packers have representatives in the terminal markets to protect their interests in the cash and futures markets.

Lastly, both packers and processors are also growers, having purchased potato land near their operations. In Idaho, the advent of the processor has brought a large increase in production and acreage since World War II. A good percentage of this is processor operated acreage. The largest food companies in the United States are involved in growing and processing potatoes, which indicates the extent of integration in this industry.

Packing and Distribution Costs

It is difficult to give accurate percentages for the profit margin of each participant in the chain, from grower to retailer. These are influenced by the prevailing price level, the pricing policy of supermarkets, the speculative position of growers, packers and wholesalers, and the degree of advertising for specific varieties.

The cost of transportation between Maine and New York is about $1.00 per cwt. It would not be unusual for potatoes, yielding the grower under $3.00 per cwt., to cost over 80¢ per 10 pound bag in a New York supermarket. This means that the distant farmer generally receives well under 50% of the retail value of his crop. The nearby farmer in Pennsylvania or Suffolk County, Long Island can expect to receive more by virtue of his lower transportation costs. The grower in Maine, who sells to a processor, might receive the same amount as from a fresh potato packer. However, since the price per lb. of processed potatoes is higher, the grower's percentage of the final price will be smaller.

This factor, which applies in varying degrees to all varieties, will be extremely important when we discuss the relationship of grower price to demand. An increase of 25% from $3.00 to $3.75 per cwt. paid to the grower might only increase the supermarket price from $8.00 to $8.75 per cwt. or about 9%. The high percentage of marketing costs thus serves to damp out the effects of price movements and contributes to demand inelasticity.

Potatoes present somewhat of a problem to supermarkets that are trying to obtain a standard rate of profit from floorspace. They try to make up bulkiness by charging a higher percentage markup than in the past. Idaho Russets and new potatoes from the South, which come in during the winter months, have been promoted and carry a much higher markup than do the storage Maine potatoes. It is not unusual for Idaho potatoes to sell in New York around 4 times the price paid to growers.

Potato Processing

The growth of the potato processing industry in the past 15 years has been in excess of 500%. The most amazing growth has come in the areas of frozen and dehydrated potatoes which have grown from insignificant amounts in the early 1950s to a total that now accounts for over 50% of total U.S. potato production. Chips and sticks have also grown at a faster rate than the growth of production. This can be explained by the higher per capita income in this country which favors the consumption of these "nicnacks." It is indeed remarkable that in 1974 potato demand from chippers was steady despite a four-fold increase in the price of the vegetable oils they use for frying.

However, it is in the area of frozen and dehydrated potatoes that the greatest growth has occurred and can be expected to continue. Production of frozen french fries increased by over 1,300% from 4.2 million cwt. equivalents to 56.8 million cwt. equivalents in 1972. Apparently, the convenience offered by these foods more than offsets any extra costs. In restaurants where labor is a factor, these forms of potatoes have become the variety of choice. This is particularly true of the flourishing "McDonalds" type of fast food operation. In homes, adaptation has been slower due to poorer frying equipment, less emphasis on economy and deep seated customs. However, the post-war baby now getting married is less sentimentally attached to peeling potatoes than was her mother and probably will move even more quickly to the new products. The variety of these products from bulk dehydrated mashed, or frozen french fries, to gourmet dishes frozen in attractive servers demonstrates the high level promotional activity being carried out in their behalf.

Potato Utilization (Million cwt.)

	1957	1961	1966	1972
Total Sales	212.3	260.1	265.0	268.1
Table Usage	148.4	153.3	133.9	111.2
Chips, Shoestring	17.4	22.6	32.7	34.9
Dehydration	3.8	8.5	19.8	27.7
French Fries	4.2	15.9	34.0	56.8

Source: Commodity Research Bureau

The Four Crops—Their Relative Importance and Marketing Seasons

Potatoes are classified into four groups determined by period of harvest.

Percentage of U.S. Crop Production

Winter	0.9
Spring	7.1
Summer	7.1
Fall	84.9

(Based on 1973)

Despite the fact that the preponderance of potatoes produced in this country are fall crop, the potatoes of other seasons are extremely significant in bridging the gap between successive fall crops. Each of the potato exporting areas of the country tend to supply the importing areas in a regular fashion. These supplies are counted on and, when not available, can cause the price to advance.

The New York market is supplied in the summer by western potatoes from Washington and eastern potatoes from New Jersey and Pennsylvania. Then, successively, Long Islands, upper New Yorks and finally Maines take over the bulk of the unloads. The Maine potatoes start arriving in November and continue to appear into the spring. In years of surplus, they may continue into the early summer. Idaho Russets appear in late November and continue during the winter at premium prices. Florida potatoes from Homestead, Fort Myers and Belle Glade appear in April and early May. These potatoes are of extreme importance during tight supply years to bridge the gap until Carolina, Georgia and Alabama potatoes appear in late May and early June.

Hastings in Northern Florida is subject to the same early winter freezes which bother the citrus crop and can be sharply reduced by them. Florida potatoes appear not to compete with Maines owing to the high premium they command. However, they are potatoes none the less and their presence helps to reduce the demand for Maines. Freeze damage to the Hastings crop can affect the price of Maines.

Weather in Idaho is also extremely important. The loss of any part of this crop will result in Maine potatoes being shipped further to the Mid-west. It can also stimulate a greater processor demand in Maine.

Factors That Influence the Demand for Potatoes

The overall demand for potatoes can be subdivided into several smaller component demands: The consumer demand for fresh potatoes; consumer demand for processed potatoes; processor demand for fresh potatoes; overall demand for potatoes for animal feed; and, demand of the starch factories.

Consumer Demand for Fresh Potatoes

The long term demand for fresh potatoes is inexorably declining at an accelerating pace as the demand for processed potatoes increases, and as diets change. However, if we include processed potatoes we find that the total consumption of all forms of potatoes is actually increasing.

The consumer demand for fresh potatoes is markedly inelastic. A small change in supply causes a much greater change in price in percentage terms. This is because potatoes are an inexpensive staple that are consumed regularly with little concern paid to prevailing price. This is more true of ordinary grades such as Maines than of luxury grades such as Idaho Russets in New York. This was reinforced in the recent bull market when concomitant increases in the prices of the traditional substitutes; rice and wheat products such as macaroni and bread eliminated the impetus for switching.

With regard to income inelasticity, potatoes have always been considered an "inferior good." This means that the higher the income level, the smaller the absolute expenditure on potatoes; higher income families can afford more expensive foods. However,

the very lowest income level (below $5,000) do not hold with this in that they use less potatoes than the groups directly above them. Thus, it is possible that the idea that potatoes are an inferior good has passed and the explanation lies in the fact that the upper income levels tend to be more diet conscious.

Consumer Demand for Processed Potatoes

It is difficult to adequately analyze this component of overall demand, due to its dynamic expansion during the past few years. Undoubtedly, demand is far more elastic for processed potatoes than for fresh potatoes owing to the higher price and the possibility of substitution of the lower priced ubiquitous fresh potato. Yet the fact that the fresh potato often represents less than 10% of the retail value of the processed potato causes changes in grower or wholesale price to be severely damped and result in a smaller percentage change in retail processed price. Moreover, since these either represent relatively higher priced convenience foods at home, or the luxury of eating out, one might be wary of the effect of either the current recession or any future gasoline rationing on the continued expansion of this usage.

Processor Demand for Potatoes

The processor demand for fresh potatoes is increasing each year which makes statistics difficult to analyze with regard to market impact. Much of this demand is satisfied by long term contracts with growers; others are taken care of by processor owned production. The processor also purchases actively during the harvest. The processor is a shrewd buyer of potatoes. At the same time he must keep his factories running during the season when potatoes are available. Thus, processors are apt to pay the going price for the quality they demand and use their acumen in the futures market with well placed long and short hedges to protect their interests.

Demand for Potatoes as Animal Feed

The demand for potatoes for animal feed is rather fixed. The largest share represents culls and undergrades. These usually sell at very low prices. In the case of a glut in a year of heavy production it is doubtful if animal consumption would increase significantly for two reasons. 1. The surplus potatoes would only be available for a short period of time and it is doubtful that farmers would want to tamper with the diets of their livestock. 2. The great bulk of potatoes makes their distribution over a wide area very costly.

Demand for Potatoes for Starch

Since starch can be made from other carbohydrates such as corn, demand for potatoes for starch production is highly elastic and shuts off when prices cease to be competitive. In recent years this point has been well below the lowest free market levels. Therefore, it has required government incentive payments to move potatoes in this direction. When prices either naturally or with the benefit of a diversion payment go below the breakeven point, various factories will open, providing a great demand. Often a starch factory is owned by a large processor or other integrated operator, so that a shut-down is anticipated and not of great economic consequence.

The Early Season Price Rise

An interesting price relationship, which may be quite significant, is the early season price rise. This occurs when either the acreage prediction or the weather have caused the early fall cash prices to be high, with correspondingly high futures prices available for hedges. Situations of this type often produce higher yields than expected owing to greater care in harvesting. They also produce a cumulative price resistance that lasts for months rather than only weeks as do the short duration rises that come in March and April. Hence, statistics determining supply and demand needs for the year should be adjusted inversely to early season prices. Actual supply may be slightly larger and demand slightly lower. These differences are not easily measured but are quite significant, considering the overall inelastic nature of demand.

Imports and Exports

There is relatively little foreign trade in potatoes involving the United States. Imports, with the exception of Canada, are restricted for fear of pests, particularly nematode. Certain countries likewise have banned American potatoes, ostensibly to prevent transference of Colorado beetle but more probably to avoid competition. Foreign trade with Canada is fairly active in both directions. The temperature in Canada during the winter is sufficiently low to prevent propagation of most of the micro-organisms which can plague potatoes. Seed potatoes from Canada are particularly valued in the northern producing areas.

There is exporting to the Caribbean although the Cuban portion has been taken over by Canada. South America is a potential customer for processed potatoes. Although it currently purchases fresh potatoes, it finds European prices cheaper. This is mainly due to transportation costs. Many ships that take beef and grain to Europe will quote very low prices for a back haul. In the mid-60s the U.S. sent a large shipment to Spain. In 1968, 322 cars of Maine's went to Uruguay.

When considering foreign trade in an economic analysis, it is important to pay close attention to production and stocks reports from Canada. Eastern Canadian production in 1973 was affected by much the same weather that affected the eastern U.S. From a supply and demand point of view, the border does not exist.

How Government Legislation and Programs Affect Prices

The U.S. Department of Agriculture is an extremely important factor in the growing and marketing of potatoes through its scientific advisory services, exchange supervision, and market news propagation, much the same as is the case for other important commodities. In addition, there are programs specifically designed to remove surplus from the market. The announcement of a new program usually has an explosive effect on the market and, therefore, should be fully understood by the trader.

The most significant program in past years had been the subsidy paid to those selling potatoes to the starch factories. This has been used in years when prices have been quite low. The subsidy has been necessary because, even at low prevailing prices,

potato starch still has trouble competing with tapioca and corn starch. This diversion program, coupled with the P.L. 480 to Uruguay in the spring of 1968, had a sufficient impact on inventories to cause the price of the May contract to double in a period of a few weeks. These programs, unlike those for grains, are not permanent. Enactment has come during periods of oversupply and will often hinge as much on political condition as economic problems.

In recent years, the U.S.D.A. has tried bolstering the potato market with food donations to the poor. For example, in 1968, 16.8 million pounds of dehydrated potatoes were purchased. In the last six months of 1972 they purchased 25 million pounds of frozen french fries and over 7 million pounds of flakes and granules. With the shortage that developed in the same period of 1973 and higher prevailing prices, french fries purchases dropped to 3.2 million pounds and dehydrated purchases were eliminated. In the future, the recession and unemployment will encourage greater purchases while the fight against inflation will tend to discourage them.

Important Factors to Consider in Price Forecasting

Any trader who makes his own decisions, as opposed to those who rely on others, also makes an economic forecast. The most sophisticated will use a formal economic model. Others will abstract several statistics they consider paramount and compare them to corresponding figures for the preceding years. Still others will do this subconsciously. Having been in the business a number of years, they listen to everything and make a decision based on the "feel" of the market.

However, no matter how they make their particular forecast, all will attempt to answer the same question. Will the fall crop be sufficient to supply the potato needs of the country until the spring and summer crops can assume most of the burden? The critical time is usually from the middle of April until the middle of June. If stored potatoes from the fall are insufficient, it will become apparent in late March or early April. At this time the law of supply and demand will have to ration the remaining potatoes. Since potatoes have an inelastic demand, prices will generally have to rise substantially before rationing becomes effective.

The converse of this situation is also true. If in late March it comes evident that there will be excessive supplies of storage potatoes, those who own them will become immediate sellers, thus driving the price very low. Potatoes are perishable. If spring and summer potatoes are reasonably priced they are preferable to the older Maines. Their competition, along with the inelasticity, will cause the inferior storage potato to be a "drug on the market." In the case of the surplus there is always the possibility that the government will step in with a diversion program. This chance causes a very nervous market toward contract expiration, with prices always slightly above true value. Should the government not enter the market, prices will plummet to actual value in the last few trading days.

Obviously, whether there will be a shortage or a glut is not known by all people on the same day in late March. Some people have analyzed it early. Others do not see the light until much later. Thus, price movements gain in intensity as the situation becomes more obvious, reaching a climax shortly before contract expiration in May.

It is not important, except at contract expiration, whether a participant has actual potatoes or futures contracts. This buying and selling of both equally affect the price, which as in other commodities, is only the sum total of what every one thinks the value is at the point in time.

The Importance of the May Contract

While potatoes are traded in four contract months, it is generally best for traders to select the May contract. The majority of volume is centered in this position as well as are all forecasts centered around it. The other months generally move in unison and occasionally offer similar movements at lower margin requirements. However, they are thinner and do not offer the same fluidity especially during violent conditions. In the life of the 1974 May contract it constantly had volumes over 10 times that of the April contract and over 5 times that of the March contract.

Season's Price Ranges of MAY CONTRACT on the New York Mercantile Exchange

Year	Open	High	Low	Close	Contracts Settled by Delivery
1974	5.15	19.15	4.76	15.50	204
1973	3.70	9.27	3.70	8.25	210
1972	3.70	4.25	2.12	2.25	150
1971	3.54	4.27	2.95	4.25	120
1970	3.40	4.80	2.99	4.30	248
1969	3.24	4.36	2.90	2.90	124
1968	3.07	3.94	1.95	3.00	1,198
1967	3.06	4.82	1.81	2.90	333
1966	3.38	5.33	2.58	4.09	169
1965	2.95	6.50	2.83	6.20	596
1964	2.66	4.49	2.46	4.47	1,939
1963	2.90	3.09	1.78	2.00	163
1962	2.98	3.23	1.94	2.00	959
1961	2.82	3.35	1.85	1.90	288
1960	2.65	4.89	2.55	3.95	194
1959	2.72	3.66	1.76	3.21	831
1958	2.60	6.10	2.07	2.49	957
1957	3.44	3.50	1.93	2.45	365
1956	1.92	6.20	1.92	5.05	75
1955	2.88	5.15	2.57	4.22	392
1954	2.65	2.65	1.37	2.46	288
1953	3.60	5.90	1.78	1.79	214
1952	4.10	4.75	4.10	4.51	

Source: N.Y. Mercantile Exchange

The May contract has a life span of 1 year. Trading begins the day after the expiration of the old May contract. Initial prices often reflect the expiration mood of the previous May contract, along with expectations based on the government acreage forecast. The opening price used to be around the $3.00 per cwt. level. In the last few years it has been around $3.50 but under the shadow of the expiring May 1974 contract, May 1975 opened around $10.00.

The open interest builds quickly in the initial weeks but much of this consists of tax straddles and March–May spreads. During the summer, trading is relatively light with attention centered on the weather. Unfavorable weather can cause activity and higher prices. However, the trader should be wary since potatoes generally have good regenerative powers and crop scares are not often as serious as initially thought to be. This is particularly true of droughts.

The period from the end of August through the harvest is one of frost scares. Many traders consider it a good rule to avoid the short side of the market at this juncture except to sell into a frost scare. However, frost and droughts do happen, otherwise there would be nothing to scare. They can materially hurt a crop, causing wide price reactions as was the case in 1973. Nevertheless, experience has taught us that there are more scares than actual killing frosts.

Government Reports

From September through December potato markets are influenced by the monthly government crop forecasts. These are highly accurate and generally considered so by all participants. Obviously, they only judge the crop as it appears at that moment and can change from month to month as a result of weather. Despite the acumen of potato traders in judging the crop, these reports are often a surprise and cause limit moves on the following trading day. However, two or more successive limit days so early in the season are rare.

The other significant report is the stock on hand report, issued monthly commencing with the middle of December. This report, in stating national inventories, shows the disappearance of the crop due to shrinkage and consumption. This is done by comparing figures either with the last crop forecast or with a previous stock on hand report. This report can cause violent reactions on the exchanges. In years when the market has overestimated the severity of a potential shortage, it has usually been a stock on hand report that sounded the death knell of the bull market. The potato market is similar to other markets in that bear moves are often much faster than bull moves, especially when they start from high levels. This is because the public prefers the bull side and are more prone to panic than the professional trader. In the bull market year 1973 volume was 694,043 contracts compared to only 151,369 in the bear market year 1971.

Throughout the season, there are frozen french fried inventory reports along with Canadian production reports. Neither of these appear to overly affect the market. At times, these reports are blamed for the succeeding day's market action although I have rarely seen these reports either set a trend or reverse one.

A french fries report, which shows greater inventories compared to the previous year, need not be bearish since it may simply reflect greater inventory needs of an expanding industry. Smaller inventories can be significant but, on the other hand, they may only infer efficiencies. They are usually used to show consumption and here they are useful, but only in a longer term frame of reference, since month to month changes can be affected by too many variables besides consumption.

The 1973–1974 bull market was perhaps the exception which proves the rule, and only because the changes were so large. The September 1973 inventory of 245.6 million pounds was down over 40% from the 415.3 million pounds of the previous year and the lowest level for that month since 1968. This was in the face of an increase in utilization of over 50% in that five-year period. Inventory changes of that magnitude are capable of affecting a trend. Nevertheless this was only second in importance to the failure of the fall crop as the major impetus for the bull market.

Day to Day Statistics

The two main day to day statistics are the cash market prices and the unloads at the terminal markets. The cash market prices are quoted by the government at each major producing area during the specific season for that area. Thus, prices will emanate from Presque Isle, Maine; Idaho Falls, Idaho; Riverhead, Long Island, New York and other major areas. Prices will be F.O.B. that point, so freight rate, size and grade price adjustments must be made.

The actual price is of little analytical significance. Its relation to the previous day's price, the previous week's, month's and year's price is the significant thing to watch. Also, the relationship of the cash price to the futures' price is important. It is a good idea to plot cash and futures prices together, considering not only the Presque Isle, Maine price, but also that of Long Island, Idaho and Red River Valley with the futures price from New York and Chicago. The thing to look for is a deviation from the normal. Once a deviation exists, the reason for it must be determined.

Unloadings by area of shipment are given daily by the U.S.D.A. at 16 major terminal markets. These also should be plotted and compared with each other as well as with last year's total and with the cash market level. The number of interrelationships really demands a computer for fine study. However, gross discrepancies can be picked up with careful analysis.

In general, the futures market can gyrate more than the cash market since the former deals with expectations while the latter always represents spot potatoes. For the most part the cash market trend is more indicative than the futures price trend. However, this is not always true and particularly early in the season.

Taking Delivery

The Maine contract calls for delivery of 50,000 lbs. U.S. No. 1 size. A 2 inch minimum Maine grown Katahdin-Chippewa type or Kennebec potatoes in straight car loads. Other grades are deliverable at premiums or discounts.

Traders Should Avoid Taking Delivery

Deliveries are made after the cessation of trading. Thus, unlike the grain markets, the trader cannot retender his potatoes in the same month. Potatoes delivered in April are redeliverable in May but must be reinspected. The fact that spreads between these months often exceed carrying charges by wide margins indicate that some of these cars do not stand for reinspection.

The N.Y. Mercantile Exchange

The pit brokers on this exchange have shown the ability to run an orderly market despite great pressures.

However, the last 30 days of the May contract is no place for the faint of heart. Potatoes are perishable and must be cleared from the market at whatever price level is necessary. It is not the fault of the brokers that price movements tend to gain in violence until they reach a final level, amidst a great crescendo at the end. It is simply that all men, even potato traders, are imperfect and tend to disagree. But then, if everyone agreed, we would have one price and no fluctuating markets in which to buy and sell futures contracts.

May (Maine) Potatoes–N.Y. Futures Delivery 1974-75

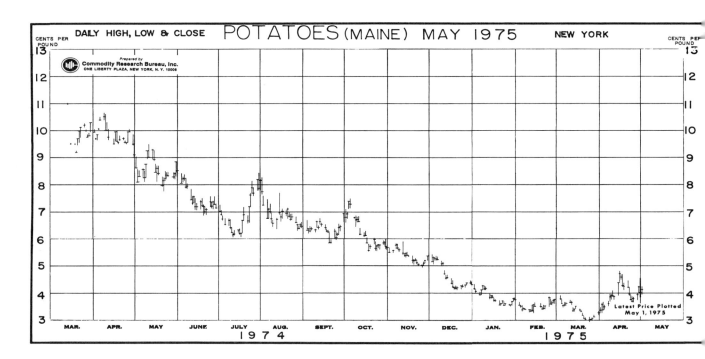

May (Maine) Potatoes–N.Y. Futures Delivery
1971-72 to 1973-74

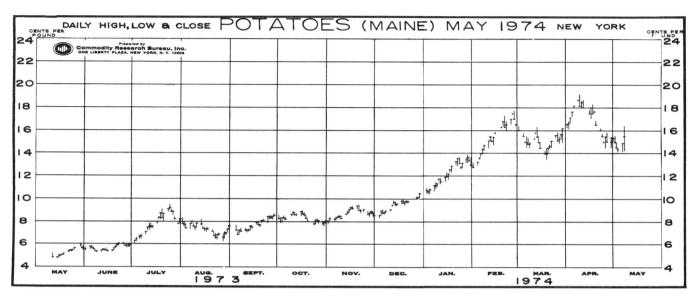

DAILY HIGH, LOW & CLOSE POTATOES (MAINE) MAY 1974 NEW YORK

Prepared by Commodity Research Bureau, Inc.
ONE LIBERTY PLAZA, NEW YORK, N.Y. 10006

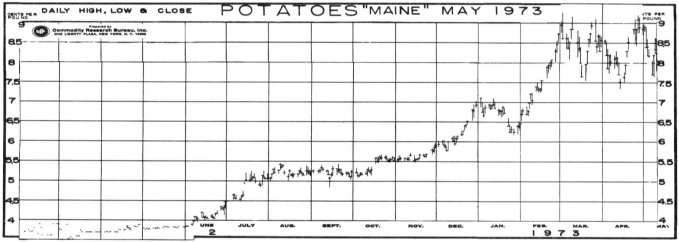

DAILY HIGH, LOW & CLOSE POTATOES "MAINE" MAY 1973

Prepared by Commodity Research Bureau, Inc.
ONE LIBERTY PLAZA, NEW YORK, N.Y. 10006

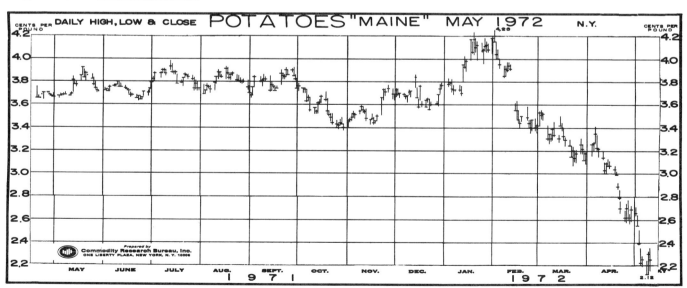

DAILY HIGH, LOW & CLOSE POTATOES "MAINE" MAY 1972 N.Y.

Prepared by Commodity Research Bureau, Inc.
ONE LIBERTY PLAZA, NEW YORK, N.Y. 10006

May (Maine) Potatoes–N.Y. Futures Delivery
1965-66 to 1970-71

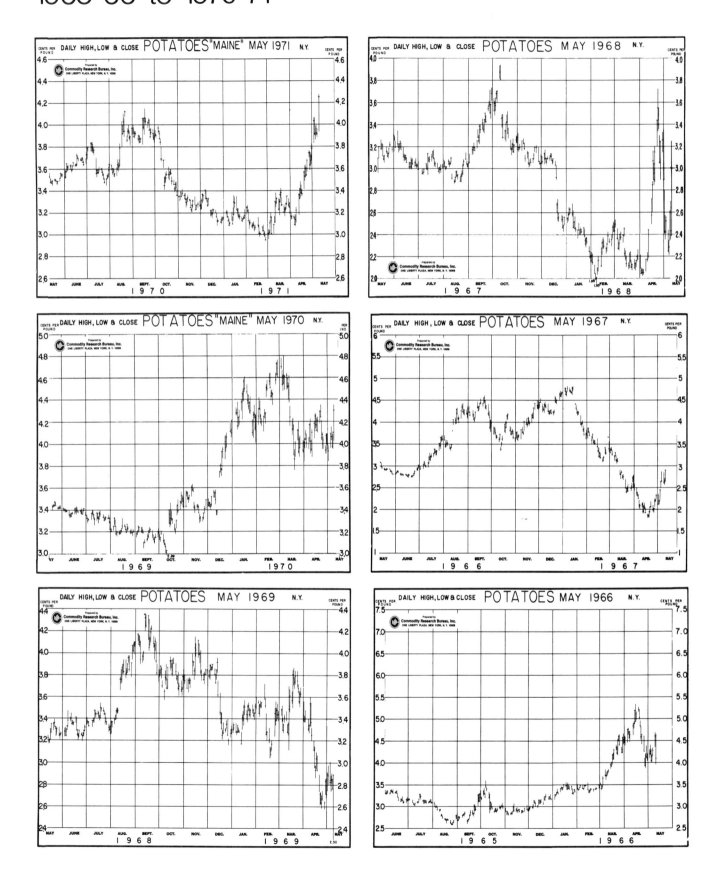

FORECASTING PORK BELLY PRICES—

THE FUNDAMENTAL APPROACH

BY MICHAEL L. MADUFF

A "Pork Belly" is the layer of meat and fat from the underside of a hog which is cured and smoked to produce bacon. It lies outside the hog's ribs and should not be confused with the stomach. Each hog yields two bellies, which typically weigh from 8 to 18 pounds each, depending on the size of the hog when slaughtered.

Pork Bellies are one of the most actively traded commodity futures and offer an excellent subject for fundamental economic analysis. The U.S. Department of Agriculture, the Chicago Mercantile Exchange and many private services publish a continuing wealth of data from which the analyst can estimate future pork belly supplies. Furthermore, since consumer demand is relatively inelastic, even small changes in supply can result in substantial price movements.

There is little substitution of other products for bellies or bellies for other products, which reduces the need to predict price movements for a whole range of products as might be the case with other commodities such as grains, edible oils, or even hogs, cattle and broilers. In the case of pork bellies, weather extremes will not kill an entire crop overnight as might happen with orange juice or potatoes, although bad weather may temporarily retard marketings or even hog growth.

Seasonal production factors require that during the period of October to early May some pork bellies be frozen and placed in storage for use during the following late May to September period. However, since bellies are relatively perishable, excess supplies from one crop year are not carried for long into the succeeding crop year.

Contract Specifications

Prices of frozen pork belly futures on the Chicago Mercantile Exchange are quoted in cents per pound. The minimum fluctuation is 1/40th of a cent per pound or 2½ points which corresponds to $9.00 per contract. The maximum fluctuation permitted in a single day is 1½ cents per pound or $540 per contract above or below the previous day's settlement price. This makes for a maximum possible daily range of 3 cents per pound or $1,080 per contract.

Minimum margin requirements set by the Chicago Mercantile Exchange at this writing (early 1975) are $1,000 per contract (higher in the delivery month) but subject to change on short notice. Minimum commissions at most brokerage firms are $45 to $50 for a round turn (one purchase and one sale).

Five contracts are traded; for delivery in February, March, May, July and August. The contract calls for delivery of 36,000 pounds (plus or minus 5%) of pork bellies uniformly weighing 12 to 14 pounds each. Bellies in other weight ranges, 10 to 12 pounds, 14 to 16 pounds, and 16 to 18 pounds, may be delivered at discounts ranging from 1¢ to 3½¢ per pound. The product must be produced and stored as a single unit

on or after November 1st of the current crop year in an Exchange-approved commercial cold storage warehouse.

Before delivery, a contract unit of bellies must be inspected and approved by a U.S.D.A. grader as conforming to C.M.E. standards for quality and workmanship. Limited deviations from these standards will result in a quality discount of ½¢ to 2¢ per pound. These quality deviations primarily measure factors relating to yield when the product is made into bacon but will generally not affect the quality of the bacon produced. All bellies must be totally wholesome for human consumption to qualify for delivery, regardless of grade.

Once a particular car lot has passed inspection, it may be redelivered any number of times against any and all options in the current crop year without any further inspection required.

Par delivery of bellies can be made only from Exchange-approved warehouses in Chicago but deliveries can be made from warehouses outside Chicago according to a schedule of allowances set up by the Exchange.

Since the industry does not use the Chicago Mercantile Exchange grading system to judge quality but relies more on the reputation of each production plant, delivered contract units which have been heavily discounted may be economically more desirable to a merchandiser. Similarly, product discounted for delivery outside Chicago may be desirable to a processor in a nearby location.

Technical Aspects

Most of the technical rules of price forecasting which apply to other commodities can be used with equal validity in predicting price movements in bellies.

Because of the large speculator interest in this commodity, technical factors can at times create self-fulfilling prophesies. Numerous individual speculators may see in the technical factors signs of an impending move. Then acting on their belief, these speculators will, by their own buying (or selling), create the move they had predicted.

In recent years technical "trend-following" trading methods have become increasingly popular among some advisory services and commodity investment funds as well as some individual traders. Since these "trend-following" traders tend to pyramid rather than lighten up when the market is going their way and tend to liquidate their position only when they believe the trend has changed, they tend to accentuate the magnitude of a price move in one direction and then cause a violent reaction once the trend changes direction.

Even the most sophisticated fundamental trader will find technical analysis helpful in confirming fundamental conclusions and in suggesting the timing of commitments. Many of the biggest losses in speculative markets come from trades based on good fundamental analysis without proper regard to the "market psychology" manifest in the technical elements of trend, price movement, volume and open interest. Frequently, after suffering heavy losses, the unfortunate fundamentalist may see the market turn around and vindicate his original judgment.

The Spring Run-Up

Often the futures market appears to stage a rally early in the calendar year for no apparent fundamental reason. For the most part, this seasonal upturn can be attributed to speculator psychology.

Several elements have contributed to this seasonal price movement. The first is the natural tendency of public speculators to be buyers rather than sellers. Most of these speculators enter the futures market with experience in the stock market where short selling is rare, difficult and often frowned upon.

A second element involves the relatively short history of futures trading in frozen pork bellies. It wasn't until 1965 that the market really became interesting. The 1965 and 1966 contracts both staged fundamentally justifiable run-ups around the first of the year and again commencing the following spring.

As speculators were analyzing the market in 1967, 1968 and 1969, they had this history to look back on and the slightest fundamental excuse was able to induce spring buying which in turn made the chart look bullish. This then set off a rally which was practically a textbook example of the self-fulfilling prophecy concept.

The market is most susceptible to this type of technical or psychologically induced move prior to June when fundamental realities are not yet able to discipline the price level.

Another factor is that in late spring the relationship between cash and futures must change from futures prices over fresh bellies to encourage building storage stocks to a relationship with futures discounted to fresh bellies to encourage liquidation of storage stocks. As fresh bellies go up, reacting to seasonally reduced hog slaughter, futures prices may rally trying to maintain the prior price relationship.

A similar, although less intense, rally can develop around January or early February as hog slaughter seasonally drops off for a few weeks. At this time, price relationships will change temporarily and in some years there will be a temporary movement of bellies out of storage.

The Crop Year

The fundamental factors affecting supply and demand for pork bellies are relatively straightforward. This may be a contributing factor to the commodity's popularity among speculators.

Trading in each belly contract generally begins one year before that contract is to mature. However, since bellies certificated for delivery on the February contract remain eligible for delivery through August of the same year, the crop year may be considered as an eighteen month period from the start of trading in the February contract until liquidation of the August contract one-and-a-half years later. As a result there is an overlapping of crop years during the March–August period when the old crop is liquidating and the open interest in the new crop is starting to build up.

For analytical purposes, we can divide each crop year into three basic phases—the *Anticipatory Phase*, from the beginning of trading in March until late November, the *Accumulation and Hedging Phase*, December to May, and the *Realization and Liquidation Phase*, May to the end of trading in August. Because there is an overlapping of crop years, each should be viewed independently in making this analysis.

Anticipatory Phase

During the *Anticipatory Phase*, the market responds primarily to speculator sentiment. The expiring contracts of the prior crop year will influence the market at this time as the new crop behaves sympathetically, tending to follow the price trends of the old. This may be the result of some of the new crop open interest being straddled against positions in the old crop contracts.

During the middle portion of the *Anticipatory Phase*, after the old crop has liquidated, the fundamental picture has not yet become clear and technical analysis can be most safely relied upon. On the fundamental side, the market is now trying to anticipate basic needs and supplies for the coming summer season.

Five basic questions must be answered by the fundamental analyst during this portion of the *Anticipatory Phase*:

(1) How much fresh production of pork bellies will be available next summer?
(2) What quantity of pork bellies, either fresh or frozen, will be required next summer?
(3) What quantity of storage stocks will be needed to make up the excess of needs over fresh production?
(4) How much fresh production will be available this fall and winter from which to build the needed storage stocks?
(5) What futures price level is currently required to divert the proper quantity of bellies from consumption into storage?

Many of the factors which will eventually answer these questions are difficult to assess because they are so far off and unexpected, intervening events may completely change the situation. The primary fundamental consideration at this time has to be breeding and farrowing intentions. Therefore, the most important market information will be the Pig Crop Reports, which survey these intentions. Sow slaughter, breeding stock retention, the hog-corn price ratio (which indicates profitability of hog-raising), credit availability, and the general agricultural economic situation may also be worth studying for a clue to future breeding and farrowing intentions.

But, for the moment, market psychology will be the predominant price factor and the market may make several false moves trying to find itself before the fundamentals become more clear.

Trading in these early months of the pork belly contract is generally light for two major reasons: The expiring contracts of the old crop year are reaching a crescendo of activity just prior to liquidation, taking the play away from the less interesting new crop year; and, the uncertainty of the distant options tends to dampen speculative enthusiasm in them.

Accumulation and Hedging Phase

Later, in the fall, the market enters its *Accumulation and Hedging Phase*. Technically, pork bellies are not eligible for board delivery if stored before November 1st, but as a practical matter the industry starts building storage stocks thirty to sixty days before that date. At this time the various storage reports; monthly U.S. Cold Storage Holdings, weekly Chicago Mercantile Exchange-approved warehouses, and daily CME-approved warehouses in Chicago, begin to take on importance. And now, as the storage stocks build, the market finds its advance estimates of these storage stocks gradually confirmed or corrected, and the price level adjusts accordingly.

At the same time, breeding and farrowing intentions are becoming reality and the future becomes clearer, causing the market to re-evaluate the need for summer storage stocks and again adjust futures prices.

Daily hog receipts at terminal and interior markets, federally inspected slaughter numbers, average weights, and weekly pork production now become important as indications of the quantity of bellies which will be available for storage. Weekly bacon slicing figures are important as an indication of current demand for bellies with which storage needs must compete.

During this period the fundamentals begin to overtake the purely technical factors of market psychology in importance as more fundamental data becomes available and conjecture on intentions is replaced by reports of actualities. Patterns which have built up on the charts for weeks or even months may be violated overnight when the market opens as much as 150 points above or below the previous day's close (the permissible limit) in response to some major report or piece of news. Nonetheless, market psychology, and particularly bullish sentiment has often caused the market to make its yearly highs during the *Accumulation and Hedging Phase*.

Realization and Liquidation Phase

Some time around May, storage holdings reach their peak and the market enters its *Realization and Liquidation Phase* as frozen bellies start to move out of storage. If this turning point comes early, it will mean a shorter storage period and smaller stocks, and prices may have to rise to stretch these supplies out over the using season. If it comes late, it will mean larger supplies and a shorter mechandising period and prices may have to drop to stimulate consumption and permit adequate liquidation of stocks before the end of the season.

It is during this *Realization and Liquidation Phase* that the market can experience some of its most extensive and dramatic moves as the factors of fresh production, storage stocks and summer consumption become clear realities rather than just an estimate of the future.

Major moves at this time are often the result of bad forecasting by the entire market earlier in the season. If prices were too low too long, adequate storage stocks will not have been accumulated; if prices were too high, massive storage stocks can depress the market. Now, with very little time left before final liquidation, the market will suddenly discover true needs and move violently trying to use up

large stocks before the fall hog run begins or alternately trying to ration limited stocks for the remainder of the season.

Even the most experienced trader will tread lightly in the expiring August option for fear of either finding himself stuck short with few bellies available for delivery or owning the actual merchandise, by now as much as eight or nine months old, and no one eager to buy it. The latter occurred in 1967 when nearly 500 cars were delivered and many later liquidated substantially below the 29.25 contract low set on the last day of trading.

Demand

The demand for bacon, and hence pork bellies, appears to be fairly uniform and responds only moderately to any but the most extreme price moves. This makes correct analysis of the supply situation most important since even a small change in supply can result in a major change in price. One evidence of this is the failure of belly prices to parallel general economic conditions on a regular basis unlike some other commodities such as live cattle.

This inelasticity of demand can be traced to the specialized uses of bacon in fairly small quantities and the absence of other products which can be substituted back and forth for bacon as relative prices rise and fall. Generally, it can be said of any commodity which has an inelastic demand that low prices fail to greatly stimulate consumer purchases and high prices fail to greatly retard them.

Spices provide an extreme example of inelasticity in demand. If a housewife needs one ounce of nutmeg, she is going to buy one ounce of nutmeg at the grocery store—no more and no less—whether the price is 9¢ per ounce or 89¢ per ounce. Certainly the demand for bacon is not as inelastic as the demand for spices but it does tend toward this direction and is definitely less elastic than the demand for other meat products.

Bacon has less nutritive value for its cost than most other foods and is not usually eaten by itself. Two major uses of bacon are as a breakfast food with eggs and as a warm weather light lunch in bacon, lettuce and tomato sandwiches. Bacon is also used as a flavoring in salads, soups and vegetables.

Because bacon is used in small quantities with other foods, the price of bacon will be less determinative of eating habits than will the price of these other foods. So, in deciding to eat bacon and eggs for breakfast, a bacon, lettuce and tomato sandwich for lunch, or a bacon-wrapped filet mignon for dinner, the consumer will be less influenced by the price of bacon than by the prices of eggs, tomatoes or filet mignon.

While some other meat products may be substituted for bacon as a breakfast food, the same is not true when it is used more as a condiment and less as a meal. This would explain why the price of bacon does not follow the prices of other meats very closely. The price of beef or poultry will tend to have only a random relation to the price of bacon. Since the production of bacon and other pork products both depend on the supply of hogs, some relationship between the two can be expected but only to the extent that supply, and not demand, determines price.

Although the consumer has few products for which bacon can be substituted, the industry is able to use bellies instead of trimmings in sausage products if price relationships are favorable. However, since trimmings are generally inexpensive, this will take place only when belly prices are severely depressed.

Furthermore, since bacon is a by-product of pork production, representing only about 12% of the live hog weight, a change in the price of bacon will have only a small effect in influencing farmers to increase or decrease hog production.

The Bacon Slice

Strictly speaking, demand is defined as the quantity of a product which consumers would be willing to purchase at various prices. Since it is virtually impossible to measure consumer attitudes quantitatively, a study of belly consumption must be accepted in the hope that it will be a reasonable reflection of demand. This can be done in two ways, measuring bacon slicings and estimating belly disappearance.

Weekly estimates of the quantity of bacon sliced under federal inspection are released by the U.S.D.A. generally three weeks after actual production. These figures, typically in the range of 20 to 30 million pounds per week at present, represent about three-quarters of total bacon production. The remainder would be accounted for by bacon produced exclusively for intrastate sale in other than federally approved plants, slab bacon and bacon used commercially in other products, such as canned soup or pork and beans. In estimating federally inspected bacon slicings, the government polls its own inspectors rather than depending on sample surveys, thus making this estimate fairly accurate. However, since this figure represents only a portion of belly consumption, it can be misleading as an indicator of total belly consumption in a given period. When comparing the bacon slice to figures for prior years, consideration should be given to an increasing number of slicing plants coming under federal inspection each year.

Disappearance

Disappearance can be estimated by a simple balance sheet method but the availability of data will generally require that a period of at least one month be used. Bellies available for consumption during the period can be estimated by taking beginning storage stocks and adding belly production during the period. (Total dressed pork production times a factor of 17½% to 18% will give a reasonable estimate of belly production.) Subtract storage stocks at the end of the period and an estimate of belly consumption will result.

The disappearance method of measuring consumption obviously contains possible sources of error and hence is likely to be inaccurate. It can, however, be useful as a check in evaluating the U.S.D.A. weekly bacon slice reports.

Very rough estimates of disappearance can be made by a daily study of storage movements at C.M.E.-approved warehouses in Chicago (C.M.E. warehouse outside of Chicago are reported on a weekly basis) and U.S.D.A. daily slaughter or weekly pork production statistics.

Role of Inventory Levels

It should be remembered that consumption of bellies is at best an estimate of demand for bacon and may at times give an inaccurate picture of actual bacon consumption. Consumers, retailers, and members of the processing industry itself each maintain inventories which may vary in size from time to time. Decisions to increase the size of these inventories may cause a false appearance of increased consumption and result in an equally false appearance of decreased consumption when inventories are reduced.

Adjustment of belly inventories by the industry can at times severely accentuate short-term fluctuations. Let us assume that something happens to make members of the industry bullish for the near-term. Bacon processors, eager to assure themselves adequate supplies of bellies, increase their normal inventories, filling their own warehouse space and making additional purchase commitments into the future. This additional buying stimulates a rise in cash prices. At the same time, packers who would normally be selling excess supplies of bellies withdraw their offerings from the cash market, hoping to sell on a higher market a short time later and thereby further stimulate the price rise.

After their inventories have reached a peak, bacon processors must cease further buying and withdraw from the market while they use up these excess inventories. Suddenly a market which has been used to a higher than normal level of user purchases is faced with lower buying levels and the price begins to drop. At the same time, packers are also depressing prices as, in addition to their normal selling, they begin to liquidate the excess supplies they have built up during the price rise.

As bearish sentiment sets in, processors permit their inventories to fall to minimum levels and packers contract sales of bellies in the future. As during the price advance, this "defensive action" by the industry in the face of falling prices now accentuates the downward price velocity and guarantees a reaction when supplies must once more be replenished.

A particularly extreme example of this phenomenon occurred in August, 1973 immediately before and after the lifting of government price ceilings on dressed meat products. Producers, processors, distributors and consumers all built up their inventories before the ceilings came off, hoarding supplies in anticipation of higher prices. Then when the ceilings in fact came off, prices fell sharply.

International Trade in Bellies

While there is some international trade in bellies and bacon, the market can be analyzed both on the supply and demand sides as essentially a domestic market. Although U.S.D.A. publishes some data on international trade in pork products, very little data is available on pork bellies as such. Canada and Japan have been buyers of frozen bellies and in 1969 both of these countries bought substantial quantities from the U.S.

The United States also imports about 12 million pounds of smoked bacon a year, 75% from Denmark and the remainder mostly from Canada. This compares with total annual domestic production of 1½ to 2 billion pounds of bacon. Annual variations in quantity of imports are generally small and not of major significance. Unfortunately, the data available on international trade in bellies and bacon is so slight that the trader must often rely on industry rumors for such information.

Supply

As mentioned above, there are only two sources of supply of pork bellies, fresh production and storage stocks.

Fresh production of bellies will depend on two factors—the number of hogs slaughtered during the period and the weight at which those hogs are slaughtered. Estimates of the number of hogs slaughtered under federal inspection are released by the U.S.D.A. each afternoon for that day. These figures are revised weekly and annually.

U.S.D.A. market reports at some terminal markets give a daily or weekly figure for the average weight of market hogs passing through their yards. This may be helpful in weighting the importance of relative daily slaughter statistics.

Federal estimates of pork production in terms of pounds are available on a weekly basis. As with the bacon slice, slaughter and pork production estimates tend to be extremely reliable since, in compiling them, U.S.D.A. is using data reported by its own employees who currently inspect more than 90% of all hogs slaughtered in the U.S. As in analyzing bacon slice reports, comparisons with prior years should be adjusted for an increasing portion of the industry coming under federal inspection.

Hog Marketing Patterns

Longer range estimates of anticipated hog slaughter can be based primarily on the U.S.D.A.'s "Hogs & Pigs Report" issued each December, March, June and September. These reports give estimates of the U.S. swine population broken down by weight groups as well as farrowing intentions reported by farmers. The March and September reports deal with only the fourteen most important hog producing states but the June and December reports cover each of the 50 states. Even the March and September reports, however, cover a significant proportion of the nation's hog production capacity and none should be taken lightly.

A study of the weight break-down contained in these reports can give an indication of future marketings of finished hogs. Typically a pig will gain 1½ pounds a day and be ready for market six to seven months after farrowing depending on weather conditions, diet, etc. Optimum market weight for a hog is in the area of 200 to 250 pounds which is something short of full biological maturity.

In determining to market his hogs or hold them to a greater weight, a farmer will be influenced by his evaluation of the near term price outlook for hogs, his marginal cost of production (the hog-corn price ratio), current and anticipated competing demands on his labor (primarily field work), weather conditions, availability of wet corn which must be used before it spoils, and tax considerations if he is approaching the end of his fiscal year or the date set for annual assessment of state property taxes where he operates.

In periods of sustained high hog prices, some farmers, unable to increase the number of animals they raise in the short term, may feed to heavier weights, thereby increasing their production. During the late summer, lighter than normal hogs will often be slaughtered as some farmers rush hogs to market in an effort to avoid the declining prices which usually accompany the seasonal fall increase in numbers. Farmers may also market hogs prematurely during planting and harvesting seasons when field work puts great demands on their time and they don't want to be bothered caring for hogs.

An increase in average market weights often indicates farmers are holding hogs back from market for any of a number of reasons, such as resistance to declining prices or bad weather. This would result not only in increased pork production per animal, but in greater marketings once the holding action lets up. Sustained periods of high average weights may indicate general confidence of farmers and, therefore, suggest that an expansion of the breeding herd is taking place. On the other hand, sustained periods of light weights may indicate that liquidation is taking place.

Hog slaughter in the short term can be affected markedly by accumulation or reduction of the breeding herd. Normally, sow slaughter will average just under 10% of normal slaughter so that failure to retain a corresponding number of gilts (female market weight hogs) or accumulation of extra breeding stock may cause short term slaughter to fluctuate 5% to 10%. While government figures do indicate the number of sows being slaughtered, measuring retention of gilts is more difficult since there are no published reports available breaking down slaughter of market hogs by sex. Periods of panic liquidation of breeding stock will become apparent when pregnant or "piggy" sows are marketed for slaughter. This type of wholesale liquidation may signal the end of a bear market.

In deciding to change the size of his breeding operations, a farmer may be influenced by many or all of the following factors, an evaluation of which in turn may be influenced by other current conditions and government and private prognostications:

1. Anticipated future hog prices.
2. Anticipated corn prices and availability.
3. Anticipated labor costs and availability.
4. Availability of physical facilities required in caring for hogs.
5. Availability of financing.

For several generations there has been a gradual consolidation and elimination of smaller farm units and a migration of farm labor to urban areas. In addition, hog raising requires considerable constant human attention and some farmers seem to have given it up entirely to specialize in larger, more efficient grain operations. This seems to have reduced the relative importance of the hog-corn price ratio and increased the importance of availability of labor and physical facilities required for hog raising operations. But, as an indicator of current profitability, the hog-corn ratio will give an indication of money available to hog producers for expansion. In the future, we may see the development of large commercial feeders entering the hog industry. However, with the exception of a few pilot operations, large scale commercial hog producers remain an expectation for the future only.

Storage Stocks

The first factor determining the size of stocks of frozen pork bellies will be the amount of surplus fresh production available for storage during the October to May period. Of even greater importance, however, will be the anticipated need for storage stocks in the coming May to September period, particularly as reflected in the price of futures contracts trading on the Chicago Mercantile Exchange.

In recent years, the futures market has become so important to the pork belly industry that today practically every major producer, storer and user of pork bellies keeps in close touch with futures prices. Many go so far as to have Exchange tickers in their offices and private telephone lines directly to their brokers on the Exchange floor.

Persons engaged in storing pork bellies—"hedgers"—will maintain constant communication with the futures market and the cash market for fresh pork bellies. If the futures price less storage and other costs associated with making delivery (about 2¢ to 3¢ per pound at this writing), is greater than the price at which Exchange quality fresh pork bellies can be purchased, hedgers will enter the market. If the bellies being purchased are less than standard grade and size, this will also enter into their calculations. If price relationships are favorable, hedgers will compete with processors to buy and store fresh bellies and at the same time sell corresponding numbers of futures contracts. The hedgers may then either deliver against their futures sales or merchandise their inventories at some profitable differential to the futures market. In many cases, a producer will store and hedge his own surplus production rather than sell it if the relative cash and futures prices indicate this to be the most profitable course.

In this way, anticipated shortages, by causing higher futures prices, result in rationing of supplies during the surplus production period and creation of storage stocks to augment supplies during the deficit production period.

Merchandising

Because most owners and merchandisers of stored frozen pork bellies have their inventories hedged in the futures market, the futures price level will be influential in determining when storage stocks will be liquidated. If the futures price drops in anticipation of excess stocks, the merchandiser, able to buy back his hedge at reduced prices, will offer his inventory for sale to users at lower prices, compete more aggressively with sellers of fresh bellies and cause a lowering of the entire belly price structure, thereby stimulating consumption.

Normally, a user will choose to buy frozen bellies rather than fresh if the frozen is available at 1¢ to 3¢ per pound less than the fresh. This discount will reflect the user's additional costs of thawing the bellies, trimming waste and otherwise preparing them for smoking. How much of a discount the user requires before choosing to purchase frozen rather than fresh bellies will depend on the availability of fresh bellies, location, brand name (associated with quality) and length of time the frozen bellies have been in storage (associated with deterioration).

Sources of Information

The *Hogs and Pigs Report* is published each March, June, September and December by the U.S. Department of Agriculture and should be required reading for every Pork Belly trader. This report deals with the swine population of the fourteen most important hog-producing states, including Ohio, Indiana, Illinois, Wisconsin, Minnesota, Iowa, Missouri, South Dakota, Nebraska and Kansas. Among other things, it enumerates hogs kept for breeding, hogs kept for market, hogs weighing under 60 pounds, 60 to 119 pounds, 120 to 179 pounds, 180 to 219 pounds, and hogs over 200 pounds. A study of these figures will give indications of the anticipated slaughter over the coming months. This report also gives information on the number of pigs to be farrowed in the coming six months. In addition to the fourteen-state information listed above, the June and December reports give less detailed information on each of the fifty states. The *Hogs & Pigs Report* should be read most carefully, particularly during the *Anticipatory* and *Accumulating and Hedging* phases of the market when it represents a large portion of the total fundamental statistics available.

Another publication which the active belly trader may wish to read on a regular basis is the *Live Stock Market News*, a weekly publication of the Consumer and Marketing Service of the U.S. Department of Agriculture. This publication contains a wealth of information on current hog marketings and slaughter. Among other statistics, it includes receipts at terminal and interior markets, federally inspected hog slaughter, pork production, average weights, numbers of sows killed, prices of various pork cuts and the hog-corn price ratio.

A number of other statistics are available on a regular basis and can best be gathered from private wire services, the Exchange ticker, or trade and some general news media. These statistics will include the daily noon and closing prices for pork bellies in the cash trade, daily terminal and interior market hog receipts, slaughter under federal inspection and hog prices.

The Exchange itself reports storage movement of bellies in Exchange-approved warehouses in Chicago on a daily basis and in Exchange-approved warehouses outside of Chicago on a weekly basis. Total U.S. storage holdings are released by the Government on a monthly basis.

The government releases a weekly figure on the quantity of bacon sliced under federal inspection although this report is not available until the information contained in it is three weeks old.

Many of these statistics, as well as daily price fluctuations, volume of trading and open interest in the futures market, are contained in the *Daily Information Bulletin* issued by the Chicago Mercantile Exchange. The *Chicago Mercantile Exchange Yearbook*, issued by the Exchange each spring, is a good source of historical data.

Many brokerage firms also issue compilations of data as well as weekly letters and periodic special reports on bellies.

March Pork Bellies Futures Delivery
1972-73 through 1974-75

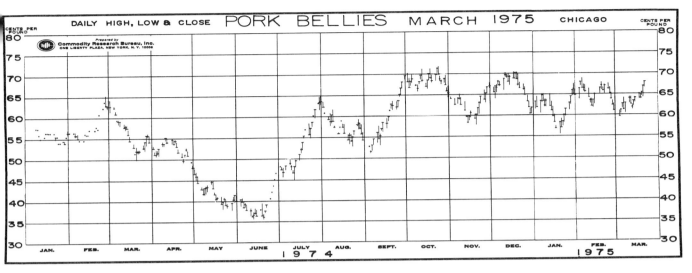

DAILY HIGH, LOW & CLOSE PORK BELLIES MARCH 1975 CHICAGO

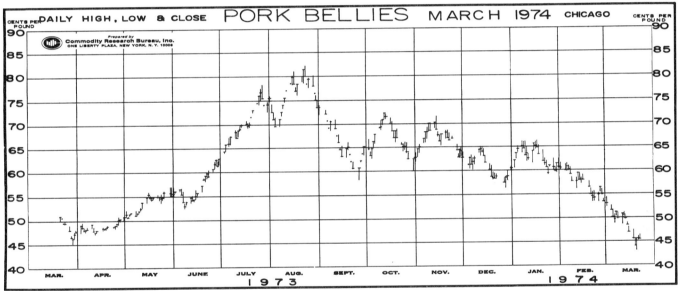

DAILY HIGH, LOW & CLOSE PORK BELLIES MARCH 1974 CHICAGO

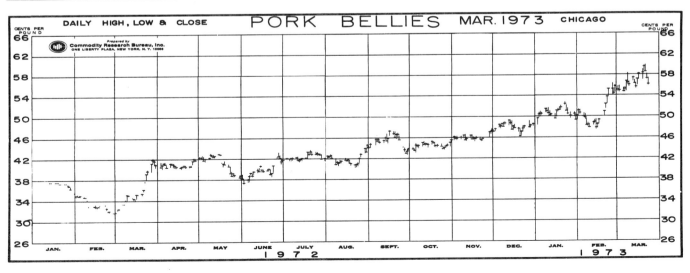

DAILY HIGH, LOW & CLOSE PORK BELLIES MAR. 1973 CHICAGO

March Pork Bellies Futures Delivery
1966-67 to 1971-72

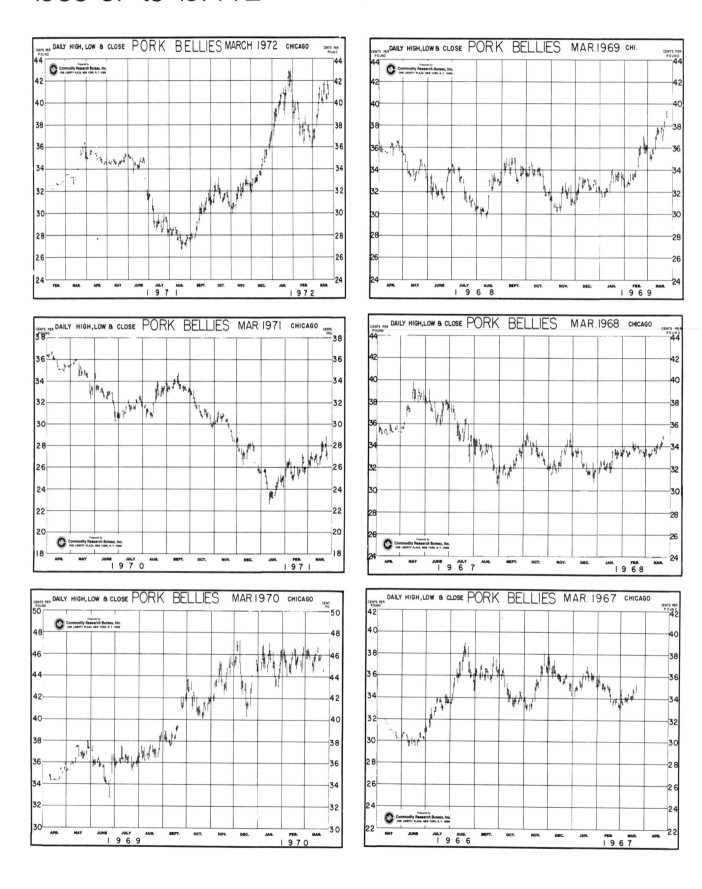

UNDERSTANDING THE SILVER FUTURES MARKET

BY DAVID M. INKELES

On May 18, 1967 the U.S. Treasury announced that it would no longer sell silver at $1.2929 per ounce to all comers. It thus removed the ceiling at that price and allowed prices to fluctuate according to the supply and demand of the free market. In the years since that date trading in all forms of silver has increased in volume until it is now one of the world's most actively traded commodities. During this period, futures trading on the Commodity Exchange, Inc. and bullion trading on the London Silver Market have increased several fold. Two additional large exchanges, the London Metal Exchange and the Chicago Board of Trade, also have begun to trade in silver futures, and the New York Mercantile Exchange and the International Monetary Market of the Chicago Mercantile Exchange have established trading in silver coins. It now appears quite likely that this expanded trading activity will sustain itself for some time to come.

The immediate sequel to the Treasury's cessation of unlimited sales at $1.2929 was a vibrant bull market which lasted a whole year and saw prices rise more than 100%. This major advance was followed by a bear move of almost equal duration through June 1969, which saw erosion of about 85% of the gain. The markets of 1967, 1968 and 1969 were influenced mainly by three major factors which governed fluctuations. These were: 1. The projected long term production deficit and the potential shortages it engendered. 2. The Treasury's policies in disposition of its silver stocks. 3. The use of silver as a currency hedge, especially in the U.S. and Great Britain, where private citizens were prohibited from owning gold.

From 1969 through 1971, silver traded between $2.00 and $1.50 except for the final months of 1971 when it plunged back to the pre-1967 levels of $1.29. During this period the price structure was largely governed by: 1. Large U.S. government sales of silver during 1969–1970. 2. A mild recession with a decrease in industrial demand for silver and consequently a stabilization of the annual production deficit at just over 100 million ounces, and, 3. A general period of optimism with rising stock markets and a winding down of the Viet Nam war.

From 1972 through 1974 silver underwent its largest bull market in history. The chart of the move had the typical hyperbolic shape of the explosive bull market. Prices advanced slowly at first. They only reached $2.00 by the end of 1972 and $3.00 by the end of 1973. Then in the first two months of 1974 prices exploded, doubling to over $6.00.

The bull market was based on several factors: 1. Increased prosperity in 1972 and early 1973 which brought about an increase in industrial consumption from 351 million ounces in 1971 to 479 million ounces in 1973. During this period, the annual production deficit increased by 85% from 133 million ounces to 247 million ounces. 2. The period was one of monetary instability, inflation and international unrest. As a result, people fled currencies and sought the haven of precious metals. During this period, gold advanced from $50 to $180 per ounce and platinum

from $100 to $300 per ounce. 3. There was a withdrawal of Comex certified stocks which declined from 115.4 million ounces in January 1972 to 48.7 million ounces at the end of November 1973. This drop occurred despite a marked increase in trading volume. At the end of 1973 there were fears that longs would continue to withdraw and that shorts would be unable to obtain supplies.

After the bull market crested in February 1974, the remainder of the year saw volatile markets. There were several gyrations of $1.00 to $1.50 in range, between the $4.00 and $6.00 level. These were due to the continued presence of economic and political instability in the world in the face of bearish fundamentals in the silver market. The erosion of prices was due to 1. decreased industrial consumption secondary to the higher price level, and as a result of the spreading world wide recession. 2. The increased marketings of demonitized silver coinage and silver hoards at the higher price level. 3. The possibility that the legalized trading in gold would draw away those who wished to hedge against inflation. 4. Interest rates over 12% prime throughout the world. 5. Reports of stocks of bullion in India which were heretofore unknown and 6. A simple reaction to the speculative excesses early in the year. The decline was violent since the bullish factors did not disappear all at once.

An investor who has witnessed the recent bull market with its talk of "irreplaceable supply," "production deficits" and "rampant inflation" might be surprised to learn that the position of silver was not always so noble.

Throughout the years, trading in silver has had a great deal of emotion attached to it. At times, owing to its precious metal status, it was felt that silver represented an absolute store of value which could withstand currency devaluation and war. However, at other times, as we shall see, it has not been treated quite so nicely. A bull market in pork bellies or cocoa will involve those participating in trade or speculation. A bull market in silver or gold catches the imagination of everyone and is subject to far greater non-economic forces. An appreciation of these emotional swings in investor attitude is essential if one is to have a broad understanding of the causes affecting the price of silver. Therefore, this study will begin with a historical review. Following this it will then cover economic forecasting and the technical aspects of trading.

Silver vs Gold in the Past

Prior to 1871, silver was an important monetary metal, accounting for most of the world's coinage and a substantial portion of the assets of the national treasuries. "It had been a tradition in Europe that only empires coined gold. Until then only Great Britain had gold as its standard of value. In the rest of Europe gold and silver circulated at a fixed ratio but gold was the minor partner."[1] In 1871 after winning

[1] Groceclose, Elgin *Monetary Services of Silver*, Institute For Monetary Research, Washington 1965.

the Franco-Prussian war with France, Germany exacted an indemnity of 5 billion gold francs (48 million ounces). Bismarck then unified the various Duchys and Principalities into greater Germany. He invalidated all their individual moneys and replaced them with the gold mark as the only acceptable standard of official settlements. This was the beginning of the gold standard. The rest of Europe and the world followed quickly. Paper currencies based exclusively on gold backing were issued. Silver remained only for subsidiary coinage. A large portion was no longer needed and hence was demonitized and sold.

Prior to 1871 the price of silver was $1.2929. The United States government had a bimetallic currency with silver and gold valued in the ratio of 1 to 16. This was equivalent to the value of $1.29 per ounce for silver and $20.67 per ounce for gold (gold was revalued to $35.00 per ounce in 1933). In 1873 the United States went on the gold standard and officially demonitized silver as a reserve metal. Since the United States was a leading silver producer with discoveries concurrently being made in the Rocky Mountain areas, this was not a popular decision in the western states. It became even more unpopular in succeeding years as prices were depressed by heavy supplies resulting from demonitized European coinage. It became known as "The Crime of 1873."

As a result of increased political pressure, in 1878 Congress passed the Bland Allison Act. This instructed the Treasury to buy not less than $2 million and not more than $4 million of silver each month. The Treasury, under the influence of Republican administrations, generally bought the minimum. Nevertheless, it managed to accumulate 291,272,018 ounces under the provisions of the act. Yet it did not achieve its goal, for by 1888 the price of silver had eroded to 92¢ per ounce. In 1890 the Sherman Silver Purchase was enacted calling for monthly purchases of 4½ million ounces per month. Prices continued to decline reaching 65¢ in 1893. In that year the program was repealed as being ineffectual after purchases totaling 168,674,682 ounces.

When Silver Was a Major Political Issue

It must be understood that a high degree of emotionalism was attached to this matter. People in the streets, who knew nothing of economics, hotly debated the silver question. It became a symbol of the class and sectional rivalry between the wealthy eastern establishment and the poorer agrarian and mining states of the West. Farmers were convinced that agricultural prices would improve if the Treasury induced inflation by buying silver at around 60¢ per ounce and then issuing money against it at the old $1.29 price. Farm prices were low and this was an attractive issue. Silver induced inflation was to be the panacea of the age. William Jennings Bryan got the Democratic presidential nomination in 1896 with his famous "cross of gold" speech directed against the repeal of the Sherman Silver Purchase.

However, it was not the eastern establishment that carried the day. It was the enormous oversupply of silver that resulted from demonitization and large new discoveries. With the exception of a sharp World War I rally, prices continued to erode until they reached a depression low of 24½¢ per ounce. Devaluation of the dollar, coupled with large Treasury

purchases of silver finally turned the tide. However, this turn was only artificial. The real turn did not begin until World War II with its large increments in industrial silver usage.

The major silver legislation of the New Deal was made up of two Acts, the Thomas Amendment to the 1933 AAA and the Silver Purchase Act of 1934. The speeches and politicking involved in passage of these acts often spoke of restoring silver to its rightful place of eminence. In reality there was little holiness involved since the measures were designed to subsidize the mine owners enough to keep the mines open. The Treasury was to buy silver from any source at prices below 50¢ per ounce and from domestic producers at prices up to 64.64¢ per ounce. The domestic price was later adjusted upward. Under this legislation the Treasury bought over 3 billion ounces of silver.

Silver Acquired by the U.S. Treasury Since 1933

Foreign Debt Silver (Act of 1933)	22,734,824 ounces
SILVER PURCHASE ACT OF 1934	
Foreign Silver	2,048,490,530
Domestic Silver	301,226,723
Nationalized (W. W. II)	113,032,915
SILVER ACT OF 1939	206,287,208
SILVER ACT OF 1946	376,686,164
TOTAL	3,068,458,364 ounces

The silver purchased under the New Deal legislation was paid for in newly issued silver certificates. However, while the Treasury paid approximately 55¢ per ounce for silver, it valued the silver at $1.2929 in issuing silver certificates. In other words a dollar could buy almost two ounces of silver but it was backed by less than 1 ounce. As a result the Treasury made a profit on its books on each ounce purchased. This profit was called seignorage. An amount of silver equal to the total value of all seignorages was set aside either to expand subsidiary coinage or for resale to industry at prices up to 91¢ per ounce.

How New Industrial Demand Helped to Push the Price Higher

Prices stayed below the 91¢ Treasury selling price until 1957. In that year the price level reached 91¢ and it became a ceiling. Silver began to be purchased for industrial uses. However, at the same time the vending industry began to expand rapidly and the amount of silver required for new coinage increased. The new coinage and the sales to industry began to eat into the seignorage reserves. Then in 1961 in order to provide for future coinage needs, the Treasury stopped selling silver to industry at the 91¢ price.

The Treasury price now moved upward to $1.2929 per ounce which was equal to the value of silver backing silver certificates. Gradually the free market price also moved to this level. The U.S. government allowed silver trading and removed the confiscatory 50% tax on silver profits that had been part of the New Deal legislation. The Commodity Exchange reopened silver futures trading on June 12, 1963.

At the same time a change developed in speculative attitudes toward silver. The commodity was no longer a glutted market in the strict domain of the U.S. Treasury. People began to see that the Treasury would eventually have to make changes in the existing policy of a fixed price of $1.2929. If not, they would surely run out of silver in the vain attempt of trying to hold the price down. This prompted hoarding of bullion, silver coins and long positions in silver futures.

What Happened When the U.S. Treasury Lifted the $1.29 Ceiling

The demands for new coins became more intense as vending and speculative demands increased. Silver allocated to new coinage increased from 46 million ounces in 1960 to 320 million ounces in 1965. To forestall a run, President Johnson introduced legislation which, when passed, provided for subsidiary coinage of a cupro-nickel sandwich for quarters and dimes and a 40% silver content for half dollars. This change accentuated the plight of the Treasury and speculators began to hoard even more silver. Purchases from the Treasury at its $1.2929 price increased. On May 18, 1967, after about a week of increasingly heavy purchases which had assumed the proportions of a run, the Treasury stopped selling at $1.2929 to all except certain domestic industrial users. Prices on the free market immediately ran up 30¢ per ounce.

The new policy also provided for redemption of all silver certificates within one year and the public sale of 2 million ounces per week to ease the transition. This continued for three years.

The Treasury clearly wanted to be out of the silver business. In addition 165 million ounces were transferred from Treasury accounts to the inflexible strategic stockpile. The Treasury wished to delay its exit in order that its new coins would be accepted and also to protect against an inflationary spiral in silver prices. Despite its efforts a bull market ensued which has already been discussed earlier in this article.

The Historic Relationship Between Gold and Silver

"Speech is silver but silence is golden." As children, through sayings such as this, we all learned that there was indeed a relationship between silver and gold, and that gold was worth more. We never learned exactly how much more. The gold-silver ratio was used by some analysts to explain the 1974 phase of the bull market. In the past two decades the ratio stood between 20 and 30. During the 19th century silver interests had the U.S. Government value the ratio at 16:1. This ratio was for silver purchases and it clearly was a support price for silver. At the end of 1974 it stood at slightly over 40. However, during the depression it was over 70. In the future the ratio may be significant since both gold and silver are now traded freely. In the past either one or both commodities was restricted and thus the ratio was artificial and not a basis for current price action.

The Supply of Silver

The supply of silver at a given point in time and at a given price is determined by the level of new mine production as well as the amounts of silver that speculators, dealers and governments are willing to sell. The demand for silver at the same point in time and price is determined by the level of industrial consumption plus the demand of speculators, dealers and governments for stocks of silver. There is nothing profound in this since the equilibrium described is arrived at in similar fashion for every other traded commodity. What makes silver unique is that available world stocks of between 3 and 7 billion ounces are equal to between 15 and 30 years of new production at the current rate. What's more, even at the current production deficit, there is a sizable cushion, and it is probable that the deficit will contract rather than expand in the short term. This is because of increased prices and poor economic conditions early in 1975.

A look at most economic forecasts published in 1975 shows careful attention paid to 5 and 10 year

Silver Statistical Summary (Non-Communist World), 1960–1974   Million Troy Ounces

Year	Consumption Industrial	Consumption Coinage	(A) Total Consumption	(B) Mine Production	(C) Primary Deficit	Secondary Supplies U.S. Treasury Sales	Secondary Supplies U.S. Treasury Coinage	Secondary Supplies Other Secondary Supplies	(D) Total Secondary	#(D-C) Net Surplus (+) Deficit (−)
1960	225	104	329	202	127	22	46	72	140	+ 13
1961	240	137	377	204	173	63	56	127	246	+ 73
1962	259	128	386	211	175	1	77	99	177	+ 2
1963	261	166	427	214	213	25	112	80	217	+ 4
1964	295	267	562	212	350	151	203	100	454	+104
1965	330	381	711	218	493	80	320	121	521	+ 28
1966	348	130	478	225	253	143	54	117	314	+ 61
1967	341	105	446	215	231	195	44	136	375	+144
1968	342	89	431	230	201	180	37	204	421	+220
1969	351	33	383	249	134	89	19	169	277	+143
1970	339	24	363	259	104	67	1	133	201	+ 97
1971	351	28	380	247	133	–0–	2	111	113	− 20
1972	391	38	430	246	184	–0–	2	108	110	− 74
1973	479	24	503	256	247	–0–	1	163	164	− 83
1974p	432	30	462	252	210	–0–	2	187	189	− 21

Source: J. Aron & Co.—Their sources; Handy & Harman, U.S. Bureau of Mines; The Silver Institute, and private sources.

projections of future industrial usage and new mine production. Very little is said about future wants of hoarders and speculators. Yet a change of a few percent in hoarder demand will have an enormous effect on price. Clearly, determination of hoarder demand is not within the scope of econometric models since it is determined by too many variables. In the short run, however, it clearly overshadows the production deficit as a price determinant.

The Speculative Hoard

Where is the speculative hoard and what are the factors that affect it? Unfortunately, trying to pin down its size or location is extremely difficult. Certified stocks of the various exchanges are the easiest to find. Slightly more nebulous is that portion of the G.S.A. sales which have not gone into production. Then there is the silver in pre-1965 U.S. silver coins which have gone into private hoards. Since these coins may be privately melted, their current form as well as their location are questionable. The Treasury originally issued slightly under 2 billion ounces in this form. Various reputable sources differ widely in their estimates of recoverable silver, with guesses from 350 million to 800 million ounces.

To go even farther afield there are large, old private hoards. In many parts of the world due to the mistrust of currencies which universally have had a blemished history of depreciation and devaluation, there are private stores of jewels and precious metals, including silver. These exist in big cities and in many smaller places. Aside from certified stocks, there are probably another 500 million to 1 billion ounces in the industrialized countries of the west. In the Far East the estimates range from 2 billion to 5 billion ounces and even higher. A great deal of this is in the form of jewelry and utensils, but, recently, heretofore unknown bullion supplies were found to exist. If we wish to scrape the bottom of the barrel, and we would certainly do this if prices ever went high enough, we could consider the vast amount of silver in flatwear, utensils and tea services in the middle and upper class homes of the western world. At a given price these would be melted and silver flatwear would become a distant memory.

What causes hoarders to sell? Probably the outlook for silver at a given time when compared to other stores of value and investments. When times are good, currencies sound and the overall world outlook is peaceful, speculators tend to switch from precious metals to higher yielding or growth promising investments. During wars or confusing periods such as the recent period of currency insecurity, people naturally acquired precious metals for security. Thus, although speculative holdings of silver produced no income, they were considered as offering a secure haven in the short run at least.

Irwin Shishko, the well known analyst for J. Aron & Co., raises the term "disturbance factor" to combine all the background conditions which cause an investor to hold silver in place of money. As world anxiety increases so does the value of the "disturbance factor." Mr. Shishko also believes that there are 3 major tiers of supply and that silver can be induced from each, but at widely differing price levels. Tier I was the U.S. Government which held over 2 billion ounces in 1960. By 1967 over 85% of this silver was liberated at the price $1.29. Tier II consisted of the private hoards of those who anticipated the price rise but did not appreciate its eventual magnitude. Most of this was available around $2.50 and it was at this level that the 1968 bull market was halted. Tier III is recycled silver from old hoards and Indian treasure troves. These were felt to be available around $5.00 which was near the top in 1974. The price needed to liberate the far eastern silver is the sticky question. Considering the state of the Indian economy and its balance of payments problems, its silver shipments in 1974 were below expectations. Probably Mr. Shishko's three tiers are all part of a single long term demand curve. Also it is retrospective since it was determined after the two bull markets which determined tier II and III. However, as with conventional chart analysis it will be valuable since the tiers are now future points of support and resistance for the market.

The Production Deficit

It is only since the early 1960's that we have an inability of new production to cover industrial consumption. Prior to that we often had deficits, but they were due exclusively to new coinage. The monetary value of the coins exceeded their silver content so there was no incentive for melting and the coins became another form of the general silver inventory. They would be available for future melting as we see now or as was the case after the Franco-Prussian War.

Today (early in 1975) the production deficit is due to an excess of industrial consumption. Silver coinage has disappeared in all but a few countries and its aggregate amount is minimal. Industrial silver has some potential reclamation but vastly smaller than the percentage recoverable from silver coins. It will take a very high price for "mama to take her tea service to the smelter."

We should subtract 60 million ounces per year from the production deficit since this only considers new mine production and does not include scrap as a primary supply. The 60 million ounces represents annual scrap before the price rise of 1967 and we can expect this to continue. Most of it comes from industrial sources and is not price dependent. If we do this, then a production deficit of 100 million ounces such as the 1970 level, becomes only 40 million ounces. This is not the stuff shortages are made of. On the other hand, the 247 million ounce deficit of 1973 is still significant even if we deduct scrap.

The current production deficit has influenced the hoarder to become more aggressive. As stocks diminish to feed the deficit, prices should logically advance over the long run. Since speculators anticipate the future, the current price level may have discounted part of this projected shortage. In the future it will be the attitude of the hoarder regarding the future size of the production deficit that determines price. The great price fluctuations from 1967 to 1969 occurred in the absence of unexpected news regarding new production or industrial consumption. Major news centered around U.S. Treasury disposition of its stocks and international currency unrest. On the other hand, the 1972–1974 bull market, while also influenced by monetary instability, was largely fueled by the jump in the production deficit.

Although the production deficit is often overshadowed in the short run by the willingness of hoarders to hold silver, it still remains the most important long term price determinant. As long as net industrial consumption of silver continues to exceed new production plus non-coinage scrap, prices will have an upward bias. One of the main reasons for this is that the projection of a long term deficit makes speculators bolder in their hoarding of silver.

Industrial Consumption

Industrial consumption should really not be lumped together as one amorphous grouping and discussed as such. The components are too varied to simply apply a growth rate based on future gains in G.N.P. The technology of any component could change drastically as could the tastes of society toward sterling silverware. Past changes in industrial consumption have been consistent but sporadic, based more on technology than any other factor.

It is not expected that price increases for silver will have much of a restraining force on consumption. Only in sterlingware does silver cost represent a large proportion of final product cost. In photography, the silver cost is between 3% and 5%. A 100 foot roll of 16 mm. color film costs about $7.50. It contains about 3 grams of silver worth around 40¢ based on a silver price of $4.00 per ounce. A 50% rise in silver prices would only change the cost of making this film by about 20¢. Hence the price elasticity of silver in photographic film is very small. A technological breakthrough in a non-silver film would be quite significant since photography accounts for 28% of silver consumption. Many companies have been researching this for considerable time but the outcome of the research is still uncertain.

Nevertheless, some progress has been made. There has been a reduction in the amount of silver used per square foot of certain grades of film. Hence, in the past 10 years the amount of silver used in photography has increased, but at a lower rate than the increases in production for that industry.

The electronics industry uses silver due to its resistance to corrosion and its high electrical and thermal conductivity. Its specific uses are too numerous to list. What they all have in common is the small amount of silver needed in each particular use. Hence this area is also quite insensitive to price changes. It should not be assumed however that technological uses of silver will continue to expand unabated. Current uses of bimetallic conductors of silver and copper are cutting into gains once projected for silver. However, unlike photographic film, the uses of silver in electronics are too varied to be displaced by a single technological breakthrough. Overall, this market should continue to expand. Indeed, consumption did increase from 25 million ounces in 1968 to over 40 million ounces in 1973.

Sterlingware

The amount of silver going into sterlingware is a big question. If the price of silver increases at a rate equal to or slightly above the overall inflation we might expect production to increase eventually. In the intermediate term, consumers get used to higher prices and catch up with deferred purchases. In 1968 when prices jumped over $2.00 sterlingware production dropped. This drop continued through 1971. Sil-

ver prices also dropped from 1969 through 1971, yet except for one month, they remained above the pre-1967 level. Nevertheless, from 1971 to 1973 sterlingware production doubled. People had gotten used to the price increase.

One can only expect severe curtailment of production in 1974 and 1975 as the high price and economic troubles make their weight felt. Should silver prices stay at their present level sterling flatware might no longer be a practical gift for a new bride. It might become a luxury for only the very rich, with a commensurate drop in production.

Brazing

Brazing is a bonding process for metals in which silver is often used as a filler metal. It involves more heat than soldering yet it differs from welding in that a filler metal is involved in fusion of the two pieces. Silver brazing uses a mixture of silver, copper, zinc and cadmium with silver the senior partner. The use of silver for brazing should not be price sensitive and should expand with the economy.

The remaining uses of silver for electroplating, jewelry batteries and medical uses do not seem to be radically changing in a broad sense. The exception to this could be the silver battery for automobiles. However, technology here is still premature and very much in flux. When and if the electric car comes into medium scale production its battery could be quite different from current concepts.

New Production Prospects

The greater part of world silver production occurs as a secondary metal obtained in the mining of other metals, principally copper. Four countries, the U.S., Mexico, Canada and Peru account for about 59% of world production. Silver generally occurs in compounds together with tin and sulfur such as Argenite and Stephanite. Although in most mines the silver withdrawn is small compared with the principal metal, in marginal mines it is often the difference between profit and loss. As a result we generally get a modest increase in production when silver prices rise sharply.

The supply of silver from new mining is expected to increase as a result of new copper and zinc mines scheduled for operation in the near future. Estimates of this increment show world production up 20% in 1979 over 1974 levels. Year to year production changes are not very great and new mines take several years to begin production. Hence the average speculator need not be concerned with the intricate details of production and metallurgy. There is usually agreement amongst the experts as to the production prospects for the coming five year period.

Secondary Supplies

It is secondary supplies that make up the production deficit. These include scrap and projected dishoarding by individuals or governments. As we have already mentioned scrap should be divided into two categories: basic scrap which is produced regardless of price, and marginal scrap which is produced in increasing quantities as price increases. It might be assumed that in 1974 basic scrap was about 60 million ounces and marginal scrap was about 22 million ounces.

The demonitization of coinage depends on the willingness of holders to melt their coins and the availability of smelter capacity. The willingness of holders to sell at a given price depends on many factors already discussed. Thus, a study of secondary supplies is only valuable in retrospect. Market forces always establish a price at which sufficient secondary supplies are forthcoming to cover the deficit.

Trading in Silver Outside the Futures Markets

Before discussing silver futures trading, we will note other ways of silver trading. Old rare coins, foreign coins, pre-1965 ordinary coins, objects of art, bullion and futures are all vehicles for trading in silver. But except for pre-1965 coins, bullion and futures, they are uneconomical owing to the high premiums they carry over the value of their silver content. Coins have been a favorite vehicle for speculation and have been a favorite vehicle for speculation and have yielded excellent profits in the past. These profits have been due to either numismatic appreciation or to the increased value of their silver content. In some cases it has been due to both, as exemplified by the silver dollar. Foreign coins and old rare coins generally have too great a numismatic premium for them to be justly considered a silver speculation.

Silver dust is a suitable medium if one is sufficiently sophisticated as to be able to obtain dependable assays. For the average speculator this should be avoided. Silver ornaments and other objects of art are in the same category as old coins. The premium for artistry makes the item cost a great deal more than the value of its silver content. Hence, they become suitable for speculation in art but not for speculation in silver.

Silver bullion is an excellent vehicle for speculation. It is the deliverable grade for futures contracts. It comes in bars of 1,000 ounces and 1,100 ounces both .999 fine. The 1,000 ounce bar is about 68½ pounds. It can be stored easily in the vaults of leading banks. Silver bullion does not deteriorate in quality. It is excellent collateral for loans. For long term speculation it offers the savings of commissions when compared with futures contracts. The reason for this is that the most distant futures contract is only 17 months forward. Once it matures it must be liquidated

and reinstated another 17 months forward. This turnover involves a round turn commission, to which the bullion holder is not subject.

On the other hand, while silver futures reflect the carrying costs through the spreads between contract months, buying futures does not involve the actual borrowing of money. The bullion speculator usually borrows from banks to finance his holdings. In periods of tight money these banks might charge the small speculator considerably more than the prime rate. They might also call his loan, forcing him to either shop around or liquidate. The holding of bullion in units of less than ten bars in New York or five bars in Chicago is in effect an odd lot since they can not be sold via the futures markets. In these cases the buyer might exact a differential for the inconvenience of handling a small quantity.

Pre-1965 silver coins are now another form of bullion since they require only to be processed. They are liquid, with an active futures market, and they are kept in line with bullion by the same processor arbitrage we find in the soybean industry.

In Europe, and of course Asia, where the fear of war and devaluation is perhaps a more vivid memory, bullion is preferred in some instances for its tangibility. Futures contracts are viewed as promises which in times of war could possibly be subject to nationalization, or confiscation. Finally, bullion offers anonymity while futures contract transactions are subject to the perusal of tax officials.

The largest organized center for trading in bullion is the London Silver Market. It is jointly operated by the three large bullion brokers, Mocatta and Goldsmid, Ltd., Samuel Montagu, Ltd., and Sharps Pixley, Ltd. Published prices are determined daily at fixings which take place at 12:15 P.M. The prices are quoted in Sterling and U.S. dollars for spot, three, six and twelve months forward. Delivery is in London within seven days of the settlement date at the option of the seller. Prices at each fixing are based on the proviso that all offerings received before the fixing time must be absorbed. On the other hand should there be an excess of buy orders all need not be satisfied at the fixing price. In addition to this once a day ritual, this market is open for specific quotations throughout the day.

World Secondary Silver Supplies by Source (Excluding U.S. Treasury) 1960–1974   Million Troy Ounces

Year	Scrap	India & Pakistan	Demonetized Coin	Foreign Stocks	USSR	China	Total
1960	40	—	10	12	—	10	72
1961	45	—	20	7	—	55	127
1962	50	—	20	4	—	25	99
1963	55	—	15	10	—	—	80
1964	60	—	20	20	—	—	100
1965	65	—	30	17	9	—	121
1966	69	—	28	10	10	—	117
1967	68	20	35	5	8	—	136
1968	79	60	50	15	0	—	204
1969	83	25	50	—	11	—	169
1970	60	25	25	10	13	—	133
1971	66	20	20	5	—	—	111
1972	68	10	15	15	—	—	108
1973	73	25	15	50	—	—	163
1974p	82	35	45	25	—	—	187

Source: J. Aron & Co.—Their sources, Handy & Harman and private sources.

The Organized Silver Futures Exchange

There are three exchanges where silver futures are traded, The London Metal Exchange, The Commodity Exchange, Inc. (New York) and The Chicago Board of Trade. The London Metal Exchange has been trading silver since February 1969. The trading unit is 10,000 ounces of .999 fine. There are two sessions during the day with two five minute rings in each session. In addition silver can also be traded for fifteen minute periods following the last session of the morning and afternoon in what are called kerb dealings. Prices are officially quoted for spot, three, and seven months forward. However, trading can take place for delivery on any specific date up to seven months forward.

Trading regulations on The Commodity Exchange, Inc. and The Chicago Board of Trade are available from the exchanges and the various brokers. They differ in contract months and in the size of the contract. New futures contracts for silver coins are gaining popularity on the New York Mercantile Exchange, and on the International Monetary Market of the Chicago Mercantile Exchange. They call for delivery of U.S. silver dimes, quarters and half dollars bearing the date 1964 or earlier and weighing not less than 54.5 pounds per $1,000 face amount.

Speculating in Silver Futures

The distant silver futures contracts usually trade at a premium reflecting the cost of money, warehousing charges and insurance. Up until 1974 the size of the premium was slightly above the current prime rate. As mentioned earlier the 1974 bull market saw significant stocks withdrawals, with the market being inverted for a short time. It returned to being a carrying charge market, but as in most other commodity markets, the back months often sell at less than full carrying charges.

After considering all of the historical and economic factors affecting silver, the trader may elect to either buy or sell silver futures. Should he feel the market only temporarily out of line, he will have his position only a short while. In doing this he should exercise prudent rules of trading. He should limit his losses. He should not become a long term holder because of a short term loss. Silver futures can be traded in many ways, as a short term buy or short sale, as a long term buy or sale, as a tax straddle or as a hedge against bullion. The intelligent trader will be wary about changing his objectives after establishing a position since emotions rather than reason are probably dictating the shift.

BIBLIOGRAPHY

Encyclopaedia Britannica, Encyclopaedia Britannica, Inc. Chicago, 1968.

Groceclose, Elgin E. *Silver as Money, The Monetary Services of Silver*, Institute For Monetary Research, 1965, Washington.

Pick, Franz, *Silver, How And Where To Buy It And Hold It*, Pick Publishing Co., New York, N.Y. 1965.

Butts, Alison, Ed. *Silver: Economics Metallurgy and Use*, D. Van Nostrand Co. Inc., Princeton, N.J. 1967.

Commodity Year Books 1966–1974.

Silver Statistics, J. Aron & Co., New York, Nov., 1974.

Various reports from:

Commodity Research Bureau, New York.

U.S. Bureau of Mines.

Handy & Harman, New York.

J. Aron & Co., New York.

U.S. Consumption of Silver By End-Use   (Thousands of Troy Ounces)

	1968	1969	1970	1971	1972	1973	1974
Electroplated Ware	15,279	12,706	11,437	10,909	12,716	14,542	13,320
Sterling Ware	28,349	20,291	19,116	22,729	27,163	40,100	28,300
Jewelry	4,538	3,011	5,119	3,447	4,870	5,778	5,240
Photographic Materials	41,607	41,380	38,044	36,073	38,251	51,979	46,280
Dental and Medical Supplies	3,094	1,591	1,804	1,485	1,991	3,022	2,400
Mirrors	1,744	1,510	1,386	1,112	1,225	2,579	3,950
Brazing Alloys and Solders	15,124	16,549	14,035	12,085	12,214	17,736	14,500
Electrical/Electronic Products:							
Batteries	5,764	3,799	6,342	5,631	6,044	4,155	3,990
Contacts and Conductors	25,805	34,555	25,183	27,954	36,434	40,209	31,660
Bearings	451	481	383	355	344	375	430
Catalysts	2,310	4,081	1,999	1,730	3,430	5,988	7,340
Miscellaneous	1,228	1,590	3,556	5,636	6,381	9,477	12,340
Total Net Industrial Consumption	145,293	141,544	128,404	129,146	151,063	195,940	169,720

Source: Bureau of Mines.

March New York Silver Futures Delivery
1972-73 to 1974-75

March New York Silver Futures Delivery
1969-70 to 1971-72

March New York Silver Futures Delivery
1966-67 to 1968-69

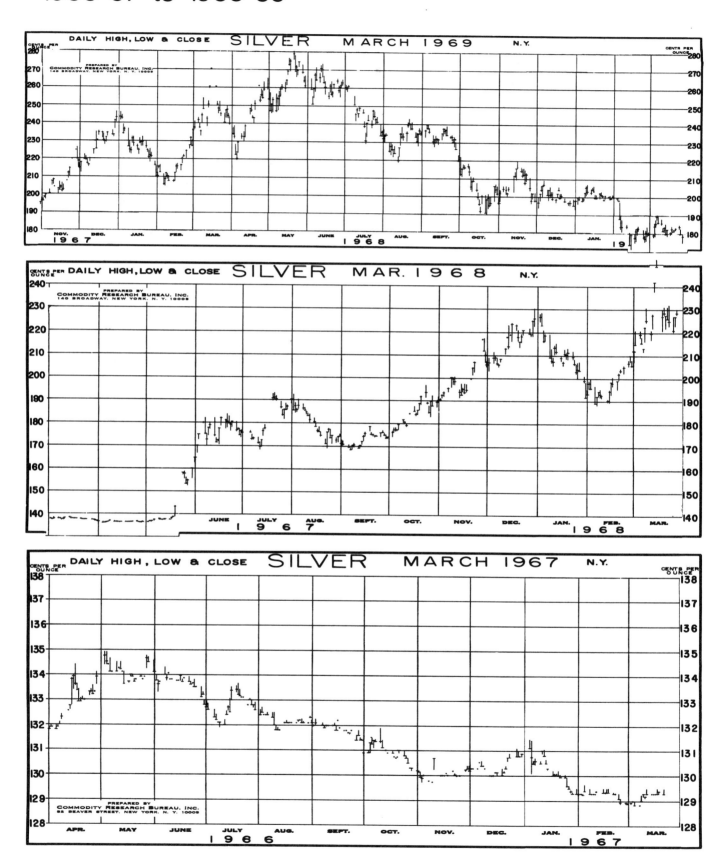

DAILY HIGH, LOW & CLOSE SILVER MARCH 1969 N.Y.

PREPARED BY
COMMODITY RESEARCH BUREAU, INC.
140 BROADWAY. NEW YORK. N. Y. 10005

CENTS PER OUNCE

NOV. DEC. JAN. FEB. MAR. APR. MAY JUNE JULY AUG. SEPT. OCT. NOV. DEC. JAN.
1967   1968   19

DAILY HIGH, LOW & CLOSE SILVER MAR. 1968 N.Y.

CENTS PER OUNCE

PREPARED BY
COMMODITY RESEARCH BUREAU, INC.
140 BROADWAY. NEW YORK. N. Y. 10005

JUNE JULY AUG. SEPT. OCT. NOV. DEC. JAN. FEB. MAR.
1967   1968

DAILY HIGH, LOW & CLOSE SILVER MARCH 1967 N.Y.

CENTS PER OUNCE

PREPARED BY
COMMODITY RESEARCH BUREAU, INC.
92 BEAVER STREET, NEW YORK, N. Y. 10005

APR. MAY JUNE JULY AUG. SEPT. OCT. NOV. DEC. JAN. FEB. MAR.
1966   1967

HOW TO ANALYZE THE SOYBEAN FUTURES MARKET

BY WALTER L. EMERY

Introduction

Soybeans have made enormous strides over the past several years, not only in terms of production, but as the leading cash crop for farmers—having pushed corn into second place. Moreover, they have become, with their products, our most important earner of foreign exchange—accounting for a record 2.8 billion dollars in calendar year 1973. The contribution of soybeans to commodity futures trading has also been a major one, over 2.7 million contracts being traded in 1973 and in 1974, second only to the leader, corn.

The influence of soybeans extends beyond the areas already mentioned. Soybean meal, one of its two products, is the most important high protein feed for poultry and livestock. The other, soybean oil, is the major oil used in the manufacture of shortening, margarine, and cooking and salad oils.

Background

The United States is, by far, the world's most important producer of soybeans. China, which used to be the second largest producer, is believed to now produce less than 20% of our production, and, in fact, has bought soybeans from the U.S. Output there is concentrated in Manchuria whose climate compares with that of our main soybean belt. China's harvest season is August/November. Brazilian soybean production has expanded sharply and has pushed China out of second place. Its major producing area is the Rio Grande do Sul whose climate and soil is similar to our mid-South. The harvest season is April/May. The North Central states are the most important growing area in the U.S., accounting for about 60% of acreage. Illinois is the largest producing state by a narrow margin, followed by Iowa, Indiana, Missouri, Arkansas, and Minnesota. Growing of soybeans has increased in the Mississippi Delta and in the Middle Atlantic states.

Planting usually starts in the main soybean belt during early May. Seeding can take place as late as early July, but yields generally suffer. Normal to above normal rainfall during the period of most active plant growth (July) when seed pods are setting, and in the mid-August to mid-September period when pods are filling, is essential to good yields. The root system of the soybean is neither as deep nor as extensive as that of corn, but the length of the flowering period is longer for soybeans than for corn, which means that drought conditions must persist over a longer period of time to adversely affect soybeans to the same degree as corn. A light frost has little adverse effect on either young or nearly mature plants. The harvest, weather permitting, is usually a fast one—most of the crop being combined within a two month period. October is normally the most active harvest month.

There are a number of crop hazards. Prolonged drought or excess moisture at planting time adversely affects germination and can result in spotty stands. Soybeans should emerge within a week after planting. Wilt may affect seedlings if cool growing conditions exist. Unfavorable weather during seed development tends to exert a most adverse influence on yields. The crop is most susceptible to drought during the mid-August to mid-September pod filling period. Hail can cut yields if severe defoliation occurs when seeds are beginning to fill. A period of high temperatures may result in increased shedding of pods and lower yields. Weeds can reduce yields, particularly when poor moisture conditions follow early season high moisture conditions. Soybean varieties resistant to most known diseases have been developed, but bacterial blight can be a problem when the weather is cool and rainy, and other blights may cause concern under warm, humid conditions. Brown stem rot is favored by cool weather in August.

Soybeans are grown for their two major products, soybean meal and soybean oil. The soybean contains about 21 percent oil and 40 percent protein (oil content tends to be higher in the South and protein content higher in the North). A 60-lb. bushel of soybeans will produce, on the average, about 10.7 pounds of soybean oil and 47.5 pounds of soybean meal. Points to remember in this connection are that the yield of oil per unit of soybeans processed is much less than for most other oil-bearing crops, while the yield of meal is higher. Moreover, some competing high protein meals, such as cottonseed meal and tankage, are by-products and their supply is virtually unaffected by price.

Over the years, the price of soybean meal has accounted for about 63 percent of combined product value and oil 37 percent. This proportion will vary, however, with the supply/demand balance for each product. Practically all of the oil consumed domestically (93 pct.) goes into food products, chief of which are cooking and salad oils which account for about 43 percent of total domestic disappearance; shortening—34 percent; and margarine—23 percent. A small amount is used for industrial purposes. Almost all soybean meal is used in the high-protein portion of feed rations for poultry and livestock. (Most of the 48–49% protein meal produced is used in the broiler industry and the 44% protein meal in livestock rations.) Close to 50% of the soybean meal consumed in the U.S. is estimated to be 48–49% protein meal. Hence, it must be recognized that one must be constantly on the alert for factors which might cause changes in both domestic and foreign demand for soybean meal and soybean oil.

The value of soybeans then, in the final analysis, is determined by the prices received for soybean meal and oil. The soybean processor must, over a period of time, receive more for the products of a ton or bushel of soybeans than he pays for the soybeans. The upper limit to the production of soybean meal, for example, in a given season is fixed by the supply of soybeans available for crushing. But, the effective supply of meal is determined by the rate of crushing operations. This is influenced over the long run by profitability of processing, which usually has been more a function of meal prices than of oil prices. While U.S. processing capacity is close to 1.1 billion bushels vs. record production of 1.6 billion in 1973/74, the rate of crush will depend primarily upon the crushing margin, soybean and product inventory levels, and the amount of uncovered forward sales commitments in products.

The soybean farmer usually markets a fair portion of his production shortly after harvest. About 60% of open market farm sales occur by January 1 following the fall harvest. Processors usually acquire close to one-third of their season's purchases by November 1, and over one-half by January 1, according to USDA estimate. This means the processor acquires a lot more soybeans than he needs to keep his plants running against orders early in the season. Soybean prices tend to be seasonally depressed around harvest time, which operates in favor of a profitable processing margin early in the season as product values tend to be firm before product supplies are built up from new crop crushing operations. This usually presents the processor with the option of placing selling hedges against his uncommitted soybean purchases in either the soybean futures or in oil and/or meal futures. The course of action taken by the processor will exert an influence on the soybean market. Less than expected seasonal hedge pressure in soybean futures may result when a favorable crushing margin exists, and more than expected pressure when the processing margin appears unfavorable.

Factors Affecting Exports

The exporter is the other major market for soybeans. He accounts for an increasingly large share of production (approx. 35–40%) and about the same percentage of distribution. Expansion of the soybean producing area into the mid-South, and a shift to increased utilization of river terminals or subterminals in recent years, coupled with expanded barge traffic and the widened use of 50-car or more unit trains, have resulted in widening the buying area for the exporter in competition with the processor. There are a limited number of large export firms in this country, with major foreign markets for soybeans being Japan—the world's largest importer—West Germany, Spain, the Netherlands, Italy, Denmark, and France. In 1973/74 the U.S. supplied 87 percent of world exports, and Brazil 12 percent. The People's Republic of China, a net exporter in earlier years, was a net importer of soybeans.

Demand for soybeans from foreign buyers reflects improved standards of living in many areas with resultant increased demand for meat and poultry products. A sharp expansion of poultry production (broilers especially) and livestock numbers has been the result. This, in turn, has been translated into a greater demand for soybean meal, especially where government import policies do not discriminate against its use and permit the following of efficient feeding practices. Demand can be satisfied by the shipment of soybeans where adequate processing facilities exist in the importing country. As foreign crushing capacity increases soybean exports will become even more important, at the expense of meal exports. Exports may be in the form of meal where existing processing plants are inadequate, or even in the form of a still small but growing, foreign market, for complete feed rations.

This demand is not a one-way street. It can, and has been, adversely affected by such major and unpredictable factors as drought which results in the reduction of feed supplies, subsequent liquidation of poultry and livestock, and consequent reduced demand for U.S. soybeans and soybean meal. Reduced foreign demand for soybean meal can also result from increased peanut meal, fish meal, or sunflowerseed meal production in foreign countries. Foreign demand for soybean meal is expected to decrease in favor of soybeans in coming years as foreign processing capacity grows—at least when soybeans are not significantly out of line on the high side relative to meal prices.

Exports of soybeans tend to be heaviest after the harvest as foreign buyers attempt to replenish locally or regionally produced supplies of oilseeds. Of course, booking of export business can, and usually does, take place many months in advance of shipment. An indication of the extent of forward bookings can now be obtained from weekly USDA export sales reports.

Price Making Influences

The soybean crop or marketing year runs from September 1 through the following August 31. The November contract is considered the first trading month of the crop year, and the August contract is usually considered the last futures contract of the season. The September delivery tends to be a between-seasons contract, tending to reflect the new crop when the harvest is early and old crop when the harvest is late. Provision is made for trading in soybean futures as much as 16 months ahead. For example, trading in the January 1976 delivery started on September 24, 1974. This enables the producer to plan his production a season ahead by having knowledge of futures prices (and the ability to hedge) that far distant.

Pricemaking factors vary with the time of season. Obviously, soybean supply factors tend to receive greatest attention at the start of a crop year, and at its end, with attention shifting to demand considerations in the interim. However, it may be of more value to look at seasonal price influences starting with the time when trading interest usually picks up in new crop futures.

Interest in the new crop, taking November as the first trading month, usually starts in the winter of the previous year (December 1974 for the November 1975 contract) when discussion on anticipated acreage, if not on any prospective price support legislation changes, receives attention. Also, in some years around that time there is considerable interest in the outlook for switching acreage, particularly to or from corn, depending upon the market prospect for each in the coming year and experiences of the past season. (It is estimated that soybeans must sell at about three times the price of corn—or weather conditions favor soybean planting—in order to expand soybean acreage at the expense of corn.) While futures trading volume in new crop contracts is usually limited, there is some interest prior to the planting intentions report issued by the USDA in late January and again in mid-March. Also, spreading activities between current and new crop months begin to influence the market to some degree.

Meanwhile, trading interest is beginning to shift away from the crop which has just been harvested (the USDA annual crop summary having rather well established production by mid January) to the demand side of the equation. It is still too early for much excitement about the new crop other than conjecture over how much will be planted and harvested, and a tentative production estimate made. This is a time when early season projections for the distribution of soybeans are put to test. It is around this time that markets which have been bid up on glowing crush and export prospects begin to run up against the hard reality of actual crush and export figures—which may or may not confirm earlier expressed optimism.

Conversely, it is often a time when statistics point to a better distribution than originally anticipated, and this finds reflection in futures. First quarter (September/November) crush and exports are usually well ascertained by late December in official reports, and there is a tendency for analysts to compare results with projections for the period under question as well as for the comparable period for previous seasons.

As the season progresses, both current crop distribution and new crop planting and growth considerations vie for attention of traders. Prospects for a reduced current crop carryover, as indicated by the unfolding distribution pattern, and new crop growing conditions along with periodic crop reports, both private and government, furnish ammunition to the bulls or bears in futures. This is a period from late spring into the summer when spreading operations attract increasing interest as cross currents between the current and new crop factors come into closer focus.

The last approximate month and a half of the season tends to be a period when most attention is centered on liquidation of current crop contracts, perhaps acquired months previously, as it becomes more evident that end of season tightness will, or will not, prevail—a consideration to which new crop progress must be a part. Both the expiring current crop contracts and the next crop futures contracts are influenced mainly by new crop weather conditions, for this is a critical growth period.

It is within this broad framework of considerations that the futures market operates within a given season. But, a closer look at more specific factors is essential to place the various market considerations in perspective.

Supply Factors

From a theoretical point of view, to obtain the supply side of the equation one must merely add indicated production for the current season to carryover from the previous season. This works out fine for the current crop year (once production is fairly well established) and the upper limit to supply perhaps may be set thus. However, the "effective" supply (that which is, or appears to be, readily available to the trade) at any given time is usually quite another matter, as will be pointed out later.

It is more difficult to estimate supply for the following season. Prospective carryover for the season ending August 31 is certainly little more than a "guesstimate" by late winter or early spring. Also, it is quite common to estimate new crop production based on private acreage ideas or on the mid-March planting intentions report, based on average abandonment and yield adjusted for trend, or some combination of these variables. Yet, assumptions are made, and the market adjusts to these assumptions. Then when a more accurate assessment of supply can be made, it often differs considerably from early forecasts—with resultant reflection in the futures market. Hence, one must allow for considerable error in the next crop supply projections, especially early in the current season.

Even when one can make what appears to be a reasonable assumption as to supply for the current crop, or for that matter even when current season supply is rather well established, "effective" supply is another matter. The most obvious factors limiting free or effective supply at any given time are operation of the price support program when there is a price support program (there is none for the 1975 soybean crop) and when prices are in the vicinity of the loan level, and a determined farmer holding movement. Importance of these factors will vary somewhat with the price level. Farmer eligibility for non-recourse price support loans is going to siphon off excess supplies when prices remain low relative to loan values for any period of time. In this connection it is well to remember that the loan is available only to the producer, and usually only up through the end of May. Once the crop is sold by the farmer it is no longer eligible for price support. This fact can be of importance if farmers have sold a larger than usual amount of their production early in the season, and prices sag later on, when the loan is not available.

A determined grower holding movement does not always have to occur when prices are low. At times producers have been strong holders not only because they feel current prices are not as high as they should be, but sometimes because of concern over growing tightness of supplies late in the season. Such action can exert a strong, but usually temporary, effect on prices for eventually such soybeans must come to market.

Some of the less predictable factors affecting effective supply include; adverse weather, which holds up harvest activity and makes for less than expected new crop supplies when inventories have been run down in the expectation of such supplies; strikes at processor plants which reduce production of oil and meal, cutting the use of soybeans, and at the same time tending to firm up meal and oil prices; rail or port strikes, which can temporarily interfere with the movement of soybeans and products and can adversely affect demand. Often when a strike is anticipated as labor contracts approach expiration without agreement on terms of a new contract, processors and others may buy products or soybeans in the expectation of a short strike. When none develops it tends to leave a vacuum in nearby demand. It can also make for a very uncomfortable position on the part of those who intend to satisfy their short futures commitments by delivery of soybeans, if a strike occurs around first notice day or in the delivery period for a maturing futures contract.

Another factor which at times can make for a tighter free supply situation than seems apparent, is the tendency for the processing trade to make heavy forward sales of products and product futures when the processing margin is relatively attractive. As the time draws near to fulfill these forward sales commitments in the cash market and in futures, there may be a tightening up of soybean supplies. They may be there, but they are committed, forcing buyers to reach to obtain requirements.

Factors That Influence Domestic Demand

Having an approximation of the "free" or effective supply situation at any particular time is only one-half of the equation. It means little without some estimate of probable demand for the marketing year. One seldom lacks for such estimates. The best known, and most heavily relied upon estimate, of course, is the initial forecast of crush and exports by the U.S. Department of Agriculture early in the season. The initial crush estimate for the oil segment of the product complex is based primarily upon the size of the soybean oil inventory, and indicated supplies of competing cottonseed oil and lard relative to per capita use of cooking and salad oil, shortening, and margarine—plus estimated export demand. The estimate for the meal segment is based primarily upon the expected number of high-protein consuming animal units for the season (both domestic and foreign), feed-price ratios, and the price and availability here and abroad of substitute protein concentrates.

The obvious means by which the distribution of soybeans can be followed are the weekly export inspection figures voluntarily provided by the trade and subsequently adjusted by monthly Census Bureau export figures several weeks after the month-end; by the weekly USDA exports sales reports; and by the monthly reports on processing activity (the crush). The futures market is usually sensitive to significant (and sometimes insignificant) departures from previously circulated expectations with respect to crush and export figures. These statistics provide a check on initial and later distribution estimates.

How to Determine Effective Supply and Demand

Bringing the foregoing considerations into focus when studying the soybean situation, one must first make an estimate of supply, bearing in mind that this can be an approximation only. A start can be made by using USDA figures on carryover from the previous season plus the most recent USDA production estimate for the current season to obtain total supply. This amount must be adjusted downward by that amount which is not readily available to the trade.

Once a month a rather good guess can be made of "free" supply. The monthly loan impounding report issued about mid-month indicates the amount of soybeans currently under loan, and remaining previous crops reseal loans not yet redeemed. To this combined total, one must add CCC uncommitted inventory as of the closest date to the month-end (this figure is available weekly). The total represents the approximate amount of soybeans under current loan, reseal loan, and in CCC uncommitted inventory as of the end of the month, and not considered readily available to the trade. This amount subtracted from total supply provides an indication of the amount of soybeans in "free" or commercial hands at the beginning of the current month. (The foregoing

applies only when a loan program is in effect, and when the CCC owns soybeans. Supply now can be obtained from periodic USDA supply/demand estimates.)

This figure must be measured against anticipated demand. The initial comparison is made with expected disappearance (crush, exports, seed and feed use) for the full season. If "free" supply is less than anticipated distribution for the season, it suggests the need for cash prices to advance sufficiently to attract soybeans back into commercial channels from any CCC stocks, or to "ration" supply.

The procedure for determining supply can be refined further, particularly when quarterly reports (as of Sept. 1—carryover; Jan. 1; April 1; July 1) on stocks of soybeans in all positions are issued by the USDA. At other times the free supply/demand balance can be approximated by subtracting known and/or estimated distribution to the date in question from the latest quarterly report on stocks and then determining the relationship between the resultant figure and estimated distribution for the remainder of the season. Periodic USDA supply/demand projections provide a check on such analysis. There can be a significant variation between estimated stocks arrived at by deducting known and/or estimated distribution from either total supply or the previous stocks on hand report, and the stocks on hand as subsequently reported by the USDA. Discrepancies tend to reflect the different sources of information for crush and exports and the stocks on hand figures.

Determination of a tight free or commercial supply/demand balance does not guarantee higher prices to come, nor does an ample free supply situation relative to indicated demand necessarily spell lower prices in the offing. But, it does provide a reference point against which to measure developing events which could cause a shift in this balance.

Seasonal Price Influences

A factor of considerable importance in some years, is the tendency for cash soybean prices to rise from a harvest low to a peak in the spring. This tends to reflect the fact that supplies are heaviest shortly after the harvest and that farmers usually market a considerable portion of their production before the calendar year-end following the fall harvest. Later in the season competition from crushers and others for remaining supplies, coupled with the cost of carrying soybeans in commercial storage (storage, interest and insurance) tends to make for a firming price structure which is sometimes less than the cost of storage into late winter or spring and sometimes more than such costs.

This phenomenon appears to have been most evident when abundance of harvest supplies drove cash prices to, or somewhat below loan levels causing farmers to either hold a large percentage of their production or to place it under loan. In either case excess supplies tended to be siphoned off the market, and once the flush of initial harvest pressure was over, prices tended to firm up. This usually took time, however. Some guide as to whether prices had recovered enough to discourage producer holding or loan entries in volume was obtainable from a comparison of mid-month prices received by farmers and included in the USDA "Agricultural Prices" report each month-end, and average loan rates. Also, the monthly loan impounding report provided an indication of the amount being held off the market.

Two observations should be made with respect to seasonal price movements. The first is that cash (not futures) prices are referred to, and marketing and price pressure may be earlier than usual (perhaps by a week or more) if weather for maturing and combining the crop has been favorable, or later than considered normal if cool, wet weather delays maturity or impedes combining operations. Moreover, at times there is a tendency for futures to anticipate harvest pressure, so peaks of harvesting activity and troughs in price do not always coincide.

The second observation is that failure of seasonal price influences to register their usual appearance serves as a warning that all may not be well. Frequently this can be traced to a poor technical condition in the futures market, whereby a sizable and stale speculative long interest initiated at higher prices operates against price upturns. In addition, a seasonal price advance is less likely to be apparent when prices are relatively high early in the season.

Having taken into consideration the indicated free supply/demand balance, and seasonal price factors, the analyst is better prepared to evaluate month to month, week to week, and day to day developments affecting this balance, and their probable effect on price.

The Cash Basis

The soybean analyst also keeps an eye on the cash basis (usually the spread between the cash article on track at Illinois points, or the cash price at Chicago on track—Toledo and St. Louis are expected to become additional delivery points—and the nearest soybean futures contract) primarily as a guide to the underpinning of futures. Basis changes occur more slowly than market changes. The basis tends to be weakest around harvest time when cash prices often are depressed relative to futures, and to strengthen later in the season as the relationship between cash soybean supplies and demand improves. Aside from this seasonal tendency in the cash basis, a weakening basis (cash losing ground to futures) perhaps reflecting an abundance of supplies on track at Illinois points, favors the placing of short hedges. A strengthening of the cash basis (cash gaining on futures) favors the placing of long hedges and/or lifting and transferring of short hedges. Changes in the Chicago cash basis, taken into consideration with movement of Chicago soybean stocks, may suggest impending price movement in futures, especially approaching contract maturity.

Soybeans vs. Product Spreads

Another factor affecting the supply of and demand for soybean contracts is the interplay between soybeans and its products—oil and meal. It is usually referred to as soybean conversion, and it arises from the simple fact that one must process soybeans in order to obtain products. The opportunities for profit arise from the frequently overlooked fact that a processor cannot crush for a strong oil demand without getting less desirable meal; or crush for a good meal demand without obtaining unwanted oil. He is fortunate when he can crush for both without building up an inventory of one or the other, and the price of soybeans usually reflects this situation. More often than not, however, one of the two products is produced in larger amounts than routine forward sales commitments can absorb without prices giving ground. Thus, strength in one product may be offset by price weakness in the other, with soybeans showing little price change.

There are almost endless varieties of combinations of soybeans and product positions or commitments in futures and in the cash market, but two basic situations exist, and as they influence soybean prices, students of the soybean market should be aware of them, and be alert more to potential or actual changes in trends in spreads than to absolute price differences.

The first situation is one in which the combined product value is several cents higher than the price of the soybeans. Seasonally the widest premium for product values over soybean prices tends to occur early in the season when soybean harvest pressure is greatest, and lowest in the spring and early summer. It is a situation conducive to active crushing activity to take advantage of favorable processing margins, and at times for processors to increase their crush capacity by "putting on crush" i.e., buying soybean futures and selling deferred product futures. This procedure has backfired on occasion, when crushers put on heavy crush spreads early in the season hoping to take advantage of an unusually large processing margin with the expectation that it would narrow as usual later in the season. However, an unexpectedly good domestic and export demand, particularly for oil, forced undoing of spreads at unusually wide differences.

The second situation arises when the combined product value is considered less than the cost of soybeans plus out-of-pocket processing expense, or when a negative crush margin exists. Under such circumstances a "Reverse Crush" may be put on; buying products and selling soybeans. If processors have crushed heavily in the early part of the season at a very good margin, it can take longer than one might expect for the relationship to return to the plus side of the ledger, but the expectation is that sooner or later product values will gain relative to soybean prices.

The foregoing observations present some of the possible effects of changing crush margins on soybean prices. In general, there has been a tendency in real soybean bull markets, for one product to hold the limelight for a time until it gets temporarily overbought, when the other takes over, with the soybean market itself eventually taking over the lead.

A knowledge of how conversion spreads operate can provide the soybean student with some idea as to whether or not soybeans are unusually high or low relative to product values even if he does not intend to initiate commitments in such spreads. (Conversion spreads can be easily followed on a weekly basis in Commodity Research Bureau's weekly chart service.)

Crushing Margins

In order to determine the relative value of soybean meal (traded in units of 100 tons), and soybean oil (unit 60,000 lbs.) to soybeans (unit 5,000 bushels), one must make certain assumptions. For "Board" purposes, it is usually assumed that one bushel of soybeans will produce 48 pounds of meal and 11 pounds of oil. A price of 30¢ per pound for soybean oil times 11 pounds yield equals $3.30 product (oil) value per bushel of soybeans. A price of $175.00 per ton for soybean meal times a factor of .024 equals $4.20 meal product value per bushel of soybeans. (A factor of .024 as a multiplier is easier than dividing the price of $175.00 per ton by 2,000 pounds, the result being 8.75¢ per lb., which must then be multiplied by 48 pounds to arrive at the same figure of $4.20 product value.) Adding the two product values $3.30 and $4.20 together provides a $7.50 combined product value. If the same month futures contract in soybeans is selling at $7.50 per bushel, the gross processing margin is zero. The wider the premium for product values over the price of soybeans the more profitable it is to crush soybeans in the expectation that increased production of oil and meal would weigh on their prices, reducing the crushing margin —thus providing a profit to those who bought soybeans and sold meal and oil futures when the crush margin was very favorable.

The other side of the coin is when the crushing margin is considered unfavorable. This does not have to be a negative margin figure, for even out-of-pocket costs of processing soybeans dictate a modest premium. Gross processing margin, Decatur basis, averaged a record 72 cents per bushel in 1973/74 compared with only 9 cents in 1971/72. An unfavorable or unprofitable crushing margin is not expected to last indefinitely, and must find eventual reflection in easing of soybean prices relative to products. It is expected this will come about by processors' curtailing crushing activity because of its unprofitability, with resultant tightening of cash meal and oil supplies and prices. This would provide a profit to those who bought the product futures and sold soybean futures (Reverse Crush) because soybeans appeared high relative to oil and meal.

Both favorable and unfavorable crushing margins have a tendency to last longer than one might suspect. One reason is that gross processing margins computed for cash soybeans at Illinois points relative to oil and meal values at Decatur, Illinois as well as "Board" conversions are based on averages and assumptions of yields; and are thus of more value for observing changes in relationships than in absolute crush margin levels. Moreover, some major processors undoubtedly obtain operating margins less from crushing and selling oil and meal as such than from selling the end products such as mixed feeds, premixes, shortening, margarine, and cooking and salad oils. Hence they are less likely to curtail soybean processing operations than an unfavorable "Board" margin might suggest. Nevertheless, very profitable crush spread opportunities do arise from time to time, and the soybean student should be aware of the possibilities.

A Check List of Important Statistical Data

Daily:

Chicago Receipts and Shipments of Soybeans— Significant primarily around the time of maturity for a futures delivery, with sizable net movement into Chicago suggestive of tenders by shorts. (Compiled by the Chicago Board of Trade.)

Cash "Basis"—The relationship between the nearest futures month and the cash price at Chicago. While the basis changes less frequently than the market, a strengthening basis especially during or near the delivery period of a futures month may presage market firmness. Conversely, a weakening basis may foreshadow an easier futures market. Occasionally strength in the basis is the result of an easier futures market while cash prices remain virtually unchanged. (Transportation difficulties tended to distort "basis" relationships in 1973/74.) Less weight may usually be assigned to a decline in futures accompanied by a stronger cash basis.

Weather Forecasts—During planting, growing, and harvesting seasons each Monday, Wednesday, and Friday before the start of trading, the government 5-day weather forecast is released and usually receives close attention. Daily weather forecasts also receive considerable attention.

Weekly:

Export Inspections—Released after the close of trading each Monday by the USDA. Amount compared with expectations, with the previous week and year, with cumulative total for the season given.

Export Sales Reports—Released after the close of trading each Thursday by the USDA, provides amount and destination of export sales commitments.

Crop Summary—A Commerce Department report released Tuesdays during market hours giving progress of the crop based on weather conditions during the week under review. State reports often precede summary by one day.

Visible Supply—Released Monday by the Board of Trade, providing stocks at major terminals. Because of relatively direct distribution channels for soybeans, it is less important for this commodity than for grains.

National Stocks of Grain—Released Tuesday by the USDA includes Soybean stocks at many more points than covered in the above "Visible Supply" report.

Deliverable Stocks—Released Tuesday, providing an indication of that which is deliverable quality in registered warehouses available for delivery against futures. Most important as first notice day (the first day a short can signify his intention to liquidate his short position by tendering cash soybeans) approaches for a maturing contract. (Board of Trade.)

Chicago Storage Movement—Released Friday and in conjunction with deliverable stocks provides an indication of demand for receipts at Chicago. (Board of Trade.)

Primary Market Movement—Released Friday giving receipts and shipments at 13 major markets, gives some indication of soybean sales from the country, but less important than for grains. (Board of Trade.)

Price Range—Weekly price range is a consideration because traders frequently protect commitments with stop orders based on the range.

Chicago Stocks—Released Monday, indicates total Chicago stocks.

Monthly:

Crush Figure—Released by the Census Bureau around the end of the third week of the month covering the amount of soybeans crushed or processed during the previous month, meal and oil produced, and mill stocks of soybeans, meal and oil.

Factory and Warehouse Stocks of Oil—Released by the Census Bureau around the month end for the previous month, provides crude and refined soybean oil stocks, consumption, production and stocks of products, shortening, salad oil, and margarine. This report provides an indication of prospective crushing demand for oil.

Exports—Released monthly by the Census Bureau, usually late in the month covering the previous month. More important for oil and meal exports which receive less publicity than soybeans through weekly export inspection figures. This report complements the weekly USDA export sales report.

Crop Reports—Issued monthly by USDA August through November, after the close of trading on the 10th of the month. Gives production and yield per acre forecasts by states and total, and provides a check on private crop estimates. Where there is much difference from expectations the market can be influenced.

Quarterly:

Stocks in All Positions—An estimate by USDA of the amount of soybeans on farms and off farms. Important indicator of the amount of farmer holding, and the rate of sales or movement from farms, re-leased on 22nd of September, January, April and July.

Fats and Oils Situation Reports—Issued by the USDA, provides supply and demand outlook, statistics. Published in January, April, June, September and November.

Yearly:

Prospective Planting Reports—Issued in late January and again in mid-March by USDA indicating farmer planting intentions These reports are followed by a *July Acreage Estimate* released usually on July 10th. These reports are the basis for estimating production for a season and if much different than expected can exert an influence on the market.

Miscellaneous:

Supply and Demand Estimates—Issued by the USDA after major crop and stock reports. These projections are revised when indicated by a significant change in the crop or stock reports; usually providing a projected range of exports—crush—carryover. They place crop and stock reports in perspective with respect to the supply/demand balance—and sometimes tend to moderate the initial reaction of the market to crop and stock reports.

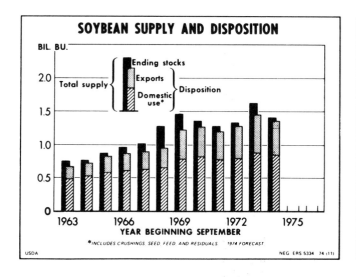

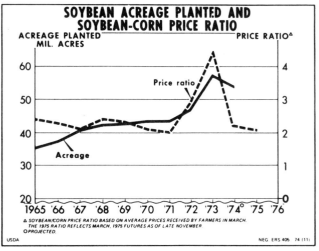

March Soybeans Futures Delivery
1969-70 to 1974-75

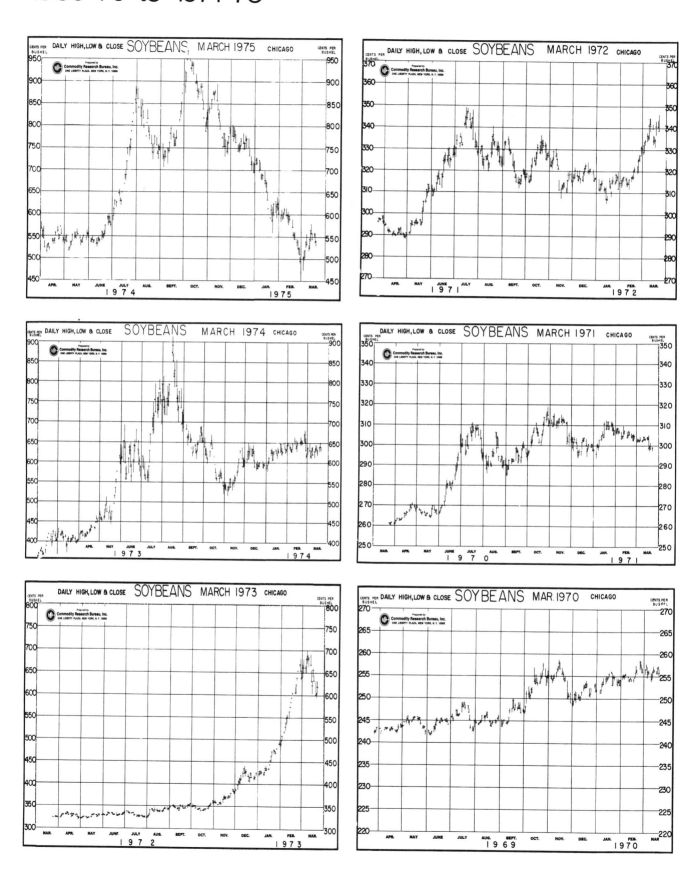

March Soybeans Futures Delivery
1966-67 to 1968-69

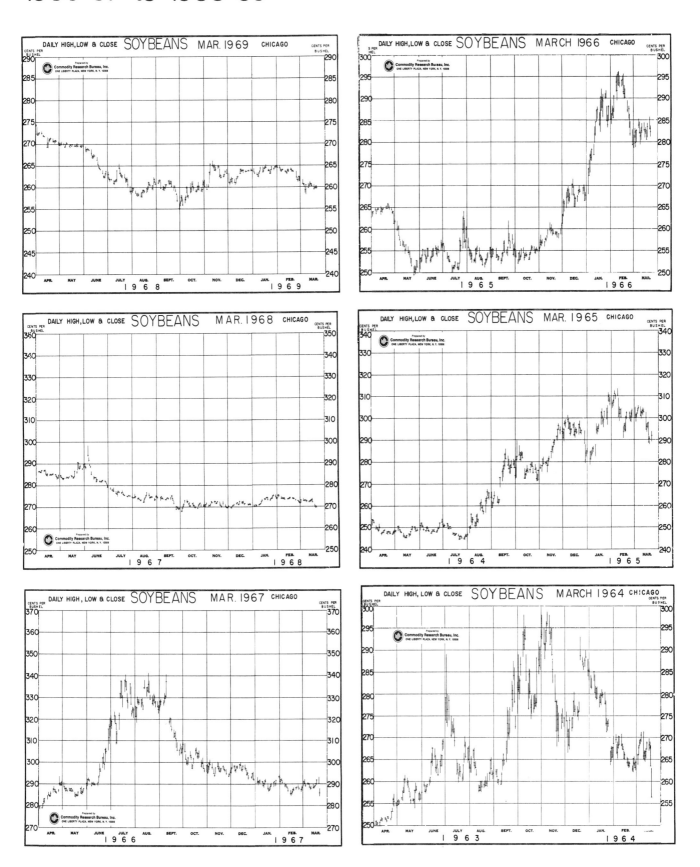

UNDERSTANDING THE SOYBEAN OIL MARKET

BY WALTER L. EMERY

The factors which influence the price of soybean oil are many and complex. They embrace not only the supply/demand considerations involving soybean oil itself, but also those which affect the supply and demand for competing edible oils, and oilseed meals.

Some Basic Observations

Soybean oil is a joint product (with soybean meal) of soybean processing. A 60-lb. bushel of soybeans yields approximately 10.7 pounds of soybean oil and 47.5 pounds of soybean meal. The meal is usually the more valuable of the two products, accounting for 60–65% of combined product value in most seasons. Thus, the demand for meal plays an important role in determining oil values. The oil content of the soybean is about 18-21 percent, depending upon the variety of soybean, area of production, seed weight, grade factors and climatic conditions. This is a much lower oil content than for most other oil-bearing materials which enter world trade, with the exception of cottonseed which contains a slightly smaller percentage of oil than soybeans. By comparison, the oil yield of some varieties of sunflower seed is as much as 40–45 percent and copra yields about 64% in coconut oil. An expansion or contraction of high oil content oilseed production can exert considerable influence on soybean oil demand (and price).

Soybeans are grown for their meal and oil. The oil's major competitors in this country (cotton oil and lard) are by-products of the cotton and hog industries, and their production is influenced by factors other than the demand for lard and cotton oil.

The soybean industry is an important one. U.S. crushing capacity in late 1974 was estimated to be in the vicinity of 1.1 billion bushels. Utilization of processing capacity has ranged between 77% and 92% in recent years (the long-term average being about 80%), with the highest crush recorded to date being the 821.3 million bushels crushed in the 1973–74 season, representing 82% of capacity. A record 8,999 million pounds of soybean oil was produced in that product marketing year. This amount of soybean oil accounted for more than 63% of total fats and oils produced in the U.S. that season, and was well in excess of even record domestic requirements. Prac-

tically all (about 93%) of the soybean oil produced is used in the food industry—whether it is consumed in the U.S. or abroad.

Per capita use of edible oils has tended to flatten out in the developed countries with gains limited primarily to population increase. Demand in these areas has tended to shift to protein meal as consumer diets have been upgraded through increased livestock and poultry production. As meal is produced to satisfy an upward trend in demand for protein, oil is also produced, for which a home must be found. On the other hand, per capita consumption of fats and oils in many less developed countries is very low, but is expected to increase as living standards rise. It is in this direction that the greatest potential for expanded use of soybean oil exists.

It is probably no accident that soybean oil is the bellwether in the world edible fats and oils field. Its big volume alone gives it deserved prominence. But, beyond this it is the one oilseed for which production and utilization statistics in the major producing country (the United States) are unusually complete, and freely available to anyone. This is a distinct advantage to users of fats and oils throughout the world.

However, this is not the case for most vegetable oils entering world trade. World vegetable oil production estimates are prepared by such organizations as the Foreign Agricultural Service (FAS) of the United States Department of Agriculture, and the Food and Agriculture Organization (FAO) of the United Nations. However, oil production figures are derived from oilseed production estimates based on assumed percentages of the crops crushed, and assumed oil yields. For some crops accurate figures on acreage and oil yields are not available, though it is considered that oil yields tend to vary much less than the percentage of a crop crushed from one country to another. For example, only about 35% of the cottonseed crop in China is assumed to be crushed, while about 85% of the Russian cottonseed crop is crushed.

Moreover, with the exception of the United States (where oil production figures are available on a monthly basis) most estimates of world oil production assign the oil equivalent from oilseed harvested to the calendar year in which most of the crushing ac-

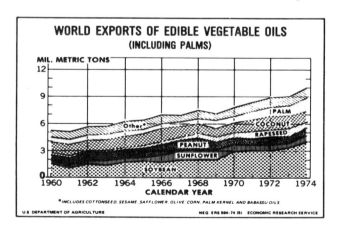

WORLD PRODUCTION OF EDIBLE VEGETABLE OILS
(INCLUDING PALMS)

MIL. METRIC TONS

*INCLUDES RAPESEED, SESAME, SAFFLOWER, OLIVE, CORN, PALM KERNEL AND BABASSU OILS.
U.S. DEPARTMENT OF AGRICULTURE   NEG. ERS 988-74 (5)   ECONOMIC RESEARCH SERVICE

WORLD EXPORTS OF EDIBLE VEGETABLE OILS
(INCLUDING PALMS)

MIL. METRIC TONS

*INCLUDES COTTONSEED, SESAME, SAFFLOWER, OLIVE, CORN, PALM KERNEL AND BABASSU OILS.
U.S. DEPARTMENT OF AGRICULTURE   NEG. ERS 984-74 (5)   ECONOMIC RESEARCH SERVICE

tivity took place. Thus, the oil equivalent of peanut (groundnut), sunflowerseed, and cottonseed produced in 1975 may be included in oil production in calendar year 1976. There are exceptions, however, and the oil equivalent of copra and rapeseed (except for Canada) and palm oil have been assigned to the year of harvest in U.S. Foreign Agricultural Service estimates. Hence, one must be aware of the methods used in reporting when evaluating oilseed or oil production forecasts, and that such estimates represent potential rather than actual oil production.

The Domestic Market for Soybean Oil

Soybean oil now accounts for about 56% of all food fats and oils consumed in the United States, and it is expected to increase its share of the domestic market in the years ahead. In addition, domestic disappearance of soybean oil accounts for by far the largest share of total soybean oil distribution. Domestic disappearance amounted to almost 7.3 billion pounds in the 1973/74 season while exports totaled about 1.4 billion pounds.

Food products account for about 93% of total domestic consumption of soybean oil. The major markets are; salad and cooking oils, which account for about 43% of the domestic disappearance of soybean oil, shortening—34%, and margarine—23 percent. Soybean oil is also the dominant oil used in their manufacture, representing 79% of the fats and oils used in margarine, 73% of the oils used in cooking and salad oils, and 58% of the fats and oils used in the manufacture of shortening in 1973.

Demand for fats and oils in the U.S. has increased over a period of years with a shift from fat use in the form of butter and lard to vegetable oils, principally soybean oil. This process has been hastened by the emphasis placed in recent years on polyunsaturated fatty acids in our diet. Of the commercially available oils only safflower oil and corn oil are indicated as containing more polyunsaturated fatty acids than soybean oil, with cottonseed oil somewhat lower and peanut and olive oil considerably lower than soybean oil in polyunsaturated fatty acids. (Sunflowerseed oil is second only to safflower oil in polyunsaturated fatty acids, but its production in this country is still relatively small.)

A major stimulant to utilization of edible oils, particularly soybean oil, has been the sharp rise in the use of cooking and salad oils reflecting increased popularity of snack food, salads, convenience foods and fried chicken and fish. Total per capita consumption of food fats and oils has risen to about 53½ pounds, of which soybean oil accounted for about 30 pounds. In 1973 per capita use of shortening amounted to 16.5 pounds, salad and cooking oils—18.1 pounds, and margarine (actual weight)—11.3 pounds.

The relative stability of overall food fats and oils use in this country places considerable emphasis on the availability of each of the major fats and oils to satisfy its principal markets. As indicated previously, soybean oil is the most important oil used, accounting for over 50% of the total food fat market and about 73% of edible oil use. However, shifts in the availability and price of cotton oil, lard and butter which follow soybean oil in importance productionwise can exert an influence on the use of soybean oil. For example, a larger than expected production of lard can capture a portion of soybean oil's market in shortening, while smaller than average supplies of cotton oil can boost soybean oil's share of the cooking and salad oils market. In late 1974 the virtual disappearance of the discount for margarine under butter prices (as a direct result of record high soybean oil prices) cost margarine—and soybean oil—some of the table spread market. Therefore, supply and price prospects for each of the major fats and oils must be examined periodically to determine whether any significant departures from usual supply relationships exist, or promise to occur, in order that some idea might be obtained as to the substitution potential.

Substitution

Thanks to technological advances, there is a fairly high degree of interchangeability among fats and oils for a number of products and uses. For example, shortening and margarine are considered to have a high degree of substitutability of fats and oils used in their manufacture. Yet, there are limits to substitution imposed by processing problems, taste preferences, and other considerations. Within these limits the amount of soybean oil used during a given season, or during part of a season, may depend in part upon the availability and price of competing fats and oils. Among the domestically produced fats and oils, lard and cotton oil (and, at least temporarily, butter) are the major competitors of soybean oil.

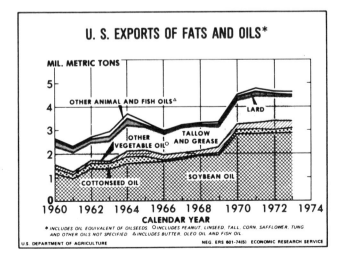

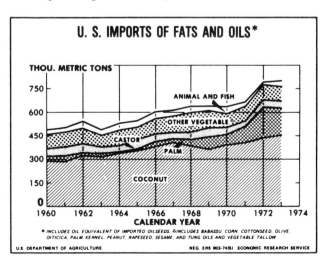

Imports

There is growing concern over the sharp rise in oil imports, although amounts involved to date have not been really significant relative to total domestic use. Palm oil poses the major threat. The oil palm yields more edible vegetable oil per acre than any other fat-bearing plant. Palm oil enters the U.S. duty free, with Malaysia and Indonesia the major sources of our imports. Its largest market is shortening, in which it competes with soybean oil. This use accounts for about 75% of its use in the U.S., but some is used in margarine and in soapmaking. Competition from palm oil is expected to increase significantly in view of expected world production expansion as recent plantation acreage comes of bearing age. Palm oil is produced throughout the calendar year. The other major import to date is coconut oil. The U.S. is the world's largest importer of this oil, which is used chiefly in confectionery and baked products where its demand is considered to be relatively inelastic. It is also used to a minor extent in shortening and margarine manufacture in this country. It usually commands a premium over soybean oil whereas palm oil has generally been cheaper than soybean oil. The degree of penetration of sunflowerseed oil (used for salad and cooking oil and in the manufacture of shortening and margarine—or safflower oil—used mostly in margarine) could exert some influence on the soybean oil market within limits imposed by crop yields and other considerations.

Importance of Crushing Margins

A major factor influencing the price of soybean oil is the shifting share of combined soybean product value represented by soybean oil. On a combined product value basis, soybean meal has been the product which has usually contributed most to the value obtained from processing soybeans (the crushing margin). Accordingly, the rate of crush, which determines the amount of oil produced, usually is influenced more by factors affecting the soybean meal market than by factors directly related to the oil market. It is seldom that a processor enjoys an active demand for both products of a ton of soybeans crushed at any given time. Yet, both oil and meal are produced in the processing operation. Soybean meal is less storable than oil and by custom moves out of crushing mills rather quickly. Over a period of time it has been more valuable than oil. Hence, there is a tendency to crush for meal demand rather than for oil—whose inventories are usually sufficiently large to draw upon for supplies. (This "normal" situation was reversed during part of 1974.) The large processors are active users of the futures markets, holding oil in inventory and placing short hedges against such holdings when the risk of price decline becomes a matter of concern, or when their oil inventory or purchase commitments exceed their forward sales commitments at fixed prices. At times, when there is an exceptionally favorable crushing margin they may place short hedges in deferred oil futures, and at times when the crushing margin is unfavorable they may place buying hedges in the distant futures contracts, provided the discounts on the deferred deliveries are attractive.

Reports to Watch

The U.S. Export Sales report issued by the Foreign Agricultural Service of the USDA provides weekly information on soybean oil export sales by destination for the current and next marketing season, and also reports cumulative exports for the current season on a weekly basis.

The monthly crush report of the Census Bureau (released around the 22nd of a month covering activity of the previous month) also receives considerable attention and may exert some influence on the soybean oil market if it fails to confirm expectations. The Census Bureau monthly report on exports (released during the last week of a month covering the previous month), and the Census Bureau monthly report on factory and warehouse stocks of oil (usually not available until after the month-end covering the previous month), as well as the production and stocks of major fats and oils products, all provide a check on production and distribution of both soybeans and the products. The aforementioned Census Bureau reports permit one to obtain a derived figure for domestic disappearance (consumption). Production of soybean oil for a given month is added to factory and warehouse stocks at the end of the previous month; from this total is subtracted exports for the month being covered, and finally, the latest month-end stocks are deducted from this result to obtain a "residual" domestic disappearance figure. In addition to these U.S. government reports, there are weekly trade services which provide statistics and comment on the oil trade.

The Foreign Market for Soybean Oil

The foreign market for U.S. soybean oil has accounted for less than 20% of total distribution of soybean oil in most recent seasons. However, its importance to soybean oil prices rests more in its unpredictability than in its volume. The U.S. is the world's largest producer and exporter of fats and oils, and soybean oil is the most important oil. But, much more soybean oil is exported in the form of soybeans than as oil. For example, the oil equivalent of soybeans exported in the 1973/74 season was 6.1 billion pounds vs. soybean oil exports of 1.4 billion. This is a fact that should not be lost sight of when evaluating export prospects. Unusually heavy soybean purchases by foreign countries, made for the primary purpose of obtaining needed meal, also produce soybean oil which can compete with our own soybean oil exports at times.

Western Europe, with a high per capita use of edible fats and oil, is by far the world's largest importer of oils and oilseeds, but this area imports hardly any soybean oil from the U.S. Europe first uses its own production. Then it takes the supplies available from former colonial possessions under a system of long term agreements and preferential arrangements. Finally, the balance of requirements may be acquired from the U.S., either as soybeans or soybean oil. The margarine industry in Europe is the major consumer of edible oils, with West Germany, the United Kingdom, and the Netherlands the most important margarine manufacturers.

Extensive oilseed crushing facilities exist in Europe, with most equipment now capable of handling soybeans. The oilseed crusher usually has access to a large number of oil-bearing materials. Which materials are favored, within limits imposed by consumer preference, technical considerations, and government regulations concerning composition of food products, depends upon the relative availability and profitability of crushing various oilseeds. In this connection, in view of the relatively low oil content and high meal content of soybeans, the widened demand for meal in Europe as a result of expanded livestock and poultry production argues in favor of the purchase of soybeans rather than oil (provided the conversion margin is favorable).

From a practical viewpoint there are little more than a half-dozen vegetable oils which are of major importance in international trade, and which exert an influence on soybean oil use. These may be classified on the basis of their consistency in temperate climates as, "soft" oils-soybean, peanut, cottonseed, rapeseed and sunflowerseed used in liquid form or in the manufacture of shortening or margarine; or as "hard" oils—the product of palm trees—coconut, and palm kernel oil which are used primarily in margarine or shortening manufacture, the baking industry and soapmaking. All of the soft oils used for cooking and salad oils are interchangeable to a large degree, and butter, lard, and palm oil are competitive as cooking fats. In the making of shortening and margarine all of the soft oils, palm oil, and lard are considered interchangeable to a major extent. Marine oil is used extensively in margarine manufacture in some countries, notably the UK.

The major edible fats and oils and their oil-bearing materials entering world trade in competition with soybean oil are peanut (groundnut) oil, coconut oil, palm kernel oil, palm oil, butter, lard, fish oil and sunflowerseed oil. Nigeria and Senegal have been the largest exporters by far of peanuts and peanut oil—their main markets being France, Italy, and the UK. The Philippines account for the bulk of copra and coconut oil exports, followed by Sri Lanka. Most of the Philippine exports move to the U.S. and Europe. Nigeria has been the largest exporter of palm kernels with the UK and Italy major customers. West Malaysia is the major exporter of palm oil, followed by Indonesia. The United Kingdom, the Netherlands, and West Germany are the largest importers of palm oil. Principal butter exporters have been New Zealand, the Netherlands, and Denmark, with the UK the major importer. The U.S. has been the largest exporter and the UK the largest importer of lard. The principal fish oil exporter is Peru by a wide margin, followed by Norway and the U.S. Major importers are the UK, West Germany and the Netherlands. The USSR has been the leading exporter of sunflowerseed and oil with Romania an important exporter of sun oil. Principal importers of sunflowerseed have been East Germany, Italy, West Germany, and Czechoslovakia. Rapeseed exports have also become of importance, with Canada the major supplier.

Concessional Sales (PL 480)

The best soybean oil export potential lies in the less developed countries where a deficiency of oil in diets persists. Demand in developed areas tends to be rather stable aside from gains afforded by population increase. Unfortunately, in the less developed countries need and ability to pay seldom are at the same level, and the requirements for foreign exchange in some of these countries dictates the export of domestically produced oil which might otherwise be used to bolster low per capita use. Hence, there continues to be a great need for concessional sales. The Food for Peace program through PL480 has played a major role in the export of U.S. soybean oil (accounting for well over one-half of total shipments over a period of years), but PL480 shipments slipped to only 19% of soybean oil exports in 1973/74. Major recipients of these concessional sales have been India, Pakistan, and more recently, Bangladesh. (PL480 export sales are not included in the weekly U.S. Export Sales Report issued by the FAS, USDA.) It seems doubtful, in view of reduced U.S. soybean oil stocks, that in the future PL480 soybean oil sales will assume their previous importance.

Price-Making Factors

Probably the most important factor which tends to establish the basic price structure of soybean oil within a season is the size of the U.S. soybean crop. This is due to the major role soybeans play in both the domestic and world market for fats and oils. The U.S. production of soybeans establishes the upper limit to potential soybean oil supply in this country.

Once the U.S. crop size is determined, usually by late December, the "effective" supply of soybean oil is determined primarily by the percentage of the crop crushed. About 52–67% of the soybean crop is crushed in a season, and the rate of utilization, as measured by monthly processing activity statistics, influences soybean oil prices as do crop forecasts prior to determination of the crop size.

If demand for both oil and meal is high, processing activity tends to be active and prices of both products rise. If demand is active for oil, but not for meal, crushing activity need not pick up significantly because meal stocks are not generally permitted to accumulate and oil stocks may be sufficient to satisfy demand at steady to firm prices. Even record meal stocks of 535,000 tons at the start of September 1974 represented only 40% of combined meal exports and domestic disappearance in that month, compared with an average of 16%.) The crushing rate is more apt to increase in response to heavier meal demand, with a resultant increase in oil stocks and subsequent pressure on soybean oil prices. (However, this was not the case in late 1973 and continuing into the fall of 1974 when record large monthly crushes were needed to permit processors to catch up on heavy forward sales of soybean oil products arising from disruptions to production and marketing caused by price controls in the summer of 1973.) A reduction in the crushing rate can bolster oil prices by reducing oil production and paring stocks. The effect on soybean oil futures of the foregoing developments depends in part upon the current and prospective cost of soybeans relative to the combined meal and oil value obtained from processing soybeans, and to trade hedge positions in futures. Trade hedges account for a significant portion of open commitments in futures for all three segments of the soybean complex—oil, meal, and soybeans.

Looking beyond shifts in the rate of crushing activity as a factor influencing soybean oil prices, there are developments which cause a change in the relative share of combined product value at a given level of crushing activity and thus influence soybean oil prices. For example, projections of increased high protein consuming animal units (as revealed by pig crop reports, cattle on feed reports, laying hen numbers, and broiler egg settings) tend to bolster demand for meal and stimulate meal prices. At a given level of processing activity, the higher meal prices permit an easing of oil values without any adverse effect on crushing margins. Conversely, a significant decline in the cotton crop or a sharp drop in hog slaughter (lard production) can stimulate demand for soybean oil and firmer prices, depending upon the level of stocks. As indicated previously, cotton oil and lard are the major competitors of soybean oil in the domestic market, and shifts in their availability and price can influence soybean oil values.

Increased imports, while still small when viewed in perspective with the overall fats and oils situation in the U.S., pose an increasing threat to soybean oil use and price in some products. Palm oil and coconut oil are the major imports.

The amount of soybean oil stocks in the U.S., and the rate of change in their size, especially during the seasonally active winter processing period (and again approaching the end of the product marketing year ending September 30 when crushing activity is seasonally reduced) exerts an influence on soybean oil prices as well as on crushing activity. End-of-season (Sept. 30) soybean oil stocks have averaged about 9% of that season's distribution over the past several years.

Late in the fall of the year, oil prices are often affected by projections of foreign oilseed crop production from which oil will be available in the following calendar year. World demand for fats and oils has been increasing at an average annual rate of one million tons a year, and the trend-line increase in world production of fats and oils is also about one million tons. However, yearly changes in available supplies have fluctuated widely and, together with a rather inelastic demand for oil, can result in significant oil price changes on a year to year basis. Accordingly, competition in the export market for soybean oil from foreign produced oil-bearing materials is a price factor of major importance with respect to commercial exports of U.S. soybean oil. The lack of accurate data on production of oilseeds and the amount of oilseed production crushed for much of the world, adds to price uncertainty in the edible oil markets.

Concessional export sales of soybean oil, through PL480 or donation programs are expected to play a reduced role in U.S. soybean oil exports. However, the level of these sales, and also the rate of shipment, particularly of PL480 oil, may influence soybean oil prices. Adequacy of storage and distribution facilities in importing countries, as well as the rate of use in the recipient nation, affects the rate of oil shipment.

The Soybean Oil Futures Market

Crude soybean oil futures are actively traded on the Chicago Board of Trade. The annual average number of outstanding contracts (open interest) has ranged between 16,000 and 38,000 contracts in recent years. Open interest tends to rise seasonally from an August/September low into December, dipping in January, then rising to a March/April peak.

In common with the soybean and soybean meal futures markets, the "trade" is an active participant in soybean oil futures trading. For example, hedge long positions accounted for about 40% of total open interest and hedge shorts 54% of open interest in recent years (5-year 1969/73 average). By comparison, small trader "longs" (those holding less than 25 contracts in any one trading month—and usually considered primarily speculative in nature) accounted for only 26% of open commitments in soybean oil futures.

There appears to be some seasonal pattern to hedge activity in soybean oil futures. Short hedges (as a percentage of open interest) tend to rise from a low around the start of the soybean oil marketing season (Oct. 1) to a high in March or April, then to decline into the following September. Long hedges tend to follow a somewhat similar pattern—but with a time lag. The seasonal low tends to occur in October/November, with a subsequent rise to a June or July peak interrupted only by a slight dip in February or March. Long hedges then tend to decline into the following October–November period.

There is much less variation in the share of total open interest accounted for by short hedges (from one season to another) than there is in the percentage of open interest accounted for by long hedges. This characteristic of the soybean oil futures market may, at times, exert a significant influence on the price structure.

March Soybean Oil Futures Delivery
1969-70 to 1974-75

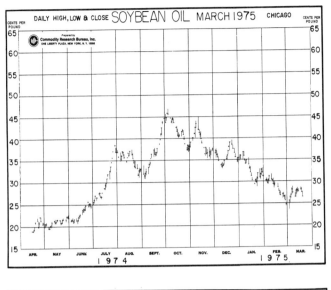

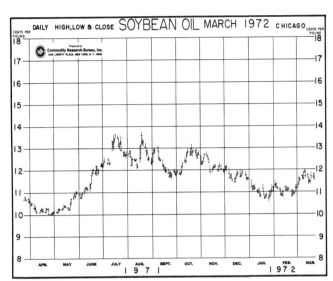

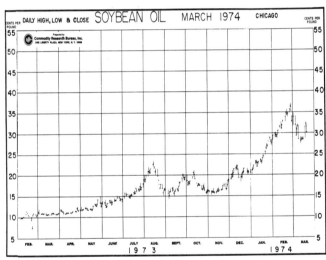

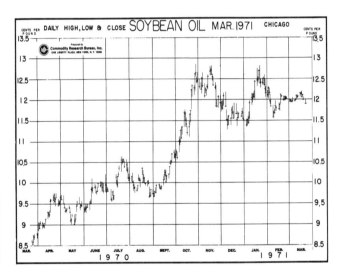

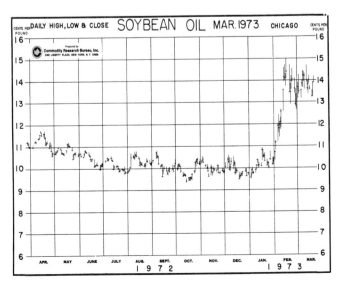

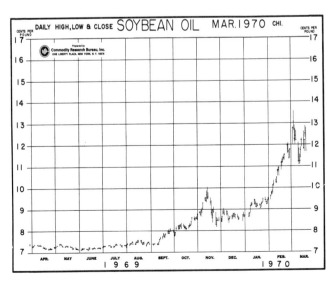

March Soybean Oil Futures Delivery
1963-64 to 1968 to 1968-69

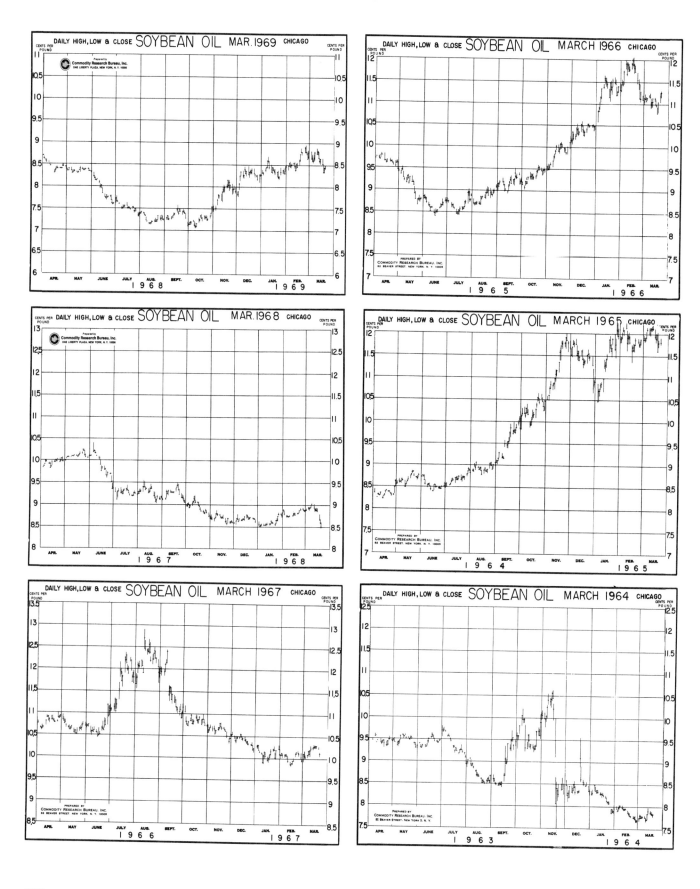

HOW TO ANALYZE THE WORLD SUGAR FUTURES MARKET

BY DAVID M. INKELES

This article is designed to help buyers and sellers in their analysis of the world sugar market in two ways. The first is the presentation of information concerning the background of the sugar industry and sugar futures. The second consists of suggestions on how to approach analysis; which material should be stressed and which material should be treated lightly or ignored. It appears that the greatest confusion lies in this second area. Information related to world sugar prices is released every day. This is important for arbitragers and day traders who must be continuously in tune with the emotion and feeling on the floor. However, much of the daily information can be confusing to one who is trying to predict the level of prices 6 months or 1 year ahead and is of little value to the speculator.

The Sugar Bull Market

A bull market in sugar does not occur often. In between, there are often years of low prices which may be quite dull from a trading point of view. However, when sugar bull markets occur, they can be bigger in scope than those of any other actively traded commodity. They become the text book case for describing the potentialities of commodity trading. They become the standard to which all other bull markets are compared and they are constantly referred to in brokerage firm analyses, economic literature and salesman presentations. This is their rightful place, for without a doubt, there is nothing in the world of commodities which can approach a full blown sugar bull market.

There have only been four major sugar bull markets in the past century. The first occurred during the Civil War, during which spot N.Y. prices moved from 4¢ to over 16¢ per pound. The major thrust carried prices from 6¢ to 16¢ in a single year of the war. This was an unusual market. Although prices declined sharply after the war, it took another 25 years for them to level out at the pre-bull market level. The second bull market started in 1915 with prices at 3¢. It included 3 years of gradual increase during the war and then a violent spurt from 7¢ to 20¢ in the 1919–1920 post war bull market.

The third bull market was of shorter duration but if anything, increased ferocity. It occurred in 1963–1964 and carried international prices from 2.5¢ to 13.5¢. Compared to its predecessors or the most recent market this does not sound impressive. However, there was a gain of almost 600% in less than a year. An investment of $500, the margin for 1 contract at the lows, could have yielded a profit of $12,800 on the first leg of the move.

The 54 Year Cycle

The fourth bull market, which we have just experienced, has dwarfed anything which came before

it. In reality it began in 1967 although probably no one realized it at the time. Sugar was selling at 1.25¢ per pound F.O.B. Late in 1974 the market reached 66¢ for March futures, a greater than 50 fold increase. The final year saw prices advance eight fold and the final month saw a terrifying advance of 12 successive limit days.

It may be significant that this market crested 54 years after the 1920 bull market. That market followed the Civil War move by 56 years and it in turn followed the famed Napoleonic shortages by 54 years. These cycles do not account for the 1963–1964 market. However, since Napoleon, that bull market was the smallest of the major advances.

The ardent student of business cycles will stop his analysis at this point. To him, cycles tend to recur and fundamentals simply cloud his view and keep him from having the courage of his convictions. In 1967 the only bullish fundamental was the price of sugar itself. Those who tried to trade the market long term saw their contracts lose value. The back months traded at considerable premiums which disappeared as the contracts approached maturity. Those wishing to pursue this subject are referred to substantial available literature on business cycle theory.

There were, of course, good statistical reasons for the price rise. The 1969–1970 season was the last in which world production substantially exceeded consumption. At that time, ending stocks stood at 23 million metric tons. This represented 32% of annual consumption. The October 1974 Licht estimate of year end (Aug. 31) stocks was 15,587,000 metric tons which was only 19% of yearly consumption. This was indeed a low figure but not very different from the 15,704,000 metric tons of the previous year. Furthermore, it was well above the 14% level of the 1964–65 bull market. Thus, while the end of season stocks created a tight supply picture it could not in itself be credited for being the cause of the bull market.

It was the bad weather in Europe and the prospective production shortfall in the coming sugar year (1974–75) which led to the acceleration of the bull market. This began in July and carried until the market crested in November. Since the European and Russian sugar is harvested after August 31, there was a production shortfall which came on top of the tight supply picture already mentioned. The hard statistics of the shortfall as estimated by Licht called for a drop of at least 10% in the production of both eastern and western Europe and the Soviet Union. In the 1973–74 season these areas produced 26.5 million metric tons.

A factor, which had firmed prices earlier in the year, were fears of massive Arab buying and increased Arab consumption. This contributed to the rise from the 10¢ to the mid 20¢ level. There was indeed Arab buying early in 1974. However, in the end it turned out that they bought approximately the same amount as in previous years. They merely bought early, and as it turned out, at good prices. The supposed increase in Middle Eastern consumption as the reason for the rise appeared to be unfounded. With the wealthy Arab nations rather sparsely populated, a significant increase in per capita consumption would not amount to a great overall increase.

Other factors were significant. Both the U.S. quota system and the Commonwealth Sugar Agreement ended in 1974. It was rumored that some countries were holding back on their quota shipments forcing the U.S. and U.K. into the free market. However, U.S. refiners were reported to be well inventoried. Their earnings reports seemed to substantiate this by showing large inventory profits.

The succession of limit moves in the climatic phase of the market made it difficult to trade physical sugar. The reason for this was that without sellers in the futures market, actuals could not be unhedged. At approximately the same time, a trader for a large firm was reported to have taken an unauthorized short position of considerable size. Once discovered this was promptly covered and the buying added fuel to the fire.

However, these were incidentals. There was a tight supply picture during the summer. Earlier production intentions for 1974–1975 had optimistically indicated a modest improvement. Then came the reports of poor weather in Europe, and there arose the spectre of a shortfall of at least several million metric tons. With this projected supply picture, there would be very little sugar available to deliver against the March 1975 contract. The market exploded.

The decline from 66¢ was equally dramatic. It was due to a reaction to the speculative excesses. It was also due to the realization that consumption was going to be substantially affected by the higher prices. We shall explore this in some detail later in this article in the discussion of the consumption of sugar.

General Approach To Market Analysis

The analysis of any market in its simplest terms is the analysis of the factors that affect the supply and the demand of the commodity involved. The analysis of sugar prices is no exception. However, no commodity market today is purely competitive as defined in economic literature. There are always factors, whether they be oligopolistic (a few large sellers who can affect prices), oligopsonistic (a few large buyers who can affect prices) or governmental, which modify the workings of a purely competitive market. Here, too, sugar is no exception. In fact, it contains many more non-competitive factors than the average commodity. This tends to severely modify normal factors of supply and demand analysis. The limiting parameters cannot be overlooked. This is perhaps unfortunate since they are the factors that reduce the accuracy of any statistical analysis.

The World Market—Its Composition

The No. 11 sugar contract on the New York Coffee and Sugar Exchange is a contract for raw sugar. The sugar involved is free sugar. No duty has been paid on it. It can be exported but remains subject to all the sugar import legislation existing throughout the world.

This free sugar represents a small portion of total sugar produced. Only 22.7 million tons or 28% of total world production enters international trade. The remainder is consumed in the country in which it is produced. Prior to the end of 1974, of the 28% exported, less than half entered the free market. The remainder moved under various protected agreements. Of these, the most significant were the U.S. quota system, the agreements of the British Commonwealth, the agreements between France and her former colonies, and the agreements between the various communist countries, mainly China, U.S.S.R. and Cuba. The U.S., U.K. and Canada import over 8 million metric tons annually, which now will come from the free market. Hence, from now on, a majority of internationally traded sugar will be free.

The sugar sold under the various international agreements usually includes premiums to the seller. With the possible exception of the communist agreements, the seller has been free to leave the agreement and it is the premiums that kept the agreement binding. The sugar sold in the free market (also called the world market) generally carried the lowest price and had no premium. In surplus years, the free market became the dumping ground for sugars produced in excess of world consumption and quota requirements. It was usually a depressed market and considered a buyers' market. In the future this will undoubtedly change, since non-communist producers will no longer have the cushion of the U.S. quota or the Commonwealth Agreement.

Participants in the World Market

The world market is made up of exporting countries, importing countries, operators, brokers and speculators. For the most part, exporting nations of raw sugar are the producing nations. Importing nations often re-export refined sugar or sugar products. Others are simply final users. Brokers are lubricants to aid the flow of business. Operators buy sugar for their own account for resale. Speculators deal in futures contracts and rarely own actual sugars. All of these parties influence the price of raw sugar. In analyzing any given piece of news it is wise to consider its effect on all of these groups.

U.S.S.R.

The Soviet Union is the world's largest producer of sugar with yearly production recently between 8 and 10 million metric tons or a little less than ⅛ the production of the world. In spite of this, Russia is still an importer of sugar with net imports in recent years averaging around 1.5 million tons. Imports are often from other communist countries on barter terms. The Russians are quite knowledgeable in dealings of the world market and from time to time will buy or sell on the London exchange. The major obstacle in analyzing Russian activity is secrecy. Published statistics are prone to be either inflated or deflated for propaganda purposes. The complexity of communist dealings is difficult to follow. Heavy production in Russia could result in heavier free market exports by Poland since Russia might not take as much of her sugar. However, it will show up somewhere. Thus I would suggest using Licht's production figure against an estimate of consumption. The latter can usually be last year's consumption increased by the previous 5 year cumulative growth rate. Statistics on home consumption are late in coming and will have affected prices long before they are published.

Russian production is entirely in beets. Since the mid-60's they have been endeavoring to increase production but have had difficulties. A large part of this has been a result of poor weather.

Cuba

Before Castro, Cuba was the main source of free market sugar. It still remains the largest exporting nation, but a large portion of its output now moves via a barter agreement with the U.S.S.R.

It also deals in the free market. However, it generally hides these activities by dealing through operators and brokers. Cuba is the third largest producer in the world at about 5 million tons. Her production has fluctuated considerably in recent years. Variations in Cuban production are extremely important since 84% is for export. The problem again is that we generally do not have good information. Rumors about Cuban production are rampant. These run a gamut from weather, which can be checked, to shortages of lubricants for mills and trucks, which are difficult to verify. It is best to pay close attention to Caribbean weather, and production statistics of neighboring islands.

Cuba profited greatly from the higher prices of the past few years. Castro has indicated that he wants production above the 10 million ton mark. However, he has been saying this now for a good many years. Perhaps with the inflow of hard currency, he will be able to achieve sufficient modernization to accomplish this.

Brazil

Brazil is the second largest producer of sugar after the U.S.S.R. She is also the second largest exporter of sugar after Cuba. Unlike Cuba, Brazil has sizable home consumption. Hence, her exports were only ⅓ of 1973–74 production compared to 84% for Cuba. For 1974/75, her production is forecast at 7,400,000 tons. This represents an 80% increase for the decade. Since her consumption has not changed greatly, her exports will have increased by over 200% for the same period.

Brazil's sugar exports are government regulated. In the mid 60's the sugar agency used to guess the market. Sugar sales were sporadic with much fanfare to influence prices. Today, with a larger export base, it has become more orderly, allowing operators to handle sugar, but imposing minimum prices.

Europe

Europe is generally a net importer of about 10% of its needs. In the current year (1974–75) this could go higher due to the poor beet crop already alluded to. Switzerland and the United Kingdom are large importers, Poland and Czechoslovakia are large exporters. European production is carefully analyzed by Licht. Consumption patterns are quite stable but production can fluctuate sharply. The latter is one of the most important factors affecting world prices. Europe, as a whole, is the world's largest producer of sugar.

Other Nations

Production of other countries contributing to the world market should be studied with respect to variances from the norm. There has been a large increase in cane production in the past 10 years while beet production has been static. The Philippines, Brazil, Mexico, Dominican Republic, Australia and Africa, as a whole, have been the most noticeable standouts. India has large variations in production and is of considerable importance. Unfortunately, production statistics are not reliable until well after the season, and rumors are rampant. A study of weather is necessary to verify the rumors.

The Role of the World Sugar Operator

A world sugar operator is a well financed company that buys and sells raw sugar for a profit. These companies are usually international in scope and have excellent information at their disposal. They are not prone to divulging this information. A speculator, who trades in the futures market, is operating in the same arena as these companies. This is a sobering thought since few if any speculators have the same information or financing as the operator.

The operator, simply by his size, has an effect on the futures market. A cargo of sugar is 10,000 tons. The hedging of a single cargo requires the sale of 200 contracts of 50 tons each. The size of this sale can affect the market. The operator must be an expert in futures market dealings since 1 point (1/100¢) on 200 contracts is equal to $2,240.

Operators can influence speculative opinion in many ways. One example is for the operator to short the futures market heavily. He then sells a part cargo or even a full cargo to another operator or even a final user well below the spot price. The news of the sale causes the futures market to decline amidst heavy speculative liquidation. The operator can then

Production of Selected Large Producers   (1000 Metric Tons)

	1934/35 1938/39	1945/46 1949/50	1950/51 1954/55	1960/61	1965/66	1972/73	1974/75
U.S.S.R.	1,924	1,249	3,217	6,630	9,019	8,150	9,000
Cuba	2,741	5,351	5,516	6,767	4,866	5,250	6,000
Brazil	673	1,318	1,814	3,354	3,851	6,164	7,400
U.S.A.	1,810	1,789	2,125	2,800	3,567	4,920	5,036
India	961	1,087	1,328	3,094	3,632	4,572	4,800
China	502	143	500	1,200	2,400	2,457	2,600
Mexico	318	589	840	1,487	2,251	2,770	3,000

Source: International Sugar Council, and the U.S.D.A.

cover his shorts and perhaps even buy back his actuals at favorable prices. In any case, he is prepared to lose money on the part cargo since he should profit by a greater amount in the futures market.

One should be extremely careful about rumors concerning the floor activities of the operator. He could be selling heavily and yet be bullish. His long positions could be in actual sugar. He might want to carry a portion of this clear but, due to his financial limitations, hedge the remainder. Thus, on balance he could be net long although selling in the ring. Operators are quick to take advantage of market movements resulting from speculative excesses.

Large Net Exporters (1000 Metric Tons)

	1960	1966	1972	1973
Poland	162	295	332	423
Czechoslovakia	320	90	229	225
Cuba	5,634	4,434	4,140	4,797
Dominican Republic	1,099	511	1,099	1,031
Brazil	854	1,010	2,054	2,376
Peru	513	433	481	407
Philippines	1,088	1,085	1,240	1,475
South Africa	284	578*	1,168*	892*
Australia	841	1,524	2,010	2,100

* Does not include Swaziland.
Source: International Sugar Council and the U.S.D.A.

The operators provide liquidity to the world market by buying from producing nations and selling to importing nations. They usually hedge at least part of their inventory. The stocks they hold are called "second hand" sugars as opposed to first hand sugars which are held and sold by producing nations. The operator needs to buy and sell sugar to make a profit, and his inventory is normally for sale. Since it is hedged it may be sold profitably, even if the spot price drops below his purchase price. Heavy stocks in the hands of operators generally tend to depress the world market. Licht gives statistcs on total stocks of sugar in the world. However, there are no official statistics on second hand stocks. Nevertheless, this is a very important figure. Although it can not be pinned down, members of the trade generally have a good idea as to the size of the stocks in second hands.

Importing Nations

For many years, the consumption of sugar was relatively static with small annual increments the rule. In the past decade and a half, this accelerated due to world prosperity and the spreading sweet tooth. 1954/55 exceeded the 1935–39 average by only 35% while it has doubled since then. The annual increments have been averaging as much as 2.5 million tons in recent years. This, of course, may change now, with the higher price level and the world economic problems.

The U.S. and U.K. heretofore were not major factors in the world market. Due to the expiring agreements, they of course will be in the future. The U.S.S.R. is an irregular participant since it obtains a great deal of Cuban sugar by way of barter.

Japan buys heavily in the world market but much of this comes from normal trading partners with the

prices determined by a formula based on the futures price. Other countries buy consistently from the world market on tenders and publish the prices. These sales are of great importance since they give an indication of what final users are willing to pay for sugar. These sales will generally change the spot price if they differ from the prevailing level. The amount of sugar offered on a tender is also an indication of the supply of second hand sugars and market strength. The sellers at these tenders are generally operators although first hand sellers also offer sugar. Among the major buyers of sugar in this manner are the Middle Eastern countries, South Viet Nam, Sri Lanka (Ceylon), Turkey and Sweden.

Selected Large Net Importers (1000 Metric Tons)

	1960	1966	1973
Europe	4,685	5,108	5,315
U.S.A.	4,633	4,076	4,746
U.K.	1,885	1,983	2,050
U.S.S.R.	1,485	680	2,633
West Germany	116	361	140
Canada	613	756	965
Chile	151	163	251
Japan	1,252	1,505	2,372
Algeria	267	271	278
Iran	337	202	150
Iraq	228	251	280
Sri Lanka (Ceylon)	260	204	169

Source: International Sugar Council and U.S.D.A.

Agricultural Factors—Characteristics of Cane and Beet Sugar

Both sugar cane and sugar beets yield sucrose $C_{12}H_{22}O_{11}$ on extraction. They also yield dextrose and levulose (both $C_6H_{10}O_5$) in smaller quantities. The latter two are called invert sugars. Sucrose is broken down by the body into glucose, the sugar used in body metabolism. Sucrose is the most desirable readily available sugar because of its high sweetening power and agreeable taste. Today about 60% of the world's sugar (sucrose) comes from cane with the balance from beets.

Sugar Cane

The sugar cane is a perennial grass which reaches to a height of 8 to 24 feet at maturity. The sugar is found in its long woody stem. The stem contains structural cellulose and a liquid containing on average 14% sucrose. Cane requires tropical or semi-tropical temperatures and an annual rainfall of at least 50 inches. Higher temperatures and winds produce greater transpiration and thus increase the water requirement. The temperature region of the cane is almost the same as that which permits the growing of the palm tree. The cane growing season can be from about 7 to 24 months. Growth is faster nearer the equator. However, cane grown near the outer limits of the tropics, such as Hawaii, give greater sucrose yields. A period of cooler weather with diminished rainfall will cause the cessation of woody growth and the building of sugar supplies in the stem. This then, coupled with abundant sunshine, is most desirable in this period just preceding the harvest.

Cane can be planted from seed but, in fact, only new breeding varieties are planted in this manner. Production cane is planted in a manner similar to the potato, except that a piece of stem bearing an eye is the vehicle of propagation in this case. This is only done once every three or four years. In other years the stubble left after harvest produces shoots from existing eyes which yields a new crop. This is called ratooning. Each ratoon crop is of successively smaller amount. After several years, ratooning becomes uneconomical and the field is then plowed and planted anew.

Cane is subject to varied pests, to hurricanes and to droughts. The latter are most serious. Hurricanes are of significance depending on the area. In September a hurricane is quite serious in Louisiana where harvesting has just begun, but it can be a blessing in Cuba. In the latter the crop has not yet reached its full height. It is resilient enough to stand most wind, while benefiting from the accompanying rainfall. The futures market generally advances anytime a hurricane is loose in the Caribbean. It would be wise to consult people in the trade or sugar analysts and inquire just how susceptible the crop really is to the storm. Drought is, of course, unwelcome at any time, but it is most serious early in the season during the rapid vegetative growth period. Sugar cane is crushed quite near its field. Deterioration and large sugar loss result if there is delay in getting the cane to the mill. This undoubtedly has been part of Mr. Castro's problem in past years.

Sugar Beet

The sugar beet is a biennial requiring two seasons to produce seed. When grown for sugar it may be harvested in 6 to 8 months. The largest part of world beet production occurs in Europe and U.S.S.R. with significant production also in North America. Uruguay and Chile produce beet sugar but the rest of South America produces cane. Beets are grown in a temperate climate with 10 to 20 inches of rain in the growing season between May and October. Like cane, it prefers a cool, dry period immediately prior to harvest in November. This checks vegetative growth and increases sugar accumulation in the root. Insufficient rainfall during the summer as well as cloudy weather before harvest during the fall, can seriously curtail sugar yield. Sunshine, necessary for photosynthesis, is desirable during the summer and fall and can compensate for insufficient rainfall. However, beets produced in a maritime climate with 20 inches during the growing season generally yield better than beets produced inland with closer to 10 inches. Much of the beets produced in the U.S.S.R. are under irrigation due to insufficient rainfall.

The beet is both a farm and cash crop. The tops make excellent silage while the beet is sold to the mill. Beets are also rotated with grains. This cycle along with farmer inertia make it difficult to sharply curtail or exand acreage in any one season. The beet should be sliced very quickly after harvest to insure maximum sugar yields. Unlike cane, beet extraction and refining are carried out under one roof. This is mainly because the beet is grown in more industrialized areas where the cheap fuel necessary for refining is readily available. The yields on sugar beets are perhaps the most unreliable part of sugar supply forecasts. They are quite sensitive to weather conditions. Crop forecasting requires a close check on the weather throughout northern Europe eastward to the Ural Mountains. Since this is generally beyond the scope of the average speculator, he should obtain this information from brokerage firms and sugar trade houses.

Subsidies to World Sugar Producers

Up until the end of 1974, 10–15% of world production was free and 85–90% was for home consumption or under some form of subsidy. The higher prices for the 85–90% enabled the 10–15% to be sold below the cost of production. It made the world market a buyers' market by and large, except for those occasional periods of shortage.

There are two main historical reasons for these subsidies: The first is that sugar is a necessity and no nation wishes to be at the mercy of international trade during war. The second is one of balance of payments. Since sugar in either cane or beet form can be grown in most areas of the world with the exception of the arid Middle East, most countries prefer to subsidize their own industry, be it inefficient, rather than use hard currency to purchase sugar in world markets. Not all consuming countries have carried this to the extreme of self-sufficiency. But the fact that two thirds of the world's sugar remains in the country where produced indicates that it has been pursued avidly.

A short look at the history of the sugar industry in Europe explains much of the present system of subsidies. During the Napoleonic wars, England blockaded France and cut the flow of tropically grown sugar into that country. Napoleon, a great innovator as well as a great general, seized upon the sugar beet which had not yet been exploited commercially. He subsidized the planting and refining of sugar beets. After Waterloo the sugar industry that he developed collapsed owing to British enforced competition of lower priced imported cane. Around 1850 a revival took place which laid the foundation for the great beet industry that now exists in Europe. By 1890 more than half the world's sugar was produced from beets. The industry growth was brought about by the bounty system. Various governments in Europe imposed taxes on all forms of sugar. However, they would rebate the taxes with a bonus added if the sugar was exported. This caused the world market to become a dumping ground since producers could sell to it below cost and yet eventually profit after the receipt of the bounty. The world price was generally below various domestic prices by at least the amount of the tax. It encouraged a "beggar thy neighbor" type of rivalry and led to extremely low world prices. The bounty system was disallowed by international convention in 1903, but subsidies and tariffs remained to protect inefficient domestic industries. The latter part of the 19th century also saw sugar go from being a luxury item to an ordinary staple in most European countries.

History of American Legislation

The sugar legislation terminated at the end of 1974 can be traced back to 1933, at least in regard to its basic idea. The hypothesis was that the U.S. would pay a bonus to certain foreign producers to make sure that they would continuously ship to the U.S. Thus,

171

in the rare periods of scarcity the U.S. would be amply supplied. Producers that defaulted on U.S. commitments when the world price was higher than the domestic price would lose their right to participate. Since the countries involved would normally sell in the free market, the U.S. premium represented a substantial profit which they would not wish to lose. Originally the domestic beet and cane producers were given 55% of a quota set by the U.S.D.A. and foreign producers were given the rest. Cuba and the Philippine Islands were given preference and were alloted the largest quotas. This system worked quite well. Besides enabling the U.S. to have a dependable supply, it served to subsidize the domestic cane and beet producers and mask a certain amount of foreign aid to countries receiving U.S. quotas.

Shortly after Castro made his communist intentions known, the U.S. suspended his quota. It then decided to purchase the Cuban allotment in the free market and keep the difference between the world price and the domestic price. This idea apparently did not consider the thinness of the free market. In 1963–1964 bad weather in Europe and a hurricane in Louisiana further tightened supplies. When the U.S. began to buy, prices advanced sharply. Here was a perfect example of the "tail wagging the dog." Sugar offerings were scarce but world stocks did not decline below 9.4 million tons. However, when a sudden stress was put on, free market stocks disappeared. That is, with the U.S. in the market for exceptionally large amounts, no one wanted to sell any inventory. Thus, it could be said that the 1963–1964 market was largely artificial. True, the weather conditions would have forced price somewhat higher, but had it not been for the tremendous buying by the U.S. in the free market, it is doubtful that the upward spiral would have been as dramatic.

The quota system came under political attack in the U.S. by early 1970 when prices for sugar had already risen considerably above their 1967 lows. The U.S. continued to pay a premium for sugar and it was felt that this contributed to inflation. Furthermore, there was some "waffling" by some participants in meeting their quotas. It will remain to be seen if the U.S., the world's largest importer, will be able to insure adequate supplies without a quota system based on bonus payments. The other possibility could be a cartel of sugar exporters such as the O.P.E.C. is for petroleum. In this case the U.S. could be caught in a price squeeze. One thing is clear, however, the quota system did not protect the U.S. consumer from being ravaged by the high prices of the 1974 shortage.

Factors that Govern Sugar Consumption

Consumption of sugar from year to year has tended to increase at a fairly steady rate. Thus, it has not had as marked an effect on price movement as has supply. Furthermore, consumption figures are often difficult to obtain and are usually available only after the year for which they are compiled. Thus, they are valuable only in retrospect to determine why the market did what it did. There are exceptions to this. An example would be the purchase of large quantities of sugar for abnormal uses. This occurred in 1966 with sugar being used for alcohol and feed due to the low price.

The demand for sugar is governed by two factors. The first is price elasticity; the relationship of a price change to consumption. The second is income elasticity; the relationship of per capita income to consumption.

Income elasticity has been responsible for increased per-capita consumption in newly developing countries. From year to year this will contribute to the annual increase in world consumption. Barring a world wide depression, it should have little short term influence on price.

Price elasticity is a different matter, since it is the key to the potential explosiveness of the sugar market. In writing about sugar, it used to be said that the demand for sugar was inelastic. This means that people buy virtually the same amount of sugar regardless of price. However, we had never seen sugar retailing at 75¢ per pound before. It is now evident that the price elasticity of sugar is related to the second derivative of price with sharp increments at higher prices. As we have found out, sugar demand is quite elastic above 50¢ per pound.

There are two reasons for the inelasticity at low prices. At these levels, the cost of sugar is a small component of the total retail cost of soda pop or confectioneries. At higher prices it is a major cost and substantially forces up the price of these less than necessities. Secondly, at low prices, the costs of tariffs, refining and distribution are greater than the cost of raw sugar. If raws are priced at 2¢ and retail sugar 12¢, then a tripling of the price of raw sugar to 6¢ will only raise the retail price by ⅓ to 16¢. During the 1963–64 bull market, raws increased by 600% while the cost to the consumer barely doubled. In 1974 when raws moved from 25¢ to 65¢, retail prices moved from 35¢ to 75¢ which was almost the same percentage.

In 1974 there was consumer reaction to the price rise. Bakers switched to products requiring less sugar. Restaurants took sugar off the tables. Soft drink makers started adding fructose and sugar substitutes to their non-dietetic products. Moreover, the price of dietetic drinks was lower and became an added source of competition. Also the threat of government investigations may have served to loosen some refiner inventories.

In some countries price elasticity was not a factor because the domestic price of sugar did not increase very much. This occurred notably in Canada and Mexico where the price was government subsidized. Americans living near the borders were allowed to import 100 pounds, and many did this each trip across.

Longer Term Consumption Patterns

Per capita consumption depends mainly on per capita income. However, there is a saturation point at which sugar ceases to be a luxury. Thus, an increase in income leads to increased consumption until a level of slightly over 100 lbs. a year is reached. Historical figures then show that despite additional income increments, sugar consumption per capita does not move above this level. The present world population is about 3.7 billion. World production of sugar this year will be around 80 million metric tons. Per capita consumption is thus 21.6 kilograms or 47.5 lbs. This figure is slightly deflated by the fact that only centrifugal (refined or semi refined) sugars are included. It does not include noncentrifugal sugars such as paneta, repodura, chancaca, papiton, muscovado, jaggery and gur. However, if for argument sake we accept the 47.5 lb. figure then, if per capita consumption were raised to 100 lbs., world production would have to expand to 168 million metric tons based on today's population. This is double current levels. It is unlikely that per capita consumption will reach that level during the present century.

War

War or the threat of war has always had a greater effect on sugar prices than on those of other commodities. A large portion of the sugar sold in the free market is exported in ships. Wars interfere with shipping and thus cause destruction and dislocations of supply. Wars in Europe have caused reduction in beet output as well. Due to the price inelasticity of sugar a world shortage or dislocation (a shortage in one area) will cause a great advance in prices. This is an old concept but it is equally applicable today.

The threat of war or threat of dislocation such as the 1956 Suez crisis, or the 1967 Middle East crisis, will cause a sharp advance in prices in the futures market. This is because an actual war will cause such a drastic advance that speculators are willing to risk a premium to be long during a crisis. Also, speculators and members of the trade do not wish to be short during a war advance where the losses could be disastrous. Thus, any crisis precipitates massive speculative buying and short covering. In the case of crises that do not lead to war, the decline that follows the advance is usually very sharp. Speculators know this but will take the risk since the potential gains are enormous should an actual war develop. It is somewhat significant that the 1973 Arab Israeli war did not have an immediate effect on prices.

Per Capita Consumption of Sugar for Selected Countries

| | In Kg. | |
	1934–38	1966
World	11.4	19.4
North America	46.7	47.7
South America	16.6	31.9
Asia	3.2	6.7
Africa	5.1	10.7
Europe	18.9	38.0
Italy	7.9	27.9
Albania	4.3	16.2
France	24.7	35.8
Netherlands	30.9	58.8
Ireland	39.3	60.8
U.S.A.	47.0	48.0
U.S.S.R.	11.2	43.7
Brazil	17.1	32.4
(Mainland) China	1.0	3.6
India	3.2	6.3
Israel	19.8	43.8
North Vietnam	1.0	1.3

Source: International Sugar Council

Sugar Statistics

The reports of F. O. Licht & Co. of Germany are the best sources of sugar statistics. Other good information is supplied by the U.S.D.A. and the United Nations. The forecasts of F. O. Licht are considered to be the best since they are of high quality and im-

partial. They are widely respected and have a market impact approaching that of the U.S.D.A. for domestic commodities. An older but complete source of sugar background information is the study *"THE WORLD SUGAR ECONOMY"* in 2 volumes published by the International Sugar Council in 1963.

Statistical computations are seriously affected by the units used, especially the 4 different kinds of tons. These are all in common use depending on the country. The accompanying figures show the more commonly used measurements, some of which differ from our own.

Short ton	2,000	lbs.
Long ton	2,240	lbs.
Metric ton	2,204.6	lbs.
Spanish long ton	2,271.64	lbs.

An Approach to Statistical Analysis of the Market

The statistical objective of an analysis of the sugar market is the determination of year end stocks. This is forecast by adding estimated production and subtracting estimated consumption from the previous figure of year end stocks. By convention the sugar year ends on August 31. This is at the height of northern hemisphere consumption and before European beet and Caribbean cane harvests. It is not as marked a carryover date as we have in corn or soybeans, however, since sugar harvesting continues throughout the year in one country or another. The estimate of year end stocks is by far the most important statistic to be derived. How the statistic is used and interpreted is another matter.

Carryover

For the market to be in equilibrium, in a surplus, or close to surplus condition the following conditions must be satisfied. 1. The pipelines must be filled and 2. Speculative holders must have all the sugar they want to own. In addition, the outlook must be for continued surpluses such that no member of the industry wishes to hold excessive inventories. Once supplies tighten or the outlook changes, then inventories become closely held and prices rise. The price rise is due to the necessity of offering more to induce the sale of inventories. These facts are axiomatic and apply to all commodities. What is not axiomatic is how much supplies have to shrink to produce a given price level above the surplus price. This is not subject to a simple equation. The price will rise slowly until expectations swing completely around to the point where users begin to panic and holders of inventories begin to believe they have gold rather than sugar. Prices then can skyrocket until either new supplies or a contraction in demand begins to loosen existing stocks.

Factors such as who owns the carryover stocks become significant. Stocks in the hands of operators are much more mobile than stocks in consuming or producing nations. Also, computers have increased inventory efficiency in every other industry. It is perfectly logical that the same could be true for sugar and that the percentage of stocks to consumption necessary to maintain a given price has declined.

Ending stocks for the 1963–64 season were only 9.7 million metric tons. This represented 14% of consumption that year. Ending stocks for 1973–74 were 15.5 million tons. This represented 19% of consumption, yet prices far exceeded those of 1963–64. Of course the poor weather in the fall implied a large potential erosion of current inventories, if we assumed stable consumption.

While I do question the labeling of any percentage (of stocks to consumption) as a crisis level and thus making one's thoughts inflexible, I do not suggest disregarding year end stocks. As in other commodities, changes in carryover will inversely affect the price structure. Trying to correlate the size of the advance with the level of stocks is much more risky since other factors besides stocks are usually involved.

Price Making Influences

Day to Day Movements. While a long range estimate of supply and demand and the resulting inventories can often predict a major move it can be clouded by day to day activities and news. These include weather reports, prices of sales, Licht reports, international news and rumors. Rumors are the easiest to deal with. They are sometimes true. However, on balance followers lose more money than they make since most are not true. Reports of sales are the most concrete. Sales to final user countries are the best. Sales to operators by operators are most suspect but still usable. All sales should be converted to an equivalent f.o.b. and stowed price since these are the terms of the futures contract and the spot price. Members of the trade who know shipping rates and conversion rates can do this easily. The important question is whether the sale was above or below previous prevailing levels. The former is of course bullish and the latter bearish. Sales that tend to change an existing trend should be suspect, but should be excluded as evidence only if apparently designed to influence the market. Wild speculative moves with increased public participation should also be suspect. However, the public is not always wrong.

The Extra-ordinary Event. News interpretation is important. A market is generally in an equilibrium regarding expectations. Extraordinary events will upset this equilibrium and cause prices to move. For example, Venezuela might sell 4 cargoes of raws to an operator at a premium to the spot price. This would normally be a bullish sale. However, if the trade had not expected Venezuela to export to the world market that year, the news of the sale could cause futures prices to decline since it upset the equilibrium of expectations. A knowledge of the industry structure and expectations is important for correct interpretation of news. It enables the speculator to spot the extraordinary event before it has had its full effect on prices.

Inflation and Devaluation. Conventional wisdom has it that commodities, especially sugar, are a good hedge against inflation and devaluation. This can be true in the case of a galloping inflation such as recently in Chile or in Germany during the 1920's. It was vehemently emphasized by virtually all commodity markets in 1973 and in 1974. However, for many years this was not true. During most of the 1960's with the exception of 1963–64, sugar in London sold at prices below those which prevailed in the second half of the 19th century. This was true despite several devaluations which severely reduced the gold value of the pound.

At the same time the cost of living based on wages paid a laborer has increased geometrically. The reasons for this divergence have been increased farm technology and sugar subsidies. Also, as mentioned earlier most countries wish to produce sugar domestically and pay large subsidies to do this. The result is that supply often outstrips demand, causing the free market to be depressed. Countries are all trying desperately to cut imports and increase exports.

Sugar had been a useful hedge against pound devaluations in the 1960's. Prices in London quickly equilibrated themselves with the prevailing world price. Thus, a person long London sugar and short New York made a profit since London gained with respect to New York, the full amount of the devaluation. An Englishman, who bought sugar before the devaluation, ended up with more pounds, albeit of lesser value. He thus insulated himself from the devaluation.

In the 1970's both the pound and dollar have tended to move together, declining vs. gold, Swiss francs and marks. Thus N.Y. vs. London sugar switches would have been of little value. Furthermore, with gold now being freely traded, it is a preferable vehicle. However, it is important for the speculator to understand the relationship of currency values to price levels in London and N.Y. and the inherent currency risk involved.

London Market

The London market is open several hours before New York. Hence any over night news can first reflect itself there. The markets are considered in line when both are open. London closes at 12 noon New York time. Major moves in New York after this time will reflect in the London opening as will early morning London moves affect New York. This is brought about by arbitragers who operate in both markets simultaneously with the aid of open line trans-Atlantic communications. The spreads between New York and London can change. However, the speculator attempting arbitrage is at the disadvantage of not having proper communications and having to pay non-member commissions. London–New York spreads should be avoided except when impending currency devaluations are a consideration.

There is also a futures market in Paris which is smaller than either London or N.Y. In the November–December 1974 price decline, this market was shaken by the failure of one of its largest operators. By exchange rules, other firms were required to contribute large sums. It will be interesting to see if this market can regain its position once again.

Taking Delivery

Taking delivery should be avoided. Sugar is shipped economically only in boatloads of 5 to 10 thousand tons. A person taking delivery of 50 tons (1 contract) can not hire a ship. He may not be able to store in the country long enough to retender it on the next delivery. The paperwork dealing with sugar in foreign countries is extensive and requires experience in handling. The speculator who takes delivery must generally employ a cash sugar broker. The broker tries to sell it to an operator who may have taken delivery of the remaining 199 lots of the same cargo. The operator must go to extra handling expense to accommodate this speculator. He probably will reduce the price he will pay for the sugar since otherwise it would be unprofitable.

Conclusion

The outlook for the next several years points to continued price activity and speculative participation. It will be extremely treacherous for the small specu-lator. To begin with, as a result of the price rise, contract size and margins are now much more important. Moreover, if history is a guide, prices will probably have additional large swings before settling down into another equilibrium. However, this type of market is home for the seasoned speculator and he should have good opportunities for testing his intellect and wallet in the coming years.

March World Sugar Futures Delivery
1972-73 to 1974-75

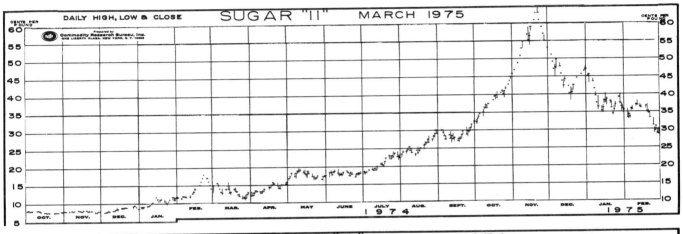

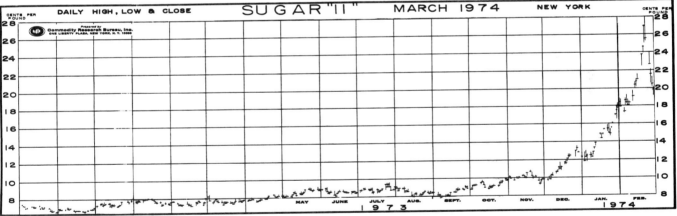

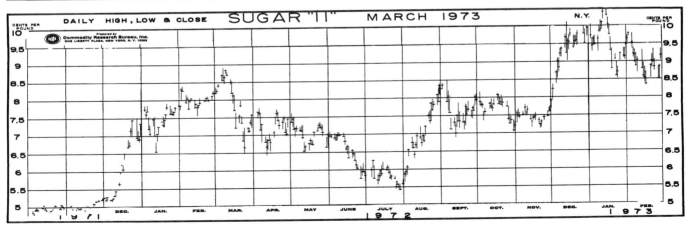

March World Sugar Futures Delivery
1969-70 to 1971-72

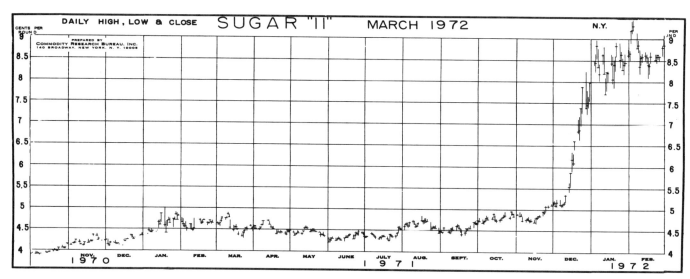

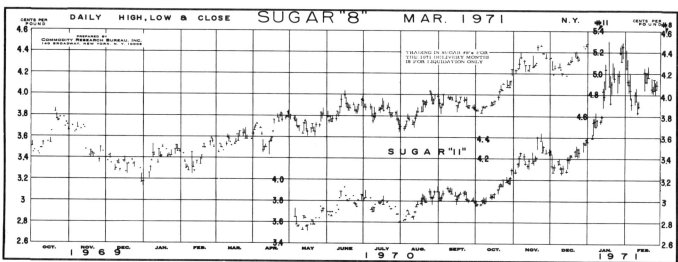

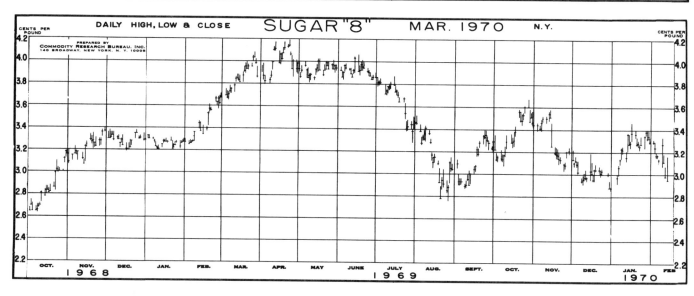

March World Sugar Futures Delivery
1966-67 to 1968-69

UNDERSTANDING THE WHEAT FUTURES MARKETS

BY WALTER L. EMERY

Wheat is, by far, the most important food staple entering world trade. Rice, the other major source of food energy, is produced and consumed primarily in Asia, where areas of both greatest surplus and deficit production exist. This is also an area where population growth has tended to exceed food production capacity. Accordingly, the extent of Asian demand for U.S. wheat is dependent not only upon their own wheat production but also upon world rice crop prospects. (At times, the People's Republic of China has sold high-priced rice and bought lower-priced wheat in the world market to obtain foreign exchange.)

The United States exports more wheat than it consumes domestically, and accounts for about 45% of world trade in wheat. Crop developments in major producing and consuming countries—particularly the USSR and the People's Republic of China—are of great significance to the demand for, and price of, U.S. wheat. The USSR is the world's largest wheat producer by a wide margin, accounting for about 25–30% of total world production, and is usually a net exporter—mostly to eastern European countries. The People's Republic of China is the world's largest producer of rice, and also produces a significant amount of wheat. Trade with these two countries was facilitated by agreements reached during the Nixon Administration, and because of crop reverses, first Russia and then the PRC became major buyers of U.S. wheat. However, changes in trade policies by the USSR and the PRC are very much dependent upon important decisions by their central governments' regarding the extent to which the diets of their people are upgraded, as well as upon crop considerations. In addition, data on grain stocks in these centrally-planned countries is not yet available. Hence, the extent to which buying in the world market by these countries represents the building of reserves of grain (rather than to make up reduced production in any one season) is unknown.

The major traditional wheat exporting countries are the United States, Canada, and Australia. A sharp decline has occurred in the level of carryover stocks in these countries—from 23% of world wheat consumption in the 1960/61–1962/63 period, to 15% in 1969/70–1971/72, and to only 4% in 1973/74–1974/75. As annual world wheat use has exceeded production slightly in most recent years, we are forced to pay increased attention to production prospects in these countries. This requires a knowledge of their crop seasons, the type of wheat produced, and their usual markets. It should be borne in mind that dislocation of supply is more likely to be encountered than actual shortage. And, it has essentially the same effect on demand and prices, for it causes buyers to reach out beyond their normal sources of supply to seek wheat in competition with other purchasers.

Increased uncertainty regarding the availability and price of desirable quality wheat means a greater need on the part of commercial interests to carry and hedge inventories and forward sales commitments. Both the "trade and trader alike" must be increasingly alert to shifting supply/demand prospects by class of wheat, area of production, and use. This changing wheat picture demands more than a knowledge of total wheat production, exports, and domestic disappearance. It requires a working knowledge of the supply and distribution pattern of the major classes of wheat and their relationship to the futures market.

Wheat, to the miller, is more than "just wheat." It must meet specific milling requirements, and it also must meet exacting baking quality demands. It is classified by its growth habit—whether it is planted in the fall in areas of milder climate and known as Winter wheat, or whether it is planted in the spring in areas of more severe climate and known as Spring wheat. It is further classified by color of the kernel, and by texture of the grain as to whether it is Hard or Soft. (Most winter wheat is soft wheat and spring wheat is hard wheat.) Hard wheats are usually higher in protein content and are used mostly for bread flour, while the soft wheats are milled primarily for cake, cookie and cracker flour.

Problems of the Seventies

At the mid-point of the 1970's, a major uncertainty concerned the ability of the world to feed a growing population in the face of increased dependence upon each season's crop output as a result of a sharp drop in world food grain reserves. World stocks of wheat in 1974 were reduced to an estimated 14% of world wheat consumption, compared to 24% of the 1969–71 period and 33% of estimated consumption in 1960–62.

About 75 million people are added to the world's population each year, with much of the expansion occurring in less developed countries which account for about 65% of the world's population but only about 20% of world food production. These countries are primarily grain product consumers rather than meat product consumers. In addition, per capita use of wheat for food has increased in these countries. Hence, world demand for food grains may be expected to continue at a relatively high level, with the focus on wheat.

It is the purpose of the following sections to bring the major classes of U.S. wheat and their distribution pattern into focus, enabling the student of wheat prices to better evaluate market developments as they occur.

Section I—The Kansas City Wheat Market

Hard Red Winter Wheat

This is, by far, the most important class of wheat produced in this country, representing about 46% to 56% of all wheat produced, and amounting to about 747–960 million bushels in recent years.

Where Produced

Production is centered in the Central and Southern Plains. Kansas alone, where production is concentrated in the south central and western portion of the state, accounts for about 40% of hard winter wheat production. Production in Kansas is usually more than double that of other major hard red winter producing areas, accounting for about as much as Nebraska and Oklahoma together. These two states are followed by Texas, and Colorado where acreage planted to winter wheat is concentrated in sections adjacent to western Kansas.

When Planted and Harvested—

Generally, planting in the major hard red winter wheat producing areas is started by early September and is practically complete by mid-October. If planting is too early growth may be too rapid, rendering the plant vulnerable to damage by freezing, while if planting is too late the plant may not be hardy enough to withstand the winter.

The harvest of winter wheat is usually active in the Texas Low Plains and starting in the High Plains and Oklahoma by early June, and is generally practically completed in Texas and Oklahoma by the end of June. Combining in Kansas usually gets underway in earnest by the second week of June and is virtually complete by the second week of July. The Nebraska harvest generally starts around the end of June and is about finished by late July. The crop in Colorado is the last in the major hard red winter wheat states to be harvested. Combining starts in early July and extends into or beyond mid-August.

Hard Red Winter Wheat Use—Primarily for Bread

Hard red winter wheat ranges between 10–15% protein. Protein content of wheat is a measure of gluten, and in turn of the baking quality of bread. High protein hard winter wheat (and spring wheat) is used primarily for yeast-leavened products such as bread, rolls, and sweet goods. Bread alone accounts for about 41% of the domestic utilization of wheat, and bakery flour, a bread flour used mostly by commercial bakers, accounts for about 65% of the total consumption of flour. Bread makes up about 69% of the total quantity of bakery products, and white pan bread represents most of this.

A relatively small number of wholesale bakers produce about 40% of all commercial bread, while large cooperatives account for about 24%. Less than 20 large milling companies constitute about 80% of wheat milling capacity in this country. Kansas mills represent about 13% of the total U.S. capacity; New York about 11%; Minnesota approximately 13%; and Missouri more than 9% of total capacity. Flour sales are made for as much as 120 days ahead. There tends to be two seasonally heavy flour buying periods—one from July through early August as new crop wheat becomes available, and the second in early December. However, there is no great consistency to this pattern either for timing or extent of coverage. Frequently mills will not press forward sales because of concern over basis change prospects, while bakers may permit coverage to decline to less than 30 days in the hopes of lower prices.

Exports—A Major Market

More hard red winter wheat is exported than all other classes combined. Exports have always comprised a high percentage of production of this class of wheat, as much as 87% in the 1965/66 season. Such a high percentage exported was possible only because carryover stocks were large—as much as 75% of all classes together. Practically all of the carryover stocks of this major class of wheat in past years were in the hands of the CCC. As CCC wheat stocks were drawn down, the percentage of hard red winter wheat production which was exported declined, to average 58% in the 1969/73 period. Realization that we can no longer rely upon these huge government stocks is forcing a reappraisal of possible effects of supply/demand dislocations by all segments of the trade.

Less than 10 percent of hard winter wheat exports in the past couple of seasons has been under government programs—mostly Title I of PL480 to such countries as Bangladesh, Pakistan, and Korea. Our best dollar customers over a period of years have been Japan and the European Community. More recently, the USSR, People's Republic of China, and Brazil have been good buyers. Most exports of hard winter wheat have been via Gulf ports such as Houston, Galveston and Port Allen in Texas, and New Orleans and Destrehan in Louisiana. Proximity to the major hard winter wheat producing area, low cost barge transportation, favorable rail rates, and excellent handling facilities all have contributed to the importance of Gulf ports.

The Common Market countries, which produce very little hard wheat, constitute our best dollar market, other than Japan which is our most important single dollar customer. Recent annual wheat imports amount to about 147 million bushels, of which Canada supplied about 50%, with Argentina and the U.S. supplying most of the remainder. EEC countries import mostly premium quality wheat for blending purposes. Thus, developments in this direction receive close attention of the wheat trade. Canada, with its high quality spring wheat, is a major competitor in the export trade for protein hard winter wheat, while Argentina, which ships a medium hard wheat, also provides competition.

Australia, the other major exporter, ships primarily soft wheat but is exporting an increasing amount of hard wheat. Southern Hemisphere wheat which comes on the market in late winter and early spring following their harvest, is often a factor in our futures market at that time, and their sales commitments relative to their exportable supplies receive consideration by traders.

Wheat Price Support

The wheat price support program operates under the provisions of the Agriculture and Consumer Protection Act of 1973 which covers the 1974–1977 wheat crops.

The Target Price Concept

New with this Act is the concept of guaranteed, or "target" prices and deficiency payments for wheat. Deficiency payments will not be made as long as the average market price received by farmers during the first five months of the marketing year remains above the target level. It is only when the average market price drops below target levels that a farmer's cash price for grain is supplemented; and then it is only supplemented on allotment production on the amount that the target price exceeds the larger of the loan rate or the five-month national average price, weighted by the historical quantity of production sold in each month. This arrangement will provide a farmer with a guaranteed return on the portion of the crop produced on his allotment, freeing him to concentrate on all-out production without fear that a market decline would drop grain prices below the level of profitability.

Target Price

The target price for wheat is established at $2.05 per bushel for 1974 and 1975.

If the national weighted average market price (the price received by all wheat farmers) of wheat for the first 5 months of the marketing year (July–November) is $2.05 per bushel or more, there will be no payment. If, on the other hand, the national weighted average price of wheat is below the $2.05 per bushel target price, program participants will receive a payment. The bushel payment rate will be the amount that the target price exceeds the larger of: (1) the $1.37 loan rate or (2) the national weighted average market price. This per bushel rate will be multiplied by the farm wheat allotment times the established farm yield to determine the program payment.

Loans

For participating farmers, nonrecourse loans will be available at $1.37 per bushel, national average for the 1974 wheat crop. This loan level is not designed to influence market price, but rather to enable farmers to borrow money on crop production to satisfy outstanding financial obligations while retaining title to the commodity for marketing at a more favorable price in a later period.

Wheat Certificates

The wheat certificate program has been suspended.

The Escalator Provision

Target prices for 1974 and 1975 have been set at $2.05 a bushel for wheat, but an escalator provision is included in the Agriculture and Consumer Protection Act of 1973 that could raise this price during the last two years of the bill. Under this escalator provision, which will be in effect during the 1976 and 1977 crop years, the target price will increase if the cost of production goes up more than overall farm productivity. The formula for figuring the 1976 and 1977 target price will be: cost of production increase as measured by USDA's cost of production index adjusted by the productivity change as measured by the national average yield for the preceding three years, compared with the yield of the three years previous to the preceding year. For example, for the 1976 crop the 1973–75 average yield will be compared with the 1972–74 average yield. This assures that if the national average costs of production rise faster than the national average crop productivity, the target prices will reflect such a change.

Set-Aside

Though the Secretary of Agriculture has already announced that there will be no set-aside in any program during the 1974 crop year, authority for set-aside is provided for years when he considers land retirement a necessity. This gives the new farm bill the flexibility needed to deal with the rapid changes that can occur in the supply-demand situation for grains. If a set-aside is in effect, producers must set aside and devote to approved conservation uses an acreage of cropland equal to the specified percentage of their allotments in order to be eligible for loans, purchases or payments. Cost-sharing for the control of erosion, insects, weeds and rodents, or for the establishment of wildlife food plots or habitat on set-aside is authorized.

The Secretary may also provide for additional voluntary set-aside at fair and reasonable rates if it is needed to help balance crop production. Grazing of sweet sorghum on set-aside is permitted.

Also, if set-aside is required under the wheat program, no additional set-aside will be required in summer fallow areas if 55 percent of a producer's cropland acreage is devoted to summer fallow. This feature remains the same as it has been for the past three years.

The Secretary has the discretionary authority to impose or suspend the conserving base requirement, and he has already announced the suspension of this requirement for the life of the new farm bill.

$20,000 Payment Limitation

The new farm bill establishes a payment limitation of $20,000 which a person (as defined by the Secretary) can receive annually under a combination of the wheat, feed grain and cotton programs. Excluded from the limitation is any portion that the Secretary determines to be payments for set-aside, public access, loans and purchases. All payments under the program for 1974 are included.

Allotments

The national acreage allotment for each crop of wheat shall be announced not later than April 15 of each calendar year for the crop harvested in the next succeeding calendar year. For the 1974 crop, the national wheat allotment was 55 million acres. This is the number of harvested acres of wheat that, based on the estimated average yield, was needed to result in production equal to estimated domestic and export demand in the 1974–75 marketing year. The 1974 wheat allotment was approximately three times as large as the 18.7 million acre 1973 domestic wheat allotment.

As in the past three years, the farm wheat allotment does not restrict the acreage of wheat that a farmer may produce on his land. It is used only to determine payments to a producer in the event that they are due.

However, failure to plant at least 90 percent of the allotment to either wheat or a crop designated by the Secretary as an eligible substitute will result in loss of allotment not to exceed 20 percent the following year.

After three consecutive years of zero planting the allotment will be removed.

There will be no reduction in allotment if the producer elects not to receive payment otherwise earned for the portion not planted.

Also, farmers prevented from planting wheat because of natural disaster will not lose their allotments.

For allotment preservation purposes during 1974 any annual nonconserving crop (excluding marketing quota crops) could be substituted for wheat.

Vegetative cover on cropland could also be used to

protect allotment history. However, on a completely idle farm, the producer must agree to forfeit program payments to protect allotment history.

Individual farm allotments will be apportioned on the basis of the preceding crop year allotment. Up to one percent of a state's wheat allotment may be reserved for new producers.

Disaster Payments

In a new provision, producers who, because of a natural disaster, are prevented from planting their wheat allotment to wheat or other nonconserving crops, or who obtain total production of less than two-thirds the established farm-yield times the farm allotment, may be considered for payment at a special rate to offset their crop loss.

Unless the 1975 world wheat crop is a "bumper" one, it is considered unlikely that a test of the "target-loan" price range will be made in 1975. However, if fertilizer, and other production costs remain high, the prospect of an increase in the 1976 or 1977 target prices cannot be overlooked.

Kansas City Futures

The wheat contract traded on the Kansas City Board of Trade calls for delivery of No. 2 Dark and Hard Winter wheat at the contract price. No provision is made for delivery of spring wheat or soft winter wheat.

This futures market now accounts for more than one-half the size of the wheat futures market on the Chicago Board of Trade. More important from the trader's viewpoint, its composition differs. Hedges account for a considerably larger percentage of total open interest than in the Chicago market, and small trader positions (considered mostly speculative) account for a much smaller percentage of open contracts than in Chicago. Over a period of years on an annual average basis, short hedge positions have represented more than 80% of total open interest compared with 39% in Chicago, and long hedges 56% vs. 23% in Chicago. Small trader long positions have made up about 30% of total Kansas City open interest versus 44% in Chicago, and short small trader commitments represented 8% compared with 32% of open interest in the Chicago market. Spread positions represented a smaller proportion of open contracts in Kansas City than in Chicago.

Composition of the market may be checked by means of the monthly Commodity Exchange Authority publication covering commitments of traders in wheat futures, released about 11 days following the period under review. While the number of open contracts varies within a given crop year on a seasonal basis, and from year to year as interest in the wheat market waxes and wanes, it is shifts in the proportion of open interest accounted for by one or another major category of trader in conjunction with market action which indicates whether or not an over-extended long or short position has been built up. Thus a study of the composition of the market as of a given month-end as indicated by the CEA commitment report, compared with the same date a year ago and the 5-year or more average for the date in order to iron out seasonal influences, is useful to detect any significant change from the normal pattern. Comparison with the previous month-end figures can also be of value.

The two major categories of traders are reporting trader hedges (long and short) and non-reporting trader positions (long and short). The latter is a residual figure obtained by subtracting large trader positions (200,000 bushels or more in any one futures month) from total open interest. While the small trader category represents both speculative and hedge positions, it is generally considered to consist primarily of speculative commitments.

Kansas City futures long hedges tend to rise seasonally from a low in the March-May period into late August and sometimes into late November or early December. The much more important short hedges also tend to increase seasonally from April-May to seasonal peaks in late August or early September.

Kansas City Market Influences

Inasmuch as the Kansas City market area encompasses the largest concentration of milling capacity in the country, and the Southwest also leads in storage capacity, the supply of hard winter wheat is a major consideration to this market . . . and to the entire wheat price structure. This class of wheat plays a dominant role in wheat pricing because of its major importance to the domestic milling and the export trade. In addition, the protein content and milling and baking quality of the hard winter wheat crop is also of major importance—not only to those who normally use the Kansas City futures market for hedging purposes but also hedgers of other classes of wheat in other markets.

Location of this supply must be considered also. If farmers are strong holders of both farm-stored and elevator-stored wheat, this places greater emphasis upon terminal stocks to satisfy domestic and export demand. Thus the size of sub-terminal and terminal stocks in the area, particularly Kansas City, must be watched closely. The degree to which such stocks are committed tends to find reflection in the cash basis. Mills buy over one-half of their wheat from terminal or sub-terminal operators, a fact which lends itself to hedging operations.

The decision of terminal elevators to buy, hold, or sell wheat depends upon a number of considerations, not the least of which are whether or not the current "premiums" or cash basis relative to Kansas City futures appears attractive, and whether or not the "carrying charges" (the premium for the more distant futures over the near month) provide a partial offset to the cost of carrying cash wheat to that trading month. At times in the late fall or early winter, the combination of an attractive premium on cash wheat at Kansas City and an insufficient premium on deferred futures may prompt an elevator to sell and move out wheat in store and replace it with feed grains when a more favorable hedging basis and better carrying charges exist for feed grains than for wheat.

The level of export demand is of paramount importance to the Kansas City market. It has been pointed out that about 70% of the approximate 100 million bushels handled by Kansas City in a season moves into export channels. Kansas City prices are very sensitive to bids for wheat having export billing, and when exporter bids for No. 1 hard red winter ordinary protein, track, Gulf, are on parity with No. 1 hard red winter ordinary, Kansas City having export billing, it tends to exert a steadying influence on domestic premiums. In recognition of the importance of the export market to hard red winter wheat, both the Kansas City and Chicago Boards of Trade in 1974 initiated trading in a Gulf hard red winter wheat futures contract, with delivery from points in the hard red winter wheat territory. It is perhaps too early to evaluate the impact of the new Gulf wheat contract on the older contracts. However, arbitrage (spread) opportunities between the Gulf and other wheat futures contracts should be enhanced.

The existence of a strong cash basis, or premium, for cash wheat over the maturing futures month at Kansas City tends to render delivery in satisfaction of short hedges less likely, for the commercial market provides a higher price than futures contract deliverable differences will permit. This tends to cause relative firmness in the maturing futures contract with resultant narrowing of carrying charges on the more distant futures months. A long hedger under such circumstances might take delivery on a maturing contract provided the wheat likely to be tendered is of a desirable quality. On the other hand, a sizable deliverable supply of wheat of a currently commercially less valuable quality tends to depress the maturing contract relative to the more distant futures. Hence a knowledge of not only the quantity but also the quality of deliverable stocks is useful in judging cash basis and carrying charge prospects. This information can be obtained from weekly reports on such released by the Commodity Exchange Authority.

The decision of an elevator to hedge on the Kansas City market will also be influenced by the relative price action in the Kansas City and Chicago markets, and, of course, by the particular quality of wheat he is attempting to hedge. If he holds No. 1 dark hard winter, ordinary protein which may be in plentiful supply and whose price tends to coincide more with the Chicago market which usually reflects the price of lower protein wheat, he may place his short hedge in the Chicago market. Favorable demand prospects for higher protein wheat might make Kansas City short positions less effective for one holding ordinary protein than a Chicago short hedge, if the supply prospect for the Chicago marketing area appears ample. The amount of wheat to be hedged is also a consideration in determining the market in which to hedge.

Section II—The Chicago Wheat Market

Soft Red Winter Wheat

Production of this class of wheat in recent years has accounted for about 9%–16% of total wheat production, ranging between 157 and 289 million bushels.

While the soft red winter wheat belt extends from Louisiana north in areas adjacent to the Mississippi River and east to the Atlantic Coast, production is concentrated in Indiana, Ohio, Illinois, Missouri, Pennsylvania, and Arkansas.

When Planted and Harvested

Planting in the major producing areas is usually underway by mid-September and continues into late October or early November. The harvest in the principal producing areas usually gets underway by the third week of June and is virtually complete by the end of July in most sections. Some soft red wheat is combined in parts of the Southeast and lower Missis-

sippi delta region as early as mid to late May, weather permitting.

Soft Red Wheat Uses

Soft wheat, whose protein value ranges between 8–11%, is milled into flour for chemically-leavened products such as cookies and crackers, cakes, doughnuts, biscuits, pies, and some pastries. All-purpose flour, cake flour, and prepared mixes account for the bulk of soft wheat mill products. Soft wheats account for about 30% of total domestic wheat used for food. The domestic use of soft red wheat is estimated to run about 133–178 million bushels a year, varying little apparently from year to year, although technological milling developments, and demand by housewives for convenience baked goods which use soft wheat flour have spelled increased demand for this class of wheat. Estimated supply and distribution by class of wheat is just that—an estimate, and figures should be taken as approximations, particularly for domestic disappearance.

Soft Red Wheat Exports

About 15%–30% of soft red wheat production has been exported in recent years, amounting to 24–68 million bushels. While wheat in the Common Market countries of western Europe is quite similar to our soft red winter wheat, these countries have at times been large buyers of soft red when their own crops were small or of poor quality. Commercial shipments of this class of wheat have ranged between 54% and 91% of total exports of this class in recent seasons. Major dollar markets have been Italy, Venezuela, and the People's Republic of China. Major beneficiaries of PL480 shipments have been Yugoslavia, Morocco, and more recently, Pakistan and Bangladesh. Saudi Arabia and the UAR have been the best buyers of soft red wheat flour.

Most soft red wheat exports have been made from Atlantic ports such as Baltimore, Norfolk, and Philadelphia, or Gulf ports such as New Orleans, Destrehan, and Port Allen. Although Lake shipments tend to be of less importance, Toledo is active at times when Lake navigation is open, as is Chicago. Thus stocks of wheat at export positions which normally ship soft red wheat are watched closely, with attention given to any unusual increases or decreases, and size relative to previous periods.

Carryover of this class of wheat has generally been rather small, ranging in recent years from about 7 to 15 million bushels, and very little of it has found its way into government stocks, partly because much production has not been eligible for the loan. Hence, exports are of major importance to soft red wheat. At times the government has deliberately held down the amount of PL480 soft red wheat authorizations because of concern on the part of the domestic milling trade over supplies.

The price of soft red wheat for export relative to hard winter wheat is an important market consideration at times. Prices should be at a sufficient discount at ports to stimulate purchases by those countries to whom price is more important than protein, aside from those countries who are regular purchasers of soft wheat. While the amount of discount needed to stimulate such interest will vary with the times and conditions, it has in the past taken a concession of several cents to move soft red wheat.

Most PL480 authorizations permit up to 5% substitution of soft red in shipments of hard wheat—a consideration when soft red prices are relatively low.

Our major export competition for soft red (and soft white) wheat is Australia, most of whose exports consist of a soft white wheat. Moreover, their production becomes available in international markets by late winter. Sometimes, depending upon their commitments, they can provide stiff competition for late season U.S. soft wheat export prospects. Conversely, U.S. soft wheat tends to be at a seasonal export advantage in the fall, and heavy shipments are usually seen at that time.

Sometimes soft red wheat runs into competition even from European countries. Common Market countries have built up an exportable surplus of soft red wheat as a result of their price support operations. At times this wheat provides competition for U.S. soft red wheat exports.

It is much easier to assess the effect of export business on the statistical picture of wheat (considered either by class or in total) than on the futures market. There is frequently a bulge in prices when either a PL480 agreement is signed or a purchase authorization announced even though hedge buying by the exporter who is the successful bidder on a tender may not take place until somewhat later, depending upon the contracting period, and actual buying of the cash wheat to cover the sales commitment may not take place for weeks or months. At times when export bookings are slow and hedge purchases light, there may be good demand from exporters for cash wheat to cover commitments . . . and downward pressure on futures as they liquidate long hedges. This, in turn, may be partly or completely offset by lifting of short hedges by elevators who made the sales, or by the exchange of cash wheat for futures between the elevator and the exporter.

Late in the season, around April/May, old crop Chicago May futures are frequently quite sensitive to speculation concerning the probable availability of soft red wheat from early harvest areas of the Southeast and Mississippi delta where there is considerable production regarded as out of position for the domestic milling industry, though some of which may be in a rather favorable export position. The concern is that existence of such supplies would mean reduced export demand for remaining old crop stocks of soft red at Chicago. New crop wheat from this area has been available as early as mid to late May.

Price Structure

A rough, though useful, guide to approximate price relationships in the Chicago marketing area can be gained from a comparison between county loan rates in important soft red wheat producing areas and the estimated Chicago loan, and between monthly average prices received for wheat by farmers (by states) during the harvest period and monthly average cash prices at Chicago. These figures should provide an indication as to the widest discounts likely to be encountered for country prices under Chicago. This basis tends to be widest, or closest to transportation costs to the terminal market during the harvest period when wheat must be moved into storage, and supplies exceed immediate demand by a wide margin. The discount for cash wheat in the country from Chicago cash prices tends to be reduced somewhat as demand for replenishment of supplies by mills and terminals increases, and particularly if exporters are bidding in

competition. In other words, the basis tends to strengthen into mid-winter or early spring. The trade attempts to take advantage of basis shifts in their hedging operations by constantly watching shifting patterns of supply and demand between classes of wheat and markets.

Soft red winter wheat is usually grown as a cash crop on small acreage as part of a cropping system in conjunction with livestock feeding operations rather than as a specialized crop as it is in the Southwest. As wheat production has meant less to an individual farmer than were it his sole crop, less use of the loan program has been made than for other classes of wheat.

Chicago Futures

By virtue of its location, the normal flow of wheat from West to East and Southeast, and because of advantages resulting from a complex grain rail freight rate structure, Chicago can draw wheat from a larger area than any other futures market. Yet it is neither a major storage center nor is it a principal milling center as are both Kansas City and Minneapolis.

The Chicago Board of Trade permits the delivery, at contract price, of No. 2 Hard Winter, No. 2 Soft Red Winter, No. 2 Yellow Hard Winter, No. 2 Dark Northern Spring and No. 1 Northern Spring. Certain other grades of the foregoing are deliverable at fixed premiums or discounts to the contract price. However, from a practical point of view Chicago deliverable stocks have usually consisted primarily of No. 2 soft red wheat. However, some hard red winter wheat usually finds its way into deliverable stocks—there is almost as much or more acreage planted to hard wheat as to soft wheat in Illinois. Occasionally some yellow hard winter wheat is found in deliverable stocks. More often than not this wheat follows soft red rather than hard wheat as it is considered less desirable than hard red wheat. The holder of a maturing long futures contract is most likely to receive soft red wheat if he elects to accept delivery. Some such wheat taken on contract moves to downstate Illinois mills or to mills in other central state locations. However, most long hedgers, realizing that the seller has the option as to what he tenders and when he elects to tender within rules established by the exchange, prefer to shift their hedges forward before first notice day of a maturing futures contract.

Deliveries

Free stocks of deliverable wheat in Board of Trade approved Chicago elevators have varied in recent years from practically no stocks at all to almost 14 million bushels. These stocks have usually been lowest in the between-seasons late May to mid or late June period, depending in part upon harvesting weather. However, as much as 4 million bushels has been on hand during this period. Seasonal highs in Chicago deliverable stocks have generally been posted in the late August-early October period, ranging in amount in recent years between 5.7 and 13.6 million bushels. Toledo has recently become a delivery point at 2¢ per bushel discount to the contract price.

The size of deliverable stocks, their composition, and whether or not they have been increasing receives close attention as first notice day (the first day a seller can signify his intention of liquidating his short futures position by delivery of cash grain in satisfaction of his contract) of the maturing futures contract approaches. If deliverable stocks are large relative to the number of contracts remaining open in the maturing futures contract, or if the stocks are increasing, there is a tendency to anticipate pressure on prices as speculative longs who have held their contracts into first notice day, not wishing to hold a position in the cash market, sell and retender the futures contracts against which they received a delivery notice. Sometimes the market advances in the face of heavy tenders if they pass into trade hands and do not circulate. Occasionally the market declines on small tenders which go to speculative longs who sell and retender through a clearing member to the clearing association, with these tenders going again into speculative hands—triggering a chain reaction of selling by those who do not wish to hold cash wheat. Trade shorts against out-of-position wheat, that which is not along the normal line of freight movement to the market, much prefer to observe the differences between the futures month in which they have their hedge and succeeding months for an opportunity to switch their positions forward at a favorable basis rather than to remain short an expiring contract.

The largest amount of wheat delivered in settlement of all futures contracts combined in a single season over the past several years has been the 73.4 million bushels tendered in the 1962/63 season, while the smallest was 14.3 million bushels delivered in the 1970/71 season. The amount of wheat tendered against any one futures contract month has varied widely. Generally the lowest amount—about 300,000 bushels—has been delivered against the May contract. Heaviest deliveries have usually been made against the December position, though there appears to be no consistent pattern in this respect. The heaviest tenders against any one trading month in the last several years amounted to 22 million bushels against the July 1962 contract.

Inasmuch as some contracts are settled by delivery every trading month, speculation centers upon how much will be tendered, and when during the month deliveries will be made. A major consideration in this respect is the cash basis on wheat making up the deliverable stocks. The basis, of course, is influenced by demand for a given class and quality at a particular location at a specific time. This must be taken into consideration with deliverable premiums and discounts on the class and grade of wheat in the deliverable supply. It should be recognized that limits of deliverable grades against futures are wider than trade tolerances within a particular grade, for milling and baking characteristics are of foremost importance to the miller who sells to bakers on very exacting specifications. Wheat might appear to be a bargain based on federal grades alone, but may be something less than a bargain considering milling and baking values. The trade will deliver that which is of less commercial than deliverable value. Premiums and discounts for deliverable grades are fixed, while commercial values fluctuate.

Most deliveries appear to be made by large merchandiser, exporter or elevator interests who have short hedges against deliverable stocks, and who, depending upon circumstances, issue most of the delivery notices—and frequently take as well as make delivery.

Composition of the Chicago Futures Market

The makeup of this market, which is, by far, the largest and which is the center of speculative interest, is of prime importance to one who attempts to forecast wheat prices. The reason for this is simply that the impact of market developments on prices tends to be governed by the character of open interest. For example, news that PL480 shipments are being cut back sharply tends to have more influence on a market when small trader long interest, initiated perhaps in anticipation of record exports, accounts for a significantly larger than usual proportion of total open interest than when small traders account for a smaller than normal percentage of open commitments in futures.

The most important segment of Chicago wheat futures open interest is that of small trader longs, which has accounted for about 44% of total open interest on an annual average basis in recent years. The next most important is comprised of short hedge positions, which have made up close to 39% of open interest during the same period, while small trader short positions accounted for about 32% of total open interest in futures.

Seasonally, short hedges tend to be heaviest in the mid-July to late October period. Small trader long interest approximately coincides with seasonally heavy hedge sales. Both small trader long and hedge short interest tends to be lighter in the late winter to mid-spring period but there is less consistency on this score than on seasonally heavy commitments.

Factors Influencing the Chicago Market

In addition to market considerations mentioned earlier in this section on soft wheat or in the previous section in hard winter wheat, attention is given to the rail car situation—a tight freight car supply available to move out wheat delivered against futures may mean additional expense and hesitancy on the part of those who might otherwise accept delivery.

The stocks of wheat on farms in major soft red states provides an indication as to potential pressure from first hands, though at times some such stocks may be committed. This figure is available periodically in the USDA report on such stocks.

The amount of wheat likely to be fed can be an important factor. More soft red wheat tends to be fed than any other class, partly because it is grown in areas of mixed livestock-grain farming, because the eastern and southeastern part of the soft red wheat belt is a feed deficit area, and partly because the loan is based on wheat's value for feed purposes and soft red wheat prices in the past have received less support from the loan than other classes.

There is a tendency for country and subterminal elevators to move wheat out of store to make room for corn and soybeans in the late fall or early winter. The amount of selling from this quarter depends in part upon the extent to which elevator capacity is utilized, and the extent to which the cash basis favors purchasing and hedging corn and soybeans over holding wheat, and comparative carrying charge premiums on deferred over nearby futures contracts.

In years when a sizable soft red wheat crop is in prospect, there is a tendency for the trade to permit supplies to decline to minimal levels, especially if Chicago stocks appear ample. However, the extent to which export commitments still have to be covered before new crop is available and the degree of coverage on the part of domestic millers must be considered.

The existence of large stocks in terminals usually associated with soft red wheat stocks and in a better export position than Chicago have a bearing on the Chicago market. At such times the composition of the futures market can be of considerable importance. If speculative long interest is higher than usual in expectation of a good export movement of soft red, and demand is satisfied without recourse to Chicago stocks, long speculative liquidation can result. Thus at times the rate of movement out of Chicago stocks, whether by barge "going South" perhaps to Texas mills, or by Lake, can exert a considerable influence on the market.

Demand for soft red winter wheat can be adversely affected by a relatively large supply of low protein hard winter wheat. Conversely, a small supply of low protein hard wheat relative to higher protein hard wheat can result in some substitution of soft red. At times such a development finds more reflection in intermarket differences, or in the basis in a given terminal market such as Chicago or St. Louis for these two classes of wheat, than in the price structure itself, but either way it affects hedge operations.

Section III—The Minneapolis Wheat Market

Hard Red Spring Wheat

This is a high protein wheat, ranging between 12% and 18% protein. It accounts for between 15% and 23% of total wheat production, ranging between 198 and 284 million bushels in recent years.

Where Grown

North Dakota is, by far, the most important producing state, accounting for more than 50% of acreage seeded to this class. It is followed in importance by Montana, South Dakota, and Minnesota. Other than in North Dakota, acreage is concentrated in the northern half of South Dakota, the western quarter of Minnesota, and along the north central and northeastern sections of Montana.

Planting and Harvesting

Seeding in much of the hard red spring belt is usually underway by early May and completed by the end of the month. Combining is generally started by the end of July or early August and virtually completed by the first week of September. Thus this class of wheat tends to have a seasonal low in prices later than winter—usually in August.

Use of Hard Red Spring Wheat

This high protein wheat produces a superior quality bread flour. The importance of bread to the overall wheat picture is outlined in the section on hard red winter wheat. High quality hard winter wheat can be substituted for hard red spring for some purposes, and in turn when the durum wheat crop is very poor limited amounts of high quality spring wheat can be substituted for durum in some products. Domestic disappearance ranges between 134–208 million bushels a season.

Exports

Countries which grow soft low protein wheat purchase hard red spring wheat to blend with their own supplies to produce better bread. There has been a wide variance in hard red spring exports. In recent years, exports of hard red spring wheat have ranged between 28% and 71% of production of this class of wheat. Major dollar purchasers have been the Netherlands, Venezuela, PRC, Japan, and the Philippines. Over a period of years a larger portion of hard red spring wheat exports have been commercial (for dollars) than any other class of wheat. In recent seasons, exports have ranged between 89 million and 217 million bushels, most of which has been for dollars.

More hard red spring wheat is exported from Lake ports such as Duluth, Toledo, and Chicago than via Atlantic, Gulf or Pacific ports. Decreased rail freight rates to the West Coast have made spring wheat more competitive with Canadian hard wheat in Asian markets.

Price Structure

A comparison of monthly average prices received for wheat by farmers in the Dakotas and Minnesota with the estimated loan and cash price at Minneapolis may provide a starting point, or rough approximation, for gauging whether or not price quotations at country points appear low enough relative to terminal prices to encourage loan impoundings, or high enough to discourage movement to terminals and a buildup of supplies at major terminals. Although at times the CCC has held a considerable amount of spring wheat, by and large, hard red spring wheat prices have held above the loan better than other major classes (whenever the loan was a general market consideration).

Minneapolis Futures

The Minneapolis Grain Exchange futures contract basis is No. 2 Northern Spring wheat of 13.5% protein. Spring wheat alone is deliverable, and there is no premium allowed for delivery of higher than 13.5% protein.

Premiums for protein vary widely in the cash market reflecting shifts in the supply situation for spring wheat and in its composition by protein, and for higher protein hard red winter wheat, and to a lesser degree the durum crop size. Protein premiums tend to be lowest when there is a relatively large supply of 13% or higher protein spring wheat, and higher when the reverse situation exists. Protein premiums cannot be hedged, and as they sometimes move counter to the general market, effective hedging of high protein spring wheat is considered to be quite difficult.

Composition of Minneapolis Futures

The Minneapolis wheat futures market is a relatively small but professional market, usually accounting for about 10% as much open interest as at Chicago. Composition of this market by class of trader is much different than that of the Chicago market.

Small traders over the years have usually accounted for less than 25% of the market. Long hedges accounted for about 72% and short hedges 76% of total open interest. Even though this is a small market, long hedges in terms of bushels have been larger than one might expect, and at times have actually been heavier than in Chicago. Spread positions of speculators have usually represented only a very small percentage of open interest, averaging less than 3% of open contracts.

Total contracts settled by delivery in any one season have ranged from just under one million bushels to more than six million. The heaviest tenders against any one futures contract month in the past several years amounted to the 3.9 million bushels delivered against the December 1965 contract. December futures have usually borne the brunt of heavier deliveries than other trading months.

In view of the relatively high percentage of hedges, especially long hedges, it is obvious that there is a tendency on the part of spring wheat elevators and mills to favor Minneapolis because it represents the spring wheat market despite its size. The probable course of protein premiums is a major consideration on the part of spring wheat mill, elevator or export interests contemplating hedge operations in this market or in any other futures market. A short hedge position can be very unprofitable even when the general level of wheat prices is declining if the cash price of the high protein wheat being hedged declines much more significantly than the futures in which it is hedged. Conversely, a long hedge can be ineffective when, during the life of a buying hedge placed against a flour sale, wheat of the protein value needed to satisfy the flour sale rises at a much faster rate than the futures month in which the sales commitment is hedged. The size of the flour order against which futures must be purchased is a further consideration in the use of Minneapolis for the hedge. At times it may be advantageous to place the hedge initially in Chicago provided Chicago appears low relative to Minneapolis, with the hedge being shifted back to Minneapolis piecemeal as intermarket differences provide the opportunity.

White Wheat

Soft white wheat is by far the most important of the sub-classes of white wheat, which include Hard White, Club White, and Western White. This class of wheat has accounted for about 10–14% of total wheat production, ranging between 171 and 250 million bushels in recent seasons.

Where Grown

Its major production area is the Pacific Northwest. The southeast quarter of Washington is the major producing section by a wide margin, with the next most important areas of Oregon and Idaho adjacent to this section accounting for less than three-quarters as much production. There is some spring wheat grown in this area, accounting for perhaps 15–20% of total production. The southern half of Michigan is the principal soft white wheat production area in the East, while some is grown in western New York.

Planting and Harvesting

Seeding of fall planted white wheat in the Northwest and in the East is usually underway by mid-September and completed by mid-October, while spring wheat plantings in the Northwest are usually completed by early May.

Harvest of winter wheat in the Northwest and the East is normally underway by mid-July and mostly complete by early to mid-August. Spring seeded white wheat combining is usually close to completion by the first week of September.

Soft Wheat Uses

Soft white wheat is used for milling of cookie, cracker and cake flour, much the same as soft red wheat, with which it competes in some areas. Soft wheat protein ranges between 8 and 11%. Domestic use of white wheat has accounted for only about 35% of total distribution in recent seasons. Some white wheat is fed in the Northwest when it is competitive with barley, considering its feed value for some livestock is about 110–115% that of barley.

Exports

Exports are a major consideration to this class of wheat, accounting for 51% to 72% of production in recent years. About 36–37 million bushels of Pacific Northwest wheat is milled for flour, a fair portion of which is exported, and the rest of this wheat is shipped abroad. Exports have ranged between 104 and 151 million bushels in recent seasons. Commercial exports have represented from 82% to 98% of total shipments in recent years with Japan and Iran our major dollar customers. Korea and Pakistan have been major destinations for PL480 program white wheat. The Pacific Northwest ports of Portland, Longview, and Seattle have been the principal shipment points. White wheat is competitive with Australian wheat to Asian destinations, and to a degree at times is competitive with eastern soft white or red wheat in the export market.

Durum Wheat

Durum is a variety of hard wheat which accounts for a very small percentage of total wheat production, having a highly specialized use for alimentary paste products such as macaroni and spaghetti. It accounts for about 8% of total domestic use of wheat for food, and much less acreage. Because of this and its specialized use it is usually of little interest to wheat traders. Most of this class of wheat is grown in North Dakota, with the eastern edge of Montana and the western edge of Minnesota also producing areas. An unusually small durum crop may result in minor substitution of high quality protein spring wheat in some product mixes.

Section IV—A Method of Procedure in Evaluating Price Prospects

Outlining market factors to consider in analyzing wheat prices must be viewed in relation to a particular class of wheat, its supply/distribution pattern, and then to the overall total wheat situation. The foregoing discussion of wheat classes, planting and harvesting periods, uses, exports, futures markets, and market influences should enable one to better evaluate market factors as they develop—to view news with some perspective.

The following should provide an overall guide for forecasting price movement, bringing foregoing sections into focus.

Supply of Wheat

A logical starting point for assessing the domestic supply side of the wheat equation is the carryover. The amount as well as composition by class is available in government publications, as is the location of the supply at the beginning of the season, and how much (if any) is in government hands. There is a tendency for commercial interests to hold inventories as low as possible at the crop year-end to avoid costly price adjustments as the new crop harvest approaches. Thus the principal holders of the carryover over a period of years have been the CCC and farmers. Now that CCC stocks have been virtually depleted, more attention is centered upon farmer holdings.

Well before production becomes an actuality, its upper limits can be approximated by the December USDA estimate of winter wheat production. Much weight tends to be assigned to planting intentions reports issued by the government, in January and in March, and how they compare with previous trade ideas on a state by state basis, and by class. The May winter wheat crop report which also includes acreage abandonment receives close attention of the trade when crop prospects do not appear favorable due to lack of moisture in the southwest winter wheat belt. During the growing season close attention is paid to daily, 5-day and longer weather forecasts as well as to the weekly government crop summary as these often exert a sharp influence on prices. USDA crop reports in season also exert a considerable influence when they vary much from private trade ideas. When a crop is threatened by adverse weather, the futures market is less prone to pay attention to its effect on the supply by individual classes of wheat than to the plain fact that the production outlook is poor. Over the longer run, changes in intermarket differences should become apparent, depending upon what class of wheat was most affected by adverse weather.

While total supply may be measured by carryover plus production (imports have usually been limited to less than a million bushels and are not significant) effective supply is another matter. The latter can at times be temporarily but acutely affected by poor weather holding up the harvest when export or domestic mill commitments have been made on the basis of expected early new crop receipts. The resultant price bulge may not last long, but it can be severe to those caught short. A farmer holding movement can offset for a time the threat of large farm stocks on a market. In some seasons farmers have proven stubborn holders, which has had quite an effect on prices. Boxcar shortages or rail strikes can cause hedge selling by country elevators who cannot move wheat to terminals and by terminal elevators who cannot move wheat stocks out. This can result in a firmer "basis" at ports where commitments must be covered. Conversely, congestion at ports can cause a backing up of supplies and pressure on terminal prices.

Other factors affecting effective supply, at times, include the amount of wheat impounded in the loan, the domestic resale price, and operation of loan reseal programs. It should be noted especially with respect to supply figures that in the first instance they are usually estimates by qualified official or trade observers made on the basis of sampling and reporting techniques developed over a period of years, but estimates nonetheless and subject to sizable revisions at times. Supplies do exist in unreported positions and some in transit do not get reported. Thus one learns to accept production and stock figures with a certain amount of reservation.

Movement of wheat is followed by means of daily and weekly USDA or Exchange reports on receipts and shipments at major markets. Receipts at major interior markets indicate movement from country points, and sometimes provide a clue as to a loosening up of producers' holding of wheat, while shipments tend to measure movement from principal interior markets to major terminals or to export. Daily and weekly Chicago movement receives attention as maturity of a given futures contract nears, and weekly reports on deliverable supplies are watched closely.

Demand

Of the two major elements on the demand side of the picture, exports and domestic business, exports receive the most attention. The basic reason for this is the fact that viewed in its entirety domestic mill grinding of wheat varies little month to month, while export bookings and exports vary widely. Yet the extent of bakery coverage on flour certainly has a bearing on mill hedging activity as does the extent of export flour buying by the government. Wheat is the only ingredient of flour, the extraction rate being about 72–73% on the average with the remaining 27–28% consisting about equally of bran and shorts. It requires close to 2.3 bushels of wheat (about 140 pounds) to produce 100 pounds of straight flour, and more for higher grade flour. The mill must price flour on wheat costs with a modest allowance for changes in millfeed value. But the problem of changing returns on wheat millfeed between the time a flour sale is consummated and the wheat ground and delivered influences not only the mills' willingness to sell ahead as far as the 120-day usual limit, but it influences their hedging activity as well. This rather overlooked area deserves more attention than it usually receives as a market consideration.

Constant attention must be paid to export movement and bookings from the U.S. and other countries; to the availability of exportable supplies by area and by class; and to the regular reports on progress of foreign wheat crops—in consuming as well as in exporting countries and to further developments in the EEC as their grain program is implemented by variable import levies, and particularly by accumulation of surpluses of soft wheat in France under protection of the Common Market. Import provisions, and prospects for U.S. Gulf export rail freight rate changes—also must be given consideration, for they will exert an influence on export prospects, and on hedging activities. The possible establishment and possible subsequent disposal of a grain reserve must also be considered.

On balance, one must bear in mind that futures markets tend to move on anticipation rather than realization of events, and that one must always judge whether or not production and effective supply will be as large as expected, and whether or not export and domestic demand will reach expectations.

Wheat–Chicago–March Futures Delivery
1969-70 to 1974-75

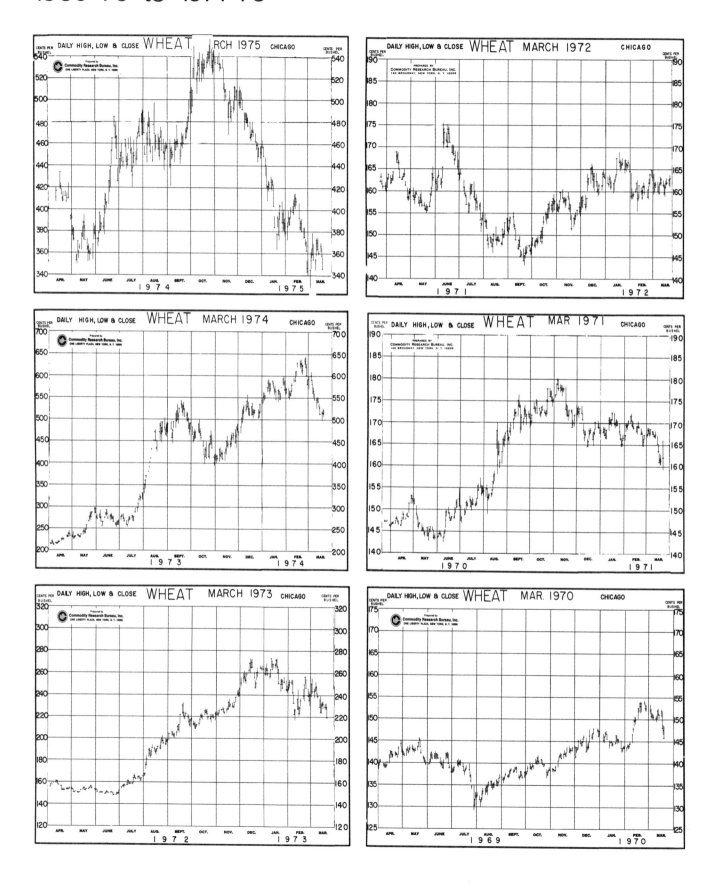

Wheat–Chicago–March Futures Delivery
1963-64 to 1968-69

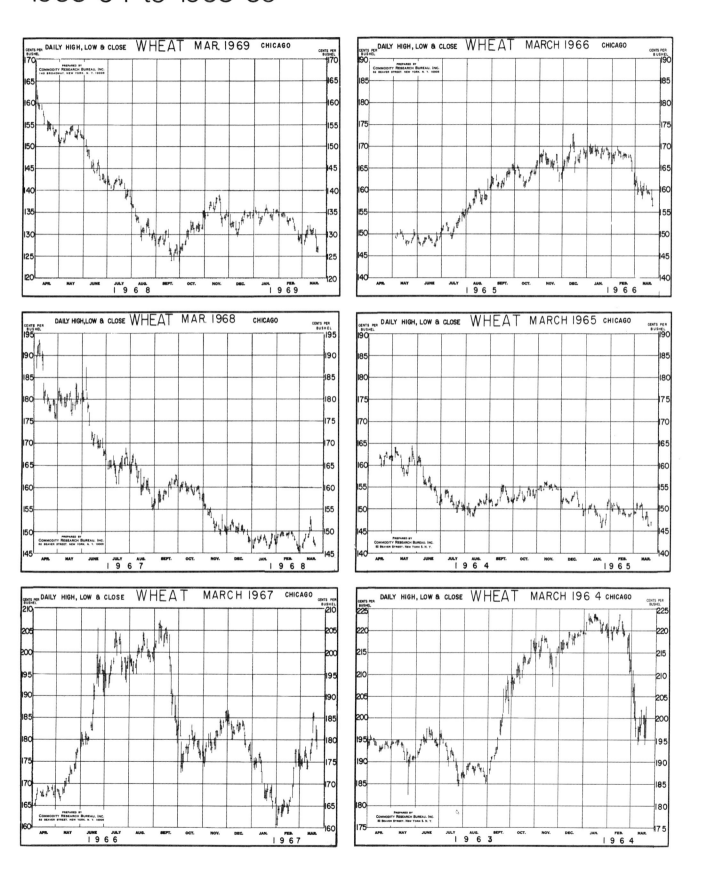

OBSERVATIONS ON PRICE FORECASTING
WITH CHARTS

BY ROBERT FEDUNIAK

Technical analysis is the art of using past market activity to forecast future price action. The technician's basic assumption is that price changes are not independent of one another, and that a thorough analysis of what a market did in the past can help predict what it is likely to do in the future. Price charts, especially vertical bar charts, have historically been the foundation upon which technical analysis builds, since they provide simple, graphic portraits of market action.

The use of charts for analyzing price movements began to flourish in the early years of the twentieth century, when Charles Dow devised the Dow Theory for identifying trends in securities prices. Significant differences exist between security and commodity futures prices, and these will be elaborated on below. However, valuable insights into any theory can be gained by studying the theory's origins, so a brief look at Dow's original ideas will serve as an appropriate starting point for a discussion of basic technical methods.

The underlying assumption of the Dow Theory is that price movement consists of a superimposition of three trends—minor, intermediate, and major. The three trends cannot be separated and identified according to hard and fast rules, but they are assumed to be confined to relatively well-defined time intervals. Minor trends last up to several days; intermediate trends for a few weeks or months; and major trends can persist for several years. A major uptrend is assumed to continue as long as the intermediate term lows and highs are higher than the preceding lows and highs while the converse is true of a major downtrend (see figures 1, 2).

The original Dow Theory was intended to be an overall economic barometer rather than a specific trading strategy, but adaptation to individual securities was straight-forward: Go long as soon as a major bull trend is signalled, and stay long until a major trend reversal occurs. Then go short and stay short until the bear trend is reversed. Obviously this approach was designed for long term trading, and did not meet the needs of those who wanted to play a more active role in the market. Because the Dow Theory did an admirable job of indicating trends, the natural reaction among traders was to refine the techniques by identifying patterns and formations that would aid in predicting shorter term price moves.

Differences in Chart Analysis of Securities and Commodities

The subsequent development of technical analysis proceeded with securities prices in mind, and the recurrent principles were carried over into the commodity futures markets. This is perfectly reasonable if we assume, as most technicians do, that important chart patterns and formations characterize any market in which trading is free and active. Stock prices depend largely on traders' expectations of future earnings, while futures prices depend largely on expectations of future supply and demand. The underlying speculative psychology should be similar, which means that technical considerations should also be closely related. On the other hand, at least three basic differences do exist between securities and commodity futures markets, and though the differences do not necessarily invalidate the use of similar technical principles, they should not be dismissed casually.

The most notable difference between securities and futures markets is that the open interest in futures markets is theoretically unlimited, while the supply of any stock is fixed and finite. Securities prices therefore depend on the relationship between demand and *available* supply, while the concept of availability does not apply to futures contracts per se, although it is certainly relevant in connection with the actual commodity. The net result is that futures contract prices should tend to vary more in line with overall changes in traders' attitudes, since bulls and bears can "create" futures contracts in order to establish market positions.

The second important difference is that futures contracts expire at a specified time, whereas securities do not. This means that the evening up of positions prior to contract expiration could play a significant role in the technical behavior of futures prices. Most technicians try to circumvent this problem by not trading in expiring contract months. However, the fluctuations of expiring deliveries have not been widely studied, and such a study could conceivably yield worthwhile information.

A third important point is the fact that most futures prices have daily fluctuation limits, whereas securities prices do not. The stated purpose of these limits is to prevent unreasonably extreme moves from occurring as a result of panic buying or selling. If limits are at all successful in doing this, then it would seem likely that they would cause significant differences from the behavior of securities during dynamic price moves. Since rapid, extensive price changes present the greatest profit possibilities, the characteristics of price action after limit moves might be a fruitful area of investigation for commodity technicians.

Philosophies Underlying Chart Analysis

One unfortunate feature in the history of chart analysis is the fact that studies concerning the utility of technical principles have, from the very beginning, tended to fall into one or the other of two widely separated categories. The first category contains pure academic research, and attempts to answer the theoretical question of whether price changes in actual markets are non-random, i.e., whether the very idea behind technical analysis is a valid one. The second category consists of practical market analysts, who assume that technical analysis is based on valid principles and set about trying to find specific functional guidelines more or less by trial and error. The fact that each of these groups has tended to work almost independently of the other has doubtless prolonged the search for an understanding of technical analysis.

To be perfectly candid, there is very little objective, explicit evidence available to support the commonly accepted rules of chart analysis—yet the rules are widely accepted as valid and seem to produce worthwhile results. The problem stems from the fact that there is no statistical method for proving randomness, so statistical research must proceed by a trial-and-error method of searching for specific types of correlations. If subtle, specific, correlations exist, they will very likely be masked by the vast bulk of data which technicians would agree provides no conclusive trading signals, and both security and commodity prices do seem to display types of non-randomness that would be extremely difficult to verify statistically. Chart signals are given by patterns built up from many days' price activity and that often are extremely difficult to define mathematically. This means that the chartist is, essentially, performing a highly complicated and subjective multiple correlation analysis in his mind as he examines his charts. And, as implied above, prudent chartists do not make specific forecasts continuously, but only after the appearance of certain formations, while academic researchers invariably check long sequences of prices for correlations, which tends to conceal and minimize the importance of the occasional patterns that technicians find most valuable.

Why Chart Analysis Is Valuable

Whether or not the reader believes that chart analysis has merit, the fact is that the discipline enjoys a tremendous following among traders, and it is scarcely possible to discuss market activity without the subject of charts cropping up in the conversation. The author's personal belief is that technical analysis is a valid and valuable tool for detecting major trend changes and for verifying the continuation of existing trends. Furthermore, since much statistical research seems to indicate that actual trends are more extensive than would be the case in random markets, it is logical to conclude that chart analysis can be of significant value simply by helping to confirm the existence of major price trends.

When technicians attempt to focus attention on short term fluctuations, they leave themselves open to considerably more justifiable criticism. There is substantial evidence that short term price changes are very nearly random, and even if they are not strictly so, it seems improbable that deviations from randomness are great enough to allow the construction of a very short-term system that would even pay commission costs, which can represent a substantial percentage of short-term price moves. Therefore, this discussion of chart analysis will center on those characteristic patterns of major trends including reversals, breakouts, support and resistance areas, and continuation patterns, that can be of particular pragmatic value to traders.

I. Trends
A. Overall Patterns

As mentioned above, the first trend theory held that an uptrend remains intact as long as each successive intermediate high is higher than those preceding it and each reaction stops at a higher point than did earlier reactions. Conversely, a downtrend prevails when each intermediate decline carries prices to lower levels while intervening rallies fall short of earlier rallies. Figure 1 illustrates a continuing uptrend, according to Dow Theory standards.

As technical analysis became more refined, the concept of a trendline gained widespread acceptance. In a bull (bear) market, an uptrend (downtrend) line is simply an upward (downward) sloping line connecting successive lows (highs), as in figures 2 and 13. Many technicians have modified the original Dow rule to indicate a trend change (or at least a caution signal) whenever prices penetrate the trendline. Using trendlines for this purpose will result in more signals and earlier abandonment of positions than would use of the Dow rule, so the trendline can be considered a somewhat more conservative approach to actual trading. Whether it is a more valid approach is debatable. While the Dow requirement that the highs and lows continue to move in the direction of the trend seems intuitively reasonable, there is no "a priori" reason to assume that sloping lines have special significance.

Another difficulty with trendlines is the problem of how to interpret them when prices move very quickly. When an extremely steep trend line is broken, technicians often disagree sharply about whether the trend itself has been broken. The question of how steep a trendline can be before it becomes meaningless is answered differently by each chartist, and seems to be largely a matter of personal taste.

B. Volume and Open Interest Characteristics

Variations in trading volume and open interest are frequently used to provide confirmation of trend direction. The accepted rule is that both items should tend to increase when prices are moving in the direction of the primary trend. Unfortunately, the matter is not quite so simple, and a cursory examination of past markets indicates that this rule might not stand up under careful scrutiny. High volume is very often a harbinger of substantial price moves, but it frequently occurs toward the end of major trends, and extremely great volume is considered a sign of an impending trend reversal. Furthermore, since the public prefers the long side, there is a natural tendency for volume to expand more on advances than on declines.

A large open interest usually indicates that the speculating public is heavily committed to the market and that volatile price action is the likely consequence. However, contrary to the usual rules, "long" liquidation declines and short-covering rallies often cause extensive price moves, and both of these type markets are characterized by declining open interest. Two other considerations deserve mention. First, the open interest in most markets follows a seasonal pattern, so that the trader who wants to get a true picture of open interest changes must consider seasonally adjusted figures. Second, commodity trading has increased tremendously in popularity over the past several years, which naturally means that open interest has tended to grow simply as a reflection of the general expansion of activity.

191

II. Continuation Patterns

Some of the most reliable chart signals are those that occur during periods of consolidation prior to continuation of the prevailing trend. Among the most common are pennants, flags, triangles and gaps.

A. Flags and Pennants

These parallelogram and triangle formations that sometimes form after rapid vertical moves indicate that another similar move is likely to follow. Both formations usually slope in the direction opposite the preceding fast move, and they seldom persist for longer than about two weeks. Because they are basically consolidation patterns or "breathing spells," volume should be smaller during the formation of the pennant or flag than during the move that preceded it. Technicians often follow the rule of thumb that flags mark the halfway point of a price move, measuring from the level of decisive breakaway from the previous formation. Figure 3 shows typical flag and pennant formations.

Many chartists rank flags and pennants among the most dependable technical signals, particularly with reference to the direction of the impending move. This fact, coupled with the relative simplicity of their structure, marks these patterns as especially suitable candidates for objective and explicit statistical study. Unlike many chart formations, flags and pennants could be given precise enough definitions to allow them to be unequivocally identified and tested for predictive value.

B. Gaps

The preceding comment concerning suitability for critical analysis applies with equal force to gaps, which are the simplest, and among the most controversial of chart patterns. Gaps are simply areas within the boundaries of activity where no actual trading occurred. Technicians generally place gaps into one of these four categories: common gaps, breakaway gaps, runaway gaps, and exhaustion gaps. Common gaps (figure 4) are blank areas between two consecutive days' trading ranges, within which activity took place in the recent past. They are usually considered to have no special meaning. Breakaway gaps (figure 4) occur when prices suddenly explode out of a congestion formation, leaving behind an empty area in which no trading has taken place for a considerable length of time (or in which no trading has ever taken place). Runaway gaps appear following an already substantial price move (figure 5), while exhaustion gaps (figure 6) are supposed to mark the final stages of a major move.

There is considerable disagreement among chartists about whether breakaway and runaway gaps should subsequently be "filled," about whether the "filling" of gaps has any significance, and indeed, about whether gaps themselves have any significance. Gap aficionados point out that the ability of a market to "jump" price levels certainly must signify a powerful underlying trend—a statement that seems entirely logical. On the other hand, it could be said that many gaps result from the purely coincidental fact that some significant announcement or development happened to occur after a market had closed; that had the news become known during trading hours, no gap would have appeared in the course of the price response, and that such gaps are merely chance occurences. On balance, it seems that unfilled breakaway and exhaustion gaps are valuable trend indications, but the question arises whether it is possible to use them as trading signals. By the time it becomes apparent that a gap isn't going to be filled, the subsequent move may be over, so technicians must exercise special caution when attempting to base trading decisions on the existence of gaps.

Exhaustion gaps pose special trading problems because the most specific characteristic that sets them apart from runaway gaps is the fact that a sudden dramatic reversal follows the appearance of an exhaustion gap. Extremely high volume is often mentioned as providing confirmation of an exhaustion gap, but high volume usually accompanies runaway gaps as well, so this is not a useful criterion. When prices open with a wide gap and then seem to go nowhere despite good volume, an exhaustion gap should be suspected. Making this judgment requires a knowledge of opening prices, which do not ordinarily appear on bar charts, but which often provide useful information for those technicians willing to do a little extra work. Before leaving the subject of gaps, one final point is in order: Many chartists feel that runaway gaps, like flags and pennants, can serve as measuring devices, marking the halfway point of sudden dynamic moves.

C. Triangles

Triangles can be either continuation or reversal patterns, but seem to fall into the former category more often. They appear when there are simultaneous short-term uptrend and downtrend lines which intersect, as illustrated in figure 7. The conventional chart interpretation holds that triangles signal an impending large move, with the direction of the move likely to be in the direction of the steeper trendline. An ascending triangle should break out on the upside, a descending triangle on the downside, and a symmetrical triangle is equally likely to break out in either direction. Volume generally decreases near the apex, increasing again following the breakout. Subjectively, triangles appear to be fairly reliable indicators, especially when no more than three or four oscillations occur before the breakout.

III. Support and Resistance

Support and resistance levels are unquestionably among the most important of all technical considerations. They are areas which prices are expected to have difficulty moving beyond, and they therefore deserve especially careful consideration in connection with buying and selling decisions. Support and resistance levels on bar charts can be divided into three basic categories: 1) congestion areas, 2) areas at which previous advances or declines were turned back, and 3) transformed support or resistance levels —i.e., former highs that have been penetrated and thereby turned into support levels. The basic idea behind support/resistance theory is simply that price levels that were significant in the past will have significant impact on price action in the future. This discussion will center on advancing prices; bear market patterns are identical but inverted.

A. Congestion Areas

These are horizontal bands within which prices have fluctuated for a period of time—preferably a few weeks or longer. As long as prices remain within the congestion area, neither buyers or sellers predominate and there is no significant price trend. As time passes a large number of positions, both long and short, are established within the horizontal band. If prices subsequently break out above the band, then the congestion area will act as support to any subsequent declines.

The underlying logic is straightforward. In figure 9 for example, many traders took long or short positions in the 9.60 to 10.80 range between September and January. When prices subsequently penetrated the 10.80 level, the longs had profits, some of which were taken on the advance, while the shorts showed losses. Since the upside breakout clearly established the trend as upward, the subsequent reaction back into the trading range was an opportunity for many shorts to cover where they sold (or at a small loss) and for many former longs to re-establish or add to positions that had proved profitable. This combined buying pressure, from both bulls and former bears, stopped the break in the previous congestion region and is typical of the effect of horizontal support areas.

Because congestion areas are assumed to provide support or resistance largely as a result of action taken by traders who initiated positions within the area, it follows that the volume of activity within the congestion zone is an important indicator of the expected strength of the support or resistance. The more traders that have a vested interest at prices within the zone, the greater will be the expected buying (or selling) power should a return move occur. A related idea is that recent congestion areas are more significant than older ones, since the potential buying or selling pressure will have had less chance to dissipate, and the prices within the zone will still have fresh significance in traders' minds.

B. Previous Highs as Resistance

That previous highs should provide resistance in a bull market is almost self-evident. Since prices were unable to move beyond a particular level during a prior advance, traders will naturally be skeptical of their ability to surpass the same level on subsequent moves and will be inclined to either take profits or risk a short sale as the previous high is approached. This selling naturally creates resistance to the advance as is typified by the action in figure 10. Resistance at former highs and support at former lows will be more pronounced if the previous formations display characteristics of major tops or bottoms, which will be discussed in detail below. Naturally, penetration of an earlier high should be interpreted as a bullish signal—especially if the move to new highs is decisive and on strong volume.

C. Previous Highs as Support

At first sight, it might seem strange that an old high should help check reactions, but the underlying principles parallel those of a congestion area. Using figure 11 as an example, consider that some longs had taken profits when futures reached the 200 area

in December. The subsequent move to still higher levels in January convinced some of these traders that the bull move remained intact, but they were unwilling to buy back in at prices substantially above where they had previously liquidated their positions. If given the opportunity, however, they would be willing to reinstate their positions in the vicinity of where they had taken profits, so these former bulls should tend to provide buying power near former highs. Similarly, bears who had sold near earlier highs and had their market opinions changed by the subsequent rally will welcome a decline to the previous top as an opportunity to cover at only a small loss, and perhaps even reverse their positions. As in the case of congestion areas, the strength of the support at an old high should be greater if the volume was substantial in the vicinity of the previous top.

The explanations of support and resistance levels given above may seem implausible since there is no "a priori" reason to expect traders to behave in the ways described. In fact, most experienced market men would expect such actions to result in consistent losses. The justification is empirical. For reasons that lie within the province of psychology, large numbers of traders, especially novices, attach inordinate importance to prices at which they previously took action. Given this simple observed fact, it follows that support and resistance will tend to appear according to the principles described above.

IV. Reversal Formations

Every commodity trader would love to be able to pick tops and bottoms, but most have made enough unsuccessful attempts to realize that this is an extraordinarily difficult task. Few can resist the occasional temptation of trying to recognize a change in trend before anyone else, but this questionable past-time is not the primary reason for studying reversal formations. The goal of such a study is to recognize changes in trend once they have occurred, rather than to predict changes in advance. Because major tops and bottoms are clearly identifiable areas on a chart, their study has been more empirical than the study of most other technical formations. Over the past three-quarters of a century, experience has taught chartists that certain formations are especially likely to signal major trend changes.

A. Reversals

The reversal, on either a daily or a weekly chart, is the simplest of trend change formations. A downside reversal occurs when prices register a new high during the course of a day (or week) and then close the day (or week) sharply lower. Figure 12 illustrates complementary weekly reversals in silver. Reversals are most likely to prove significant if they occur on heavy volume after a prolonged move. Such reversals often occur after a piece of dramatic news propels prices to new highs (or lows) from which the market turns abruptly because of a sheer exhaustion of buying (or selling) power. Price action immediately following daily and weekly reversals varies considerably. In some cases key reversals mark the beginning of dramatic and extensive retracements of the preceding move, while in others the reversals merely mark the beginning of a more gradual trend change.

B. Island Reversals

These are small top or bottom formations set apart from the rest of the chart by gaps on either side. A top is illustrated in figure 13. The island can consist of a single day or of several days, and the entire formation is closely related to the daily and weekly reversal phenomena. The key difference is simply that, following the gap to the island area, prices hold for one or several days before the buying (or selling) power disappears between trading sessions. Like the daily and weekly reversals, the island formation frequently occurs on relatively high volume, and the subsequent trend change can either occur suddenly or develop over a period of time.

C. Head and Shoulders

The head and shoulders top (as well as the inverted head and shoulders bottom) has historically been one of the most popular and widely followed of chart formations. The name is descriptive of the formation, as illustrated in figures 14 and 15. The left shoulder results from an advance followed by a relatively similar decline; the head is formed by a larger rally and another setback to the vicinity of the starting point; the right shoulder is completed by a third rally falling short of the top of the head and a subsequent decline that carries prices below the line connecting the low points of the head—called the "neckline." Several ideas concerning head and shoulders formations have gained widespread acceptance by technicians. First, the pattern is not complete until the neckline is decisively penetrated. Unless and until this occurs, no reversal signal is considered given. Second, after this confirming penetration, prices frequently rally back to the vicinity of the neckline before the final move begins. Third, the vertical distance from the top of the head to the neckline provides a measure of the extent of the decline likely to occur from the neckline level. The existence of this concrete measuring rule perhaps accounts for part of this formation's popularity among chartists. Fourth, a market is considered especially vulnerable to a steep decline if the rally forming the right shoulder is unable to carry as far as the top of the left shoulder.

The head and shoulder pattern is a direct descendant of the original Dow Theory in that the sell signal is given by a lower high (right shoulder) followed by a lower low (penetration of the neckline). It has been so widely publicized and studied that in recent years it seems to have become something of a victim of its own popularity. With virtually every technician aware of any impending head and shoulders patterns, chartist selling alone can frequently cause a false breakout via a penetration of the neckline. Another possibility is that non-technicians who are aware of the pattern might attempt to force prices through the neckline in order to generate chart selling and enable themselves to buy at artificially lowered prices. In either case, the chartists who sell become sources of buying power in that they are likely to cover their short positions on a return move through the neckline. By their own well-known actions they mitigate the validity of their own signals. Technical analysis assumes free and liquid market conditions, and these can be destroyed by a large block of chartists as well as by any other artificial source of supply-demand imbalance. The implications of this bootstrap effect have not been widely examined, but they will become more and more important as the popularity of technical analysis increases.

D. Double Tops and Bottoms

These patterns form when successive intermediate term highs or lows stop at approximately the same level, as in figure 10. A double top should be considered complete only after the decline from the second peak carries prices below the first stopping point. Double tops can be subdivided into two rather distinct types, which might be called short-range and long-range. Short-range double-tops generally form within 8–10 weeks, and result from the kind of activity described above under "Previous Highs as Resistance." Because the bull market is running out of steam, volume on the second advance should be somewhat smaller than on the first. Long range double tops develop over much longer intervals and are frequently associated with a widespread reluctance to pay prices much above levels that have gained a certain historical respect. For psychological reasons, round numbers are often especially likely areas for long-range double tops.

Because most technicians adhere to the rigid criterion that the two peaks of a double top should differ by no more than 3–4%, the formation is not very common. Furthermore, chartists who try to anticipate double tops prior to the break below the first stopping point invariably wind up being frustrated, since every new intermediate high or low represents a double top or bottom that might have been, but wasn't. Still, because double tops and bottoms often signal sizable trend changes, they are well worth watching for, although the importance of awaiting a confirming breakdown (breakout) following the second top (bottom) cannot be overemphasized. Besides double tops and bottoms, triple and higher multiple reversal patterns occasionally appear. These are relatively scarce and follow the same basic principles as the double formation types.

E. Triangle Tops and Bottoms

Triangular reversal patterns, while rarer, have the same general characteristics as do the triangular continuation patterns discussed previously. The significant difference is merely that the reversal patterns forecast a breakout in the direction opposite that of the preceding trend. There is also a tendency for an ascending triangle to portend a major reversal, while a descending triangle would point to further weakness. Triangular bottoms seem to occur more frequently than their bearish counterpart, the triangular top.

F. Round Tops and Bottoms

These patterns, also known as saucers or bowls, occur during very gradual trend changes, but are often harbingers of sizable price moves. They are rather uncommon formations, and tend to develop most often in relatively thin markets, with volume decreasing as prices reach the top or bottom, and increasing as they turn in the direction of the final move. As illustrated in figure 16, prices gradually turn upward during the formation of a round bottom, indicating that the selling pressure is conquered only slowly. When bulls and bears wage a prolonged battle, the final outcome is usually a substantial price change, and in the case of rounded formations, chartists often assume that the extent of the move will be proportional to the time taken to form the top or bottom. No specific measuring formula is widely accepted, but the formations themselves are quite reliable indicators of the direction of an impending move.

Conclusion

The concepts and formations discussed in this article represent only the very tip of the technical iceberg. Besides the dozens of more complicated formations considered by vertical line chartists, there are point and figure charts, moving averages, oscillators, computerized models, and numerous other technical tools. As mentioned previously, all such technical approaches to price forecasting remain objects of spirited debate. Because the underlying validity of technical analysis as a whole has never been either proved or disproved, it seems logical for chartists to base most of their trading decisions on formations that can be defined precisely enough to be identified with a minimum of ambiguity. Another important characteristic is that patterns should justify predictions whose validity can be readily tested—at least subjectively via a careful and honest examination of past charts. Above all else, the technician must guard against the tendency to introduce so many "refinements" into his interpretations that his charts become capable of saying anything at anytime, depending on how he happens to look at them. The chart formations and technical concepts discussed here have been chosen with these principles in mind, and therefore should provide interested readers with a foundation on which to build a deeper understanding of technical analysis.

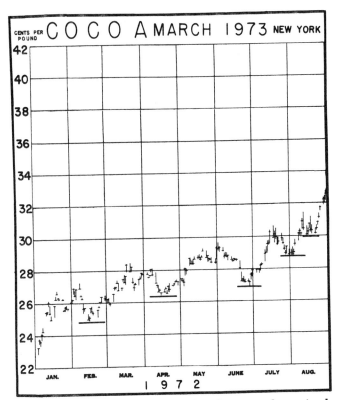

Figure 1: Dow Uptrend. Note that the uptrend remained intact because successive lows and highs were at higher levels than earlier lows and highs. A Dow downtrend would be just the reverse.

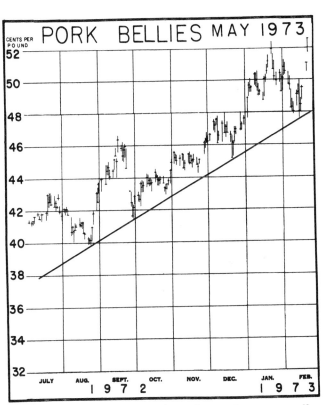

Figure 2: Uptrend Line. At least three points are usually needed to define a trendline. Here four lows lie on the line, with four others very nearly touching.

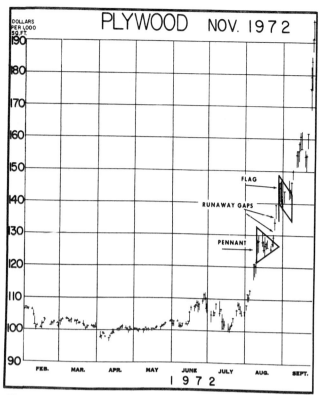

Figure 3: Pennants & Flags. The small pennant marked the halfway point of a move to the 160 area. A flag in the 145 area proved later to be the halfway point of the entire advance. Note the numerous runaway gaps during the upmove.

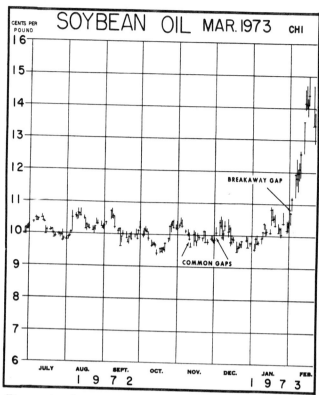

Figure 4: Common Gaps & Breakaway Gap. Notice the numerous common gaps that occurred within the trading range. The action following the February breakaway gap, which cleared all highs of the previous seven months, typifies the value of this signal.

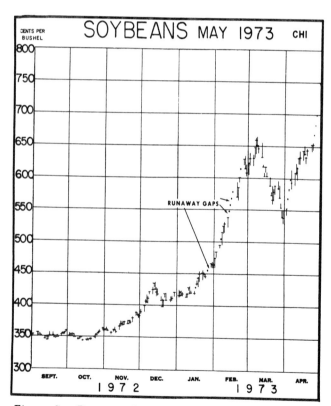

Figure 5: Runaway Gaps. The historic soybean advance of 1972–73 was marked by numerous runaway gaps, most of which were never filled.

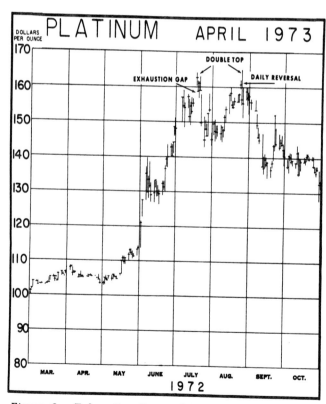

Figure 6: Exhaustion Gap and Double Top. Exhaustion gaps such as this are very difficult to recognize until a substantial decline takes place. Note the daily reversal that formed the second half of the double top.

196

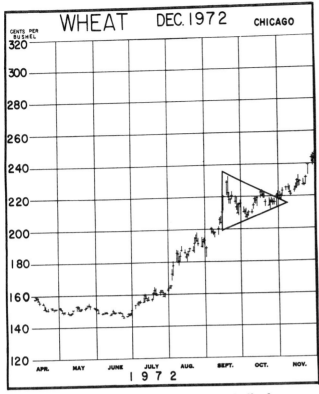

Figure 7: Symmetric Triangle: The big bull wheat market of 1972 featured this classic symmetric triangle. Prices later continued to move steadily in the direction of the breakout.

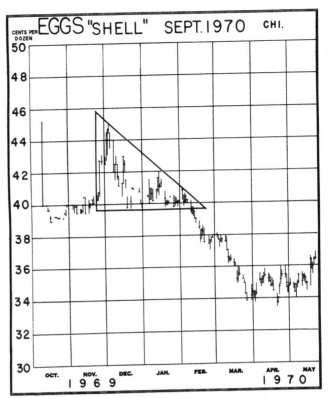

Figure 8: Descending Triangle. The prevailing downtrend continued following the breakdown from the triangle formation. An ascending triangle would be the same formation, but inverted.

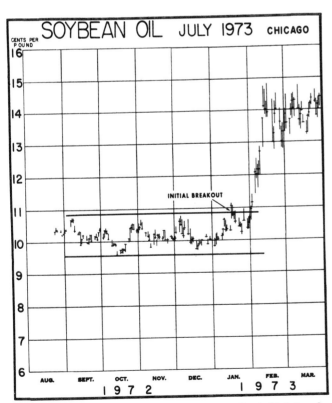

Figure 9: Congestion Area. Following the initial breakout, prices found support upon returning into the congestion area, and then launched a major advance.

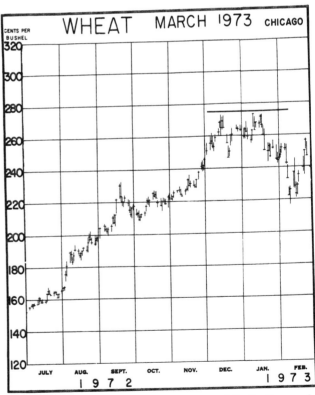

Figure 10: Resistance at Old Highs and Daily Reversal. The top of the market was marked by a daily reversal. The January return move met strong resistance at the December highs, and the formation subsequently evolved into a major double top.

197

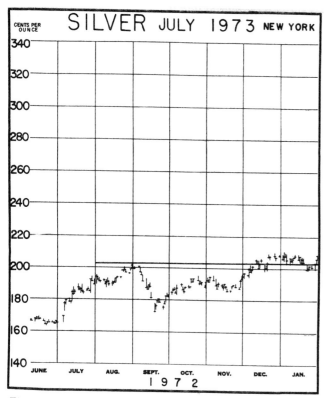

Figure 11: Support At Old Highs. In December and again in January, declines met good support in the area of the August highs.

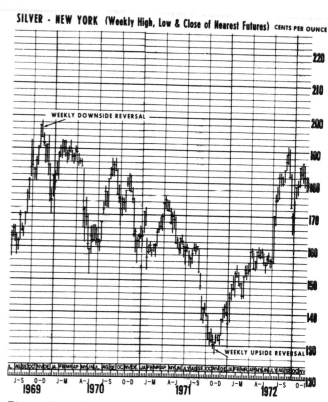

Figure 12: Weekly Reversals. The weekly continuation chart on Silver shows how weekly reversals signaled major moves down in 1969 and up in 1971.

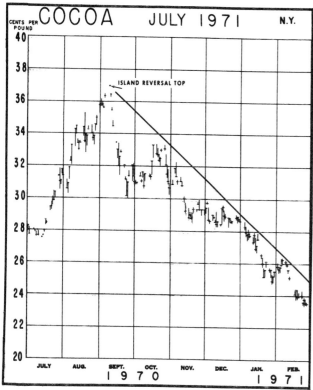

Figure 13: Island Top. The one-day island top marked the beginning of a sustained downtrend. The downtrend line held for six months.

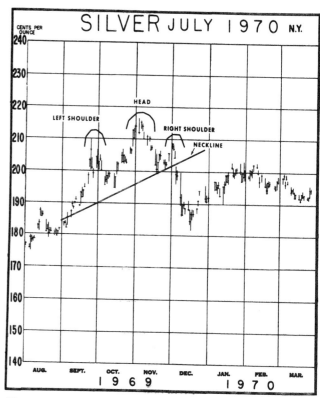

Figure 14: Head & Shoulders Top. Following the initial breakdown, prices fell the measured distance from head to neckline without making a return move.

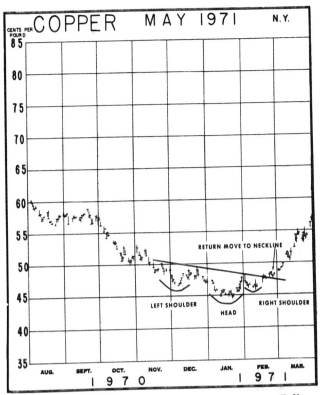

Figure 15: *Inverted Head & Shoulders Bottom. Following the initial breakout, prices returned to the neckline, then rose sharply. The advance carried beyond the head to neckline objective.*

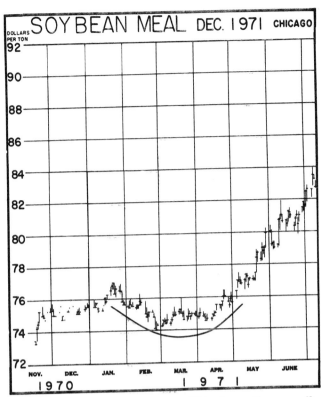

Figure 16: *Rounding Bottom. This formation usually develops when markets are not trading actively.*

Conversion Factors

The following equivalents are among those most commonly used in international agricultural trade:

METRIC EQUIVALENTS

1 meter	(m)	equals	39.37	inches
1 hectare	(ha)	equals	2.471	acres
1 liter	(l)	equals	.9081	dry quarts, or
		equals	1.0567	liquid quarts
1 kilogram	(kg)	equals	2.204622	pounds
1 quintal	(100 kgs)	equals	220.462	pounds
1 ton	(1,000 kgs)	equals	2,204.622	pounds

TON: The "metric" ton of 2,204.622 pounds is the weight unit most widely used in reporting international trade statistics. Other "tons" include: "short" ton of 2,000 pounds; the "long" ton of 2,240 pounds —also called the "gross" ton, "shipper's" ton, or "shipping" ton; and the "freight" ton, a volume for cargo freight, usually reckoned at 40 cubic feet or 1 cubic meter.

To convert short tons to metric tons multiply the short tons by 0.907185—or divide by 1.102311.

To convert metric tons to short tons multiply the metric tons by 1.102311—or divide by 0.907185.

HUNDREDWEIGHT (Cwt.): The "short" hundredweight (one-twentieth of a short ton) is 100 pounds in the United States. The "long" hundredweight (one-twentieth of a long ton) is 112 pounds in England and some other countries. The "metric" hundredweight (one-twentieth of a metric ton) is 110.23 pounds.

Pounds per bushel / Bushels per ton

		Metric ton (bushels)	Short ton (bushels)	Long ton (bushels)
Wheat	60	36.7437	33.3333	37.3333
Corn (shelled)	56	39.36825	35.7143	40.0
Oats	32	68.89444	62.500	70.0
Barley	48	45.929625	41.6667	46.6667
Rye	56	39.36825	35.7143	40.0
Sorghum grain	56	39.36825	35.7143	40.0
*Rice, rough	45	48.991	44.4444	49.7778
Soybeans	60	36.7437	33.3333	37.3333
Flaxseed	56	39.36825	35.7143	40.0

* Milled rice is sold in bags—sometimes called "pockets" —of 100 pounds each.

SELECTED COMMODITY CONVERSION FACTORS

100 pounds of	Can be obtained from	
White flour	2.3	bushels of wheat (72% extraction)
Cornmeal (Degermed)	3.16	bushels of corn
Cornmeal (Nondegermed)	2.00	bushels of corn
Rye flour	2.23	bushels of rye
Milled rice	152	pounds of rough rice
Soybean oil	549	pounds of soybeans
Soybean meal	127	pounds of soybeans
Cottonseed oil	588	pounds of cottonseed
Linseed oil	277	pounds of flaxseed

USUAL LOADINGS OF RAILROAD FREIGHT CARS

	Bushels per car	*Short tons per car*
Wheat	1,925	57.8
Corn (shelled)	2,035	57.0
Oats	2,712	43.4
Barley	2,198	52.8
Rye	1,880	52.6
Sorghum grain	2,000	56.0
Rice, rough	2,180	49.1
Soybeans	1,825	54.8
Flaxseed	1,778	49.8

Source: Agriculture Handbook No. 411, U.S.D.A.

APPROXIMATE CONVERSIONS FROM CUSTOMARY TO METRIC AND VICE VERSA

	When you know:	*You can find:*	*If you multiply by:*
LENGTH	inches	millimeters	25
	feet	centimeters	30
	yards	meters	0.9
	miles	kilometers	1.6
	millimeters	inches	0.04
	centimeters	inches	0.4
	meters	yards	1.1
	kilometers	miles	0.6
AREA	square inches	square centimeters	6.5
	square feet	square meters	0.09
	square yards	square meters	0.8
	square miles	square kilometers	2.6
	acres	square hectometers (hectares)	0.4
	square centimeters	square inches	0.16
	square meters	square yards	1.2
	square kilometers	square miles	0.4
	square hectometers (hectares)	acres	2.5
MASS	ounces	grams	28
	pounds	kilograms	0.45
	short tons	megagrams (metric tons)	0.9
	grams	ounces	0.035
	kilograms	pounds	2.2
	megagrams (metric tons)	short tons	1.1
LIQUID VOLUME	ounces	milliliters	30
	pints	liters	0.47
	quarts	liters	0.95
	gallons	liters	3.8
	milliliters	ounces	0.034
	liters	pints	2.1
	liters	quarts	1.06
	liters	gallons	0.26
TEMPER-ATURE	degrees Fahrenheit	degrees Celsius	5/9 (after subtracting 32)
	degrees Celsius	degrees Fahrenheit	9/5 (then add 32)

Source: U.S. Department of Commerce

COMMODITY FUTURES CONTRACTS
*VOLUME OF TRADING

No. of Contracts

18 YEARS - 1957 thru 1974

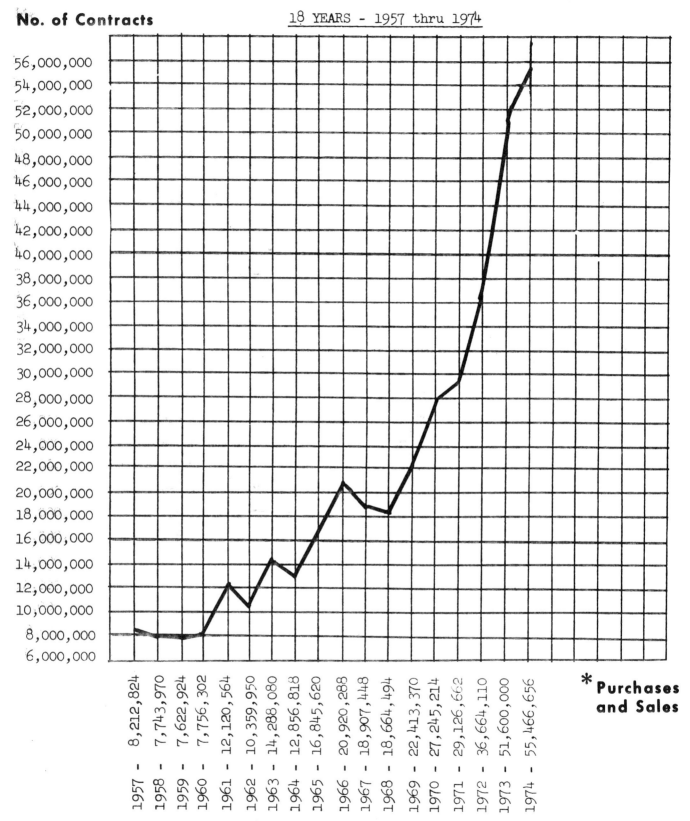

1957 –	8,212,824
1958 –	7,743,970
1959 –	7,622,924
1960 –	7,756,302
1961 –	12,120,564
1962 –	10,359,950
1963 –	14,288,080
1964 –	12,856,818
1965 –	16,845,620
1966 –	20,920,288
1967 –	18,907,448
1968 –	18,664,494
1969 –	22,413,370
1970 –	27,245,214
1971 –	29,126,662
1972 –	36,664,110
1973 –	51,600,000
1974 –	55,466,656

* Purchases and Sales

Source: Association of Commodity Exchange Firms, Inc.

COMMODITY FUTURES CONTRACTS TRADED 1970 - 1974

	Per Contract	1974	1973	1972	1971	1970
*Wheat	5,000 bu	2,376,611	1,567,483	855,813	549,773	559,514
*Corn	"	4,679,042	4,075,075	1,942,120	2,073,652	2,140,044
*Oats	5,000 bu	199,486	182,963	36,282	45,006	91,816
*Rye	5,000 bu	- - -			3	3,957
*Soybeans	5,000 bu	2,731,297	2,742,513	4,043,474	3,113,038	2,031,272
*Soybean Oil	60,000 lbs	1,620,316	1,762,856	1,110,776	1,485,519	1,907,436
*Soybean Meal	100 tons	878,182	660,305	630,916	474,911	868,333
*Live Chce Steers	40,000 lbs	- - -	- - -	- - -	149	4,577
Iced Broilers	28,000 lbs	221,128	328,346	23,264	55,136	95,280
Silver	5,000 ozs	1,462,195	1,632,298	813,492	559,330	191,006
Gold	3 kgs	1,143	- - -	- - -	- - -	- - -
Plywood	60,120 sq ft	383,322	274,134	217,631	222,987	47,426
Stud Lumber	100,000 bd ft	3,258	8,059	411	- - -	- - -
*Winter Wheat	5,000 bu	1,455	- - -	- - -	- - -	- - -
CHICAGO BOARD OF TRADE		14,557,435	13,234,032	9,674,179	8,579,504	7,940,661
*Butter	30,000 lbs	- - -	4	- - -	- - -	- - -
*Frozen Eggs	36,000 lbs	14	6	86	- - -	19
*Fresh Eggs	22,500 doz	361,257	617,395	474,948	379,850	678,627
*Nest-Run Eggs	22,500 doz	405				
Copper	12,500 lbs	6,129				
*Idaho Potatoes	50,000 lbs	9,063	9,532	6,137	23,916	78,030
*Pork Bellies,Fzn	36,000 lbs	735,246	1,154,873	2,057,064	1,695,386	1,778,443
*Live Hogs	30,000 lbs	1,083,512	1,061,770	543,257	261,001	115,108
*Live Ctle, M-W	40,000 lbs	2,517,341	2,547,827	1,370,471	745,835	578,525
*Hams, Fzn, Sknd	36,000 lbs	- - -	9	2	71	216
Turkeys, Tom	36,000 lbs	4	- - -	- - -	- - -	- - -
Lumber	100,000 bd ft	238,427	194,792	66,539	100,149	85,513
*Frozen Beef	36,000 lbs	- - -	- - -	- - -	128	1,584
*Grain Sorghums	400,000 lbs	1,344	2,271	1,354	8,155	- - -
*Live Feeder Ctle	42,000 lbs	30,999	22,752	7,423	520	- - -
British Pound	25,000 lbs	14,033	31,412	14,790	- - -	- - -
Canadian Dollar	$100,000	3,699	29,164	38,807	- - -	- - -
Deutschemark	250,000	49,447	77,272	19,320	- - -	- - -
Italian Lira	50,000,000	- - -	144	592	- - -	- - -
Japanese Yen	12,500,000	7,239	125,660	43,989	- - -	- - -
Mexican Peso	1,000,000	90,941	120,342	9,717	- - -	- - -
Swiss Franc	250,000	42,505	22,013	17,722	- - -	- - -
Dutch Guilder	125,000	1,527	11,327	- - -	- - -	- - -
U.S.Silver Coins	$5,000	86,977	18,555	- - -	- - -	- - -
Canadian Sil.Coins		281	509	- - -	- - -	- - -
French Francs		11,359	- - -	- - -	- - -	- - -
Gold	100 ozs	2,131	- - -	- - -	- - -	- - -
CHICAGO MERC. EX. & IMM		5,293,880	6,047,629	4,672,218	3,215,011	3,316,065
Copper	25,000 lbs	411,073	564,589	251,219	235,374	177,467
Gold	100 tr. ozs	2,550	- - -	- - -	- - -	- - -
*Hides	40,000 lbs	- - -	- - -	- - -	- - -	7
Lead	60,000 lbs	- - -	- - -	- - -	- - -	35
Mercury	10 flasks	84	25	115	177	466
Propane	100,000 gal	- - -	- - -	- - -	347	674
Rubber	22,040 lbs	183	- - -	- - -	- - -	10
Silver	5,000 ozs	1,365,915	1,237,860	815,168	616,244	693,697

Per Contract		1974	1973	1972	1971	1970
Tin	11,200 lbs	- - -	- - -	- - -	10	71
Zinc	60,000 lbs	- - -	- - -	- - -	- - -	3
COMMODITY EXCHANGE, INC.		1,779,805	1,802,474	1,066,502	852,152	872,430
*Cottonseed Oil	60,000 lbs	- - -	2	4	25	25
Fishmeal	100 metric tons	- - -	5,361	5,700	235	406
Pepper	11,200 lbs	- - -	0	696	1,037	5
Foreign Currency		- - -	0	24,531	14,603	1,340
*Pork Bellies,Fzn	18,000 lbs	- - -	0	2	52	- - -
British Pd.Sterling		- - -	0	- - -	- - -	- - -
Swiss Franc		- - -	0	- - -	- - -	- - -
French Franc		- - -	0	- - -	- - -	- - -
Deutschemark		- - -	101	- - -	- - -	- - -
Italian Lira		- - -	40	- - -	- - -	- - -
Japanese Yen		- - -	396	- - -	- - -	- - -
Canadian Dollar		- - -	0	- - -	- - -	- - -
Dutch Guilder		- - -	4,707	- - -	- - -	- - -
Belgian Franc		- - -	2,991	- - -	- - -	- - -
INTERNATIONAL COMMERCIAL EX.			13,598	30,933	15,952	1,776
*Wheat	5,000 bu	426,686	346,118	292,921	150,452	179,485
*Corn	"	8	354	- - -	- - -	3
*Grain Sorghums	280,000 lbs	0	1	2	100	466
KANSAS CITY BD. OF TRADE		426,694	346,473	292,923	158,552	179,954
*Wheat	1,000 bu	623,939	74,662	15,544	7,601	14,196
*Corn	1,000 bu	760,521	102,572	12,579	10,443	11,338
*Oats	"	5,161	9,323	2,132	724	1,224
*Rye	"	- - -	- - -	- - -	2	80
*Soybeans	"	557,348	56,546	81,205	46,076	25,555
*Live Hogs	15,000 lbs	34,352	- - -	- - -	- - -	- - -
Gold		421	- - -	- - -	- - -	- - -
Silver	1,000 ozs	587,256	400,048	80,800	49,805	4,267
U.S.Silver Coins	$5,000 value	3,850	141,712	43,092	- - -	- - -
MIDAMERICA COMM. EX.		2,572,848	783,863	235,352	114,651	56,660
*Wheat	5,000 bu	174,574	171,660	116,874	54,229	49,732
*Corn	"	- - -	- - -	- - -	58	8
*Oats	"	3,974	- - -	- - -	- - -	4
*Rye	"	- - -	- - -	- - -	- - -	- - -
*Pork Bellies,Fzn	36,000 lbs	- - -	- - -	2,294	3,337	- - -
*Durum Wheat		14	417	- - -	- - -	- - -
MINNEAPOLIS GRAIN EX.		178,562	172,077	119,168	57,624	49,744
Cocoa	30,000 lbs	345,264	430,836	278,416	212,802	312,667
NEW YORK COCOA EX.						
Coffee "C"	37,500 lbs	151,913	182,605	7,669	160	102
Coffee "U"	32,500 lbs	- - -	- - -	- - -	- - -	2
Molasses	40,000 gal	- - -	- - -	- - -	- - -	53
Sugar-World(#8)	112,000 lbs	- - -	- - -	- - -	2,552	266,667
Sugar-Domes(#10 & 7)	"	43,273	21,797	19,644	7,658	11,179
Sugar #11	"	736,941	1,029,588	875,178	454,964	75,944
Sugar #12	"	302	- - -	- - -	- - -	- - -
N.Y. COFFEE & SUGAR EXCH.		932,429	1,233,990	902,482	465,334	353,947
Petroleum		14,446	- - -	- - -	- - -	- - -
*Cotton #2	50,000 lbs	396,434	450,272	365,372	358,847	33,657
*Orng Jce, Fzn Con.	15,000 lbs	96,525	151,970	123,493	157,926	73,347
*Wool	6,000 lbs	2,350	4,677	3,778	3,559	3,741
*Wool Top	5,000 lbs	- - -	- - -	- - -	8	66
Propane	100,000 gal	8,293	7,013	925	1,544	- - -
Tomato Paste	26,500 lbs	- - -	- - -	100	222	- - -
N.Y. COTTON EXCH. & ASSOC.		518,048	613,932	493,668	522,106	110,811

Per Contract		1974	1973	1972	1971	1970
Aluminum	50,000 lbs	- - -	- - -	- - -	- - -	2
Apples	840 cartons	- - -	- - -	- - -	- - -	124
Palladium	100 ozs	2,277	1,888	489	106	757
Platinum	50 ozs	199,623	147,802	159,272	112,413	98,867
Plywood	70,000 sq ft	- - -	- - -	4,020	9,581	792
*Potatoes, Maine	50,000 lbs	770,781	673,672	246,603	151,369	316,691
*Idaho Russets	50,000 lbs	- - -	- - -	9	19	119
Nickel	2,000 lbs	- - -	- - -	- - -	1	382
*Butter		- - -	4	- - -	- - -	- - -
Indust'l Fuel Oil		6	- - -	- - -	- - -	- - -
Heating Oil		11	- - -	- - -	- - -	- - -
*Shell Eggs	22,500 lbs	- - -	2	- - -	87	26
*Imp Fzn Bn Bf	30,000 lbs	4,803	2,645	964	556	- - -
Silver Coins	$10,000 value	90,852	89,978	26,437	17,985	- - -
Gold	32.151 troy ozs	1,230	- - -	- - -	- - -	- - -
Belgian Francs		18,840	- - -	- - -	- - -	- - -
British Pound		8	- - -	- - -	- - -	- - -
Dutch Guilder		4	- - -	- - -	- - -	- - -
Deutschemark		8	- - -	- - -	- - -	- - -
Swiss Franc		10	- - -	- - -	- - -	- - -
Japanese Yen		8	- - -	- - -	- - -	- - -
Canadian Dollar		4	- - -	- - -	- - -	- - -
Mexican Peso		5	- - -	- - -	- - -	- - -
N.Y. MERC. EXCH.		1,088,470	915,991	437,794	292,117	417,760
*Coconut Oil	60,000 lbs	16,870	12,742	1,812	- - -	- - -
*Shell Eggs	22,500 lbs	107	3,498	- - -	- - -	- - -
*W. Live Cattle	50,000 dzn	1,605	848	- - -	- - -	- - -
Silver		1,767	- - -	- - -	- - -	- - -
PACIFIC COMMODITIES EXCH.		20,349	17,088	1,812		
Copper	25,000 lbs	765	11,374	3,191	5,009	423
Diamonds	20 carats	- - -	- - -	3,574	- - -	- - -
Gold	200 troy ozs	- - -	- - -	- - -	475	- - -
Silver	5,000 ozs	17,939	149,966	76,557	53,739	6,379
Cocoa	15,000 lbs	68	4,955	5,235	6,618	2,510
Sugar	56,000 lbs	762	45,975	38,033	10,929	820
Silver Coins	$5,000 value	- - -	- - -	18	756	- - -
Coffee		10	2,494	- - -	- - -	- - -
WEST COAST COMMODITY EXCH.		19,544	214,764	126,608	77,526	10,132
TOTAL ALL REGULATED CONTRACTS		21,101,622	18,285,377	14,345,711	11,810,383	11,547,271
TOTAL NON-REGULATED CONTRACTS		6,631,706	7,541,370	3,986,344	2,752,948	2,075,336
TOTAL ALL FUTURES CONTRACTS		27,733,328	25,826,747	18,332,055	14,563,331	13,622,607
CHANGE FROM PREVIOUS YEAR		+7.37%	+40.90%	+25.88%	+6.91%	+21.56%

*Regulated Commodities

Source: Association of Commodity Exchange Firms, Inc.

The World-Famed "Blue Sheet"

PUBLISHED EACH WEEK FOR 41 YEARS
WITHOUT INTERRUPTION

Futures Market Service

Popularly known as the "blue sheet" by two generations of commodity traders, FUTURES MARKET SERVICE has been published every Friday since 1934 as a source of information and market opinion for those who trade in the futures markets.

The first page of the weekly eight page presentation at times discusses factors influencing commodity prices generally. However, in the majority of weekly issues, the front page is devoted to an in-depth study of a specific commodity that the editors think is unusually timely because of prospective statistical change, seasonal price considerations, etc. Two additional pages each week show charts to illustrate the front page discussion.

Four pages each week are divided into separate sections for each commodity actively traded on futures markets. They are listed on this page. Every one of these commodities is analyzed separately in each issue.

The final page is reserved for timely statistical and factual data such as open interest, volume, trading facts and a calendar of coming commodity events.

Present subscribers to FUTURES MARKET SERVICE include banking institutions, commodity brokerage firms, investment trusts, commodity traders, bakeries, department store executives, dairy products firms, importers and exporters, marketing and purchasing cooperatives, agricultural producers, shoe manufacturers, textile mills, candy manufacturers—in fact, all types of companies and individuals who produce, process, distribute, finance or trade in commodities. Their common interest is in WHERE COMMODITY PRICES ARE HEADED AND WHY.

If you have a similar interest, you should subscribe to FUTURES MARKET SERVICE.

SUBSCRIPTION RATES—You can subscribe **now** to the weekly **FUTURES MARKET SERVICE** at the following rates; three months—$28; six months—$49; one year—$85.

Commodities Analyzed In Every Weekly Issue

- **BEEF CATTLE**
- **BROILERS**
- **COCOA**
- **COFFEE**
- **COPPER**
- **CORN**
- **COTTON**
- **EGGS**
- **GOLD**
- **HOGS**
- **LUMBER**
- **OATS**
- **ORANGE JUICE**
- **PLATINUM**
- **PLYWOOD**
- **PORK BELLIES**
- **POTATOES**
- **SILVER**
- **SOYBEANS**
- **SOYBEAN MEAL**
- **SOYBEAN OIL**
- **SUGAR**
- **WHEAT**

Brochure available on request

Commodity Research Bureau, Inc.

ONE LIBERTY PLAZA · NEW YORK, N.Y. 10006

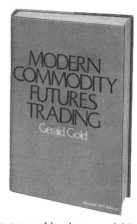

The Daily Commodity Computer Trend Analyzer

HELPS YOU OPERATE SUCCESSFULLY IN THE COMMODITY FUTURES MARKETS

The publication **DAILY** COMMODITY COMPUTER TREND ANALYZER is undoubtedly the most useful working tool we know of for daily trend following, which is the basic requisite for successful trading. This unique service identifies existing trends and trend changes for all active commodity futures markets every trading day. This technique employs a strictly mathematical formula for determining trends and trend changes.

Although the original decision models were implemented in 1963, continuous research led to a new series of models with progressively improved results culminating in the most recent program introduced in March, 1975. Besides utilizing all new formulae, the fantastic calculating ability of the computer enabled our research to be customized for each commodity. In effect, the "Trend Analyzer" is made up of a series of models designed to give the maximum performance for identifying trends of each individual commodity.

DAILY COMMODITY COMPUTER TREND ANALYZER is coldly impersonal, completely objective. It rules out emotions—often a speculator's worst enemy; it continuously labels the trend; calculates in advance the level where the trend may change; and can help establish a plan of action.

Each day, after the market closes, pertinent market information is assembled in machine readable form and then a large sophisticated computer performs all of the essential calculations necessary to complete the formula established for each of 170 different futures contracts, and prints out the results in minutes.

The daily report—mailed to subscribers within two hours after the futures markets close—is actually a reproduction of the final computer printout. (For convenience in printing and mailing, the size of the actual printout is reduced in size.) The report consists of two printed pages.

The Daily Commodity Computer Trend Analyzer continuously monitors the market each day:

It identifies the existing major price trend

Pinpoints levels in advance where the trend could change

Identifies the trend change on the day it occurs

The illustration below is a reproduction of part of the daily report sent to all subscribers after the markets close for the day. Approximately 170 specific futures deliveries in the top 39 commodity markets are included. Each subscriber is sent a complete explanation of the twelve columns of information appearing in the specimen in a study entitled "Understanding The Daily Commodity Computer Trend Analyzer." The salient points are:

1. The existing trend—when it started and at what price.

2. **"Support" and "Resistance" prices. (The price levels which, if penetrated by any day's closing price, will signal a probable change of trend, i.e., stop-loss points for traders.)**

3. **Current Market Data—today's high, low, and closing prices, net change from the previous trading day's close, individual volume and open interest.**

4. **Relative strength—an additional market indicator, explained in the subscriber's manual, "Understanding The Daily Commodity Computer Trend Analyzer."**

5. **Ten Day Moving Average—a short range trend indication.**

6. **Composite Moving Average—A composite of three moving averages, which can be used as a trendline.**

7. **Commodity group indices and technical market indicators.**

```
                  D A I L Y   COMMODITY COMPUTER TREND ANALYZER        MON JUN  2, 1975
  VOL. 05   ISSUE  106        ---------                                                              PAGE 1

           N TREND STARTED   INDICATED STOPS          T O D A Y S   M A R K E T        OPEN   REL STRENG  TEN-DAY   COMPOS
      TRND E ------------------  ------------------  -------------------------------------------------  INTER  ----------  MOVING    -ITE
           W  DATE   PRICE    SUPPORT   RESIST    HIGH     LOW     CLOSE   NET CHG H/L   VOLUME   EST   CURR HIGH  AVERAGE   AVERAGE
BARLEY WPG
  JUL  SIDE  05/30  233 1/2   220 1/2    237     233 1/2   229     229 1/2  -  4          278    2346    1    66  228.75+   228.90+
  OCT  DOWN  05/06  219 3/4             218 1/2   213       210     210     -  2 3/4       115     955  -60  -498  214.10-   217.35-
BROILERS
  JUN   UP   03/24   39.90     43.27              44.60    44.00    44.45  +   .35         426    1161   81    81   43.50+    42.44+
  JUL   UP   03/26   40.30     42.89              44.30    43.75    44.07  +   .22         482    2221   74    78   43.23+    42.26+
  AUG   UP   03/24   39.75     41.39              42.85    42.10    42.80  +   .75          64     729   71    71   41.35+    40.48+
  SEP   UP   03/24   38.75     39.40              40.00    39.90    40.00  +   .05          22     413   43    43   39.65+    39.06+
CATTLE LIVE
  JUN   UP   03/17   38.90     48.81              51.45    50.87    50.97  -   .43        3321    7959  131   238   49.51+    47.44+
  AUG   UP   05/15   44.12     42.73              46.95    46.30    46.75  +   .05        5590   16974  104   164   44.63+    43.37+
  OCT   UP   05/15   40.72     39.40              42.52    42.00    42.45  +   .13        1456    6383   61   116   40.88+    40.15+
  DEC   UP   05/30   40.90     38.40              41.15    40.65    40.97  +   .07         574    3706   44    91   39.86+    39.35+
  FEB   UP   05/30   39.97     37.33              40.10    39.70    39.90  -   .07         315    1874   28   142   39.17+    38.82+
CATTLE FEEDER
  AUG   UP   05/30   34.05     32.72              34.50    33.75    34.50  +   .45          70     343   35   136   33.61+    33.31+
  SEP   UP   02/26   30.50     32.85              34.00    33.45    33.80  +   .35          23     141   31   108   32.96+    32.80+
  OCT   UP   05/30   33.30     31.95              33.72    33.15            27                    1328   43   135   32.4
  NOV
```

In addition to the daily reports, up-dated charts of prices, relative strength and composite averages are sent every other week.

For Samples and Subscription Information, Write to:

Commodity Research Bureau, Inc.

ONE LIBERTY PLAZA • NEW YORK, N.Y. 10006